W9-BCG-070

How I Got That Story

Also by Members of
the Overseas Press Club of America

I CAN TELL IT NOW

AS WE SEE RUSSIA

MEN WHO MAKE YOUR WORLD

DEADLINE DELAYED

how I got that story

by Members of the
OVERSEAS PRESS CLUB OF AMERICA

Edited by
DAVID BROWN and W. RICHARD BRUNER

E. P. DUTTON & CO., INC.
New York   1967

Published simultaneously in Canada by Clarke, Irwin & Company Limited, Toronto and Vancouver

Library of Congress Catalog Card Number: 67–11370

FIRST EDITION

Grateful acknowledgment is made to Cambridge University Press for permission to quote material from *The Universe Around Us*, by Sir James Jeans, published in 1929, in William L. Laurence's "The Greatest Story"; and to Clifton Daniel for permission to quote from a speech by him in Tad Szulc's article, "*The New York Times* and the Bay of Pigs."

Acknowledgments

THIS, I FEEL, is the best book the Overseas Press Club of America has ever done. All of the contributors have met their deadlines with élan, éclat and new insights into how imaginative, responsible newsmen and women work. A special word should be said about the dedicated editors, David Brown, chief story executive for the Twentieth Century–Fox Film Corporation, and W. Richard Bruner, a former war correspondent who is now an advertising executive. This is the same editorial team who handled the previous Overseas Press Club volume, *I Can Tell It Now*, and once again they have outdone themselves in the management of outstanding editorial material. In the complex task of arranging and assembling contributions by thirty-four geographically far-flung authors, the editors and I have been greatly aided by the work of Mrs. Beth Fine of the Overseas Press Club staff, whose tracking of contributors was a brilliant display of editorial logistics.

The volume was started under former OPC President Merrill Mueller, and his successor, Victor Riesel, maintained the momentum. Five former presidents of the Club are associated with the book as contributors or members of our Book Publishing Committee (including the chairman). The committee consists of:

Will Yolen, *Chairman*
Director of Book and Magazine Services
Hill and Knowlton, Inc.

Simon Michael Bessie
President
Atheneum Publishers

Richard P. Cecil
President
WCC Books

Bennett Cerf
Chairman of the Board
Random House, Inc.

Robert Cousins
Executive Editor,
General Books
McGraw-Hill Book Company

William Doerflinger
Editor
E. P. Dutton & Co., Inc.

Beulah Phelps Harris
Freelance Editor

Fred Kerner
President
Hawthorn Books, Inc.

Kenneth McCormick
Editor-in-Chief
Doubleday & Company,
Inc.

Jerry Mason
President
Ridge Press, Inc.

Mrs. Eleanor S. Rawson
Editor
David McKay Company,
Inc.

Frederick R. Rinehart
Vice-President
Holt, Rinehart & Winston,
Inc.

M. Lincoln Schuster
President
Simon & Schuster, Inc.

Roger W. Strauss, Jr.
President
Farrar, Straus & Giroux,
Inc.

Victor Weybright
Chairman and Executive
Officer
Weybright and Talley, Inc.

Will Yolen

Contents

Contents

A Prefatory Note

SOME OF the most exciting stories rarely see print. They are the stories behind the stories that make the headlines. What reporters go through to bring the world public its news is often as interesting or even more interesting than the actual news stories themselves.

The purpose of this book is to reveal how great reporters obtained some of the world's major news stories—the preparation, the danger, the luck, the sagacity that go into making an assignment pay off.

We believe this book will prove enlightening and entertaining for the general reader and instructive for students of journalism as well as for all those who must deal with the press.

DAVID BROWN

W. RICHARD BRUNER

Foreword

TURNER CATLEDGE

Executive Editor, *The New York Times*

FOR A MAN called Turner Catledge to write a foreword to a book about how reporters got their big stories is a little like a man called Martin Luther King writing an introduction to an autobiography of Governor Wallace of Alabama: the casting is adventuresome but you would not expect total uniformity of opinion.

The fact is that around the news room of *The New York Times* I believe I have acquired a certain reputation for a certain coolness toward newspaper stories about how reporters have suffered, how real rough things were for our hero covering the story, how he persevered in the face of chilling difficulties and how if some information just happened to be missing it was because some cruel news source would not talk to him. If I have not acquired that reputation, I will have to do something about it because I certainly have been trying to get the idea across.

Reporters are fine, intelligent, industrious people; some of my favorite executive editors were once reporters. But I cannot really convince myself that newspaper readers put down their dime to read about reporters. I labor under the belief that the newspaper reader wants to know what the reporter saw and heard and not about his troubles in seeing and hearing. When I get a carpenter into the house to build a bookcase I am interested in what he builds. I may be willing to hear about how he banged his thumb with a hammer three weeks ago but, cold heart that I am, I am not keen on paying for the privilege.

It is not that I don't like shop talk. I have been talking newspaper shop talk for a handsome number of years now—around the country at newspaper conventions, at my home and at the homes of my colleagues and in a little room behind my office stocked with water and ice cubes. It is simply that I think shop talk is just that—talk for the shop.

There are a number of professional reasons for my asking reporters and editors on the *Times* to keep stories about us unsung heroes out of the paper as much as possible. One reason is that I don't really think my professional purpose in life is to reminisce with reporters about the stories they got. I suspect I get paid, rather, to visit with them from time to time about the stories they did not get, or the ones they might get.

A deeper reason has to do with something called objectivity, a strange commodity we all know we can never quite own but which we also know we have to spend our lives trying to attain.

We know that pristine objectivity is by definition impossible in newspapering because the very process of selecting facts to go into a story and deciding how much space to give it is of itself a subjective process. But the point is that if we do not strive for as close an approach to objectivity as the nature of the human beast allows then we have to wonder what our purpose in life is.

There are techniques that make for objectivity and there are techniques and habits of thought that work against it. And among these last perhaps the most dangerous is the injection of the reporter into the newspaper story. It is dangerous because the reader begins to think of a reporter as a participant rather than observer and is likely to lose trust in him. The reader's trust is the only real stock in trade any reporter has. It is even more dangerous because the reporter who injects himself into a story begins thinking of himself as a participant, a shaper, and pretty soon he is writing about himself for himself. Reporters do not spend many dimes on newspapers; if we write for the trade we will find ourselves taking off weight just a little too fast.

There are, of course, exceptions and I am a man quite as interested in exceptions as the rule. There are times when a reporter or an editor directly affects a story materially and this the reader has a right to know. If an investigation by a newspaper turns up a vital bit of information, the reader has the right to know that it was uncovered by the reporter, not by the police or any other government agency. If a statement is made during the course of an interview, the reader has the right to know that, too, because it makes some difference as to whether a politician is volunteering information in public or is responding to questions he would not otherwise have been asked.

These are the most simple and obvious exceptions to the rule and there are many others. The point, I believe, is that the reporter should enter the newspaper story only when that is absolutely essential to the reader's understanding of the event— and then he should get out of the story as quickly as his type-writer can carry him.

Having said all this, do I believe there is any value or purpose to a book of reporters' inside tales about how they get the story? I do, indeed, because there is an "on the other hand"—and as a newspaperman I am grateful that there are always at least three.

It has to do, this other hand, with time and place. When you pay your money to hear Heifetz, you don't want him to break off a concerto with a speech about his background or about the trouble he had getting to Carnegie Hall. But that doesn't mean you are not interested in hearing and reading about Heifetz and his life and personality. The concert hall is simply not the right place to listen to Heifetz talk about himself and a newspaper is not the right place to read about reporters—as a rule.

But to pretend that newspapermen really are not interesting people and really do not have interesting lives and really do not expend of themselves in energy, initiative and courage in getting stories is not something I could do with a straight face. They are and they do.

Most of the newspapermen who have contributed to this book are foreign correspondents. A foreign correspondent is a reporter with a passport—and something more. Let's leave aside the qualifications we trust every foreign correspondent has— knowledge of his area, some language, intellectual curiosity, good education. You can take a man who speaks Hindi among twelve other languages, graduated summa cum laude from Harvard and spent seven years in India—and he still might not make a foreign correspondent you would ever send to New Delhi for a week.

The foreign correspondent is a man who relates; his whole life is spent relating. He relates what goes on in the country he is covering to journalism—he sees the world in news terms. He relates the country he is covering to other countries he has been in and even to countries he has not been in. He relates one development in a country to another. He can relate from one specific incident to something broad and generic in a country or a continent; a meeting of Buddhist priests in Japan is not just a meeting of Buddhist priests but something that tells him about a re-emergent country's movement away from the religion of its fathers or its groping for a lost unifying movement.

Above all, the foreign correspondent, the good foreign correspondent, relates to his readers, most of whom have never been anywhere near the country or crisis about which he is writing. The good foreign correspondent is constantly writing letters—to his readers, telling them what he has seen, heard and learned for them.

There is value in knowing what these men and women have gone through, interest in how they have done it—and a book, this book, is the right time and place.

How I Got That Story

Burnet Hershey, onetime newspaperman, war correspondent, radio news commentator, author, playwright and screenwriter, is founder-member and past president of the Overseas Press Club. He has written for the *New York Sun, New York Tribune, New York Times, New York Post, Philadelphia Ledger* and *Liberty* magazine. His awards include France's Legion of Honor.

Germany's Meekest Hour

BURNET HERSHEY

WOULD you believe that I remember a Germany that was *meek?* And I remember a *me* that was not? Thus do times change.

Let us for a moment recall the Paris of the 1919 Peace Conference, when the German delegation came to get the peace terms, was held incommunicado—symbolic of Germany's defeat and humiliation.

I was then on the Paris staff of the old *New York Sun* and, because I spoke several languages, including French and German, I was assigned to cover the various continental delegations. It was the off-limit Germans—representatives of the new Weimar Republic—and their activities which went uncovered by our papers, that made me want to bloodhound a historic story being lived but not told.

The fallen German enemy were restricted to the old Hotel des Réservoirs in Versailles; not exactly a punitive cell, since it was the handsome onetime villa of Madame de Pompadour. Neither were they feeling exactly welcomed by the people of France. Many citizens, with unbridled passion and in frenzies of emo-

tional war memories still fresh and painful, had thrown stones at
the German leaders who had arrived to accept the peace terms.
For this reason, the French Committee on Arrangements had
thought it essential to build a high stockade around the hotel. The
stockade embraced part of the Park of the Palace of Versailles and
connected with another hotel, the Vatel, which lodged German
newspaper correspondents and a clerical staff. An extension of the
stockade led to the Palace of the Petit Trianon where the diplomatic drama was taking place, for here were the beaten but still
quibbling German representatives who had been handed the
peace terms. In less than diplomatic language they were told by
the Allied chiefs to read and sign.

The delegation was headed by the royal carriage of Count von
Brockdorff-Rantzau, a Junker of the best Prussian aristocracy.
With him were a round number of the usual military and naval
experts (experts who had lost a war) and some 220 clerical
workers, interpreters, orderlies, and telephone and telegraph
technicians whose job it was to maintain direct lines to the
government of the new German Republic in Weimar. One barber
and seventeen trusty gentlemen of the Teutonic press completed
the enemy roster.

The Trianon was carefully guarded by *poilus* with fixed bayonets. There was great curiosity about our defeated enemy. Except
across a gunsight, few in the Allied countries had seen a German
in four years, though many had seen the results of their devastation of Belgium and northern France. We all itched to have a
personal look at this gang.

I found my itch unbearable and decided to scratch around for
a solution. I wanted desperately to see and talk to those Germans,
but was well aware of the "unbreakable" regulations. This is as
far as one could go with a press pass: one could be admitted by
the French guard to the stockade near the Vatel, and then the
final privilege was to walk the half block down the palisaded path
to the conciergerie of the Hotel des Réservoirs where one met
"total impasse" in the figure of Colonel Henry, a toughened
French veteran who presided as warden.

Henry was no Pierre Salinger or Bill Moyers. His idea of an
important press announcement—of "opening up" for the press—
was to announce that the Germans had taken a stroll in the
gardens of Versailles.

The frustration was nerve-wracking. The biggest news in Versailles was how the Germans were taking their defeat, but none of us was anywhere near the reporting line to get the picture. Some of my older colleagues were a lot more passive than I about it—they said I'd be smart to adopt the same philosophical attitude—but I was in my twenties and, in those years, I never accepted the inevitable. I had a job to do for Mr. Munsey's *Sun.* How could I ever give him any whatever-reason for not getting in to see those Boches? When I imagined Munsey's predictable contempt, maybe even an uncontrollable rage (the old man had a temper), it propelled me into action that normally I might not have taken, although I was, within myself too, very anxious to get the story somehow, and vastly annoyed at the censorship.

Experienced and responsible newspapermen never resent reasonable censorship based on military necessity. Most of us held to the World War I motto: "The best story in the world isn't worth risking a single Allied soldier's life." But now there were no lives at stake and I couldn't see any valid reason for concealing what was going on inside where the peace terms were being discussed.

I recall feeling a good deal of satisfaction at a cartoon that was published at this time in the Paris edition of the *New York Herald.* It portrayed President Woodrow Wilson as "The New Wrestling Champion," and the adversary he was throwing was "The Press," a figure dressed in old newspapers. The caption read:

"It is forbidden to publish what Marshal Foch says!"
"It is forbidden to publish what Lloyd George thinks!"
"It is forbidden to publish what happened at . . . (censored) . . . !"
"To make sure that nothing else will be published, the censorship delays the transmission of every wire message."

As often as I could, I would peer inside the stockade and see that the group of German correspondents left the Hotel Vatel every morning after breakfast. They would walk down to the Hotel des Réservoirs and vanish inside. This appearance was my first impression of the new "meekness" of the Germans. They had, in general, a hangdog air, like ex-bullies who were now misplaced in a world of stronger men who had slapped them down.

Furthermore, they looked badly underfed and wore makeshift clothes, mostly ill-assorted improvisations of morning coats and striped pants of prewar fashion.

In those days, I could match the skinny look of these men, and being fair-skinned, with light blue eyes, and not particularly hairy in the face, I was also pale enough to look like one of them. The obvious thought was that I had to get myself a costume just like theirs. In such a disguise, it was possible that I could slip by Colonel Henry's guards, join the German press group and get an earful.

Needless to say, I didn't ask for permission when I went on a shopping expedition in Paris to gather my masquerade. I rounded up striped pants, a cutaway then called a "Prince Albert," round Teutonic spectacles, a green-feathered Tyrolean hat and, most important, a large and shabby dispatch case like the ones I saw the Germans carrying.

Next morning I summoned an old, black, chauffeured Renault limousine, temporarily on the *Sun* payroll, which dropped me on the Boulevard de la Reine, right around the corner from the Réservoirs. I told the driver to wait just in case I was forced to take some emergency action where I was going, such as fleeing for my life. That chauffeur was such a nice chap, and I've often wondered how long he did wait, and in what fashion he must have cussed out "that mongrel with all the gall"—me, looking like a halfway Boche in my semicamouflaged German journalist costume.

At the gate of the stockade, I had shown my Allied press pass and the guard had said *"Passez"* in a very bored voice, concentrating on the validity of my *"coup fil"* and overlooking me entirely.

After walking, seemingly, in toward the Vatel, I did a fast turn on my heels and headed for the Réservoirs, and now I began to feel the shakiness that comes with such boldness and deceit, albeit for an honorable cause. Should I be caught in the masquerade, there would be an inquiry, I knew, and a good chance I might even be arrested and thrown out of the country. However, I couldn't afford to let my thoughts panic me. At the Réservoirs, I quickly pulled out the tails of my cutaway, propped the Tyrolean hat on my head, put on my round German specs, shuffled my dispatch case from hand to hand and waited for the German journalists to show. As usual, they did.

I flattened against a wall and they walked by, talking, and didn't notice me. As the last of the three-abreast group filed by, I fell into the rear beside an older man who eyed me tentatively and tipped his hat. I tipped mine back. He introduced himself as Herr Wolff. Taking the bull by the horns, I spieled off to the chap, in German, that I was an American newsman and had taken a chance to come inside so I could get both sides of the story for American readers.

Wolff was wearing blue glasses which fairly popped out into a rainbow as his widened eyes distorted the lenses. He was aghast. He couldn't realize how I could break the rules, and he was certain something horrible would happen. His reaction was a first-class example of the manner of the conquered German; having been beaten into submission, he was apt to give such an exhibition of fawning, cringing and the desire to obey, as to make one forget any admiration for his "efficiency" of yesterday.

When Wolff passed the whispered word to his colleagues that I was an American reporter in their midst without permission, they all sidled away from me, saying: *"Streng verboten!"* (strongly forbidden). Finally, when they saw they weren't shaking me, at least, Herr Wolff, who was correspondent for the *Berliner Tageblatt,* warmed up to some conversation. To my surprise, he spoke excellent English with a London accent, but it was German above all I wanted to be talking with him when we walked past Colonel Henry's guard. To my relief, he did switch languages when I elbowed him frantically to do so, and, again, a bored guard overlooked me completely.

Wolff relaxed somewhat once we were inside the press hotel, but now it was my time to get really nervous. Unexpectedly enough, Wolff was cooperating, and I was getting deeper and deeper into forbidden territory. I was taken to Count Brockdorff-Rantzau's aide, who said he would inform the Count of my presence and determine whether or not the Count would receive me under the irregular circumstances.

In the meantime, all the German correspondents seemed to get more comfortable about having me around and we talked for hours. They answered lots of questions for me, after I assured

them I would repay them for their kindness with things they
wanted me to get them from Paris, since shopping was not
allowed for them beyond the stockade. One asked wistfully for a
bottle of French brilliantine so he could dandy himself up with a
product he hadn't seen in four years (due to the blockade of
Germany). Another asked for Uridonal, the equivalent of our
Little Liver Pills; others wanted lighthearted magazines, such as
La Vie Parisienne. My promises to see to these favors strength-
ened my position with the German newsmen, and I was making
progress, but my hoped-for audience with the Count never
materialized.

Two days later I repeated the performance, but not without
running into some menacing obstacles—not only in the form of
the French guards, who seemed to me suddenly very watchful
and suspicious, but also my own fellow newsmen, who had spied
me getting out of the Réservoirs. Costume or not, they had
recognized me, but I had disappeared so fast that I was able to
deny later that I had ever been near Versailles and said I had
been in Paris all the time, that their powers of observation were
failing them.

Came the celebrated day that the Peace Treaty was to be
formally delivered to the Germans. For the first time, the delegates of the twenty-seven Allied and Associated Powers and the
German plenipotentiaries were to meet face to face in the great
hall of the Petit Trianon, and the "press invited" sign was out.

The atmosphere was impressively solemn as Count von
Brockdorff-Rantzau took his place at the head of the German
delegation and sat facing France's Clemenceau, Britain's Lloyd
George, the U.S.A.'s Woodrow Wilson, and Italy's Orlando.

Clemenceau made the opening remarks:

"Gentlemen plenipotentiaries of the German Empire . . . the
time has come when we must settle our accounts. . . . You have
asked for peace. We are ready to give you peace. We shall
present to you now a book which contains our conditions . . .
this second Treaty of Versailles has cost us too much for us not to
take on our side all the necessary precautions and guarantees that
the peace shall be a lasting one."

Then he announced, "Count von Brockdorff-Rantzau has the
floor."

While everyone present expected the Count to rise, instead he

remained seated, and indeed, began to speak from his chair with
a defiance and bitterness that shocked his audience.

"Gentlemen," he said, "we are deeply impressed with the
sublime task . . . to give a durable peace to the world. We are
under no illusion as to the extent of our defeat and the degree of
our want of power . . . We know the extent of hatred which we
encounter here, and we have heard the passionate demands that
the vanquishers shall make us pay as the vanquished . . . those
worthy of punishment. It is demanded of us that we shall confess
ourselves to be the only ones guilty of the war. Such a confession
in my mouth would be a lie."

President Wilson leaned forward with intense, incredulous gaze
as the Count fairly hissed his naked words. As the meeting was
adjourned and the Germans exited, holding a copy of that fateful
document, the Treaty of Versailles, there was only one topic of
conversation. Among the Allied delegates and journalists alike, all
we could recount was the strange and unabashed insolence of the
Count as he had made his address without rising to his feet.
Wiser men might have seen in this deliberate insult to the heads
of state at the conference an omen that the resurrectionists were
already on the horizon singing the song of their uniform shirts:
"Color Me Brown."

As all the correspondents returned to Paris to write much the
same story—the inexplicable impertinence of the Germans, now
fawning, now defiant—I hoped to get an inkling of what really
lay behind the German strategy, what was really in the Boche
mind. In my striped pants and cutaway once again, I hurried to
the Hotel des Réservoirs to await the return of the German
delegation from the Trianon, where I scored, at last, one of the
few real beats of the Peace Conference.

My old acquaintance Herr Wolff again led the way, ushering
me into the old ballroom of the hotel, which had been refitted as
a communal dining room. Three immense oval tables, large
enough to seat three hundred people, were set with shining coffee
cups and huge platters of sugared *Kuchen*. Most of the German
delegation was already seated, waiting for their leaders to return.

Wolff deposited me discreetly at the end of a table opposite to
the seat presumably set aside for Count Brockdorff-Rantzau and
his associates.

I was the only non-German there—the only American newsman—the sole outsider in the room—the single ex-enemy! Except for the German journalists, who knew me well by now, I trusted the others thought me one of the members of the mission. I tried to keep poised, but anyone noticing my hands would have seen them shaking like fried bacon in a hot pan.

After all, I wasn't exactly built like Agent 007. These German faces represented the enemy, vanquished or not. What if they suddenly spotted me, or already had, but were biding their time to pounce on me? And the French military—how would they react when they found out?

When Wolff turned to talk to me, he noted the heavy perspiration on my face, and this time a certain hysteria really gripped me.

"I think I'd better leave," I whispered.

He was a pillar of sense and calm—my friend, really. "Keep quiet, and no one will notice you. If you get up now, everyone will look," he cautioned. "Sit there," he directed firmly.

The thought crossed my mind. Could I really trust Wolff? What if he had schemed to be my betrayer? At that precise moment a door behind us opened, and everyone in the hall stood up and looked in *our direction.* Turning around, I saw it was Count von Brockdorff-Rantzau who had entered in back of us. Two seconds later, the seat next to mine was occupied by the Count. I had been misdirected to the head of the table! But, just because I was at his side, the Count ignored me altogether as he looked, instead, out ahead at the others.

His mouth was pulled tight and his eyes seemed at once hard and preoccupied. He arose. He spoke in German, of course.

"That Clemenceau, that senile old man hurling insults at our people!" he said between his teeth. "We are not so to be treated! "Ah, but what could I do? The only way for me to articulate my feelings was deliberately to keep sitting as I gave them my answer to the Treaty. . . ." He paused and surveyed his delegates with a softer, almost paternal look.

"And now, *meine Kinder* [my children], the Fatherland has been dealt a heavy blow. There is work to be done. This treaty must be studied and altered. I shall expect all of you here after supper to begin it, for it surely is only the beginning. We must work. We are Germans! We will not forget! We will rise from this shame."

That was it. He got up and quickly disappeared through the same little door in back of us.

As for myself, no Batman ever traveled faster out of there. I knew I had heard something never intended for the ears of outsiders, particularly for the ears of an American reporter. And I was lucky beyond my own belief to have played "I Spy" with safety and success.

That evening in the press room of the Hotel Crillon in Paris, every correspondent was giving his own account of how the German insolence would be making the morning headlines in the States, while I raced on to my newsroom in Paris to get in a slightly more inside, more sinister, version.

Lawrence Hills, of the *Sun's* Washington Bureau, was sitting pounding the typewriter when I exploded in and yanked him by the sleeve.

"I've just come from Versailles!" I yelled, expecting him by some miracle to know what had happened.

"That's certainly Page One," he said sarcastically. "We've *all* been to Versailles, or haven't you heard? Or maybe you had an interview with Marie Antoinette?"

"Smart aleck," I said. "*I*, yours truly, was in the room with the German delegation when Brockdorff-Rantzau brought back the Treaty and said some fascinating things not intended for anyone but Germans to hear!" Then I filled him in on the many hours I'd spent as a "German" in the confidences of the German press.

That brought the action. He grabbed his portable typewriter, he grabbed me, and we rushed madly to the Crillon trunk room, in the basement, out of sight and earshot of other reporters.

"Wait a minute," I said. "I've got to get in the mood." I donned my round specs and Tyrolean hat.

We sat down on two boxes, used a trunk for a desk, and wrote the story.

James P. Howe has covered Germany, England, Russia, Poland, India, China and Japan for the Associated Press. He has also written for the *Washington Post, Portland Oregonian, New York Evening Journal, San Francisco Chronicle* and *New Orleans Times-Democrat.* He is now self-employed in what could be a newsman's paradise—the Gopher Gulch Wine Cellars.

"If You Dare Do That, I'll Shoot You!"

JAMES P. HOWE

TO HAVE a noted character threaten to shoot you doesn't always work out to one's advantage as it did in my case. I won an outstanding promotion.

I was a news reporter in London. One day, out of a perfectly clear sky, I distinctly heard a literary light known wherever the English language is spoken warn me that he was resorting to the use of a gun.

This Fleet Street incident of 40 years ago involved the great and grizzled George Bernard Shaw.

Three others heard the threat: Mrs. Shaw, Mr. Shaw's secretary, Miss Blanche Patch, and the family cook and housekeeper.

The Irish author of *Pygmalion* (which developed into *My Fair Lady*) had often tongue-lashed anyone who dared take sides against him. It was his habit. Also now and then he appeared eager to bring his fists into violent action if necessary to indicate just how he stood on any subject under the sun. He was a prankster of the first order. Thrived on it.

But as far as I know, I'm the only individual, living or dead, whom this genius of stagecraft endeavored to intimidate by threatening to use a firearm.

The several interviews I had with GBS concerned his winning of the 1925 Nobel Prize for literature. Mr. Shaw accepted the honor with dignity and grace, but turned down the prize money with a vengeance.

That started the rumpus.

The Swedish Academy was in an uproar. Some members considered the action of the London Fabian in refusing the prize money as an out-and-out insult—tantamount to refusing the award itself.

During several years with the AP in London, one of my most cherished possessions was a little vestpocket black book. In this I had recorded the unlisted telephone numbers of various officials and other persons of note who were apt to figure in the news from time to time.

In addition to that of G. Bernard Shaw, as he signed himself, I had written down the secret phone numbers of the United States ambassador; two of his secretaries; the personal physician of King George V, Lord Dawson of Penn; the King's chef de cuisine, André Cedard; the chef of the famous Savoy Hotel, François Latry; Sir Oliver Lodge; Sir Arthur Conan Doyle, the head man of Scotland Yard and other newsworthy individuals.

My first interview with Shaw was based on an AP dispatch from Stockholm which related the dismay of the Swedish Academy at the dramatist's acceptance of the Nobel honor but sardonic refusal of the money prize. There were considerable differences of opinion among the members as to how the situation should be handled—whether this world-famous figure should be rapped on the knuckles, or what should be done.

With this dispatch in hand, I called Mr. Shaw's secret number. Miss Patch answered the phone. I informed her that I had a dispatch I thought would be of considerable interest to her boss.

"What's it about?" she queried.

"Oh, some of Mr. Shaw's idiosyncrasies, perhaps," I said.

We sparred another minute or so, then Miss Patch asked, "Does it concern this Nobel business?" Told that it did, she replied: "Just a moment, please, and I'll see what Mr. Shaw is doing."

Within seconds a gruff voice thundered into my earpiece: "Bernard Shaw speaking."

He was quickly briefed on the gist of the Stockholm developments, and we then settled down to quite a comfortable chat.

Although the hard-boiled critic had more or less of an aversion to the telephone, he apparently was in a delightful mood that morning—mellow in spots, sarcastic in Shawlike flashes, tauntingly serious at times and bubbling over with good humor.

(Miss Patch, longtime secretary to the tall, bearded figure, confided to me later that at no time over the years had she ever seen Mr. Shaw enjoying himself quite so much, especially on the phone, as he did that morning when I happened to call up.)

"It's up to the Swedish Academy," is what I heard as sort of a growl. "I'm not worrying—let them do that. But I'm certainly going to be a most interested front-row spectator in the discussion which I hope will now develop around the question of giving prizes to writers!"

It was here that Mr. Shaw was asked if he agreed with Sinclair Lewis, who had turned down the Pulitzer Prize on the contention that prizes were really bad for literature, and he snapped: "I don't agree with anything!"

He went on: "I had heard of the Nobel Prize, I believe, before I wrote the work which won the award—whatever it was—but I certainly did not try for it.

"Understand me," snarled the voice, "I did not try for it."

The author of *Back to Methuselah* and numerous other successes went on and on for perhaps another ten or fifteen minutes. And I had a pocketful of notes and my interview made up a thousand words or more for the transatlantic cable.

Frank H. King, now of Dallas, Texas, was also a member of the AP London staff. Frank, a habitual reader of the newspapers, soon had compiled a fat scrapbook of the Shaw interview from papers coast to coast.

Frank suggested that possibly Mr. Shaw would be interested in seeing the scrapbook. I agreed that it was an excellent idea.

I called Miss Patch, informed her of the wonderful "play" the Shaw interview had—the big headlines, some in color, and all that. Miss Patch was somewhat skeptical as to whether her employer would actually be concerned.

And here's where my guardian angel again came to my aid. I heard Miss Patch remark, in an aside: "Here's that Associated Press chap again," and Mr. Shaw himself took over with "What's this all about, anyway!"

An opportunity of a lifetime. As I told it to my listener, Frank King's scrapbook had just about tripled in size and undoubtedly was the greatest thing of its kind that had ever been put together.

Mr. Shaw said emphatically that he was not interested in clippings about himself or anything else.

"But, Mr. Shaw," I pleaded, "please understand that these clippings are historic. There are all kinds of caricatures and very old photographs. Snappy headlines, in black ink and in red and green and pink. I'm sure you'll have a hearty laugh out of this assortment."

The voice on the other end of the line took on rather a mean and nasty edge. The voice said: "If I should see that scrapbook, I'd drop dead."

That remark stumped me for a moment, but I did manage to say that such an event would assuredly be an international calamity. And I added:

"I'll bring the book along and leave it on your desk. You may glance through it at your convenience."

The voice bristled. It was sort of gruff, but very clear, and it said, "If you dare do that, I'll shoot you!" And hung up.

Within minutes and the taxicab-meter click of one shilling six pence, I was at the iron gate, with its prongs and wire netting, that barred the stairway to Shaw's second floor apartment in Adelphia Terrace, overlooking the Thames Embankment, not far from Trafalgar Square.

Miss Patch appeared. "I'm the fellow Mr. Shaw threatened to shoot a few minutes ago," I said meekly.

"Of course," Miss Patch laughed, "I thought you'd take the hint," and the gate opened and clanged behind me as we climbed to the forbidden den. I left the scrapbook in Miss Patch's hands with the suggestion that perhaps Mr. Shaw would care to make some comment on the contents and honor me with his autograph.

Within a few days the following note came in Miss Patch's handwriting: "Your book will be ready for you on Monday morning if you care to call for it. The message is in it, but I don't know if you will like it."

Running over with curiosity, I was johnny-on-the-spot that Monday morning. And in the scrapbook, Mr. Shaw had written: "The contents of this scrapbook form a masterpiece of modern journalism. This testimonial is to be interpreted in the most unfavorable sense. G. Bernard Shaw, London, 26 Feb. 1927."

Due chiefly to the sprightly individual to whom I was talking (even if I do say so myself), the Shaw "shooting" incident came out a light and breezy story widely used in the AP papers. Additionally, in many instances, caricatures accompanied the layout, with original and amusing headlines.

Not long after Mr. Shaw had thumbed through the Frank King scrapbook, a suit regarding royalties had been filed in the British courts involving one of the Shaw plays, *Arms and the Man,* which had been popularized as a light opera in the United States and Europe under the title of *The Chocolate Soldier.* To straighten out a legal point, I called the Shaw residence. Neither of the Shaws was at home. Miss Patch answered and was in a talkative mood. So she took advantage of the opportunity to give me a peek behind the scenes at the reaction of her cynical employer to the book of interview clippings.

Several times as he went through the pages, Miss Patch said, she heard a chuckle coming from his study. Then suddenly Mr. Shaw himself appeared at the entrance to the secretary's quarters, scrapbook in hand, and burst into laughter as he read one of the headlines:

"Bernard Shaw poses as Gunman."

I thanked Miss Patch for her hearty cooperation in helping out in the scrapbook adventure and also mentioned my appreciation of the autographed snapshot of himself that Mr. Shaw had sent me. In the photo the mischievous wizard is stretched comfortably on a sofa, apparently content with everything. Shoulders propped up on pillows, arms folded, lengthy legs very much in evidence, the playwright gazes cunningly directly into the camera. His whiskers are well combed and relaxed, and all and all there are no indications of any of the antagonism that was one of the tricks of his trade.

This was his favorite photograph, Miss Patch stressed, and he passed one out but seldom.

Kent Cooper, at that time general manager of the AP, had noted the Shaw interviews both by cable and in letters. Now, if the reader will kindly overlook a bit of ego, it's sort of satisfying to admit that I am still fond of thinking that perhaps Mr. Cooper had gotten the idea that I was a pretty good reporter. Anyway, the first thing I knew, there I was on the other side of the globe in China—covering a war and revolution.

Bruno Shaw has had a long career in Far Eastern journalism—Overseas Editor of the *Hankow Herald*, Associate Editor of the *China Weekly Review*, General Manager of Trans-Pacific News Service and an executive in the Far Eastern Division of the OWI.

Train Ride

BRUNO SHAW

THE FREIGHT cars strung out behind the panting, struggling engine were of medium size, somewhat larger than the French World War I 40-and-8s, somewhat smaller than our American railway cargo carriers. They were crawling to the battleground of the moment, from the Yangtze River port of Kiukiang southward to Nanchang, on the eighty miles of rail that lay between the two cities.

The pace was necessarily slow. On either side of the roadbed lay broken, overturned freight cars similar to the one from the open door of which I viewed them, and noisome, unburied bodies clad in moldering cotton-padded uniforms, residue of the fighting which during the past two weeks had driven the defeated Kiangsi provincial warlord, Sun Chuan-fang, northward across the Yangtze. Some of his more courageous holdouts were making a blazing but futile last-ditch stand outside the wall of Nanchang, where they would be annihilated before the sun of this day would set.

I was a voluntary passenger, on my way to becoming the first newspaperman ever to interview General Chiang Kai-shek, Commander-in-Chief of the Northern Expedition—the revolutionary

armies whose goal was the overthrow of the provincial warlords
and the unification of China. I was willing to take my chances on
being able to get into the city of Nanchang, about whose walls
the flame and smoke of battle still raged, and out again without
mortal injury. I did not expect, however, on what I thought
would be an uneventful ten-hour train ride, in a freight car with
some forty soldiers and a half dozen shaggy Mongolian ponies, to
be nearly murdered on the way.

I had set out on November 17, 1926, by the Jardine River
steamer *Kungwo*, which arrived at Kiukiang on the south bank of
the Yangtze the following morning. I was armed with two letters
of introduction to General Chiang. One was from General Chen
Ko-yu, local commander of the forward elements of the Fourth
Route or "Iron" Army, and the other from Chen Kung-po, labor
minister and concurrently acting commissioner of foreign affairs
of the Kuomintang's left-wing government, which had been
established in Hankow only a month previously.

Eugene Chen, the flamboyantly voluble West Indian non-
Chinese-speaking minister of foreign affairs, had not yet arrived
in Hankow. When he came, soon afterward, it was his custom for
the first month or two figuratively to stand on a soapbox in his
office and deliver to H. J. Timperley of the *Manchester Guardian*
and me bloodcurdling manifestoes which, when we cabled them
to London and New York, would arrive on each side of the
Atlantic just in time to spoil the breakfasts of millions of readers
of the morning papers.

Both letters, in addition to serving as introductions to General
Chiang, endorsed me as "a friend of the Chinese people." With
these credentials, I was sure I would receive a friendly reception
from soldiers of the Kuomintang army I would encounter on the
way.

Ideologically speaking, the Northern Expedition, which began
its march from Canton in the spring of 1926, was by no means a
homogeneous force. It had enrolled under its banner many
diverse elements of rebellion. There were the *hung hutze*, "red
beards" from Honan, outright bandits and highway robbers,
picturesquely decorated with handy daggers in braided cord
sheaths. There were high-school and college students eager to
avenge their fellows who had died in mass executions at the
hands of know-nothing provincial warlords. There were peasants.

miners, artisans, factory workers. All had been indoctrinated, before the march northward, by fiery Chinese Communist propagandists trained in Russia, aided by Russian advisers and instructors. Heading the entire political department of the revolutionary army was Michael Borodin, known to Chinese by the transliterated name of Bo Goon-won.

Allied with the Communist wing of the Northern Expedition was General Tang Sen-chi, a pint-size, vicious and volatile Hunanese with personal ambitions of his own. His troops, together with the propaganda corps under Teng Yen-ta, chief of the revolution's political office, had arrived in August of 1926 in the Wuhan cities that were my home.

Wuhan is a metropolitan area made up of three cities at the confluence of the Han and the Yangtze rivers. Hankow, the larger of the two on the north bank of the Yangtze, was the principal commercial and residential area for foreigners. Here Britain, Russia, France, Germany and Japan all maintained transplanted bits of their homelands, known as Concessions, one next to the other along the river edge.

On the south side of the Yangtze, slightly to the west, is Wuchang, the capital of the Province of Hupeh. On the north, just west of Hankow, is Hanyang, built against a steep slope and separated from Hankow by the Han River, which flows from north to south, meeting the east-west-flowing Yangtze head on.

The commanding officer of the provincial forces at Hanyang was General Liu Tso-lung, whom Teng Yen-ta overpowered with "silver bullets," a common phrase in China for a cash bribe in time of war. Hankow was under control of Marshal Wu Pei-fu, then the most powerful warlord in all China, and regarded by the governments of most Western countries as the head of the nation.

I had talked with Marshal Wu at his railway station encampment at Changsintien, a few miles below Peking, only a week or so previously. He was engaged at that time in a futile attempt to dislodge the "Christian General" Feng Yu-hsiang from the northwest area beyond the Great Wall, with feebly ineffectual field gun and rifle fire that reached scarcely beyond his own front lines. When I asked him what he intended to do about the Northern Expedition under General Chiang Kai-shek, which was then on its way to the Wuhan cities, Wu assured me that he "would take care of that boy" very shortly. The morning after he

arrived in Hankow a few days later, he was sold out by Liu Tso-
lung in Hanyang, making it possible for Tang Sen-chi's army to
ferry the narrow Han River from Hanyang to Hankow, instead of
having to cross the broad, fast flowing Yangtze with its tremendous expanse of muddy foreshore in the autumn season,
which would have subjected Tang's attacking forces to withering
rifle, machine-gun and mortar fire from concrete abutments on
the north shore. With the arrival of Tang's troops in the outskirts
of Hankow, Wu Pei-fu's army melted away northward on the
Peking-Hankow Railway, without a fight.

Within the stoutly defended city of Wuchang across the river, a
quite different story was unfolding. The provincial capital, then
massively walled, was under attack by General Chen Ko-yu's
"Iron Army" and defended by General Liu Yu-chun, a loyal
adherent of Marshal Wu Pei-fu, who had already fled northward
with his troops. Wuchang had been under siege now for forty
days, during which nothing moved in and nothing moved out
without permission of attackers and defenders both. Together
with Suffragan Bishop Logan H. Roots of the American Church
Mission, I made several trips across the Yangtze, on barges towed
by tugs of the China Merchants Steam Navigation Company, to
evacuate women and children who were literally starving.

It was now early in October of 1926, and the anniversary of the
revolution that was launched on October 10, 1911, was approaching. It would be a great triumph, for propaganda as well as
military purposes, if the defenders of Wuchang could be made to
capitulate on that particular day. Teng Yen-ta conceived the
strategy. The ten thousand troops holding the city, under General
Liu Yu-chun, would be allowed to march out through the east
gate without surrendering, carrying away with them only side
arms with which to defend themselves if necessary on their way
back to their home villages. Any who wanted to switch allegiance
would be enrolled in the revolutionary army, Teng Yen-ta promised, and their past sins forgiven.

By now, after forty days of siege, every dog and cat inside the
walls of Wuchang had been eaten. With his troops and the
civilian population facing starvation, General Liu agreed to
evacuate the city in accordance with the terms offered him. He
demanded, however, that two foreign hostages must accompany
his men, to ensure the good faith of his enemy. The two he

designated were those with whom he had already become acquainted in the course of the evacuation of women and children,
Bishop Roots and myself. We were to be escorted across the river
to Wuchang at daybreak on the morning of October 10, and a
few hours later we would march out of Wuchang at the head of
General Liu's largely disarmed columns, through the east gate.
Treachery by their enemy would result in instant death to us.

I'll probably never know why I agreed to be a party to this
suicidal scheme when Bishop Roots came into my office on the
morning of October 9 and asked me to enter into it with him. It
was his business to save souls, and perhaps the bodies in which
they were housed; mine only to report on what happened to
them. And besides, I had already made acquaintance with Teng
Yen-ta and many of the other Communist political and military
leaders in Wuhan and had acquired a total lack of confidence in
the promises of any of them. Nevertheless, said the persuasive
bishop, we are not going to do this merely to help resolve a
military impasse. We will be doing it to save the lives of
thousands of innocent men, women and children—particularly
children—who will starve to death if we fail them. And so,
probably to prove that a pawn could be as foolhardy as a bishop,
I agreed.

Fortunately for us, we were never called upon to lead that
march. Informed by their commander of the arrangement for
their evacuation without reprisal the next morning, the troops
inside Wuchang relaxed their watchfulness. They fraternized that
evening to the extent of allowing a few enemy soldiers, without
their guns, of course, to be hauled by ropes to the top of the city
wall, bringing gifts of baskets of food and wine. Not many of
them. Just enough of them so that, on signal, they were able to
drive knives deep into the throats of the defenders at that spot,
make their way down the stone steps inside the wall quickly and
silently, speed to the north gate where they cut to ribbons the few
guards on duty, unbolt the ponderous wooden door, drag it open,
and make way for the "Iron Army" assault ready, waiting,
unexpected, and overwhelming.

Of the ten thousand northern troops whose weapons already
had been tossed into heaps in preparation for break of day
departure, not more than half, by my rough count of the quick
and the dead as I walked through the city that afternoon,

horrified by this wanton inhuman butchery, survived the bloody treachery of that day.

At noon of this infamous day the consuls general of the nations represented at Hankow were invited by Chen Kung-po to attend a reception in celebration of the Wuchang Double Ten (October 10) "victory." It was a rare sight indeed to behold the members of the foreign diplomatic corps lifting their glasses and drinking the toast "Success to the revolution," while wishing in their hearts that this particular wing of it would drop dead before their eyes. It was doubly rare, because the Communist sponsors of the reception were very well aware of what the members of the diplomatic corps were thinking.

Chiang Kai-shek, Commander in Chief of the revolutionary armies, was a man of mystery. At the head of an army that had routed every provincial warlord from Canton to the Yangtze, his exploits had already become legend and his name a magic symbol of victory. It seemed astonishing, therefore, that on this day of rejoicing not one Chinese or Russian official present raised a glass in his honor, and that his name was not so much as even mentioned. And so I decided here, at this victory celebration, to beard the military lion in his revolutionary den and learn for myself what manner of man it was who commanded an "ever-victorious army," the Communist sector of which, having established a revolutionary national capital at Hankow, refused him this mark of respect on so important an occasion.

Cheng Kung-po was enthusiastic about my proposal to interview Chiang Kai-shek, and the next morning he sent me his personal letter of introduction to General Chiang. General Chen Ko-yu, with whom I had become very well acquainted during the siege of Wuchang, was equally obliging. I wired the Kiukiang correspondent of my newspaper, a young Chinese middle school student, to meet the river steamer on which I would arrive, and to arrange to accompany me to Nanchang.

Chiang Kai-shek's forces had already taken Kiukiang. But they were still fighting a rearguard, last-ditch resistance at Nanchang, eighty miles farther south. It was not surprising, therefore, that no passenger trains had run on the Kiukiang-Nanchang line for several weeks, and it seemed highly unlikely that they would resume normal operations for some time to come.

My young Chinese friend, Jimmy Yung, met me at the wharf,

and from there we walked through the quiet and meticulously well kept British Concession of Kiukiang, which comprised only a few square blocks of lovely, flower-gardened, suburban England, to the railhead outside. There we found a train of a half-dozen freight cars, with armed Kuomintang soldiers climbing aboard.

"Is the train going to Nanchang?" I asked one of them.

"Yes," he said.

"When will it leave?"

"Soon."

Jimmy and I clambered aboard the last car and found ourselves in the company of a half-dozen scrubby, dirty, Mongolian ponies, and as many soldiers sitting on the floor nearby. It was another hour or so before the train pulled out, and during that time many more soldiers joined us. I was surprised that my presence did not arouse any curiosity. It was only later that I learned that Russian propaganda and military advisers had accustomed the Chinese revolutionary troops to an occasional foreigner in their midst, and that, because of the chino trousers and khaki shirt I customarily wore on trips into the countryside, they simply assumed that I must be a Russian comrade.

The railroad bridge near the southern terminus, across the Kan River where it flows by Nanchang, had been built by Japanese engineers many years before. When I first knew it, it seemed to have been broken at one time or another in every conceivable place a bridge could break, and to have been repaired with bamboo poles, ropes, chains, and whatever else may have been at hand at the moment. When I had previously traveled across it by passenger train, I had wondered how, as the bridge teetered back and forth several hundred feet above the river, it could possibly hold together under the weight of the joggling cars creeping inch by inch across it. Watching it shudder and buckle, and hearing it creak as the train crawled across it, a betting man would be inclined to give odds that the cars would go down through the middle or topple over the side. Somehow, they never did.

As our freight cars bumped along at about eight miles an hour, stopping often for inspection of the surrounding countryside and to make sure the rails were on their roadbed ahead where they should be, several of the soldiers came over to engage us in talk, which is the friendly custom of Chinese everywhere.

"Are you a soldier?" one of them asked me.

"No," I said, "I am a newspaper reporter."

"Where do you come from?"

"My home is Hankow," I said. "I am going to Nanchang only for a day or two, and then will return to my home."

This was wonderful news indeed, to have someone with them from the great city their armies had just taken. What had happened in Hankow, they wanted to know. Had all the capitalist oppressors been killed? Had all the imperialist foreigners been driven out? Their excited questions came fast, and the anti-foreign tone of the sentiments revealed in them was quite disturbing. In a little while I feigned tiredness and expressed a desire to lie down and sleep.

By then, however, the manner of my replies must have disturbed them as much as their questions had me. There was some whispered talk which, since it was in southern dialect, was wholly incomprehensible to me. Then one of them asked me point-blank, in Chinese I could understand: "What nationality are you?"

I pretended I did not know what he meant, and that I did not even hear. I did not like the question and had no desire to answer it. "Tell the foreigner to answer," one of them barked at Jimmy Yung, who by now was pale with fear. I was far from comfortable myself, but I knew that Jimmy would be killed out of hand if he offended them, and I did not want to see him done in before my eyes because of me. I was still under the pre-Communist delusion that, being a foreigner protected by extraterritorial jurisdiction in China, my corporal presence was inviolate.

I sat up and answered for myself in Chinese, "I am an American."

Had I suddenly started shooting Roman candles or blowing flames out of my nostrils and ears, I could not have created more astonishment than I did with those four words. There was total silence for a few moments. Then one of them muttered: "Kill the *ta pitzu* [big nose: slang for foreigner]."

The atmosphere in the car had become heavy and tense. Soldiers were in a ring about us, three or four deep. Some held rifles in their hands. A silent, black, mass hatred was closing in upon me. Again the same one said, "Beat him down. Kill the foreign devil."

One of the soldiers, gathering a mouthful of phlegm raucously from the depths of his lungs, spat it at my feet. Any outward evidence of anger or resentment on my part would have qualified me instantly for interment in the local Potter's Field.

Not trusting my own Chinese, I said to Jimmy: "Tell them I have letters from General Chen Ko-yu and Commissioner Chen Kung-po to deliver to General Chiang Kai-shek, and that I am going to Nanchang at the personal invitation of the Commander in Chief."

While I wondered why no one had yet whacked me over the head with a rifle butt, Jimmy interpreted for me. "Let me show you the letters," I said, drawing them from my pocket and offering them. I felt like an amateur magician at a cocktail party who, approaching a group intent on the subject of their own conversation, proffers a deck of cards with "Take a card, any card," and is rewarded with hostile glares or utterly ignored.

My life, however, depended on what came of this. Only a few days previously Basil Lang of the *Times* of London had been beaten to death by Communist students in the Loyang, Honan, YMCA, when he attempted to discuss with them the merits of democracy versus Communism.

My hand dropped back with the letters that no one cared to see, and again there came from someone in the midst of the group: "Kill him. Kill the American dog." I made one more try at name-dropping. Not in the hope that it would do much good, but probably feeling that as long as I heard myself talk I knew that I was still alive.

"I have been a friend of the Chinese people for many years," I said in Chinese as rapidly as I could, to try to prevent interruption, vocal or physical, and without quite knowing what I was going to say next. "Yesterday when I was talking to Borodin he asked me to be sure to report to him about the situation in Nanchang as soon as I return to Hankow."

The words had scarcely left my lips when I knew with absolute certainty that I had traveled from my way out of this world, in the space of little more than a second, back into it. With that one name I had hit the jackpot.

"You know Bo Goon-won?"

"Know him," I said, "we are very old friends."

"How can an American be a friend of Bo Goon-won?"

"Don't you know that we have oppressed people in America too?" I demanded. "And," I added, hoping I would be forgiven on Judgment Day for what I said in this extremity, "that many of us in our own country are fighting for liberation of oppressed people everywhere. That is how I know Bo Goon-won," I said, "because we are fighting together for world liberation. Someday," I said, feeling that the time had come to go all out with the large economy-size package, "you Chinese liberators will come over to help us free ourselves from our own oppressors. We will fight for freedom of the slaves of the world together—in China, in America, everywhere."

By now I was in excellent form. The soldiers, gathered in a circle on the floor about me, were wholly absorbed with my harangue, as Jimmy interpreted it for me. One soldier offered me a cigarette and lit it for me. The previous terrifying few minutes seemed never to have been. We were all good friends, all comrades, in the glorious crusade to bring the Marxist-Leninist utopia to all mankind.

"Tell us," one of them said, "what it is like in America."

As I looked at them, forty-odd Chinese peasant soldiers on their way to war in a lumbering freight car, sure that they were fighting for a righteous cause, hating me with a violent, flaming hatred only a few moments before because, as an American, I was a symbol of imperialism and oppression—I marveled at the complete job of brainwashing the Communists had done among these simple people who constituted the backbone of Chiang Kai-shek's army.

With fingers crossed, I embarked upon a description of a bleak America that no American, past or present, could possibly have recognized as "the land of the brave and the home of the free." The picture I drew brought assurances from my listeners that one day we would all fight together to liberate the downtrodden people of my country from their capitalist-imperialist yoke.

Long before our train rumbled at snail's pace across the bridge to the south bank of the Kan River and we went our several ways, we had become old friends, of each other, and of oppressed people everywhere. We had exchanged cigarettes, and much pleasant small talk. Jimmy Yung, caught up in the spirit of good fellowship, grateful that he continued to remain with me among the living, had embroidered fascinating ornamentation onto the tall tales I had spun for him to interpret in local idiom and dialect. This wisely kept the conversation in the realm of minute details of faraway places, preventing it from returning to ourselves.

When we parted, the soldiers to join their regiments, and I to have my interview with Chiang Kai-shek, we shouted good-byes and see-you-agains to each other that echoed pleasantly to our listening ears as Jimmy and I strode through the tunnel under Nanchang's north wall, and through the gates into the city. The train ride was over, and we were on our way to a meal, a bath, and sleep for one night instead of forever.

Three days later I was back at my desk in Hankow, and the following morning, November 23, 1926, the *Hankow Herald* carried my interview with General Chiang Kai-shek for the full seven columns of the entire front page, surmounted by this streamer headline:

GENERAL CHIANG KAI-SHEK REVEALS STARTLING PROGRAM
OF THE NATIONALIST REVOLUTIONARY CAMPAIGN IN CHINA

Following my by-line, the lead paragraph of the story said: "The revolution which is now in progress by the Nationalist Forces in China will not be completed until all existing treaties with foreign powers will have been abrogated and all Foreign Concessions returned to the Chinese Government, was a declaration made to me in a personal interview with the Commander-in-Chief of the Nationalist Army at Nanchang, Kiangsi, on Friday afternoon, November 19th."

For many weeks Reuters, the British news wire service, and Japanese and French news services, had been cabling reports that were being published in European and American newspapers, that Chiang Kai-shek was "dead as a doornail," that he was "wounded," that he was "mortally wounded," and that he had "died of wounds." And so I commented in my story that "For one who is dead, General Chiang Kai-shek seemed extremely healthy and in good spirits when I met him last Friday afternoon in Nanchang."

The full-page report of my interview with General Chiang concluded with this comment: "The statements which he has made in this first and exclusive interview, to the *Hankow Herald,* should give the Powers an idea of the purpose of the present Nationalist Revolution."

My Associated Press telegraph accreditation cards were good

for collect news cables to London, New York, San Francisco, and Shanghai. I could pick the city I thought best for distribution of a particular story, or for the time of day it was likely to be received.

In Shanghai at that time, AP was represented by a stringer, Charles Laval, who was editor of an English-language daily, the *China Press*. I decided to send my Chiang interview story via Laval in Shanghai, rather than directly to England or the United States because, as a domestic telegram, it was less likely to be brought to the attention of Percy Chen, Eugene Chen's son, who was telegraph censor at Hankow, and who had told me with considerable glee only the previous week that he had canceled out altogether every news story filed during the previous two weeks by Charles Daley of the *Chicago Tribune*. And Daley learned about it only after he received a rocket from his home office. A rocket, in newspaper language, is a wire of very few words which the recipient understands to mean: "You are on our payroll, remember? Where the hell are you?"

My precaution paid off. The entire story went through without a hitch. It got full-page, front-page, banner headlines in the next day's *China Press*. There was only one thing wrong with it.

Charlie Laval was as happy-go-lucky a character as ever graced a newspaper fiction yarn—a companionable drinker who would down a few with a friend at any time of day or night. A news bonanza such as my out-of-the-blue interview with General Chiang called for a celebration, and Charlie wanted everyone within reach of his voice and his phone to celebrate it with him. With the story safely in good hands in his composing room, the AP was as far out of Charlie's mind as it was out of his sight.

The next morning my story was appropriated by every foreign correspondent in Shanghai, who lifted it from the *China Press*, and who wired it to their papers and news syndicates as their own, scooping me out of my own hard-won exclusive story everywhere in the world.

W. W. Chaplin now views the world from the relatively serene precincts of Bradenton, Florida, where he is News Director of radio station WTRL. Life was not always so serene, as the following article reveals. Mr. Chaplin has worked nearly forty years as a foreign correspondent and news commentator for the Associated Press, International News Service and the National Broadcasting Company. He is a former president of the Overseas Press Club.

The Impossible Takes a Little Longer

W. W. CHAPLIN

THIS IS a tale of two interviews, perhaps the shortest verbally in the history of journalism. Yet they both made headlines and column-long stories featured across America.

In 1930 I was on the Associated Press staff in London. The AP was then housed on the ground floor of the old red brick and stone Reuters Building on the Thames Embankment near Black-friars Bridge. The chief of bureau was Dewitt McKenzie, who had been one of the few war correspondents of World War I.

Mac looked more like a college professor or a preacher than a war reporter. But he had been through the mill of combat and he had learned many things. One was that the word "impossible" is simply a meaningless screen for the timid to hide behind. His credo was put into words in a later war by the Seabees, whose slogan was: "The difficult we can do immediately; the impossible takes a little longer." To him the word "impossible" was just a challenge which he always accepted. One day he called me into his office.

"Bill," he said, "J. P. Morgan is arriving on his ocean-going yacht today, and tomorrow he's being given some sort of honorary degree at Oxford. Get an interview."

Everybody knew that the head of the House of Morgan, the Maharaja of Money, never talked to the press, but that was just the sort of challenge Mac liked and even sought out.

In the morning I took a train to Oxford and obtained a press pass to the ceremony. Morgan had come in by car and was sequestered at the home of the university chancellor, which was walled around and otherwise secured against intrusion by a tall iron gate.

Promptly at high noon the gate was opened and Morgan and the chancellor walked out, followed by a small procession of dignitaries in the colorful robes of their doctorates. Morgan was the only one in a business suit, a crow with a bulbous beak among a flock of peacocks.

The little group walked up the main street, cleared of traffic for the occasion, to the austere chapel of Christ College. All along the way, on both sides of the road, students were sitting on their bicycles against the curb. And as the marchers passed, the students gave lusty utterance to what the British call the bird and we call the Bronx cheer.

Morgan must have been informed in advance of this traditional reception for famous visitors, because he never batted an eye and the parade entered the gloomy chapel, with me as the tail of the dog.

There was a lengthy ceremony, conducted all in Latin, which was beyond me and I suspect beyond Morgan too. But at last it was over and J. P. Morgan was some sort of honorary doctor, perhaps Doctor of Money.

The chancellor placed around his shoulders a long black cape faced with scarlet satin. And a flunky in knee breeches plunked on his head a hat that looked like a squashy black velvet ice pack with crimson piping. The party moved back to the street.

The students had escalated their war against pomp and ceremony and the troops of derision had been doubled. The Bronx cheers, loud and clear, followed the gaudily gowned party all the way to the chancellor's house.

There the big gate was swung open and the privileged walked in. As the gate clanged shut, I called to Mr. Morgan through the grillwork and asked if he would give me a message for America about the great honor done him. He turned with a smile and faced me through the gate. He said: "No." And that was that. An interview in one word and a negative word at that.

But my story describing J. P. Morgan at Oxford, Bronx cheers and all, got bannered treatment in many American papers, and McKenzie got a complimentary message from New York. Once more he had proved that there is no such word as impossible. For a week he strutted around looking like a canary that had swallowed a cat, and then he called me into his sanctum again.

"Bill," he said, "for four years I covered the Allied action against Germany. It was all due to one old man who blew the spark of a Balkan incident into the holocaust of a world war. He was exiled in 1918, Kaiser Wilhelm II of Germany. He was exiled to Holland, to the village of Doorn, and there he has lived ever since. In a week or so he is going to be seventy-five years old. Take a run over to Doorn and get a birthday interview with the ex-Kaiser."

I started to remind my boss that under the terms of his exile Wilhelm II was forbidden to make statements, but I saw the light of battle in Mac's eye and I said: "Yes, sir!"

I took a train to the North Sea port of Harwich (pronounced "Harridge" over there), where I boarded an overnight steamer to the Hook of Holland. A Dutch train took me to Utrecht, a sort of poor man's Venice with almost as many canals as streets. In the morning I took a bus that dropped me off at Doorn. It isn't much of a village: one main street of small stores and taverns and people in baggy blouses clattering around in wooden shoes. But it was on the world map because it was the exile home of aging Wilhelm II.

I went first to the tiny shop of our local stringer, who sold postcards and souvenirs to the tourists who stopped briefly every day to gawk at the ex-Kaiser's home, by far the biggest house in town.

This man told me it was impossible to get an interview with the former Kaiser and I was about to agree when I remembered that look in Mac's eye that said the impossible just takes a little longer. So I said I'd look around.

I walked fifty yards or so up a side road from the highway to the main entrance of the former Kaiser's residence, which on that side was protected by a stone wall with a great iron gate. Above the gate was an arch of decorative iron, in the middle of which were two large golden letters—"RI," Rex Imperator, king and emperor of a kingdom and empire which had long since ceased to exist. Everybody in the world recognized that except the Exile of Doorn himself. He preferred to live in a dream world, surrounded by the glories of his past. I rang the bell.

A coldly polite flunky talked to me through the grillwork.

"May I see the Kaiser?"

"No. He sees no one."

"But my great Uncle Poultney Bigelow, son of the late ambassador, went to school with the Kaiser and they still correspond."

"Sorry. There are no exceptions."

I walked back to the highway on which Doorn House faced and where there was, strangely enough, no high wall but only a two-bar wooden fence. Perhaps, I thought, the old man likes to be looked at even if he won't talk.

The white three-story exile mansion stood well back from the highway, at the crest of a gentle knoll. Resting my elbows on the upper bar of the fence, I looked up at the house and saw, close to the building, an old man with a white goatee sawing wood with one hand, his withered left arm swinging. This was the former Kaiser of Germany.

Every time a length of wood fell from the log a small man appeared and carried it around the house, presumably to a woodpile. Then the log was readjusted on a sawbuck and Wilhelm II would begin sawing again.

I wasn't ready to quit yet, so I gave the story the little longer that sometimes does achieve the impossible. Also I didn't see that I had anything to lose. So I straddled the fence and started up the rise of greensward.

Suddenly two large men in forest green uniforms materialized, possibly from a lookout behind a clump of shrubbery to one side. They picked me up as though I had been a shred of distasteful litter on a well-barbered lawn and tossed me back across the fence.

After dusting myself off I decided there was still one source of information open to me, and I strolled through the village. I asked people on the street how they got along with their exiled visitor. They all thought he was just great; it was an honor to

Doorn to have such an important man living among them. And they noted that his presence brought in many tourists, who spent much money in the shops. I dropped into a local tavern and asked how their exile busied himself besides sawing wood.

"Oh," said the publican, "he often walks around town, between the buses that bring the gawkers. He drops in here quite often for a stein of beer. He doesn't enter into any conversations but he's always polite."

I asked how the people of Doorn addressed him.

"Well," said the tavernkeeper, "when we pass him in the street, we always greet him in passing as 'Your Royal Highness.' It pleases him, and it doesn't cost us anything."

So I returned to London, sketching in my story on the way. McKenzie said: "I hope you got at least twice as many words as you got from J. P."

"Subtract two from that," I said and went to my desk.

When I handed in my completed picture story of Doorn and the Master of Doorn House, Mac read it carefully and then smiled. Off it went to New York and in due course Dewitt McKenzie got another cable of praise. This story too had made a hit.

And once more Mac had proved that the word "impossible" is nonsense.

In 1919 Rhea Clyman was "leg woman" for one of the first (and most
famous) American correspondents in the Soviet Union—Walter
Duranty. Later she was herself a correspondent for the *London Daily
Express*, the London *Daily Telegram* and the New York *Herald
Tribune*. She is a Canadian now in the Madison Avenue battle zone—
with the advertising firm of McCann-Erickson.

The Story That Stopped Hitler

RHEA CLYMAN

VICKY WAS pregnant. Stan, her husband, was away on leave. This
left us very shorthanded in covering the news fully in Munich. I
was fairly new in my assignment, having been posted there only
some months previously. But the Simpsons, Stanley and Vicky,
were old hands. She, German-born and fluent in the thick
Swabian dialect spoken in parts of Bavaria and Austria,
handled a multiple of jobs: listening in on shortwave Nazi
propaganda broadcasts intended for overseas listeners, translating
Nazi publications, etc., and occasionally giving a hand in writing
news dispatches; Stanley was also word-perfect in German, but
he had never lost his North country burr, or his diffidence in not
being a product of an English public (private) school. They were
the first, and only, successful husband-and-wife newspaper team
operating in Nazi Germany, and between them they represented
about four-fifths of the entire Anglo-American press coverage in
Munich. And I the remaining fifth.

We were in the midst of another political crisis. Hitler, who
had set forth his timetable for world conquest in his book, *Mein
Kampf,* was at his usual ploy of pleading for appeasement but

bent on subversion. He told the British he would forego his
demands for the old German colonies if they would only recog-
nize his right to terminate the Polish Corridor. He told the
French he would not reclaim the "lost" provinces of Alsace and
Lorraine if they would let him have the Saar back without
trouble. He told Mussolini he had no interest in the German-
speaking part of the Tyrol ceded to Italy after World War I. But
more than half of the Austrian Nazi Legion that was being
trained on German soil for the war of "liberating" Austria from
the Christian Democrat regime headed by Dr. Dollfuss came
from the Italian part of the Tyrol.

How shaky Hitler's regime was at home in those early months
of Nazism only those of us actually on the scene in Munich knew.
On the international scene he had scored one success after another: he had successfully defied the League of Nations by pulling
Germany out of it in 1933. In March of 1934 he had regained the
Saar in a faked plebiscite. In April of that year, at a birthday
rally, he had given notice that he would oust the Poles from the
Polish Corridor and the Lithuanians from Memel. His greatest
tirade was reserved for the Czechs, who were keeping the
Sudetenland—a name that was to figure over and over again in
the Hitler tirades—from him. But we in Munich felt that the
greatest danger lay just over the frontier where a weakly defended Austria, split by internal political and royalist factions,
dangled like a ripe plum for Hitler's delectation.

Before relating the course of events that led up to the scoop
that was to set Hitler's plan back by at least four years, I should
state that neither Vicky nor I was aware of how matters stood in
Austria. Our news coverage was limited to Bavaria and some
parts of Württemberg and Baden. But it stopped short at the
Austrian-Bavarian frontier. Anything happening beyond the frontier was handled by the correspondent stationed in Vienna, who
was just as jealous of the "no poaching" rule as we were for our
part. Thus, when it seemed that we were on the eve of another
Sarajevo and that only determined action on our part might save
the world from another holocaust, it never occurred to me to do
other than to meet the challenge. Nor did it to Vicky when I
presented all the facts to her.

Actually, it was facts that we needed. We had plenty of
rumors; lots and lots of circumstantial evidence that a "Hitler

surprise" was in the making. But though Dr. Emilio Enenkel, our Italian colleague of whom more shall be said later, furnished us with lintlike bits of evidence he gathered as our motorized legman, and my own sources of information—including my gabby hairdresser who culled news items for me from his barbershop clients—none of it would have done more than raise an eyebrow among our London editors, so inured were they to Hitler's alarums. In fact, the august editor of the London *Times*, for which Stan served as "our own Munich correspondent," riposted to a story of a Nazi beating of Jews and the arrest of a Roman Catholic priest who protested with: "This is as usual, and not news any more."

Those readers who are old enough will recall that scare headlines over dispatches datelined Berlin were the usual fare throughout the years of Hitler's rule. But we in Munich were in a particularly vulnerable position of crying "wolf" too often and not being taken seriously. It was because of this that I enlisted Vicky's help to get the facts from *inside* the Nazi Party by having her infiltrate the Annex which served the Austrian Nazi Legion as administrative headquarters. I figured that a woman in her ninth month of pregnancy, and looking as overslung and ungainly as poor Vicky did then, and wearing that placid cud-chewing look of a heifer some women have in their late stages of pregnancy, would excite no more attention than any other woman in a like condition were she to go and be a sit-in eavesdropper at the Annex. Since Hitler had issued his edict that German women must be fruitful and bear more children in order to be worthy of the benefits of the Third Reich, half the women in Germany were in varying stages of pregnancy that year. This included the women working in the Brown House, the Nazi Party headquarters, and at the Annex. Illegitimacy was another high Nazi mark of distinction, so to make it look plausible I suggested that Vicky should pose as an abandoned expectant mother, worried about the nonappearance of a fictitious Otto Schmidt who had fled from her arms into the Austrian Nazi Legion, and in whose whereabouts she had an economic as well as an amorous interest. Since Otto Schmidt is as common a name in Germany as Joe Smith would be here, she could sit there in the Annex for a month while they were searching through the records.

Vicky played her role perfectly, and we got the facts we

needed. The story, first published by me and then confirmed by
Vicky, brought results that have now passed into history.

The reader will no doubt ask what a woman with a non-Aryan-
sounding name like mine was doing in Munich, the birthplace of
Nazism and the seat of some of the worst excesses of anti-
Semitism. This is easily explained. After serving four years in
Russia as a news reporter and having witnessed and described
some of the worst Stalinist terrors, I was requested to leave the
Soviet Union quite politely but very, very firmly. This was the
winter of 1932–33. I returned to my native country, Canada,
where I was given a heroine's welcome, asked to do a by-lined
series of articles in the Toronto *Telegram* at space rate (a lot of
space and very little rate), and received lots and lots of invita-
tions to be guest speaker at women's clubs at no fee. By late
autumn, after having seen a beloved younger brother expire of
TB, and with no paying job offered by any of our three hometown papers, I decided to go where the news was: Germany,
where Hitler had assumed power.

I had a longtime friend of my Moscow days in Berlin, Junius B.
Wood, then head of the Chicago *Daily News* bureau. He encouraged me to come, provided I got some newspaper credentials
and would keep my mouth shut and my personal feelings to
myself. Another friend, John Scott of the Toronto *Globe Mail*,
gave me my credentials for space rate coverage. So on a bleak
November day, at the height of the dismal 1933 depression, I set
sail from New York on the North German Lloyd liner *Bremen*. I
had almost the entire liner to myself because, since Hitler's
advent to power, German passenger traffic was almost all the
other way. I arrived in Berlin on November 11, Armistice Day
among Germany's former foes, and now chosen by Hitler for his
first plebiscite to win approval for pulling Germany out of the
League of Nations.

Junius Wood, at my request, had good-naturedly reserved the
cheapest room he could get at the Hotel Adlon. I had hardly had
time to check in when he rushed me off to join a motor cavalcade
of British and American journalists setting out to inspect polling
booths to see if the balloting was really secret. (It was not.)
During the ride I met Eustace Waring, a rotund little Englishman

with a pedantic manner who had been transferred from Rome to take charge of the *Daily Telegraph* bureau in Berlin. I also remet his bearded assistant, Martin Moore, whom I had previously known in Moscow. Moore informed me that he was merely on loan from London, and that there were two vacancies on the *Daily Telegraph* staff: his own when he returned to London, or the one in Munich, where their man had been arrested and expelled.

I applied for the Berlin post, which Martin Moore assured me was mine for the asking. A young man named Hugh Carlton Greene (now Sir Hugh, head of the BBC), was the favored contender for the Munich post. But London decided otherwise. After due consideration, Arthur E. Watson, managing editor of the *Daily Telegraph*, decided that Hugh Greene, having no previous newspaper experience, should be tried out for the Berlin post. And I, with my background of work under a Communist dictatorship, was thought best equipped to cope with the Nazi one and should therefore have the Munich job. For both of us the appointments were on a two-week trial basis. Added to this, Waring devised two more hurdles for me. One, I had to pass muster with the British consul general in Munich, a stickler for protocol, which meant knowing what is vulgarly called the German and British stud books (*Almanach de Gotha* and Debrett's *Peerage*) inside out. The second test was that he wanted to see if I could obtain a personal interview with the notorious anti-Semite Julius Streicher, the gauleiter in Nuremberg, and how I would handle the assignment.

It may amuse the reader to know that I accomplished the second much more easily than the first. Whereas my relations with G. St. Clair Gainer were always frigidly correct, Streicher— who claimed that he could smell a person of Jewish blood on an instant—welcomed me most effusively when I turned up at his Nuremberg suite without previous appointment, merely sending in my visiting card and asking for an interview. The room he received me in was about the size of a ballroom. It was littered with debris of a previous-night carousal: broken glass, spilled wine, festoons of popped champagne corks sticking to mirrors, ceiling and even to a crystal chandelier. On a huge buffet table pushed against the wall there were surprisingly enough among all this Bacchanalian litter dozens of vases crammed with expensive-looking long-stemmed roses varying from pale white to the deepest American Beauty red. The scent of them was almost overpowering, but it did not quite hide the sour breath belched up frequently by my host.

Noting my amazement at the profusion of flowers, Streicher explained that some of his friends had tendered him a "surprise party" the night before to celebrate his forty-ninth birthday, and the roses were all birthday offerings from the distaff side of his Brown House staff. (He presented me with an armful of them, and also a signed photograph, which I dumped into the nearest ash can on my way back to the station.) The interview, which began with Streicher striking a rather Mussolini-like pose behind a large desk and me in a small castered chair facing him, ended with me wedged against the wall and Streicher almost in my lap; I kept pushing away from him with his wine-laden breath and the droplets of saliva oozing from the corners of his mouth, and he kept bringing his chair forward to emphasize some point. He remained entirely good-tempered throughout, even after I rather brashly asked him whether he was entirely sure he had no trace of Jewish blood. His answer, which my Berlin colleagues never got tired of having me repeat to them, was: *"Mein Vater war Franken, meine Mutter war Schwabin: das gibt Temperament!"*

At the conclusion, he escorted me to the door, assured me that I had made a good impression on him both as a woman and as a journalist, and that I must not be backward in calling on him if I needed any help. Strange to relate, throughout the nearly seven years I remained in Germany, Streicher was my constant standby whenever a British or American visitor fell victim to the charms exerted by the Propaganda Ministry or by Herr von Ribbentrop's special office. An interview with Streicher was enough to cancel out all their good impressions. "And Streicher, being the ham actor he was," Charles Hathaway used to say, "never cared what anyone wrote about as long as they wrote about him."

Dr. Charles Hathaway, Jr., to give him his full name, was the United States consul general in Munich, and the antithesis of his British counterpart. St. Clair Gainer was always being shocked by my breaches of protocol, such as when I stuck my tongue out at a deputy gauleiter when he tried to make me give the Nazi salute; or when some sportive SS men blocked my way on the stairway of the old Bavarian Landtag building and refused to let me proceed until I had returned their "Heil Hitler" greeting—and I responded with "Rule Britannia," which rocked them right back on their heels. All this Gainer disapproved, but Hathaway only laughed and said: "You have my full permission to shout 'Hail Columbia' if Gainer doesn't think it proper of you to say 'Rule Britannia' in place of heiling Hitler."

Charles Hathaway was in his middle fifties, rather frail-looking and generally wrapped in shawls because he suffered so from cold, and the consulate was located in the draftiest building in Munich. But he could move with the speed of a hawk if anyone or anything required his immediate attention. Ours was a case of mutual affinity at first sight, and I rarely did anything in the way of breaking a news scoop without consulting him first. His advice was always carefully weighed as to cause and effect, and invariably right.

My Streicher interview, which I wrote up on my return to Berlin, pleased Waring and also London, and I was ordered forthwith to go back to Munich as staff correspondent. The New York *Herald Tribune* also asked me to serve as their Munich correspondent, part time, with a sharing of expenses between my two papers. I got to Munich on Christmas eve of 1933.

The Simpsons were to have been first on my calling list, since both James Birchell of *The New York Times* in Berlin and Norman Ebutt of the London *Times* bureau had each told me to be sure and look them up. Stanley served as Munich correspondent for both the *Times* of London and *The Times* of New York. However, through a series of mischances, it was not until mid-January that I made the trip out to Nymphenburg, where the Simpsons lived in a new housing unit known as the "Amerikaner Blok" (American block) because it had been built in American apartment-house style and with Dawes Plan money.

I took to Vicky at first sight because she was so unlike anyone I had imagined. In the first place she was short, squat and dowdy. It took me nearly five years to persuade her to use a lipstick and to wear a girdle because she did not believe in any artificial aids for feminine beauty.

"I know I'm no beauty," she used to tell me roundly, "and I'm not going to pretend that I am."

However, she did have beauty, the beauty of a soul which could be seen in the welling depths of her eyes when she regarded her towheaded babies, and the goodness with which she received anyone in trouble. And there were so many, many people in trouble in Munich in those days, even some who required to be passed over the Swiss or Austrian frontier quickly to escape Nazi vengeance. I know of at least two occasions when Vicky took all the inherent risks to accomplish this. She was decisive and quick-thinking, and all my problems such as finding an apartment, furnishing it inexpensively, etc., dissolved immediately as soon as I mentioned them. A British vice-consul was on the point of retiring and I could have his apartment, which was in the same block; I could buy some of his furnishing for a few English pounds. Later, I could get rid of the stuff and have some new furniture made to my own design. She knew the very man who could do it. All these problems were dealt with briskly in the first half hour of my visit, while the two towheaded babies were having their afternoon nap and while Stanley, her husband, also towheaded, was sleeping it off.

Someone once said of Stanley that if he had not married Vicky he might have ended up as a beachcomber on some South Pacific island. He was as deliberate as Vicky was brisk. And whereas Vicky spoke English with a crisp, unaccentuated accent, Stanley retained his north Sheffield burr which always gave him a bit of an inferiority complex in dealing with the class-conscious British consul-general.

That afternoon, over a tea of fresh homebaked bread and honey, the Simpsons and I formed a working friendship pact that was to endure throughout the six-and-a-half years I served in Munich. For Vicky I was a woman confidante, a neighbor she could talk even home problems with. She had been very lonely living as a German-born British subject-by-marriage in a hostile sea of Nazified Germans. To Stan I represented the comfort of having another nonconformist in Hitler-heiling at press functions.

The question of heiling or not heiling was a burning issue with the foreign press corps in Berlin and Munich. In Berlin, the then head of the Foreign Press Association, Louis Lochner, had won a ruling from the Reichs-chancellery that members of the foreign press were exempt from giving the Nazi salute. But in Munich, where the Brownshirts were a law unto themselves, poor Stan had been having rather a rough time over this. He said to me:

"They've threatened to kick my teeth in any number of times. But they would hardly dare with you, and I shall just hide behind your skirts, if you don't mind."

I did not mind, and we shook hands on it. That compact of comradely friendship was never broken throughout the nearly seven years I served in Munich.

Within that same week I also met Dr. Emilio Enenkel, a small, wispy-looking Italian with a slight cast in his eye, who spoke with a slight lisp. His appearance belied his character utterly; he wore many hats, literally as well as figuratively. His ostensible duty was serving as correspondent for the official Italian news agency Stefani, and when I was introduced to him at some press conference, I mentioned that I had known a colleague of his in Moscow who, as it happened, was now his news editor in Rome. From that moment on, Dr. Enenkel became a member of our team and a trusted friend. Even during the British-Italian embroilment over Abyssinia, and also after the signing of the Rome-Berlin axis pact, Enenkel would not let Rome policy deflect him from our personal friendship. He was really to prove the most invaluable part of our team, because besides serving as our motorized legman he spoke German as fluently as the Simpsons, and had a high-priority license plate and could on occasion "pull rank."

Contrary to latter-day experts, in the first years of Nazism, Hitler's command of the Nazi Party and rule of the Reichs-chancellery in Berlin was never of the strong-man type, but rather straw-fingered. He acted more like a coy, much-sought-after debutante than a national leader. In the first place, he allowed his favorites almost limitless autonomy in recruiting and uniforming their particular brands of followers. Thus, Alfred Rosenberg's men could be identified by their green and brown livery; Hermann Goering's by a dust-blue uniform which later became the Nazi air force color; Himmler's ubiquitous Gestapo and SS were black-uniformed, and Dr. Goebbels, not to be outdone, dressed his men in black and silver with gold facings. Since Hitler was the sun round whom all this revolved, each of them was constantly jockeying for position, and within the Party hierarchy there was intense rivalry, encouraged by Hitler himself. This was particularly true in South Germany.

In Munich there was a terrible feud between Hermann Esser, who held Nazi Party membership card Number Two, and the mere upstart in point of membership seniority: Rudolf Hess. Hess won because he was more financially and verbally useful. (Hitler dictated most of *Mein Kampf* to Hess, which was well for Hitler, as otherwise no one would have made any sense of it at all, since he always mixed his metaphors so.) There was also a long-standing rivalry between Theodor Habicht, who controlled the South German radio network, and Dr. Goebbels, who was setting up his propaganda ministry in the North. Habicht, a Bavarian, thought that if he could outshout Goebbels in diatribes, he would give Hitler his first international conquest: a Nazified Austria united to the German Reich. Goebbels merely howled at the Poles for clinging to the Corridor, and the Memel people for not turning on the Lithuanians. But Habicht carried on a nightly vendetta via the Munich radio with Chancellor Dollfuss and Prince von Starhemberg, whom he threatened with everything from emasculation to murder. Thus, Theodor Habicht's hate campaign was bearing fruit: though Hitler had closed the Bavarian frontier to German tourist travel into Austria as a spite measure, Nazi recruits from Austria were constantly entering Bavaria to become the nucleus of the "army of liberation"! This rabble, really, were called *Flüchtlinge* (refugees) by the Nazi press, but I shall refer to them by the name my friend Dr. Enenkel gave them, namely, Austrian Nazi Legionnaires.

The Simpsons and the Italian were most concerned with the Legionnaires in the early months of 1934. Vicky could follow the Habicht broadcasts, spoken in Bavarian dialect and intermingled with *schimpfung* (cursing) which I could not understand. Dr. Enenkel, as Il Duce's representative, was interested in preserving the status quo in the Tyrol and on the Brenner Pass because, naturally, the Italians, regardless of political adherence, did not want soldiers of a Greater German Reich breathing down their necks. I followed my own line of news reporting. My paper was not greatly interested in political stories, of which they got a surfeit from Waring, but they did like my reports of royal romances, a subject on which I later became the Daily Telegraph's expert.

It was Dr. Enenkel who recalled me to my duties of political news reporting. He came to my flat late one evening, his face hidden in a huge muffler and visored cap with earflaps down, not so much against the cold as for protection against a nosy neighbor who always peered out of her door peephole whenever she heard my door buzzer. He startled me by asking whether I had attended any of the Ash Wednesday services?

I answered rather crisply that I had not since I was not a communicant. He hastened to say, "I'm not prying into your religious belief. I only asked because, if you had, you would have noticed the absence of any legionnaire. The Austrians are still practicing Catholics for the most part, but there were none at any of the Frauenkirche services. Nor at any of the other churches in town, because I have just completed a check of them. Where have they gone to?"

I could see that Enenkel was really disturbed, but all I could tell him was that the Simpsons had skied all over the Berchtesgaden area several weeks ago and they had seen no legionnaire encampments. We discussed various possible reasons for the legionnaires being withdrawn from Munich but reached no solution. After he left, I flung on a wrap and went out to see if Vicky were still up. She was, because there was a light in her front living room.

She was looking rather wan. She was in her early months of pregnancy, her worst time, she had told me, because her babies came easily. Stan was away, as usual. Vicky said that the thought of becoming a father for the third time in as many years had so unnerved him that she had sent him up to Garmisch for a few days of skiing. I told her of Enenkel's visit and his concern that we were on the eve of a Nazi invasion of Austria.

"Enenkel is talking through his hat," Vicky said flatly. "Even the Nazis are not so stupid as to start something at the beginning of a spring thaw, when all the roads are mired in mud and the Alpine trails flush with avalanches. Besides, there is the Oberammergau Passion Play which goes into rehearsal next month. With the scarcity of valuta in Germany now, no one is going to undertake anything to scare the tourists off."

Vicky's reasoning seemed sound, and I returned home to go to bed, but not to sleep. After catnapping I woke with the thought: "Why not take a train to the frontier and look for the legionnaire camp yourself? You did it in Russia, why not here?"

By eight A.M. I was on the Vorarlberg Express and by eleven A.M. in Freilassung, the last stop this side of the Bavarian border. I was the only passenger on the final lap to the frontier, and though the station restaurant looked inviting with pretty dirndled waitresses standing by and yawning their heads off for customers that did not come, I passed right through to the outside where I saw a decrepit motor vehicle labeled "taxi." I got inside and told the driver in my best German to drive me to the *Lager*. As I had anticipated, the driver asked no questions, but drove off first in an easterly and then northerly direction (away from the frontier which I could see round a turn of the road) and then taking a very bumpy, rutted road, drove steeply downhill until we came to what appeared to be a large compound of wooden buildings which, judging by the stacks of rotting cut timber, must once have served as a lumber mill. There was a drive-in gateway; the driver let me out, then backed off a few feet when I told him to wait for me.

There was a makeshift sort of air about the place, and the sentry, a pimply-faced youth armed with a rifle, looked very amateur too. I told him I wished to speak to the camp commander, and presented a personal visiting card and also my Brown House–issued press card, asking him to take it to the commander. The sentry stood scratching his head undecided what to do; all the men were at mess, he said, and the commander might be too. But then he decided I looked harmless and, abandoning his rifle—which on closer inspection I saw was all wood—he went across a muddy field in the direction of the mess hall. I had time to have a good look around from the doorway. There were rifle ranges, and some locked sheds which could have held small arms. The barracks from where I heard the babble of many voices, could, if tiered with bunks like the Russian *casernas*, easily hold six to eight hundred men. But I could not see this as an invasion force.

I was recalled from my thoughts by the appearance of a very tall, soldierly-looking man dressed in khaki fatigues but wearing, incongruously it seemed to me, a monocle dangling from a ribbon. He clicked heels smartly, bowed and said in unaccented English: "Colonel Frauenfeld at your command. How may I serve you?"

I said that I represented an English newspaper that was greatly concerned with the plight of the Austrian refugees and I wished to interview him, and also some of his men. It had nothing to do with politics; I merely wanted the information for a color story.

The colonel had screwed the monocle into his eye while I was speaking and stood regarding me rather unnervingly. I had a feeling that he did not quite believe me. I was right, for he barked out an order to remain where I was and not to speak to anyone or take one step farther. He went off with my press card to some inner office whence I could presently hear that he was putting in some urgent telephone calls. I could not help feeling rather pleased with myself that I, the greenhorn, had found the legionnaires' camp, when neither Enenkel's nor the Simpsons' sleuthing had succeeded. But this pleased feeling turned to chagrin when the colonel returned and said without preamble:

"I have been informed by the Brown House press department that you have not received permission to come here. I have also learned that you are a very enterprising reporter, and that you succeeded in gate-crashing a Soviet prison camp and remaining there for several days because their rail system was not working. Here our trains function admirably. I suggest that you take the next one back to Munich. If you hurry, you can get the two P.M. express and also have time for an excellent lunch at the station restaurant."

There was no arguing with this edict. Besides, I had seen all I had come to see. I held out my hand for my press card, but instead of giving it to me immediately, he first clicked heels, bowed, and raised my outstretched hand to his lips, murmuring "Good try, Fräulein," in a truly Rosenkavalier manner.

I got back into my taxi and told the driver to take me to the station. Halfway up the hill we were flagged by four legionnaires requesting a lift into town. Three of them came inside to sit with me and the fourth sat with the driver. I obeyed the colonel's order of not talking to them, but I made no attempt to stop them from talking to me. But all their talk was grousing about poor conditions in the camp, bad food, and no recreation, etc. I was glad when the driver opened the car door and said "'raus!'" (out) just before we reached the station.

I further followed the colonel's advice by ordering lunch, after learning that I would have an hour's wait for the incoming train. There were only two other guests in the huge dining room: a pair of green-clad Bavarian Jaeger police officers (they did both guard duty and forest ranger's work). They seemed interested in me, and when one of them asked if they could join me for coffee, I said, "Of course," and the hour passed quickly. So did the next one on the train, which they were taking as far as Bad Reichenhall, their home barracks.

They were Bavarians of the pre-Hitler breed. When I mentioned that my maid's brother served in the Jaeger corps, they accepted me as a friend. During the journey they told me all about the Austrian refugee camps, which they regarded with disfavor, and even obligingly marked their locations on a Baedeker map I had with me. There were six of them, the largest of which I had just seen. Both gave it as their opinion that the presence of these men so near the frontier posed a threat. But they were not one yet because they had no arms and they were undisciplined and untrained.

When I returned and reported all this to Vicky, she said, "I told you so." But Enenkel was positively delighted with the marked map I gave him. I knew without his telling me so, that they would be as well watched as a mouse hole by a cat!

Vicky was right. The forthcoming Oberammergau Passion Play took the first importance in Nazi press and radio propaganda, pushing plans for the conquest of Austria into the background. Though we did not know it at the time, it was Dr. Hjalmar Schacht, Hitler's astute minister of finance, whom the Austrians had to thank for this reprieve. He insisted that foreign valuta was more important for the German rearmament program than a near-bankrupt Austria, and that as long as there was the slightest threat of warlike action, the valuta-bearing tourists from Europe and the United States would not risk coming to Germany. His will had such sway then that even Julius Streicher had to hew to the new line of not offending the sensibilities of foreign tourists, and copies of his obscene anti-Jewish *Der Stürmer* were no longer publicly on display where they might offend foreign eyes.

Schacht's policy even had an influence on the casting of the Passion players. It was first planned, in keeping with Nazi ideology, to have a blond-bearded Aryanized figure portraying the role of Savior; the Simpsons and I were informed of this in mid-March when we went up to Oberammergau to interview the cast. The storm raised by our published reports made them select a less Aryan-looking actor and stay more with the old text. Thus, James Birchell, then a roving reporter for *The New York Times* after having finished a stint of duty as managing editor, was able to quip that it should have been Dr. Schacht and not Anton Lang who was called to take all the bows at the conclusion of the opening performance.

With the departure of the foreign tourists, the anti-Austrian campaign was resumed. Habicht spewed such venom over the air nightly that it was hard to believe that the object of his hate was only five feet three and the legally elected chancellor of Austria. In Habicht's terms Chancellor Dollfuss' Christian Democratic regime were the oppressors, and the Hitlerian Nazis the "liberators-to-be." Habicht, it was believed, was trying to out-thunder Dr. Goebbels, whose job as chief propaganda minister he sought.

For me it was hard to believe that there could be so much hate in the world. It was my first spring in South Germany, and Munich with its many flowering chestnut trees and its lovely flowing fountains along the Leopold and Ludwig avenues was as lovely as Paris. I did not see very much of the Munich spring because I was kept shuttling back and forth to Berlin, filling in while first Greene and then Waring went on leave.

As I have said before, Waring had almost a jinx on him for choosing the wrong time to go on leave. On the day he departed for a long holiday in Rome, Von Papen made his now almost forgotten "Marburg speech," which was the curtain raiser for the June 30 blood purge, a day which really lasted seventy-two hours, took countless thousands of lives, including an innocent Willie Schmidt mistaken for someone else, and is now referred to by people who were not there as the "night of the long knives." Those of us who were there knew it as the day when Hitler told his Big Lie, a lie about an alleged plot, a lie about who were

involved, and a lie about the number and personalities of the
victims of the purge. It was in giving Hitler the lie to the last that
Greene and I pulled off our biggest scoop.

Greene was playing tennis in the grounds of the British Embassy on that Saturday afternoon, and therefore had a ringside
seat for the execution squads at work in the Brownshirt headquarters yard next door. I was at the hairdresser's, waiting for the
electric power to go on to get my hair dried. I did not know that
Berlin had been cut off from the outside world, and that, in
pulling the phone switches, Himmler, the chief executioner of the
day, had also pulled the electric switch.

We had no Sunday paper to work for then, and therefore
Saturday was our free day. Of course, by evening, when we all
foregathered at our newspaper hangout—the Taverna—we knew
pretty well that it was a case of Nazi massacring Nazi, SS men
versus Brownshirts, and that since Hitler appeared to be siding
with the SS men, they were bound to come out on top. Only
later did we learn that the real instigators were the shadowy
general staff of the yet unavowed German army who refused
their support of Hitler's assumption of the presidency in the event
of Von Hindenburg's death, unless he curtailed the power of the
Brownshirts. Hence, everything that followed was a case of dog
eating dog.

For the first three days following the purge, Hitler maintained
that only seven persons were involved and these had been
summarily executed. On Thursday, before a hastily summoned
meeting of the Reichstag, he upped the figure to thirty-three.
However, earlier that day, the postman had delivered two large
volumes of a new Nazi *Who's Who* ordered by Waring some
weeks previously because he felt we ought to have exact information on the spelling of Nazi names appearing in the news. We
blessed our rather fussy absent boss that day. For looking
through those two thick volumes, we found dozens of hastily
pasted-on adhesive strips to blot out entries. We guessed that this
had been done since the purge, and that the entries blotted out
were Nazis of importance who had been liquidated by Himmler's
execution squads. It was Greene who hit on the method of
reading what lay behind the obliterating strips. Since we could
not tear off the strips without ripping the paper, he tore the
bindings off. Then by holding up each printed page to a naked

light bulb, we could easily read what the Nazis had sought to hide. Thus, in the morning's edition of the *Daily Telegraph*, there was Hitler's speech and the thirty-three names of alleged plotters in one column, and, in a double-column spread, our story of the directory find, and a listing of eighty-eight additional names with their place, rank and everything, thereby giving direct lie to Hitler's Reichstag statement. This feat won us a rare "jolly good" telegram from our editors.

When Waring called up a few days later to say he was cutting his holiday short and returning to Berlin, I scuttled back to Munich.

The atmosphere in Munich was still overhung by the Roehm affair—the plot for which the blood purge was the excuse was alleged to have been staged by Captain Roehm, head of the Brownshirts. But it seemed to me that the tension I sensed in the streets, among my neighbors, everywhere I went, emanated from the people as a whole rather than from the Nazi factions controlled by the Brown House. The Bavarians were, and are, a very phlegmatic people who rarely open their mouths except to put in food and drink. However, here and there I got the whiff of a war scare. From my hairdresser, whose front parlor barbershop catered largely to Brown House personnel, and whose top-floor back room apartment looked out directly onto the courtyard of the Annex, I got the word that we were on the eve of another Sarajevo. He was a Bavarian monarchist, had served in World War I and had been taken prisoner by the French. What he saw going on in the Annex courtyard at night, and what he overheard from his Brown House customers by day, gave him the impression we were on the verge of war.

Enenkel was worried too. Not by the visible activity of the legionnaire headquarters, but by the added guardedness he found at their camps. They now had roadblocks and sentries at campsites, and security was at a maximum, he told me. Vicky also thought that something was in the offing, but did not think it would happen before August or September, when Hitler would announce it as a surprise to his Nazi Party congress. Gainer was eager for every scrap of information to add to his weekly report to the British Foreign Office, but had no real information of his own to give. And Dr. Hathaway, with whom I often took counsel,

was also interested in any item of news I brought in, but he was
even more concerned with preventing me from jumping to some
rash conclusions and thereby incurring Nazi vengeance.

"Remember," he said during those tense days, "the line between legitimate news reporting and espionage is very fine here.
You have a pretty neck and I should hate to see it stretched on a
block."

This was no idle warning. Less than a year later, two German
girls of noble birth were beheaded for allegedly giving information to the French.

My own sensitive news antennas told me that the danger was
now, and something would have to be done immediately to
prevent Hitler from presenting the world with a *fait accompli.*
But I needed a few more facts to support my theory that the
Nazis were planning an invasion of Austria with the Nazi Austrian Legion forming the spearhead. Those facts might be obtained by someone who could infiltrate the Legion headquarters.
Who?

Sunday afternoon I was visiting with Vicky. The children were
out with their nurse, Stan was away—he had left for England
immediately after my return from Berlin—and Vicky was sitting
placidly knitting baby garments. She was in her final month, and
hugely pregnant. It was then and there that the idea came to me
to send Vicky to the Annex to enquire for a missing Otto Schmidt.

It was thus that Vicky became a sitter-in in the Annex the week
of July 21, 1934. She took a little persuading before she fell in
with my plans. but she wanted to prevent Hitler from grabbing
Austria as much as I did, and she went off willingly to play her
part.

The first day's eavesdropping netted us little except some
operation called "Javelin" that was in the making; she had heard
that word in a shouted telephone conversation with someone,
presumably Rudolf Hess, since the rest was about Austrian
sloppiness, and no one would dare say that to Hitler. She had also
picked up a half-sheet of paper in the yard that might have been
dropped by one of the many motorcycle couriers who were
constantly coming and going with written orders. This one read:

> "Auf Befehl des Fuehrers:
> Jederman muss zur Stelle sein ab Mitternacht. . . ."

The rest was illegible because of wet tire marks.

We had a sort of council of war that evening with Enenkel. He thought "Javelin" might be the code word for the operation against Austria, but he did not think that the half-sheet of paper denoted anything immediate. Hitler, it had been announced, was going to spend the week in Bayreuth listening to his favorite Wagner operas, and Enenkel thought that he would more likely be at his chancellery in Berlin or here in Munich if immediate action were contemplated. Vicky took the same line. But I did not agree. I thought the Bayreuth visit was a ruse to point away from contemplated action. However, I decided to wait just a little longer while Vicky went back to pick up some additional facts, if she could.

Tuesday Vicky left her listening post early. She said the Annex had suddenly become very quiet—no running couriers, no constantly buzzing switchboard. In this quiet she had felt rather conspicuous and had come home. She was certain that whatever action had been contemplated had been postponed. I did not agree. I thought it was the lull before the storm and wished to break the story immediately. I felt strongly we were on the eve of planned action, and the absence of activity at the Annex confirmed it. Vicky hesitated about going all out on that limb with me, a much more dangerous venture for her since it involved the future of her whole family. Enenkel, too, wished to sleep on it for another night. Thus it was I who broke the story that saved Europe from the abyss of war for at least another four years.

Here, in brief, is a sequence of events, as gathered later from Enenkel, my *Daily Telegraph* colleagues in London and Rome, and what Count Ciano, the Italian foreign minister, was to tell me on a drive to the Munich airport some months later:

> At 4:30 P.M. on Tuesday, July 24, 1934, on a prearranged call from the *Daily Telegraph* newsroom in London, I dictated a carefully worded dispatch listing all the invasion preparations by the Austrian Nazi Legion I had observed over the past ten days, and also mentioned the existence of the code name "Javelin" for the forthcoming operation. At ten P.M. London time the first editions of the *Daily Telegraph* were on sale; my story had received "prime space" treatment and also earned a poster "Warlike Preparations in Munich," worn by the news hawkers.
>
> At about that time, the Italian military attaché on his way to a party caught sight of the poster, purchased the paper and read the contents of the dispatch. Instead of continuing on to the party, he rushed to a telephone booth and relayed the contents to his minister. They thought the matter sufficiently serious to put a call through to

Count Ciano (Mussolini's son-in-law) in Rome, who, in turn, communicated the matter post haste to Il Duce. At about 11:30 P.M. simultaneous calls were put through to the Italian official press attachés in Munich, Berlin and London for verification of my veracity. Enenkel was out on another night prowl of the camps and his minister, Dr. Attolico, vouched for me. Also, at the same time, my counterpart in Rome, Beatrice Baskerville, was startled to be summoned from the bridge table to receive a personal call from Il Duce. He asked her one question: Was the Munich correspondent of the *Daily Telegraph* reliable? She answered haughtily that *Daily Telegraph* reporters were always reliable as he, himself, should know.

At midnight an order stemming from Il Duce's office was issued in Rome, ordering the two divisions of the Italian Alpine troops to take up battle positions all along the Brenner Pass. They did so without any loss of time, and were there standing eyeball to eyeball with the massed Nazi Legionnaires when the Nazi plotters in Vienna, acting under prearranged orders, seized the radio station and chancellery, shot poor little Chancellor Dollfuss six times and left him to die without medical help or the solace of a priest. They held the chancellery and radio station for six hours, constantly sending out signals for help from their massed confederates, who were armed and at the ready, only waiting an order from Hitler to set the invasion in motion. The order never came because, forewarned by my dispatch, Mussolini had beaten Hitler to the draw.

The Nazi plotters had cut off all telephone communications with Vienna, so we in Munich knew nothing of what was happening there until late in the afternoon when Eric Gedye, our Vienna correspondent, managed to get across into Budapest and file his dispatch from there. By late evening, our wires were humming with requests for all the backup information possible. So I induced Vicky to go back to her listening post in the Annex. I figured that a demoralized set of would-be conquerors would soon be descending on the Austrian Legion headquarters and what they would have to say would be worth hearing. I was right. For never did so many quarrel so loudly and with so little restraint. All of which was, of course, grist to our mill, since we were bent on proving that the whole invasion plot, including the murder of Dollfuss and the putsch attempt, was Hitler-made and nurtured. The Reichs-chancellery made some feeble attempts to deny this, but the proof was too overwhelming even for them, and so in the end they obliquely admitted it by removing Habicht and disbanding the Legion.

Since my part in this Nazi fiasco was well-known, Mr. Watson, our managing editor, decided I should put in a few weeks in Berlin until the hue and cry died down in Munich. It was August, and Waring, deciding that nothing ever happened in August, was leaving to resume his interrupted holiday. Of course, he was wrong again. First, President Hindenburg died and we had a state funeral to cover. Following that, a hastily held "Ja" plebiscite to confirm Hitler's assumption of the presidency along with his Reichschancellership. By the time I returned in September, Vicky was the lighter of a baby boy, then six weeks old, and I was assigned to cover the Nuremberg Party Congress, the first of the Nazi regime. As a special mark of favor, I was issued press card No. 1 by the Nuremberg gauleiter Julius Streicher, which entitled me to the only room in the Württemberger Hof Hotel with its own telephone, a convenience the rest of my colleagues could hardly omit to use.

Because I described the congress as a gathering of German tribes doing a war dance, I was never again allowed to cover the congresses in person but did it from the comfort and safety of my Munich flat via radio.

In October, I went to London on leave. Though most of the summer's éclat was gone, sufficient remained for the great Mr. Watson to take me to lunch at his St. James's Club, an honor, I was told, never hitherto conferred on a female reporter. As we parted he said with a twinkle at the back of his eyes: "You've done very well indeed, and we are all highly pleased with your work. But whatever you do, please don't stick your tongue out at any more Nazi leaders!"

I was back at my Munich post in time to cover the Nazi November 9 anniversary celebration. Stan was gone as soon as I arrived. And Vicky was pregnant again.

Sigrid Schultz was Correspondent-in-Chief for Central Europe for the *Chicago Tribune* during the fifteen eventful years between 1926 and 1941. Following this, she became Berlin correspondent for the Mutual Broadcasting System and for the *Chicago Tribune* from 1938 to 1941.

Hermann Göring's
"Dragon from Chicago"

SIGRID SCHULTZ

IN THIS divided world, there is one point on which major and minor officials of state chancelleries can agree: it is the conviction that most foreign correspondents are weird, baffling characters.

Why? Dignified officeholders and professional image-shapers complain that they find it impossible to keep our interest focused on what they believe should concern us most or to guess what our reactions to events in their areas will be. From their standpoint, this is upsetting if not reprehensible.

I confess that I take pride in this appraisal of our breed. It shows that we continue to demonstrate a certain independence and a will to search for truth. Unlike that other breed known as "junketeers" or "earbiters" who never, never ask embarrassing questions at press conferences and tactfully fail to report stories that might annoy the powers-that-be, we foreign correspondents for the most part pay scant attention to the efforts of governments to foist their pet views and propaganda on us by means of flattery, preferential treatment, boycott and even threats.

Actually, we correspondents get a fair measure of enjoyment from the permanent tug-of-war with officials bent on withholding news, and therefore we probably deserve to be considered "weird and baffling characters."

How dangerous that tug-of-war can become, even in peace-time, Americans and others who were stationed in Germany learned well in the days of Adolf Hitler. A case in point is a battle I had with mighty General Hermann Göring. Thanks to the general, Nazi circles referred to me, for a number of years, as "that dragon from Chicago." Naturally, the title was meant to be uncomplimentary, since the word "dragon" has a nasty, shrewish connotation in German. Nevertheless I still like it.

The story goes back to 1935, when Führer Adolf Hitler and his chieftains told the world that they were rebuilding Germany's military might. They strutted around proudly, carefully omitting any mention of the fact that the quick buildup of their forces was made possible by officers and arms manufacturers who had banded together in the fall of 1918, long before they knew what the terms of the peace treaty would be, to prepare for their war of the future. Nor did anyone mention the fact that in the days of the Weimar Republic, when Soviet Russia and Germany were allies, German units trained in Russia, and German industrialists built experimental stations and war plants to produce weapons of new design and to construct airplanes in the far reaches of Soviet lands.

The Nazis spared no effort to convince Germans and others of their efficiency and superiority. But the majority of foreign corre-spondents failed to be impressed. They wrote about arrests, persecutions, rigged trials and similar aspects of the Nazi regime. At first the Führer's sundry outfits figured that we could be brought into line by bestowing favors on some and boycotting others, or summoning us to highly unpleasant questioning ses-sions by the secret police.

By 1935 they were in a quandary: they had discovered that correspondents they expelled scored big successes on their return to their homelands, in the press, on the radio and on the lecture circuit. In fact, to be kicked out of Germany was such a reward-ing business that I know of one American correspondent—one of the "earbiters"—who deliberately courted expulsion by speaking in front of two snoopers (against whom I had warned him) and succeeded in winning fine publicity.

Hermann Göring, the second most powerful man under Hitler,

decided that he could do a better job of taming the correspondents than the Propaganda Ministry or the Foreign Office.
One of the many posts he held was that of chief of the secret
police. He put some of its sinister planners to work. They hit on
an idea. What could be more satisfactory than to seduce this or
that reckless correspondent into sending a report containing
secret military information, arrest him for espionage and stage a
spectacular trial that would intimidate all his colleagues? If
nobody fell for the temptation of using compromising documents
slipped to him or her, there was always the possibility of smuggling them into offices or homes, where they could be discovered
in a well-timed raid.

Naturally, we did not know about this scheme at the time it
was being perfected. But luckily, Nazis, like other mortals, did
get sick on occasion, and some of them, when they felt very bad
even consulted a physician who was on the Nazi blacklist, such as
Dr. Johannes Ludwig Schmitt, one of the finest and most brilliant
men I have had the honor to know. He gathered enough hints
about the secret police plan to warn me to be extra careful with
military news and suspicious of people I did not know well.

In the course of the fall of 1934 and winter of 1935 some of my
American, British, French, Swiss, and Czech colleagues and I
noticed that a surprisingly big number of supposedly anti-Nazi
characters were calling on us. They would insist on talking to the
correspondent-in-chief alone and offer us a wide variety of secret
military information, ranging from new plants, new weapons, and
new training centers to figures on the strength of sundry military
units, and so on.

The Nazis did not know one of the heartwarming traits of
international correspondents: the comradeship that unites us
when danger threatens. Nor did they apparently know that we
compared notes, pooled information. Thus, when I had thrown
out a man offering me details on some weapon that could interest
only a spy, I would tip off colleagues to be on the lookout for
him, and they would do the same for me. Most of my callers
arrived with letters of introduction from people I knew. They
were generally forged, which showed that the bearers were
agents provocateurs sent out by some central office that kept tab
on me and my circle of acquaintances.

In April, 1935, one of these characters went to my home in my

absence and entrusted a big sealed envelope to my mother,
saying that it contained important information for me, but that it
would be all right to keep it until I got home late that night.

Knowing that speed is essential in newspaper work, Mother
called the office, suggesting that somebody come by and pick up
the important-looking envelope. I rushed home myself, looked at
the contents of the envelope and burned them in the fireplace,
making sure that no scrap was left that could be identified. Her
description of the man who had left the "important information"
tallied with that of one of the men who had been to the office and
whom I had thrown out sometime earlier. Whether the designs
of an airplane engine which I burned were accurate or not, they
would certainly have been compromising and would have led to a
spy trial if the secret police had raided my home and found them
there.

As I walked down the street to return to the office, I saw the
man I suspected come down the street, heading for the house in
which I lived, together with two chunky individuals who looked
very much like the type of secret police fellows I had met when
summoned for questioning about this or that cabled report I had
sent. I stepped in the path of the trio and told them not to waste
their time going to my home, that the envelope one of them had
left there had been destroyed with its contents. Before they could
close their gaping mouths, I stepped into a passing taxi, saying
loudly and clearly: "To the American Embassy."

My friends at the embassy and consulate agreed that the time
to act had come. Some of them had met Göring at my house
when he had been a mere deputy. The thing to do was to lodge a
protest with him personally. But should I face him alone or in the
company of one of the official representatives of the United
States?

The problem settled itself: at the office I found a message to
the effect that the Berlin Association of the Foreign Press was
giving a post-wedding gala luncheon at the Hotel Adlon in a few
days (May 2) to honor Göring and his bride, the gentle, shy,
blond former actress Emmy Sonnemann.

As the only woman on the board of the club, I acted as co-
hostess with its president. Thus, thanks to protocol, the mighty
general would be seated right beside me and would be at my
mercy from hors d'oeuvres to dessert, mocha and speeches. That

I'd be taking a risk by "speaking my piece" I knew well in view of the mysterious disappearances and kidnappings that marked those days, not to mention the big number of murders that were carried out in the blood purge of June 30, 1934, on order of Göring himself, to get rid of his personal enemies.

His aides had fished for the invitation with such persistence that we had no doubt he wanted to impress the international correspondents with some new development of his air force. Its existence had been admitted in March. It seems a little spooky to see in my reports sent in those days that, on March 19, Berlin's first air raid rehearsal and blackout was applauded as a "triumph of Prussian discipline." Only 150 streetlights were turned on, dispensing a ghostly glimmer since they were shrouded in thick mourning crape, which now seems like a symbol of the holocaust the elated Nazi leaders were preparing for Germany and the world.

There was nothing elated about Göring when he reached the festive hall of the Hotel Adlon with his obviously nervous bride. He took his stance in the middle of the hall, scowling, every inch the disapproving noncom, ready to bawl out his unit, as he looked up and down three long banquet tables flanked by correspondents from most countries of the world.

After everyone was settled, I asked Göring why he looked so mad. Before answering, he made me point out American, British, French, and Swiss correspondents whose names were listed on a little card. After studying their faces intently, he muttered words to the effect that foreign correspondents had better realize the time had come to pay due respect to the new Germany. He was getting tired of people who kept writing about the arrest of churchmen and being sentimental about concentration camps and such. Then he raised his voice a little to say clearly: "We need those camps to teach discipline to elements that have forgotten all about it in the days of the weak Weimar Republic." The correspondents near us pretended not to have heard him.

We'd had a hot exchange of arguments on that tragic subject of concentration camps on a previous occasion. There was no use in taking it up again. Then I started to talk to him in a very quiet voice as if we were exchanging chitchat about the opera and such, to tell him in no uncertain terms about the siege by his *agents provocateurs*, supplying ample details. He was so flabbergasted at first that for once in his lifetime he stopped eating. He kept saying: "You are imagining things." I stressed that none of us would be fool enough to buy or send information that was meant for spies, but that his agents were obviously underpaid, to judge by their seedy looks. There was always the danger of their getting together to cook up lies about us to earn an extra bonus.

When I finally told him that our embassy and consulate had been kept fully informed about the siege, he finally lost his temper and snarled: "Schultz, I've always suspected it: you'll never learn to show the proper respect for state authorities. I suppose that is one of the characteristics of people from that crime-ridden city of Chicago."

Göring's poor bride kept signaling to him, sensing that there was something wrong, but he paid no attention to her. Trying to look lighthearted to make her feel better, I concluded the long conversation by reminding him of his days spent with Swedes, "who, like Americans, think that the greatest respect one can pay a man is to tell him the truth, and that is what I have done."

By the time the "happy couple" had been properly toasted and news-hungry correspondents formed a circle around him, Göring's traditional buoyancy had returned. It turned out that the purpose of his speech was to claim that "Germany's remilitarization really represented a service to peace," that his air force was "purely defensive," and that the Reich would not allow "big or small nations to provoke it into a war."

He could not resist boasting that the Reich had "not one old plane, not one old motor," and everybody thought of Germany's neighbors who were saddled with old crates. He added that to speed up plane production, he was buying American plans, blueprints and parts.

Those were the days when German bankers and officials were telling their creditors that they could not pay their debts, and when the question period was nearing its end, I had nothing better to do than to add insult to injury by asking how Germany planned to pay for its purchases in the United States.

Göring stepped forward, shaking a big, pudgy fist at me and roared: "Schultz, you'll never learn to show the proper respect toward state authorities."

The little sycophants, who were pretty numerous in those days, snickered, but otherwise there was absolute silence. Göring half

closed his eyes and looked through little slits to see how correspondents of important papers the Nazis were courting took to
his outburst, only to discover that the representatives of the
London *Times* and of the Paris *Journal* had moved over to my
side, looking as grim and forbidding as my other colleagues. I
noticed that one of them seemed ready to say something, but I
shook my head at him, and in the silence Göring grew more and
more flustered. His outburst had saved him from answering my
question, and it also had shown him expressions of revulsion that
could leave no doubt in his mind about the reaction of most
correspondents.

The party disbanded quickly. When I told my friends why
Göring was so mad at me, they really became alarmed. But not
for long. Short, squat Ernst Udet, the World War I flyer, who was
to become one of the generals in Göring's Luftwaffe, turned up in
my office.

Usually gay and boisterous, my good friend Udet looked very
serious. What had I done to get his poor Hermann so mad that
everyone in his ministry and in the foreign office called me "that
dragon from Chicago"? As I began to tell him, I realized that he
knew pretty well what had happened. His Hermann was really
quite upset about losing his temper, said Udet; then he asked
whether a single obnoxious character had been around since the
post-wedding party? None had. "Nor will there be any more, but
you had better not be quite as rough as you were with my
Hermann at that luncheon," and he grinned happily, obviously
enjoying Göring's embarrassment.

Naturally, the Nazis thought up other ways to try to intimidate
us, but for many a month no obvious agent descended on us, and
I felt as proud as if I had scored a scoop and netted gratifying
headlines. Thanks to my many run-ins with the Nazi authorities, I
retained my title of "that dragon from Chicago" as a souvenir of
the day when I had taken "the bull by the horns"—and a big one
at that—and won.

Paula LeCler (Mrs. Walter D. Wood) has been a foreign correspondent for International News Service, *Liberty* magazine, the *London Daily Telegraph, Paris Soir* and the North American Newspaper Alliance.

Imprisoned in Loyalist Spain

PAULA LeCLER

THE MOST horrifying misadventure of my kaleidoscopic journalistic career befell me in Civil War Spain in 1937, when, having started at the top in the foreign news field, I was still a virtual tyro, short in the savvy of more seasoned colleagues and almost incredibly brash, naïve and sanguine.

Acutely claustrophobic from childhood and never before afoul of the law, I was dragged from my hotel room after midnight by agents of the Loyalists, whose cause I had espoused, to a secret police headquarters, third-degreed in a locked room for seventeen sleepless and foodless hours, then held under armed guard for twenty-one days, five in solitary confinement and incommunicado in a medieval prison cell. Why this happened to me when all I had asked was a frontline visit and an interview with the wartime prime minister is still a mystery. I can only tell you how it happened.

In London I had readily obtained a two-month visa for Republican Spain, the side I deemed to be defending freedom, as a special correspondent for the *London Daily Telegraph* and *Opéra Mundi* in Paris and to get material for a scheduled American lecture tour. I had never been in Spain. But being a Loyalist admirer with antidictator views, I foresaw no trouble beyond the usual hazards and discomforts of newsgathering in a wartorn country, and in these I had already been baptized.

My love affair with the Loyalists lasted less than two August weeks, in Barcelona. The city fascinated me. Beautiful even in wartime, it was a city of paradoxes. I marveled at the seemingly close-to-normal, orderly aspect of everyday living under the incessant Franco bombardments.

Those first days were marked by what seemed to be mutual acceptance and approval. The only frightfulness I saw or suffered was the air raids, and that only incidentally. The ruins they left were mostly in outlying factory districts housing munitions works and near the waterfront, where the masses were huddled precariously together. Astounding after each raid was the calm with which the survivors dug themselves out and resumed their meager housekeeping, their work, errands and even pleasure outings, always under the threat of instant death from the skies.

The sturdily built central sections, along the stately tree-lined boulevards such as the Paseo de Gracia on which my hotel fronted, showed few scars at the time. There, unless direct hits occurred, the raids were endured as annoyances rather than the perils they were: sudden power suspensions blacking out meals and baths and cutting water supplies; abrupt interruptions to business, shopping, movies or even hair-coloring sessions.

Surprisingly, the many beauty shops were still working, and crowded into the evenings. Most had young men operatives, often soldiers on furlough. Business was better than in peacetime the managers told me. The platinum blond craze was at its height, and war or no war, the señoritas were having their lovely black hair bleached and blonded.

Similarly, hotel maids refused the white bread and rolls I saved them from my meals, rare luxuries even for foreign visitors, explaining they were too fattening. Local girls, I found, were on a dieting binge, starving themselves amid the involuntary starvation of tens of thousands in the food-short war economy, to hasten the slimness popularized by American movies.

In the regional propaganda and other government offices where I made the daily rounds, getting their communiqués and handouts and attending briefings and press conferences where real news was rarely given, my debut seemed warm and auspicious. My occasional news dispatches and cautious interviews, the best to be elicited from top local figures, went through unchallenged. The chief one was with Catalonian President Luís Companys. Beaming in the interview photo I later used in a lecture circular, he was eventually to be arrested and in 1940 executed by the Franco government.

But when I began broaching projects outside the tours and inspections arranged by the Propaganda Bureau, I met reservations and withdrawals. These came mostly from central Spanish officials now in controlling background posts in Barcelona; among them, seldom seen, hovered shadowy individuals definitely not Spanish. With unity indispensable to Republican victory, a deep schism, barely concealed, divided transplanted Spanish and native Catalan officials.

Off record Catalan officials confided they actually feared their Republican central government; it was as arbitrary and dictatorial as the opposition Franco government. They said Catalans were Catalans, not Spaniards; anti-Fascists and no Franco sympathizers, they nonetheless wanted independence. One, studying a paragraph somewhat critical of Soviet Russia in a lecture folder I had heedlessly filed with my credentials, darkly murmured that "the Republic is the tool of sinister foreign masters."

Another slipped me a pamphlet I still have: *La Problème de la Catalogne.* Published in French in Geneva in 1935, only a year before the Franco revolt, it denounced the Republic's failure to honor its pledge of full autonomy to Catalonia and petitioned the League of Nations for this or complete separation. Illustrating it was a 1934 photo of Catalan ministers in prison garb in a Spanish Republican prison, jailed for separatist activities; conspicuous among them was their leader, Catalonian President Companys.

Curiously, this pamphlet was not mentioned when the secret police later finecombed my papers in Valencia, nor withheld when they returned them. Its possession may have played a part in my mystifying arrest and detention, but certainly less than my incidentally-Soviet-disparaging lecture folder.

Meantime as I delved ever more objectively and deeply, down to the murky subsurface labyrinth, my disenchantment zoomed. I knew better than to give the least hint of it in my dispatches or behavior. It did appear in my notes, but these were couched so cryptically, in a self-devised code in which criticisms read like encomiums, that later even my shrewd persecutors eventually dismissed them as incoherent and inconclusive.

Nevertheless I detected a change at the Propaganda Bureau. Delays lengthened in previously approved projects. Bureau officials, principally those previously most friendly and communicative, were newly evasive and uneasy.

For the first time, my permit to take pictures within specified limits was questioned and taken from me, but it was returned the next day. I knew the police repeatedly searched my room in my absence, but this had been routine, with no nasty consequences, in other countries I had worked in. Thus it never dawned on me that I might be in serious trouble.

Finally I was summoned to the U.S. consulate, where I had duly registered on arrival. The cynical vice-consul in charge stunned me by insisting I leave Spain immediately. The police had strongly urged this, he said. When I protested I had done nothing wrong or irregular, he wearily explained that guilt or innocence had no bearing on the matter. Many unoffending Americans, especially newsmen, had been jailed by the Republic; one, John Finley, the respected, elderly editor of *The New York Times*, had been held two days in a Valencia prison.

I had a legal visa and would stick it out, I persisted; the police had not directly approached me. "Special correspondent" was just a fancy name for free lance, I babbled; I had gone to great effort to get my accreditations. My professional future hung on filling my commitments, especially to my newest outlet, *The Daily Telegraph*. I had promised *The Telegraph* an exclusive with the seldom-interviewed new Republican premier, Dr. Juan Negrin, and he was in Valencia. I had to go there.

That meant a special police travel pass, the dumbfounded vice-consul reminded me. Muttering that I couldn't say I hadn't been warned, and that only a fool would take such a chance in the face of the menacing attitude of the regime, he washed his hands of me and my temerity with the grim admonition that his office could do nothing to help me if or when I hit disaster.

For the first time, I was genuinely frightened. But not to the extent of giving up. I had two big problems and started tussling with them. One was how to get to Valencia without the police permit I dared not ask for. I had planned to ride there by train, as my funds would not stretch far enough to provide private transportation, even if there was any. The second was how, meanwhile, to avoid the police and a possible official expulsion order.

I found out how a stalked criminal feels. The government offices seemed relatively safe, but I visited them less often. Mostly, by daylight, I roamed the main streets, aimlessly but still with an open reportorial eye. Oppressed by the feeling that I was being shadowed, I slunk into the obscurity of the nearest movie theater and any single empty seat in an otherwise filled row, staring at the same outdated American or foreign thriller again and again without seeing it. I joined queues, and invaded the smelly marketplaces with their chattering shoppers. All this was silly and futile and I knew it, but somehow I felt better in crowds, and I sighed with relief as each hour passed without the dreaded expulsion order.

A female in a man's field hunting exclusives, I had avoided the foreign press corps. Now I sought it and made new acquaintances. Not confiding my fears, I learned that simply my passport with its visa and entry stamp might cover me if I traveled in an authorized private car with someone holding the requisite Safe Conduct pass. Eventually I met a kindly couple who had been long in Spain, the *London Times* correspondent and his wife. They owned such a car, had the mandated police and gasoline permits, and were returning to their base in Valencia, then the Republican capital. They agreed to take me with them, and the journey proved uneventful, besides giving me an incidental view of the ravaged countryside.

Thus I attained my Waterloo quite pleasantly. Eschewing the more pretentious and expensive Victoria Hotel where most of the foreign newsmen and Ernest Hemingway were staying, I moved into a comfortable room with bath at the Spanish-frequented Hotel Regina.

It was a new Spanish world, with no apprehensions. At the U.S. Embassy, I was warmly welcomed by the harried-looking chargé d'affaires pinch-hitting for our absent ambassador. Skimming over my previous alarms, which now seemed absurd or exaggerated, I outlined my aims for my stay in Valencia, and in the telling they emerged wholly uncomplicated and achievable. To facilitate them, the chargé d'affaires wrote me a special introduction to the central Propaganda Bureau.

There and in the other central government offices I was received affably as at first in Barcelona, though more formally. I confidently entered my requests, primarily for the interview with the Premier and for the *Salvo Conducto* required for an individual frontline visit. Promised quick action, I was only momentarily stymied by the daily "*Mañana, mañana,*" and meantime cheerfully resumed the prescribed propaganda program with its prearranged group excursions, wholly umproductive of the fresh, authentic material essential to a special correspondent.

Resilient, I shed the last personal unease. Afternoons, in the golden September sunlight, I sipped coffee on café terraces, alone or with acquaintances. I crisscrossed the city, then less bombed than Barcelona, in solitary, cautiously exploratory walks, especially in working-class sections.

Here, too, I found the Guardia d'Asalto and the dread they engendered secretly dominating the life of the city. There were over 600,000 of them in Republican Spain, an army to police the Army and the hapless civilians. Here, too, anonymous background figures lurked like malign puppeteers. The people, mostly wanting peace and caught between the warring sides, fearing both and with families often divided, were the real Civil War victims, I decided. They were also its heroes and heroines, merely in managing survival and even laughter under unspeakable hardships and harassments.

Then one morning, during my usual trusting stop at the Propaganda Bureau, I was called to the inner office of its angular, highstrung woman director, who had been routinely courteous. At last, I exulted, my Safe Conduct or Negrin exclusive.

One look at her stony face killed my hope. Icily she thrust a ticket for the evening train to Barcelona at me. I must use it to get to the border and out of Spain she decreed, just shaking her head when I demanded an official order or explanation.

I went straight to our chargé d'affaires, who soothingly told me such complications were unhappily not rare in the involved and often contradictory wartime government, but happily were usually surmountable. He telephoned government minister Zugazagoitia, head of the police, explained the situation, and asked him to see me. A meeting was set for the second day following. Meantime, the police minister assured the chargé, I would not again be molested.

That very evening, however, a uniformed messenger conspicuously toting a big rifle came to me in the hotel dining room with the ticket and an unsigned note on Propaganda Bureau stationery saying only, "Your train leaves at ten P.M." I returned the ticket with a note advising of my appointment with the government Minister. Soon I was called to the telephone. The unmistakable acid voice of the woman director snapped: "You lie! You have no appointment with the Minister!" and the phone was slammed.

Next noon another messenger appeared, with a rifle but no note or credentials. He said the Propaganda Bureau had sent him to stay with me and make sure I left by *that* evening's train. He followed me everywhere, even into my room when I went to wash, later planting himself at my table as I lunched. When I persisted I wouldn't go till I had seen the police minister or been served an official order, he left me.

The chargé d'affaires had invited me to dinner at the embassy, so the evening passed reassuringly and pleasantly, and next day came my meeting with government minister Zugazagoitia.

Amazingly, he said he had known nothing of the propaganda director's actions and could find no reason for them. There were no charges against me on police records. He asked if *I* had any complaints. I said I just wanted to get on with my interview with the Premier and visit to the front lines. If he thought advisable, he might send me a translator or police escort to check my doing just this and guard me against further interruption.

The Minister couldn't have been friendlier. I could count on working unimpeded until my set leaving date and he would so inform my embassy. His secretary would get my frontline *Salvo Conducto* and send the interpreter I had suggested. Lightning relief actually shoved me into asking what I really knew he couldn't give, a Police Ministry interview with himself. He amiably said I could have it "sometime next week."

Of course I never got that police exclusive. No interpreter or *Salvo Conducto* appeared, but I attributed that to the *mañana* spirit. All seemed regular and aboveboard again, and again, having bounced back like a yo-yo, I picked up my schedule, though a trifle more warily.

At the Propaganda Bureau, the woman chief avoided me but issued no more ouster threats. Much later, in America, I found she was Constancia de la Mora, an out-and-out Communist and leader of the Spanish "comrades." Unquestionably she detested me. The carefully inoffensive pieces I airmailed to my Paris agent, mostly as covers for factual reports I planned after leaving, were passed by the bureau in her absences, rejected summarily when she was there.

Thus when I fortuitously learned she was to be out of the city several days, I really bent my wits to getting that Negrin exclusive. I had already visited the Premier's offices, not reaching him, for he spent much time in threatened Madrid at this juncture, but striking immediate spontaneous friendliness in a charming girl, one of his secretaries. Now I looked her up again, took her to a café, and asked her to lunch at my hotel next day.

During this interval when my anxieties were stilled by the police minister's assurances, and the week ahead stretched open and clear except for a little innocent professional maneuvering, I had not the slightest suspicion that I had already unwittingly become a character in a tortuous spy drama with farcical interludes. An important character: the intended victim.

A fellow hotel guest whom I had instantly found unprepossessing and even repulsive, and had rebuffed though he seemed harmless, had persistently sought me out in the lounge, trying to scrape up an acquaintance. Tall and sallow, smartly suited in British sports style but strongly Slavic in appearance, he had introduced himself in fluent British English, of which he seemed proud, as "Joe Cook," an American movie actor on holiday, and alluded glibly to stage exploits in New York and Hollywood.

Now when, as a possible avenue to my interview, I had the Premier's pretty secretary as my guest, this equivocal figure stopped, uninvited, at our table and tried to flatter her into conversation. He left when I rudely dismissed him but with sharp, undisguised resentment. Toothy and saturnine, with a grimacing smile, he was not a type to attract women, and evidently I had hit a sore spot.

I was delighted when trust in my little secretary friend paid off and she told me the Premier would be in his office all the following afternoon, a Sunday and a good time to reach him. A noted physician and former physiology professor at Madrid University, he was a fine man who spoke English well, she said, and might give me my interview if I asked for it directly.

I decided to waylay him as he walked into the building to his office. This seemed feasible, as the building guards already had a smiling acquaintance with me, had shared my American cigarettes, seen my press pass and photographing permit, and had admitted me to the outer offices several times. Thus, I was chatting with an entrance guard about the time the Premier was due when I saw him coming in, and I darted to him before the guards and his startled entourage could stop me.

Breathlessly, I pushed my credentials and a lecture leaflet picturing me in interviews with Haile Selassie, Chiang Kai-shek and Gandhi under his nose and told him I had come to Valencia expressly to interview him, had been put off by the Propaganda Bureau, and was now close to leaving. Promptly sensing my sincerity and frustration, and amused at how I had bearded him, he waved aside the guards and his aides and in the kindest manner said I could have my interview, but only later that afternoon.

I had caught him just in time, he explained, giving me news immediately. He was flying to Geneva Tuesday with a Republican delegation, to urge the League of Nations' help "against the rebels and their allies," and had to keep scheduled appointments with delegates. Smiling at my skepticism when he suggested that I return to my hotel and come back in two hours, he agreed I might wait in an anteroom.

Summoned as promised, I had the exclusive. The Premier shut out his impatient aides and visitors and we were alone for my first unsupervised Spanish interview. We talked over an hour. English was his first foreign tongue as a child, he felt close to "the nations speaking it," he said; he had friends among the foreign reporters in Madrid, particularly the Americans, and understood their problems. A professor in politics, he had been in its forefront only a year. I instinctively felt he might welcome a safe respite from diplomatic duplicity, and before putting my interview questions I laid all my cards on the table, down to my misgivings about freedom and liberty in his Republic. Once convinced he could trust my promise to withhold his off-record remarks, he spoke with astonishing candor.

For the record, his answer to my query as to how many Russians were in the Republic was the permitted one: "Just a few diplomats and some technicians," as I reported it. Off the record —unmistakably discussing Russia and the Russian and Spanish

Communists in Spain but without once naming them—he said *inter alia* that the Republic desperately needed help but was "paying too dearly for it." Not in the Republican gold "I have been slandered for sending to the east," for that was due payment for war matériel imperative to Republican defense, but in the "accompanying alien stranglehold." He was "a Liberal Socialist by long conviction, nothing more as some are hinting," and wanted Spain to remain the *Spanish* Republic, not destroyed by Franco's Nazis and Fascists but not dominated, either, "by another foreign force and ideology." Yet the Republic could not survive without effectual foreign aid and "only the one oppressive power" was really giving it. Sole hope, for the Republic and the free world, lay in "aid without dictation from the free nations of the world," but it had to be "actual and immediate." That was why he was going to Geneva.

Everything he said was true and no secret in the world's chancelleries. But no one was saying it openly at the time, certainly not from the Spanish Republic. Had I quoted him fully and smuggled the words through, it would have been a sensational interview—and instantly disastrous to him and perhaps to the Republic.

As it was, the actual interview, as sent, was adequate and even a small scoop in carrying Dr. Negrin's own announcement of his forthcoming first appearance outside of Spain since assuming the wartime premiership the preceding May, and also in giving his estimate of the probable duration of the war and developments in it. As informative as the internal imbroglio allowed, it was the most comprehensive interview Dr. Negrin had yet given—or was to give before becoming a virtual captive of his Communist partners and fleeing to France on the defeat of the Republicans in March, 1939. But it was definitely not extraordinary. Just a good straightforward interview, its readers could not be expected to surmise the heartaches and perplexities which had led to it—and were to follow it.

At my request, Dr. Negrin called in an aide to snap us with my Leica as we talked. Knowing my anxiety about getting it out, he let me work over and type the interview right in one of his offices while he resumed his delayed conferences, then signed it, with a special permissive note to the Propaganda Bureau. Thus when I took it there directly, I was able, in the continued absence of the woman director, to telephone it uninterruptedly to Paris and to London—where it got top billing next morning in *Daily Telegraph, Paris Soir* and my other outlets, though it was to be weeks before I saw it there.

Pleased by at least one success, which looked big to me, and refreshed by the Premier's off-record frankness, I headed for the Propaganda Bureau that morning. In the lounge I was intercepted like a long-lost pal by "Joe Cook." Guilty about my brusqueness at the lunch with the secretary, I let him wangle me into chatting. As he was never around evenings, I idly asked what he did then. "Night work," he grinned. I mentioned I was making a final stab at my frontline Safe Conduct but with or without it was leaving Spain that week. He said he had "influence" and would get it for me, then drew me out a little about my difficulties with the Propaganda Director. "But you got your interview with the Prime Minister anyway!" he stressed slyly and significantly, and I wondered how he knew this.

My enemy was back but out of sight when I got to the Bureau; I was never to see her again. I drew another *"mañana"* from the man at the desk.

That evening, as I finished dinner at the hotel, two rough-looking young Spaniards in plain clothes walked over to me. One said, in halting French, that they were from the police and had to question me. "Joe Cook" showed up, ostensibly by accident, as always; I was surprised to see him around so late. He pretended not to know the other two men but offered, needlessly, to translate for us. Thanking him, I turned down the offer.

Abruptly dropping his mask of goodwill and noninvolvement, "Cook" ordered that we all go up to his room for the questioning. I refused, but the two "policemen" showed concealed revolvers. My request to phone my embassy met a flat refusal. I looked around the dining room, recognizing only the waiters. But no one, not even the waiters, seemed to see what was going on. For the first time, I wished I had chosen the Victoria with its American clientele.

In "Joe Cook's" room, he and the two Spaniards launched rapid, unconnected queries at me, simultaneously in French and in English. I protested when "Cook" deliberately mistranslated

my replies to the other two, and he was furious. Soon the pretext
of questioning was dropped. They were going to search my room,
"Cook" announced. I demanded a warrant. They ignored me.

My clothes and other effects, all lying out unlocked, got
minute, ungentle examination. They zipped off my coat lining
and felt under it. My wristwatch was pulled from my arm and
"inspected." They were rough with my prized Leica camera,
starting to yank out its partly exposed filmstrip with the Premier-
and-me shots; I showed them how to remove this without spoil-
ing it. The room got still tougher treatment. Wallboards were
torn away, carpets lifted and shifted, upholstery ripped and the
bed completely dismantled, with its mattress and even hollow
cornerpost thoroughly probed. Finally they dumped out the contents of my handbag, and put my passport, papers, wallet and
the eyeglasses I have always needed for distance, into separate
envelopes.

Wryly gratified at their chagrin in uncovering nothing hidden,
I thought the hours of empty search must prove their suspicions
were nonsense. Their ostensible boss, the police minister, had
promised the embassy I would have his protection; they couldn't
be acting by his order. But midnight had passed. I was worn to a
frazzle. I prayed they would finish and leave me.

Instead, they bundled my effects together to take out. Then, to
my unbelieving horror, they said *I* had to come with them. Again
I begged to be allowed to call the embassy, vainly. I was denied
even my coat and a handkerchief. Only my massive room key,
after they had pushed me through the door and locked it, was
handed to me, an apparent good omen. I was half-shoved, half-
dragged down the stairway.

How we got there I didn't know, for I must have blacked out
momentarily, but we were in what was plainly a police building.
I was thrust into one locked room, then into another. Both were
hung, I was startled to see, exclusively with big portraits of Stalin
and of Lenin. Official-looking circulars on the desks bore the
hammer and sickle insignia. "Joe Cook" leered as he saw me stare
at them.

So began the first and longest phase of this travesty of a
hearing. Later I learned that any three police agents could hold
such a "court" entirely on their own recognizance, on the barest
hearsay evidence. In my case, it was actually a third degree by

just one man, my nemesis "Joe Cook." The more articulate of the two "policemen" merely stood by, unable to follow the English proceedings. His mate went to sleep on a bench and snored intermittently throughout them.

Jolted wide-awake by the glaring lights which only later became hypnotic, I cursed my magpie habit of saving every scrap, letter or receipt accumulated through a journey, and—though they were sometimes useful—the vanity or need for self-reassurance which at that stage prompted me to drag clippings of my own best previous pieces and newspaper lecture publicity abroad with me. Not that I feared any disclosure from my heterogeneous collection, but because "Cook" pored over each written, typed and printed word with the same intent, prolonged, skeptical scrutiny, hour upon hour upon hour. Black eyes unblinking, he seemed to relish his "work."

Certain items he put in a special pile as "important"; they would be examined further, he threatened. My lecture folder with the brief unflattering reference to Soviet Russia went in this heap. Items I thought relevant as proving my democratic views, he threw aside as "unimportant." I held my breath while for some time he irritably tried to puzzle out my cryptically unintelligible notes on Spain, but he finally tossed them disgustedly into the second pile. Every name, with or without address, on cards and scraps or in notebooks and letters, was "important" and would be investigated to expose my "accomplices," he warned.

When I begged him to dim some of the overly bright lights which were now making me unbearably sleepy, he barked: "Why should I consider you? You didn't consider me when you kept me from speaking to your friend at lunch." He refused me even a drink of water.

Now and then he rapped out sudden questions, permitting only categoric answers. Most of them were about places I had never visited, large sums of money I had never owned, or people I had never heard of. It was as if in the absence of real evidence he was trying to stumble on some detail to pounce upon.

My inquisitor dwelt at length on several unsigned articles, evidently unfavorable to the Loyalists, in old issues of the *Daily Telegraph*, which he took from a file and allowed me just to glance at. I pointed out that my pieces were invariably signed, that these, as their dates and subjects showed, couldn't have been

written by me. He snarled that my objections meant nothing. I
never lost the impression that the entire "examination" was a
screen to hide some already determined motive.

The night crawled by in this way. Morning came, then noon,
with no cessation. Seventeen unbroken hours, by the clock on the
wall of the room, had passed, despite my repeated pleas, before I
was assigned a woman to search me, and when she had gone over
every inch of my apparel and person, permitted briefly to relieve
myself.

I was then led to a smaller room where I was greeted with my
first smile that night, by a new figure. He spoke English but
looked Russian, and was treated by "Joe Cook" with the only
respect I had ever seen him show anybody. Under guise of casual
conversation, he asked specific questions about my attitude to
Soviet Russia. I stated the facts. I had visited the Soviet Union on
my first foreign news trip in 1932–33, stayed seven months and
been unfavorably impressed, and had so reported on my return to
America. I could not comment on conditions since then, or
currently, as they had refused me a visa to go back. But at least
they had never arrested me, I blurted in my last burst of bravado.
The shortest, I felt this was the most crucial phase of my verbal
inquisition.

I was led immediately to a desk in a dim hallway. Two closely
typed documents, in Spanish, were thrust at me and I was
commanded to sign them. I tried to read them though they
blurred before me, but was told there was no time to read. The
intimation was that they were release papers. I was still clutching
my big hotel key; now I looked at it with sudden hope. It was
almost evening again. Groggy from a night and close to a day
without sleep or food and no longer too clear about what was
going on, I signed.

Two uniformed armed guards then conducted me across an
inner courtyard—to freedom, I thought. But they impelled me
into a separate inside building in the police compound, then up a
short flight of steps and along a narrow corridor with a blank
windowless wall on its outer side and a row of cages on the
other.

Petrified, I realized I was in a prison. Prodded by the guards'
big rifles, I passed cell after cell with small barred apertures in
their doors. Faces, unshaven and animal-like, peered silently

through the apertures. The door of one cell stood open. The guards edged me into it.

Even as I shrieked, incredulously, "You are not going to lock me up? What for?" the steel door clanged to, the lock clicked, and I stood alone and desperate in dank semigloom, within close stone walls broken only by a naked stone slab as a cot.

Today I still feel the terror of that moment. The hotel key fell from my fist and thudded on the cement floor. Reason left me. I struck and kicked the door, then beat my whole body against it. I hurled myself at the constricting walls to try to budge them. As if listening to someone else, I heard myself wailing and howling.

Air raids and wartime gunfire had frightened but not panicked me. All through my intimidating nightlong and daylong inquisition, I had kept some pride and even cockiness. But to be sealed in like this was the ultimate horror. It broke me down utterly.

A voice from the next cell called in broken French: "Remember us. Don't make us feel worse than we do already."

I stifled my outcries in my arms against the far wall. I stumbled the length of the cell, three paces; its width, two and a half paces. I huddled on the bare stone bench, its chill cutting through my thin clothing, and despairingly counted to ten, over and over.

Please, dear God, I prayed, just let me be free and I'll never complain about anything again.

Soon, despite efforts to stop, I was whimpering and screaming anew. I rubbed tears from my face with grimy hands. There was no place to wash them. In the dim cold, I shivered.

After what seemed hours, the cell door was unlocked. A guard held out a wedge of bread. I refused it. Too sick and terrified to eat, all through the time I was penned there, at first I fancied a hunger strike might help free me.

Sleepless despite total exhaustion in the dead of night, I heard a scraping in a corner. Drawing myself back as far as possible on the stone cot, I strained my eyes vainly through the darkness. When a new guard looked in later, something big and black scurried into the hall in the sudden blaze of his electric torch: a great rat.

Even high noon came faint and gray through the narrow door-grating that admitted the only light and air. By it I deciphered some of the rudely penciled and scratched inscriptions on the dirty whitewashed walls. Scrawled last messages, they indicated the cell had been used for condemned prisoners. One with the words "Please tell him" and a name and address was subscribed with a pierced heart. Another, with no name, read "They are coming for me now" and ended there.

Some such fate would be mine, I thought. No one would find where I was. I would die in the cell, or perhaps below in the courtyard from which, in the nights, ominous shots occasionally sounded. Sometimes I heard a distant boom as of an air strike. I prayed a bomb would shatter my cell walls, even at the price of my life.

Nothing was provided to pass the interminable hours. I had no exercise periods. Crouched before the little grating, I peered through it hour after hour as I had seen the other prisoners doing. The two bars crossing it were fastened roughly with big nails; they looked like a crucifix.

Meals were black bread or a small bowl of dry rice or beans, or a slimy soup or porridge, pushed onto the cell floor and removed later. I never touched them. No one was let out of his cell except at the two sketchy mealtimes, around midafternoon and again late in the evening, when the guards unlocked each cage in turn and led its occupant to the single filthy malfunctioning toilet at the end of the passage, the stench from which permeated the already stinking cell tier. In the wall near it was a solitary faucet, under whose thin tepid trickle the guards let one stoop a second in passing. There was no drinking cup, soap, comb or towel.

I was the only woman in the cell block. I had no means of unsnarling my badly matted hair or of cleaning myself. I never took off my thin dress for a minute, both because of the cold and because the guards, when changed every hour or two, looked into each cell, day and night. Again and again I implored them to leave the door ajar, at least a hairsbreadth, but vainly. Picked men between the ages of about twenty-three and twenty-eight, some were surly, a few friendly. In the Stygian night watches, adding to my terror, several tried to be too friendly.

In the single line of cages, I could not see my fellow prisoners and seldom heard them. Most were silent and apparently un-moving. One shrieked orations in choice Castilian, punctuated by demonic hoots, but was soon led out, the guards tapping their heads significantly. In snatches during the guards' rare absences, my neighbor tried to comfort me. He and the rest were all far worse off than I, he said. Sooner or later my embassy would find me. I had hope of salvation; they next to none, if any.

It was a political prison. He had been there thirty days, abducted in the street one evening with no chance to inform his wife and children. Others had waited months to be taken before a tribunal and told the charges against them. All were just suspects or they would already be corpses, he reasoned. Some must be innocent.

I was black and blue all over from repeatedly heaving myself against the stifling door and walls. But these frenzies lessened as I grew weaker. I had had dengue fever and malaria in Ethiopia; in the moist chill such attacks recurred. I shook uncontrollably.

I lost track of day and night. I never really slept, or thought I didn't. But I spent hours or maybe days in comas and trances. In some, I was sure I heard English voices. I seldom cried now. I no longer had energy to prop myself half-kneeling against the cell door, as one had to to see through the grating.

The guards shook their heads when they looked in on me, sprawled on the stone slab. In rational minutes I still pleaded that my embassy be called. Over and over I entreated this. I was told a doctor would be sent me, but none came.

By the end all hope had left me. I thought I had been entombed weeks or months, but it was my fifth day. I was in a semistupor when, around noon, a guard came to get me. I had a visitor, he said. I didn't even get excited. I could hardly see or stand. My sandal straps had broken. My feet moved like a stranger's. The guards had to help me out of the cell and almost carry me down to the inner courtyard and across it to a public waiting room in another building.

The young man expecting me gasped at the apparition tottering toward him. I was unbelievably dirt-smudged, disheveled, bruised and wild-eyed, he said later. He was secretary at our embassy, he told me, sent by our chargé d'affaires. He looked like an American and spoke like one, with a Midwest accent. I burst into tears and just stared at him.

I wanted to believe him, but in my fevered and disordered state couldn't. Normally too trusting, I now trusted nobody. He was another "Joe Cook," a Communist in disguise trying to fool me, I ranted. I was convinced of this when he said he could not

immediately take me out with him. He had to report back to the
embassy but would surely return for me later. I sniffled that I
knew he would never come back.

To reassure me, he showed me his diplomatic passport and
credentials, and told how the chargé d'affaires had traced me.
Finding me "out" repeatedly when he called my hotel, he had
deduced what had happened and set to work to find me. Informed that I was being "held for questioning"—by implication
in an ordinary hotel room—he had needed two more days, with
the sternest official representations, to learn where I was actually
being held.

The embassy secretary wanted to help me back to my "room"
but was told this was forbidden. My dread returned when he
tried to leave. I clung to him. At last he literally had to tear
himself away while I still screeched doubts, pleas and protests
like a madwoman. Back in the cell, I collapsed wholly.

Sometime later, another guard came for me. Again the embassy
secretary waited, and this time, as I staggered against him, led
me out of the headquarters compound. The five days had been an
eternity. I couldn't accept that I was really free.

Soon I was gulping hot tea and sobbing my woes to the chargé
d'affairs. He had hardly known me in my haggard, frowzy and
frenzied condition and was aghast at the transformation. My
"mishap" was the worst of its kind he had yet encountered, he
said. After I had washed off as much dirt and smelliness as I
could in an embassy rest room, he told me he had seen an
apparent reprint of the Negrin interview, uncredited and unby-
lined, on the front page of the leading Valencia paper, had
guessed it was mine, and wanted to congratulate me. But I had
lost interest in interviews. I just wanted to get out of Spain.

Then he gently said he had news I wouldn't like. No charge
had been brought and I was released in embassy custody. But the
police insisted it would take three days to finish their investigation and return my passport, with an exit permit. Only then
would I be free to leave for my Paris plane. Meantime they were
returning my effects to my hotel room, which had been held for
me, and expected me to go back there.

I recoiled; I could never feel safe in the room I had been seized
from. I beseeched that I be allowed to spend the three days in
any free odd corner of the embassy, even a maid's room.

The chargé carefully explained that in effect he and his staff were themselves in the Republic on sufferance, in an extremely delicate internal and international situation. Sheltering me in the embassy, against the police's instruction and as if he did not trust it, might create an "incident." No question of safety existed now that the embassy had assumed official responsibility for me. The three days were probably just face-saving. My accustomed room should be the best place to bring myself back to normal. I could visit the embassy daily.

He looked as if he hadn't slept much himself, and infinitely grateful and with new realization of the ticklishness of his job, I agreed, though reluctantly. He drove me to the hotel himself, and after the clerk had handed me my key and said I had no mail as casually as if I were back from a short stroll, went upstairs with me to check my room and belongings.

No sign of the room's "inspection" remained. After the cell, it looked positively palatial. But all my effects were still missing. The chargé promised to trace them and to drop in next afternoon. He would try, maybe through the hotel housekeeper, to scare up an immediate clothing change for me.

Uneasiness recurred the minute he had left. But my healthy, sometimes dubious gift of swift rebound had already started working. The appalling claustrophobic fever could not revive in the big room with its large window fronting on the street. Its bathroom alone was twice the size of the cell. I could lock or unlock my door whenever I wished to. The food I ordered tasted delicious. A maid brought me clean clothes which almost fitted, and toilet articles, and I gave her everything I had been wearing for quick renovating. A blissful long hot bath and shampoo worked wonders. I fell into the marvelous soft-sheeted bed and slept fourteen hours.

I woke to bright midday sunlight. The inner scars were still there and would stay, but my exterior bruises, though livid, would heal soon, and meantime I had powder to cover them. I felt almost new physically, and hungry. I decided to lunch in the hotel dining room.

Were this fiction, my story would end here. I had survived a living death so profoundly disquieting that every instant is burned in my memory and I have never, to this writing, been able to bring myself to retrace its details on paper or in lectures. Anything that happened to me in Spain after it, however distasteful or distressing, must be anticlimactic.

But as this is an authentic account, I must report that when I opened my door, almost blithely, to go down to lunch, a uniformed guard with a gun was stationed behind it. I could ring for my meals, he said, but any move outside my room, even within the hotel, was prohibited. So was my telephoning.

I ate in my room, locking the door against the unprotesting guard. Nor did he deter the chargé d'affaires, who came soon looking more worried than ever, from entering and speaking with me privately. Tracking my effects, he had already learned the unforeseen development. I was under room arrest for the three days, my door to be guarded throughout them. My belongings would not be returned till I was leaving. But I would be undisturbed in the room and he had brought me old paperbacks and periodicals—no newsmagazines or papers, as these were also taboo. It was just two more days, he consoled, likelier to be boring than alarming. He would be back on both of them.

The three days stretched to five, then a full week, with no explanation. The chargé d'affaires showed up only once again, very apologetic. The police minister had advised that as I was safe, in a satisfactory setting, it would be better not to check too often; appearance of the embassy car before the hotel was drawing undue attention.

During those days I read more whodunits than I had ever had time for in my hectic life. Rested and fed, I was able to school myself, but began to feel shut-in tremors. The waiter's appearances and the maid's entrances to make up and turn down my bed were welcome diversions, though neither spoke to me. I spent more and more time at my first-floor window.

Once I saw an embassy car roll by, unable without my glasses to distinguish its occupant. But I saw the red, white and blue flutter from it, and it gave me a great thrill, like a glimpse of heaven. More fervidly than ever before I thought: How lucky I am to be American, where even in wartime justice, legality and freedom mean something.

I started worrying about my October commitments, in Rumania and Turkey, and even whether I'd get back to New York in time to launch my November lecture tour.

Then, in the evening of the seventh day, José Mendez walked into my life—to stay in it day and night for nine days, though I didn't then know this. He announced we were leaving in an hour on the Barcelona train. My belongings were already on it. He had my passport, permits and money in his pockets.

A hairy heavyset, uniformed and gun-bearing stalwart of the Guardia d'Asalto, he was crude and barely literate like most of the band, but better intentioned, I was to find. I wanted to phone good-bye thanks to the chargé d'affaires but Mendez and my room guard vetoed this. I had nothing to pack, so I followed Mendez and his gun down the steps without a backward look. At the desk, there mysteriously still wasn't any mail, but the clerk handed me a bill already made up for the last two weeks of my stay. It included my five days in the prison and week under hotel room arrest, but I didn't quibble. Mendez gave me my wallet and I paid in full.

On the funereally lighted train with its shades drawn down, we sat in the last seat, so were somewhat secluded. Mendez, with gun protruding, never left my side, even escorting me to the *retrete* and awaiting me at its door, but the other passengers showed not the slightest curiosity. My portable typewriter and two bags were on the bench opposite; Mendez said I could check their contents in Barcelona. We would be there two days, after which I would be put on a plane for France.

Two days! I sickened, wondering if that meant another prison cell. I doubted if I could take it, even with release in sight. But the stolid, fatuously smiling José, even with his gun, was somehow reassuring. He had said "we" and to call him José, and surely wouldn't look like that if our destination was a prison. He had a wife and three children in Madrid, he said. What was it like in America? He had always wanted to go there.

Happily, our Barcelona destination proved a hotel of sorts, outlying and one I didn't remember. A tall building, it—or at least its ninth floor, where we landed from a creaking elevator—was apparently used for hotel arrest cases. I never saw the other floors except for the entry.

Thus began a fantastic period of my detention, when instead of the police badgering me I badgered them, and my armed guard and I ate in dead silence in a spooky ninth-floor dining room with all around us, at other tables, other "guests" apparently similarly companioned, and neither "guests" nor waiters exchanged a single word, among themselves or to each other. The adequate meals were served without menu, "American Plan" style. Even

napkins were provided. But it was like a dining hall in a
mortuary. It didn't bother José, who with guard's discipline
seldom spoke to me in public anyhow; he ate prodigiously, as if
better than in a long, long time.

Nights could have been a problem. The high-ceilinged room to
which we were led on arrival held a big double bed, neatly made
up, under a narrow barred window in an alcove; across from the
bed stood a folding cot, for the grinning José. No man could sleep
in my room; it simply wasn't done in America, I expostulated so
indignantly I frightened him. His orders were to guard me every
second, day and night, he stammered; he wouldn't hurt me.

Eventually his cot was set in a wall angle just outside my door
and I wheedled him into lending me its key overnight and locked
myself in as at the Valencia hotel. Each evening he yielded the
key more reluctantly, as despite the wife and three children he
grew progressively more amorous, but he yielded it. He slept in
his uniform, with his beloved gun; his gargantuan snores punc-
tured my sleep even through the locked door.

Otherwise, we became boon companions of a curious kind, for
I was still very much under arrest, strictly incommunicado and
not allowed to telephone even my consulate, and José had to
check me in each morning at a local police station. I gave the
funds for all the small expenditures and excursions we made—
though room and board must have been on the house, for I never
got a bill. José confided that he drew little as a Guardia. He had
obviously never had it so good in the corps, and delighted in his
assignment with its relative freedom, except for gnawing anxiety
and mounting alarm at what his Valencia bosses would think as I
cozened him into one minor unorthodox liberty after another.

We attended movies, went to cafés and took short tram rides,
carefully avoiding the central parts of the city. José always with
no embarrassment presented cash payment for me and his "free"
Guardia pass. Licking coarse ungummed papers with fat lips, he
rolled us cigarettes with smuggled haylike Andorra "tobacco." He
even bought me the forbidden local newspapers. No one but I
ever seemed conscious of the strange juxtaposition of the armed
Assault Guard and myself. Alone, we talked and talked, by
mutual discretion not about Spain, but usually about America,
José's Elysian dream.

That the two days before I was put on a French plane

stretched to nine days was not the fault of José or wholly of his Valencia superiors, but rather of my own rearoused brashness.

Everything, down to the last scrap of paper, including my notes and folders, was in my bags when I checked them the first morning under José's watchful eye—everything but my most cherished possession, my Leica with its exposed filmstrip. The camera was more of a professional badge to me than my portable; I had bought it for my first wartime assignment, to Ethiopia, and had since worn it over my shoulder around the world. To it, I owed pictorial proof of the top exclusives I had scored, including the snaps of Negrin and myself. It was a good-luck symbol, almost a fetish, unreplaceable by even an exact duplicate.

Thus when we reported that morning at the police station, apparently an ordinary one, I insisted that José tell the desk officer of my missing treasure and that it must be returned to me. On his doing this too timidly to suit me, I lit into the surprised officer myself in vehement ungrammatical Spanish, demanding immediate action. It was certain the camera and filmstrip had just been overlooked, he assured me; he would phone Valencia and have them in the morning when we checked in.

Next morning it was the same old "*mañana*" stall; the Valencia police were tracing the Leica and I'd surely have it "*mañana*." Supposed to enplane the following morning, I refused to leave without it. This went on, day after day, for over a week.

Each morning my increasingly apprehensive Guardia took me, or rather I marched him, to the police station where I again and again demanded my camera. The police had arrested and jailed me for no reason at all, and now I would tell the world they were thieves, too, and had stolen my camera, I boldly charged, not once but many times. This really seemed to get to them, and they actually apologized. I baited them till they were sick of the very sight of me. How did I dare? It may have been reaction from my abjectness in the cell or my growing sense of nearness to the liberty of America.

Against his orders, worried José let me phone once, briefly, to the U.S. consulate. The answering officer may not have been my vice-consul for he didn't say "I told you so." But he knew of my experience and almost implored me to forget my camera "which you'll certainly never see again, anyway," and to flee Spain while

I still could, that very day if possible. Barcelona jails were even more terrible than those in Valencia, he warned solemnly.

The ninth morning, looking as relieved as I was, the police officer triumphantly produced my Leica, though without the filmstrip of the Premier, which I never got. "See," he beamed, "it was mislaid, not stolen, and you must tell them that in America." He asked me to sign a paper saying I had been well treated, but didn't demur when I said I wouldn't sign anything.

Almost immediately, my inseparable guard with his inseparable gun, still holding my passport and special exit permit, and I with Leica over my shoulder, left for the airport. One more taste of Republican justice awaited me there. Ordered into a cubicle, I had to strip to the skin for a woman inspector. Though I told her they had been double-checked by the police and under constant Guardia supervision, she dumped everything out of my bags and pawed through the mess. Finally, she pushed rude fingers through my hair, completely disarranging it. I emerged infuriated.

José, practically in tears at our parting, couldn't understand my rage at what to him was merely standard procedure. In a fearful whisper, as if about to be hanged, he beseeched me to promise I would take his wife and three children to America "if we lose, or something happens to me." I soothed him and got on the plane. As it took off, I could see him, through my restored glasses, still standing there, a somehow wistful uniformed figure with a very visible gun, waving at me.

It was a French plane but its passengers were mostly Spanish officials—none I recognized—and though still fuming at the final insult of my stripping, I held fire till our stop an hour later. For all I knew the Spaniards might be able to order the plane back, and I wasn't taking any more chances.

But the first out of the plane at Toulouse, where I had a short wait for my Paris plane, I almost kissed the ground. "Are we in France?" I shrieked, to the amazement of crew and passengers. "Oh, blessed land," I raved, "a real Republic, not like Spain."

"*Diablos!*" I yelled at the Spaniards. "Spain is a tyranny, another Russia. I never want to see it again."

The Spaniards looked as if they'd like to murder me. But I was free, in a free country.

Gregor Ziemer was Berlin correspondent for the Paris edition of the *New York Herald Tribune* and for the *Chicago Tribune* and *London Daily Mail.* He has written much about Germany, including many books.

Phoned in on
the Nazi Hot Line

GREGOR ZIEMER

DATE: October 1, 1938; location: Sudetenland, northwestern Czechoslovakia, and the key city, Eger; assignment: to prove Adolf Hitler a liar when he claimed, at the Munich appeasement conference, that the Sudetenland really wanted him.

Result: the only invasion story telephoned in over an official German Wehrmacht telephone, in double-talk, by a reporter who wasn't supposed to be there. . . .

I was working for Sigrid Schultz, correspondent-in-chief for Central Europe, *Chicago Tribune;* and doing part-time work for the Paris edition of the *New York Herald Tribune,* as well as the *London Daily Mail.*

I was also headmaster of the American Colony School in Westend, Berlin. On September 30, 1938, a cool, clear Thursday, jittery members of the colony were huddled in the school library, devouring the shortwave radio reports from the appeasement farce in Munich.

It was Bill Shirer, I believe, who signed off with: "And now begins the most horrible arms race in history. The Sudetenland is only the first piece of the pie."

But we *were* relieved to get off the fishhooks we had been

squirming on for fifteen days, wondering—would it be peace or war?

School classes Friday morning were relaxed, almost too much so. My wife, Eddie, and I got the idea simultaneously—at recess. "Let's do it," I suggested. "Find the German army? But where?" she wanted to know. "One spot is a sure bet," I said. "Somewhere near Eger, which has been in the news for months." "Poor Eger," said she. "Deliriously happy Eger," said I. "Didn't you hear Hitler say so last night?" "When do we start?" she asked. "Right after school is out. At one," said I. "Can you be ready?" "I'm always ready," said she. She's that kind of girl.

The tank of the Mercedes was full. Gertrude, the maid, was never surprised at anything. Our eleven-year-old daughter, Pat, didn't want us to go, but submitted when told she could have a friend in.

By four o'clock we were 180 kilometers southwest of Berlin near Leipzig. The weather was clear, snappy. The peaceful autobahn, winding through the landscape of Saxony, showed no evidence of the Wehrmacht. That meant the main push into the Sudetenland, which the democracies had just handed Hitler for a mess of "peace in our time," would come from farther south—Nuremberg, Bayreuth, Plauen or Hof.

We reached the rugged Fichtelgebirge before sundown, and took the Hof-Naila exit. We rolled slowly south on Route 15, uphill and down, through dense pine forests. Nowhere did we see a sign of the German army.

It was pitch-dark by now and we called off the hunt in a spot named Karkleuthen. It had one hotel, the Post, and we got the last bed, a single. It was fun.

Breakfast was routine, and by eight we were bumping along again over crooked mountain roads. The day was cool, with scudding clouds. We were glad we had brought our jackets.

Everything was weirdly silent.

"Maybe they're not going to invade after all," said Eddie.

"Sweet dreamer," I said. "Let's try Schirnding. It's a border town."

But a mile before Schirnding a heavy barricade decorated with the words *Grenze Geschlossen* stopped us.

"Border closed," I complained. "And no way to get through this barricade. Got to turn back."

"To Berlin?" asked Eddie, disappointed.

"Let's have just one more try. Hitler's gang must be around here somewhere. What does that sign say?"

"To Mitterteich."

"To Mitterteich it is."

And suddenly there it was—the Wehrmacht! Overflowing the small, plateau village with trucks, artillery, tanks, motorcycles with and without sidecars, half-tracks, staff cars. . . .

"My God!" Eddie gasped. "Thousands of them."

It was lunchtime and the boys were feasting, chatting, laughing in their trucks and beside them, smoking big, black Brazilian cigars. Many still had the farewell flowers in their lapels, stuck there by their women. They were professional soldiers—big, neat, efficient—men in their prime.

"If anybody asks, we're tourists—lost," I said. "Ah, another sign. Sixteen kilometers—ten miles to Eger. Let's go."

We inched through the village and headed northeast. The road was crammed edge to edge with assorted Wehrmacht. Our Mercedes (now in Minnesota) carried the number IA 4004. Curious faces sticking out of the backs of trucks grinned when we occasionally managed to overtake a vehicle or two. The boys from Berlin recognized the Berlin IA. "Tell 'em we'll bring back plenty Prague ham—*Prager Schinken*," they shouted.

Our luck died at the next town, Waldsassen, when we ran smack up against a full colonel, small, scholarly, precise, decorated from his Adam's apple down. He waved us to a stop.

"*Wohin?*" he barked.

"I must get to Eger," I answered in my best German.

The colonel removed his glasses, wiped them, snickered, "Eger? Why?"

I hadn't done my homework. "I—I'm studying at the—the University of Berlin," I temporized. "Doing research for a paper—" I stopped. "What's the name of the general from the Thirty Years' War who was killed in Eger?" I whispered to Eddie.

"Afraid I don't know," she whispered back. The colonel glared, suspicious.

"Colonel, sir," I began again, "I'm on my way to Eger—"

"Yes, yes, you said that. To do what?"

"I just thought of it," Eddie mumbled. "Wallenstein."

"Colonel," I carried on brightly, "I'm doing a paper on Wallenstein—you know, the famous general of the Thirty Years' War who fought so well for the Emperor." I didn't remember which emperor.

The colonel stared myopically. "Why is a Britisher interested in Wallenstein?"

I whipped out our passports. "Americans, sir," I announced. "And here is my University of Berlin enrollment card. . . ."

"Ah, *Amerikaner*," smiled the colonel, less hostile. "But you speak such good German."

"My father was a German pastor in America," I explained. "My grandfather came from Pomerania. Ziemer's the name."

"Oberst Waldmeister," he snapped, raising his hand in the Hitler salute. "So you want to go to Eger across the border for scholarly research?"

"Yes, sir, to dig up some material on Wallenstein. He was murdered in Eger, as you no doubt know."

"Ah, yes, yes, of course," he said. "About 1630 or so. In the old city hall. I remember visiting it when I was a young lieutenant." He scowled. "But that man Wallenstein was not as good a leader as our Führer."

"He was too ambitious," I agreed. Then I looked around me simulating amazement. "But, Colonel, I had no idea I'd be running into the great German army on this trip. . . . You certainly are well equipped."

"Yes, yes. We are invincible," he declared. Quickly I handed him two cigars. He stowed them away, pondered awhile. "Eger, eh? Wallenstein? For a paper? Well, why not? I'll let you pass. But you still have the German *Zollamt* to deal with, of course. The border is only five kilometers. Follow Route 303."

"That was a squeaker. Thanks for the Wallenstein tip," I told Eddie as we drove off—trying to act casual.

The hard-top road to the border was narrow, with tall pine forests on both sides. Not a soul was on it.

Thanks to my rehearsal with the colonel, I had my story ready when we arrived at the red and white customs barrier. The pudgy German official on duty was arrogant. "Those miserable Czech officials," he shouted scornfully, pointing to the booth on the other side of no-man's land. "They've already fled. Soon we won't have to bother with them. There will be only one ruler around here—ours." He glared at me. "Ridiculous time to do research in Eger," he growled.

"It's only for a few hours," I said, sneaking him a few cigars.

He accepted them eagerly. "On one condition you go in. You must leave your passports, your money, and your car registration with me," announced the dictator. "Pick them up on your way out."

I wanted to flare up. I didn't. "May I have a receipt?" I asked innocently.

He wrote one out, complaining bitterly about suspicious American professors who didn't realize what a historic day it was.

"Feels spooky," Eddie said, shivering a bit as we covered the last five kilometers to Eger. "The first Americans into the violated Sudetenland."

"I feel naked and vulnerable without our passports," I confessed.

Eger, the once-proud, free imperial city, which in medieval times had the privilege of making its own currency, and which eventually became a modern industrial center, was a sepulcher. The few pedestrians slinking along the Bahnhofstrasse and the wide Markt Platz seemed to be in a stupor. Staring down on the unhappy city the eleventh-century ruins of the Kaiserburg and the dignified towers of Gothic churches stood darkly silhouetted against the autumn sky.

The city which Hitler insisted was wild with anticipation and joy was dreary.

Everything in it seemed frightened.

"Let's find a few people to interview," I suggested. "Look for some sort of restaurant."

We drove about aimlessly in the deserted streets and finally found the *Ratskeller* near the post office.

Inside three poorly dressed Czechs were silently sipping beer at an oval table. A moment after we sat down a furtive weasel of a man in a black leather jacket came sneaking in, on his arm a red band with a black swastika in a white circle.

As if on command the Czechs came to life and dashed out through the kitchen door.

The Weasel ambled over. "*Heil Hitler!*" he shouted.

"Good afternoon," I answered in English. That puzzled him.

"Heil Hitler!" he repeated. "Who are you?"

"My God," I whispered. "No passports." But I yelled brazenly, "We're American students. Leave us alone."

"I've got an old Minnesota driver's license," said Eddie, starting to dig in her handbag. The Weasel inspected it. To our unutterable relief his interest in us was temporary. He scowled and disappeared, after bigger game.

"*Schweinehund*—damned German pig," mumbled the host, coming over. He was pale as putty.

We concentrated on him. It took nearly half an hour to persuade him to talk. I explained that I was curious about what the people of the Sudetenland thought of the so-called liberation. I promised not to use his name, or even describe him.

"It's so sad," he concluded with great melancholy. "Why did the democracies give in? Why, why did they betray us? It's the end for all free Czechs. Did you see that pig? A Hitler guerrilla fighter. Tonight there will be many dead in Eger—all over Czechoslovakia. Why did you give in? Why did you give in?"

It was pathetic to see a big, fat man cry.

I remembered something. "We must go to the city hall and pick up proof we've been there. For the colonel," I said.

We hurried past the fancy fountains to the ornate city hall. It was deserted except for a mousey gray-haired guide who sold us two tickets and led the way to the ground-floor room where Wallenstein was murdered by two of his lieutenants, because his Emperor, Ferdinand II, no longer needed him or trusted him—to quote the inscription under his picture.

"Have you come from the border? Are the Germans there yet?" asked the guide in a shaky voice.

"We left them at Waldsassen," I told him.

"My God! That close?" he exclaimed, shocked. "Forgive me, but I must hurry and move my family out of Eger. You are Americans, no? Why did you let Hitler take the Sudetenland? Tell me! Why?"

"I really don't know," I admitted helplessly. "Lack of vision, probably."

"If you ever get back, please tell the American people to stop Hitler before it is too late. Please, tell them."

"I'll tell them," I promised. "But before you go, sell me some postcards and literature to prove I was here."

He reached behind the counter and tossed a handful of cards and brochures at me. "Never mind the money," he said running off.

Outside a few furtive figures were hurrying stealthily across the marketplace. I stopped a woman, pale and thin. "Are you the Gestapo?" she whimpered, sweat breaking out on her forehead.

"No, no, I'm an American. Tell me, are you glad the Germans are coming to liberate you? Hitler says you are all waiting eagerly. Are you?"

"Waiting?" mourned the woman with a pathetic sigh. "Waiting for death. Now excuse me, I must arrange for the funeral of my poor husband. He shot himself this morning because he knew they were after him—the Nazi guerrillas. He was a city official. Oh, my God—the pity of it."

"Well?" asked Eddie. "Had enough?"

"Enough," I admitted. We barreled out of town as if the devil were after us. Neither of us spoke until Eddie shouted, "Look out! There's a man with a gun—in the middle of the road!"

I saw the swastika armband and stopped with squealing brakes. A pimply face came in through the open window. "What are you doing here?" the man snarled.

We had to put up a lengthy argument to convince him. The Minnesota license helped. "This car is commandeered," the pimply one announced finally, creeping into the back seat. "Drive on."

"Where to?"

"I'll direct you. Going to pay a call on my former boss who's been lording it over me." He patted his military rifle.

We soon came to a cutoff angling to the left. "Turn here," commanded the Swastika.

Another kilometer and we could see a farmhouse—more like a rural castle. "Stop," the Nazi ordered. "Turn around and get out of here."

We did. In the mirror I could see my passenger stalk toward the house. At the corner I turned left toward the border, and pulled off into the first lane leading into the woods. It was too narrow for the car. "I'm going to have a look," I announced, dashing off in spite of Eddie's alarmed protestation.

The narrow tongue of woods was clear of underbrush, and soon I could see the white house again. I heard shots. My hitchhiker came running out, entered a shed, and backed out a big, black limousine. He raced away. Undoubtedly he had killed the owner and was stealing his car.

I ran back like a lunatic. If the scoundrel turned left toward Waldsassen, he'd see Eddie and our car. I found my wife pale but safe. The Swastika had turned right to Eger.

We retrieved our precious possessions, and got back to Waldsassen just as it was getting dark. The small village was bursting with jolly, cigar-smoking Wehrmacht giants, anticipating their first bloodless victory.

"Now I've got to get through to Sigrid Schultz in Berlin and give her this inside stuff nobody else has," I mumbled, nervous as a prospective father.

"The only telephone in town is probably at the hotel over there, next to the monastery," said my red-haired wife.

The hotel owner glared at me. "*Fernsprechen?* To Berlin? Man, are you *verrückt?* Every telephone is cut off between here and everywhere. You couldn't telephone for a midwife in the next village if your wife were having quintuplets."

I winced. I had a story but no way to get it out. Probably all telephones in the entire area were blacked out for security reasons. But if I'd have to drive to Dresden or Leipzig to phone my story to Berlin, I'd miss Sigrid's deadline.

I remembered Colonel Waldmeister. "It's worth a try," I said.

The colonel was enjoying a champagne supper at the home of the town's mayor. "Ah, the professor," he grinned. "Well, did you get to Eger?"

"*Jawohl, Herr Oberst.* Mission accomplished." I said the last two words in English.

"English I do not understand," he growled impatiently. "Speak German."

"See," I said, holding up my Wallenstein literature, "a very successful trip. But, sir, what's more important, I'm now having another opportunity to see the German army at close range. Amazing—really amazing! Sir, I have a friend in Berlin who reports to America every Friday. I am most eager to give him information about the high morale of your invading army—about to invade, that is. But the telephones seem to be blocked."

"Military orders," he said, sipping champagne.

"But, sir," I insisted, "couldn't you permit me to make just one call to Berlin? Wouldn't it be a wonderful thing if the American people knew how peaceful and orderly and gigantic this occupation is? It would really impress my government."

"I cannot give permission," he said with finality.

"Then the world will never know how magnificent is this entire project of yours."

The colonel finished his drink, polished his glasses. "Well," he pondered, "we do have our own command post Wehrmacht telephone in a schoolhouse—but no, it would not do!"

"Why not?" I persisted eagerly. "Wouldn't it be a great service to your country if you'd let the world know what's going on here?"

"Yes, that it would," he admitted. He thought awhile. "You Americans are smart—you are not interfering with us. So you want to tell the world how strong we are—right?"

"Right!"

The colonel was a man of quick decisions. "Come," he commanded.

Eddie and I were stunned by the modern switchboard the Wehrmacht had set up in the old stone schoolhouse—manned by a battery of ten men.

I gave one of them Sigrid's unlisted number at the Columbus Haus, Berlin. "You will no doubt wish to monitor my English?" I asked, trying to sound cheerful. "My friend does not speak a word of German, silly man."

"Does anybody here understand English?" barked the colonel. To my great relief, nobody did.

"*Ach,* go ahead. We give you five minutes. We trust you," the colonel decided magnanimously, thanks to the champagne, perhaps.

The connection was established in a few seconds. Sigrid was her usual efficient self. She seemed to catch my meaning when I said, "*Herr Staatssekretär* Schultz, I'm at the border, near Eger. I thought you could perhaps use some firsthand color stuff for your report to Washington tonight in the diplomatic pouch." I put it on thick, just in case somebody did understand English.

I could almost see Sigrid bat one eye—only once. "Shoot," she said eagerly.

I couldn't possibly reproduce the double-talk that followed—spoken in the cheerful voice of a foolish tourist—describing the efficiency and strength of the Germany army, its fine spirit, discipline, seeming invincibility. Between sentences I sandwiched biting comments about Eger, murder, suicide, desperation, gloom, misery, hopelessness, death. I delivered the message of the city hall guide about stopping Hitler before it was too late. . . .

Any clever Ministry of Propaganda chap working for Goebbels would have caught on at once. But obviously nobody thought of monitoring an official Wehrmacht telephone line.

When it was done Eddie joined the colonel and me in a brandy.

Not wishing to press our luck we left at once, drove all night, and were back in Berlin in time to attend Sunday morning service at the American Church on Nollendorf Platz—bleary-eyed but grateful Americans, even though we had the depressing suspicion that the message from Eger wouldn't really make any impression on anybody.

But at least Sigrid Schultz had an exclusive. I had the satisfaction associated with getting out a story nobody else had.

Every newsman and woman knows the feeling!

Ben Lucien Burman is best known for his classic Catfish Bend stories and for *Steamboat Round the Bend.* A new glimpse of this eminent author is provided by this account of a journey with his wife and illustrator, Alice Caddy, to Africa where he found himself among the Free French rebels in the Congo and managed to get an interview with that elusive and aloof world personage, General Charles de Gaulle.

I Meet Charles de Gaulle

BEN LUCIEN BURMAN

LIFE plays us queer tricks. I had no idea when I took that Pan-American Clipper one bitter winter morning early in 1941 that I was going to witness the miraculous rebirth of a great nation that was considered to have died, and that I was to become the lucky one privileged to tell the world of that miracle. I had not the faintest notion that I was going to become the American champion of the lonely Free French rebels fighting the traitorous Pétain government in the far-off Congo. I had no inkling I was to live in the house of the then almost unknown Charles de Gaulle, and that I was to become his champion as well. Until I met him—after which I viewed him with horror.

My friends had urged me not to go. My health had never been too good since I had unsuccessfully tried to stop a German shell in the First World War, and I was quite a bit past sixteen. But having been involved in one world war, I loathed even more than most Hitler and Mussolini, who had started the second and made war again the reigning fashion. My long-suffering artist-wife Alice felt the same way.

For months, ever since the fall of France, I had been trying

without result to obtain permission to join the French rebels in
Africa, who I had vaguely heard were resisting the Vichy armistice. Again and again I was told by sympathetic Frenchmen in
New York that such permission was impossible. The rebels were
engaged in a conspiracy that meant death if they were caught;
their leaders wanted no outsiders, however enthusiastic, who by a
careless word might bring about their betrayal. And then one day
I met Roger Brunschwig, a leader of the rebel movement in
America, and after that was introduced to Zuleina, his American
wife. And thus I learned one of life's basic truths of which I had
been only dimly aware: never underestimate the power of a
woman. Zuleina had been born in Iowa along the Mississippi;
because she liked my books about the river she pleaded that I be
allowed to join the conspiracy. Within ten days I was invited by a
then unknown French general called Charles de Gaulle to be the
first writer to visit the rebels. My purpose was simple—to find an
answer to a question. Was Marshal Pétain, hero of the First
World War, who had become head of the Vichy government, a
heroic old man taking the post only to lessen his country's agony,
or was he a traitor?

Quickly I secured assignments from the *Reader's Digest* and
the Newpaper Enterprise Association of the Scripps-Howard
organization; some weeks afterward my wife and I were boarding
the luxurious Clipper bound for Lisbon, and I hoped Africa and
the war. As we took our seats I felt like an actor in an old-time
three-a-day melodrama; our instructions on leaving had been like
those given to a secret agent in some bizarre mystery story set in
the shadowy conference rooms of the Kremlin or the mythical
palace halls of Ruritania. I patted the thick brown envelope filled
with secret documents to make sure it was still safe inside my
coat pocket.

On arriving in Lisbon, the first lap of our journey, I was to find
a certain Monsieur X, the chief Free French conspirator in the
Portuguese capital. The finding was to be a strange and mysterious
procedure, the sort of thing where one goes to a certain furniture
store and asks to look at a certain piece of antique furniture, and
there is directed to a phonograph shop, where the inquirer asks
the clerk to play a certain unusual record, never asked for by the
casual music lover; if his credentials are satisfactory, he is then
led to the master, Monsieur X himself.

The Clipper took off and settled down to a steady droning above a somber ocean. I began to explore the luxurious cabin and its occupants. Most of the passengers were diplomats; among them was Anthony Biddle, better known as Tony, Ambassador to the Invaded Countries, which of course included France. We talked pleasantly. But probably nothing would have happened if a violent storm had not swept the Atlantic, forcing us to wait in Bermuda for twenty-four hours until it passed. Biddle, a highly literate person, and I talked again, and I confided to him that I was going to visit the French rebels in the Congo. To my surprise, he informed me that the United States had no representative in the area; he asked me whether, after I had studied the situation carefully, I would cable my opinion to him in London. He would forward it at once to Secretary of State Cordell Hull and the White House. He did not add one fact I already knew; the State Department policy was pro-Pétain and pro-Vichy.

This was a startling development, my becoming willy-nilly a diplomat. I felt a little like those African gorillas I expected soon to be seeing, who, legend said, pounded their chests as they swelled with hairy pride. I was now not only a character in a mystery melodrama; I was also by proxy a U.S. Ambassador without portfolio and without expense account.

We arrived in a Lisbon crowded with spies, diplomats and refugees whose weary faces were marked deep with the lines that came from constant fear of the fatal knock in the middle of the night. Here and there were gay-moustachioed Italian officers, toasting Mussolini in expensive wine, or fat Nazi storm troopers talking in loud voices and gorging mountains of meat and fish and foaming cataracts of beer.

In the morning I hurried off to the British Embassy to present the first of my secret letters. I mentioned to the English official I was visting that later I must find the mysterious Monsieur X.

"Perhaps I can save you a bit of trouble," he remarked. "Mr. X has just moved to our embassy. Just one flight up those stairs."

I felt cheated and gravely disappointed. It would have been much more exciting to visit the furniture store and the music shop and ask for the period chair and the record of which no ordinary customer had ever heard.

I was further disappointed when I met Mr. X, a mild-looking little man with more the air of a bank clerk than of one whose

daily routine was plots and counterplots and stern matters of life
and death.

But when he spoke, his words quickly belied his appearance.
They were charged with excitement and mystery. "We are putting you and your wife on a Portuguese ship," he declared. "The
Lourenço Marques. She will land you at San Antonio Do Zaire, a
village in Portuguese Africa you will not find on your map, at the
mouth of the Congo. We are rebels, and the Portuguese will not
bring their boats into our waters. From San Antonio Do Zaire you
will make your way to Brazzaville, the capital of French Equa-
torial Africa. That is the center where our men are now
gathering."

An English secretary entered, bearing a letter. Mr. X signed it
and passed it across his desk. "On the *Lourenço Marques* there
will be a lady with her daughter. I cannot tell even you who she
is, for secrecy is vital. But I will tell her you are aboard;
in case of emergency she will reveal her identity. . . . Your boat
leaves tomorrow at four."

Day after day the *Lourenço Marques* steamed on her way, past
Madeira and the Canaries, with the white peak of Tenerife
suspended in the sky above the clouds like a ghost mountain in a
Japanese painting. Often we traveled close to the African shore.
With field glasses I could see a stretch of silvery beach and palm
trees and sometimes a tiny village or town. There were five or six
women with daughters aboard, and I played a guessing game
with myself, trying to imagine which was the mysterious lady of
Mr. X.

My destination was no longer secret, and I was chatting with
some passengers one evening when I chanced to remark that I
was going up to the radio room to send a telegram to the Free
French authorities in Brazzaville, advising them that we would
soon be arriving. As I spoke I noticed that one of the ladies in the
group turned white as the paint on the nearest lifeboat. It was a
Madame Radowski or some such name, a smartly dressed
woman, with a quiet-spoken daughter who claimed Poland as her
home; I had decided earlier she was probably the Lady of whom
X had spoken.

As soon as she could without attracting attention, she drew me
aside. To my amazement she asked me not to send the telegram.

I demurred politely, as in my arrangements it was a highly
important wire.

She hesitated. "You are, are you not, the gentleman Monsieur X spoke to me about in Lisbon?"

"I am that person, madame."

"You are sending your telegram, are you not, to General de Larminat, the High Commissioner of Free French Africa?"

"Yes, madame."

She grew hesitant again. "My name is not Radowski. I am not Polish. I am a Frenchwoman, traveling on a false passport. I am Madame de Larminat."

A sailor approached to fasten down a tarpaulin cover. She waited until he had moved away. "For months I was in occupied France, trying to escape with my daughter from the Vichy government and the Gestapo. After many attempts I succeeded, as you see. Because of my husband's importance, the Germans are furious. I am a valuable hostage and they have put a high price on my head. They would use any means to bring me back."

She glanced off toward the starry horizon where during the day, through the field glasses, I had noticed new stretches of silvery beaches and waving palms. "I have just sent a radio in code to my husband in Brazzaville. We are only a few miles from Dakar, where the Vichy governor is very powerful. His men are watching the signals from every ship so they may give their information to the Germans. No one ever sends a telegram from a ship passing here to Brazzaville. If you send yours, that will make two telegrams. The governor is likely to become suspicious, and order out a destroyer to take us both away."

I did not send the telegram.

We crossed the Equator and, on landing at the mouth of the Congo, boarded a rickety launch, and made our way up the stormy, crocodile-infested Congo. Disembarking at Matadi, we changed to a little caricature of a train that soon was rumbling and screeching through the jungle, and at last arrived at the railroad station of Léopoldville, busy metropolis of the Belgian Congo. Two miles across the river lay Brazzaville, the capital of the Free French rebels, our goal.

A stout, ruddy-faced Frenchman was waiting on the station platform, clad in immaculate white cork hat and white tropicals. He came forward inquiringly.

"Monsieur and Madame Burman?" he asked.

"Yes, monsieur."

He faced me with solemnity. "I am the representative of

General de Gaulle in Léopoldville. In the name of Free France and General de Gaulle I welcome you to Free French Africa."

He reached out his hand.

The trip had been so long, so full of delays and difficulties, and in his white shirt and shorts he was so much the perfect African explorer, it was difficult to keep from saying, "Dr. Livingstone, I presume."

The aide of General de Larminat, the Free French High Commissioner, took us across the Congo to drowsy Brazzaville; quickly he installed us in the stately colonial house beside the river which was General de Gaulle's home when he was in the colony, but which in his absence was used as a guesthouse. That night at dinner I met the leaders of the revolt, General de Larminat and the great French patriot, the gentle-voiced General Sicé. One of the highest medical officers in the French Army, General Sicé had sped from army post to army post and village to village in the jungle, urging Frenchmen and natives alike to resist the Vichy armistice. By the sheer force of his personality he had overthrown the authority of Vichy in this vital strategic area, and in the opinion of many thus saved Africa for the Allies.

I lunched with General Sicé and his associates each day thereafter, and each day learned more and more of the Vichy treachery. The shocking facts were becoming evident. The Pétain many Americans believed to be a hero fighting nobly for a lost cause was a weak old man, who like those about him was royalist and totalitarian by nature; he and his associates preferred to deal with the foreign dictatorship of Hitler, who held authoritarian views similar to their own, rather than trust their own people in a democracy.

Occasionally at the table some impressive figure would sit down beside me and be introduced as a Parisian gentleman called Dupont or Duval, names as common in France as Smith or Jones in America. Later I would learn he had held some post in the Vichy government or perhaps had served as a senator in the Vichy parliament. After incredible risks he had managed to steal away unnoticed and would soon go back to his pretended duties as a sort of Scarlet Pimpernel, to rescue French patriots in person and bring them out here to their friends.

Each day new refugees kept arriving, scholars and aristocrats, peasants and fishermen, sailors and carpenters, bakers and doc-

tors and pale bank clerks. Often on the radio I could hear a
message in secret code going out to some escaping camel troops
in the burning, Vichy-held deserts of Senegal, to help them find
their perilous way across the Sahara to Free French Fort Lamy in
the Tchad or British territory in Nigeria; later I could hear the
Vichy radio sending out orders to stop them at any cost. Sometimes they arrived safely, and those about me would rejoice;
sometimes there was only silence, and we knew they had either
been captured or had died in the desert of thirst.

There was no longer any doubt in my mind as to the truth. I
hurried over to the tiny telegraph office to send my first dispatch.
Carefully the black soldier at the key, with no knowledge of what
he was sending, tapped out each letter telling America how
France, believed dead beyond hope of resurrection, was being
reborn thousands of miles away in the jungles of Africa. The
heart of France, tapped the black finger, was no longer in Paris
along the gentle Seine; it was here in Brazzaville, along the banks
of the fever-ridden Congo.

I had time now to think of Tony Biddle and my weighty
diplomatic responsibilities, which soon were to have a direct
effect on my activities as journalist. I prepared a long telegram to
Biddle in London, pointing out what was obvious to anyone on
the spot: the strategic position of the Free French in preventing a
German sweep down from North Africa. If the Free French lost
the French Congo and the neighboring territories to the enemy,
there was nothing to prevent the Nazi tanks from seizing the
mineral riches of the Belgian Congo and splitting the continent in
two. Even more important was the psychological value, also
obvious to any but willfully blind men, of creating a resistance
inside France itself. I concluded by stating, in effect, that if we
did not come to the rescue of these rebels we were crazy.

I took my telegram to the American consul in Léopoldville, an
amiable individual whose chief duties consisted of stamping
missionaries' passports, and despite the wilting heat, attending
Belgian functions in top hat and tails.

He looked at the two close-typed pages and gave a gasp of
horror.

"Good God!" he exclaimed. "It's impossible! It would use up
my telegraph allowance for twenty years!"

Nothing daunted, I went back across the river and took it to

the British consul at Brazzaville, an astute if somewhat odd
English civil servant direct from the pages of Somerset Maugham.

"Perfect," he said. "I'll send it at once."

So it happened absurdly that the first on-the-spot report about
the Free French to the American State Department was made
through a Somerset Maugham British consul by a wandering
Kentucky-born Mississippi River novelist traveling with money
paid him by Paramount Pictures.

The news of the contents of my cable spread, as such news
always spreads. The reaction in Brazzaville to this and to my
dispatches, now published in America, was startling. Before I was
merely a well-disposed journalist. Now I was a fighting champion. No door was closed if I wished to enter, no information was
too secret to be given to me. I shared in the conferences held by
the patriots planning to create a resistance in France itself.

Now I was a full-fledged conspirator, beyond my wildest
dreams.

And then came General de Gaulle. Until I met him I had
written about him with unstinted enthusiasm. After I met him,
whenever I could avoid it, I did not even mention his name.

We had only a few hours' notice of his coming; my wife and I
had moved with painful haste out of his stately mansion, which
we had occupied for so many days we had come to consider it our
own. I went with General Sicé and my other friends to meet him
at the shabby little airport; he invited me to have tea with him
that afternoon at five o'clock. The meeting place would be, of
course, his house on the Congo.

I arrived promptly, as is my habit, and was met at the door by
one of the general's aides, who courteously ushered me into the
house—My house. An instant later the lanky De Gaulle himself
appeared and with ceremonial politeness received me in the
living room—*my* living room. Then he led me into the study—*my*
study, sat down at *my* desk, and offered me a cigarette—one of
my cigarettes that I had left the night before.

I learned then how deep-seated is that instinct so common to us
all—squatter's rights. I resented the general's reception, however
polite. I felt I should be receiving General de Gaulle.

Our talk started in this amusing fashion. It ended by becoming
the most uncomfortable hour and a half of my life.

As De Gaulle gave me a cup of tea, I studied him closely. He was a striking figure as he sat there, of extraordinary height, even in his chair; he seemed at first far more like a reserved Englishman than the usual figure of the electric Frenchman.

We talked about inconsequential matters for a moment, and then he made a revelation that came with the suddenness of a bomb dropped out of the hot African sky. I had asked what caused him to rebel against the Vichy surrender.

"There was no other way," he answered. "It was not a matter of minutes, not a quick decision. The debacle was a long time coming. I saw it arriving. More than that, I saw the debacle being prepared."

He sat silent an instant, in thought. "As you remember, when Marshal Pétain took over the supreme command of the army, all France believed he was going to rally the great powers of the country to resist the Germans. That was his first duty, the purpose for which he was appointed to the post. Unfortunately his actions were exactly the contrary. At that time I was in the War Office. I shall never forget the occasion when Pétain arrived for his first conference with Premier Reynaud. To my astonishment, instead of advancing plans for halting the enemy, with his first words he urged that Reynaud ask for an armistice. 'We are finished,' he said. 'We must capitulate.' Remember, this was almost a full month before the armistice, when the resisting powers of France were still enormous. From that moment, every time he saw Reynaud, at every slightest opportunity, he continued to repeat his plea. 'France is done. We must surrender.' For a general supposed to be defending his country, an officer of the French Army whose tradition was to die before surrender, his attitude was beyond belief."

I asked if he had any explanation of Pétain's extraordinary conduct.

"It lies in the personality of Pétain," he answered. "He is of the old French military school, brought up in the tradition of the Franco-Prussian War of 1870. When the mechanized war of 1939 arrived, he could not see any difference. He tried to fight it with the strategy of seventy years before. Moreover he was always a pessimist. And so when he took over the government and had the power in his hands, he asked for the armistice."

He talked for a long time in similar vein and I should have been very happy at the interview. His startling disclosures bore out officially what I had heard vaguely elsewhere. I had been told by some of the officers in Brazzaville how they suspected that they had been removed from posts of high command in France so the treasonable pact with the Germans could be more easily accomplished. I had heard often of Pétain's profound royalist sympathies and his great personal ambition. I knew De Gaulle's revelations confirming these rumors would make a sensational newspaper story in America.

But instead of being happy I was troubled as I had never been troubled before. For the general himself came as a terrific shock. I had heard he was an egotist. I was totally unprepared for the reality. There was an intellectual arrogance in his speech and manner, a disdain for the rest of humanity such as I had never encountered in a human being. Here was a man so wrapped up in his own consciousness it was as if no one else in the world existed. I agreed completely with every word he spoke, but they were uttered with a bitterness, a fanaticism, that might lead anywhere.

The responsibility of a sincere journalist at times can be appalling. Through an extraordinary combination of circumstances I was fortunate enough to be the only writer within thousands of miles, and because of that fact had been able to make the Free French and De Gaulle sympathetically known to my countrymen. Now I wondered if, after seeing De Gaulle in person, I had made a terrible mistake. Was this towering figure who was the chief of the Free French a possible fascist, who when he achieved power would be little better than the dictators he sought to overthrow?

Yet I knew that the pro-Vichy policy of the American government was as strong as ever. If I expressed my fears, the struggling rebel cause about which I was so enthusiastic would be greatly damaged. After much soul-searching, I reminded myself that in time of battle the defenders inside a beleaguered fort do not turn their guns inward but outward. I decided that I would keep my innermost thoughts to myself, and, writing the interview as fairly as I could, put down the facts, without any dubious personal interpretation.

I have thought many times of those days of the general's visit. If the American government had not opposed the Free French movement so foolishy, so blindly, I would certainly have

written what I felt; many important Free Frenchmen who I
found later had the same deep misgivings would have expressed
their opinions in the same way. De Gaulle would probably have
been replaced by General Sicé, he would never have come to the
command of France, and modern history would have been
different.

There followed many weeks of journeying through the steam-
ing jungles of the Congo and the sleeping-sickness infested forests
where the pygmies dwelt and the saucer-lipped women of
Ubangi; there came the finding of the dashing Leclerc, then only
a captain, in the broiling deserts of the Tchad; there followed
more weeks in Egypt and Syria in the fratricidal war where the
Free French aided the British in fighting Vichy French to prevent
the Vichyites from helping the Germans seize Suez; there came at
last the incredible climax in the dusty mountains of the Druse
where I was the startled witness to another bit of history—the
bizarre episode in the remote Druse capital of Es Soueida, where
the Churchill–De Gaulle feud began.

We came back to America after ten months, and for the first
time I saw my dispatches in print. I had ceased being a newspaperman many years before; now to my astonishment I found
that without the remotest idea of doing so I had realized the
newspaperman's dream of a lifetime—a world scoop.

Life plays us queer tricks.

Joseph Newman, a longtime foreign correspondent, author and broadcaster, has worked for the *New York Herald Tribune* as chief of its bureaus in Tokyo, Moscow, Berlin, London, Latin America and at the United Nations. More recently he was an editorial writer for the *Herald Tribune*. His published works include *Goodbye Japan, Report on Russia* and *Cuba S.S.R.*

A Spy—for
the *Herald Tribune*

JOSEPH NEWMAN

THIS IS not so much a story of "How I Got That Story" as of how I almost lost it. And it taught me that crystal-ball gazing into the great international events of the future is a perilous profession in which youth and inexperience need not necessarily give way to established and highly regarded diplomats and foreign correspondents.

The story is set in the spring of 1941. Hitler, in the west, had overrun France and was standing on the coast, looking across the Channel to England. In the east, having made a pact with Stalin, he had rolled up to his new borders with the Soviet Union and had come to a halt—or so it seemed.

A few rumors had begun to circulate that Hitler, hesitating to move across the Channel, was toying with a wild notion of moving on in the east. But they were rumors without substance, emanating from the rumor factories of neutral capitals and discounted as the work of enterprising Allied propagandists trying to stir up mistrust and trouble between the Hitler-Stalin pacters.

But in Tokyo, where I had recently succeeded Wilfrid Fleisher as correspondent for the *New York Herald Tribune*, the story, as I got it, began to take on substance. And over a period of several weeks it passed from the stage of rumor, and in my mind at least, assumed the terrible proportions of truth.

But what was I to do with it? Did I dare send it? A dispatch from Tokyo announcing that Hitler was preparing to invade the Soviet Union would be a bombshell. It would be the next thing to a dispatch from Berlin itself, because Japan was an Axis partner; and if the dispatch cleared Japanese censorship (as all news reports had to do before they could be sent abroad), it would appear to carry certification by the Japanese government.

Could I be sure it was correct? The primary source for the report was Branco de Vukelitch, a Yugoslav-born correspondent in the Toyko bureau of the French Havas news agency. I asked Vukie, as we American correspondents called him, why *he* didn't send it if he was so convinced that the Nazi invasion would come in a month or two. His answer was that Havas no longer was a free agency; like France, it had fallen under Nazi control. And since he hated the Nazis for having seized his country, among others, he was anxious that the outside world should know in advance and be prepared for what Hitler was about to do. And the only way it could get to the outside world was through one or more of the four American agencies and newspapers represented in Tokyo—the Associated Press, United Press, the *New York Herald Tribune* and *The New York Times*.

Vukie was not playing favorites with his information. He offered it to all of us. But the other correspondents, older and more experienced than I, would not touch the story. How then could I, the baby of the correspondents' corps?

Early in May, as chance would have it, I found myself seated at lunch one day at the American Club with Charles ("Chip") Bohlen, newly arrived from Moscow to take up an assignment in the U.S. Embassy; Otto Tolischus, of *The New York Times*, newly assigned to his paper's Tokyo bureau after long service in Berlin; and Walter Duranty, who had made his mark as a Moscow correspondent for *The Timeses* of both New York and London. One could hardly find anywhere three men at one table who were greater authorities on Hitler's Germany and Stalin's Russia.

I threw out the story about Hitler's plan to invade before the end of June—before the Russians could gather the harvest.

"I'm almost convinced of it," I remarked rather apologetically, fearful that I might be laughed out of court as an impertinent fool. "What do you think about my filing it to New York?"

Bohlen was the first to answer. The gist of his remarks might be summed up something like this: I can't believe Hitler would attack Stalin. There is no need for him to do so. Hitler can get what he wants from Stalin simply by asking for it. Stalin is too weak to resist Hitler's demands. A Nazi invasion of Russia would bring down the Soviet regime like a deck of cards, and Stalin knows that.

It was Duranty's turn next, and a phrase he used impressed his words on my memory: "The chance of a war between Germany and Russia is about as good as frying snowballs in the summertime." He liked the parallel so much that he repeated it a few days later in an article he wrote for the English language weekly edition of the Tokyo newspaper *Asahi.*

It was said that Tolischus and Duranty, each a star in his own right, could seldom agree. This was one occasion when they did. Tolischus was in accord with his colleague, and both of them with Bohlen.

This was formidable opposition. If I were to proceed with the story, I would be presuming to be right and judging the representatives of the State Department and *The New York Times* to be wrong.

I hesitated for weeks, and sent nothing on the subject. Toward the end of May, I interviewed a Scandinavian who had managed to escape the Nazi occupation, made his way across Finland, reached Shanghai and finally got to Tokyo. He brought with him details of Nazi activities, including intensive road construction, indicating preparations for an attack on Russia. A check with my best Japanese source—closely connected with the Japanese government—disclosed considerable nervousness about Hitler's intentions and did not exclude the possibility of an attack. With the month of June—invasion month—right before us, Vukie's pleas became more and more insistent; and he warned me that if I waited much longer, I would lose the greatest story of my career.

I was inclined to believe him and to trust his sources, though I had never been able to establish exactly what they were. I was told only that they were in the Japanese Foreign Office and within the armed forces—men who were deliberately disclosing state secrets because they were opposed to the Axis alliance and to Japan's entering World War II on the side of the Nazis. I trusted his sources because they had proved accurate the previous month. They had disclosed beforehand Foreign Minister Matsuoka's decision to conclude a nonaggression pact with Russia and to enter into negotiations with Hitler in Berlin on the terms for Japan's entering the war. They had revealed the substance of these negotiations and I had transmitted them to the *Herald Tribune* in New York.

By this time the invasion story had reached the point where I could feel it in my bones; where perception reached out beyond the limits of reason—beyond the studied and serious arguments advanced by my colleagues.

I sat down and wrote the story. I was not unaffected by the strong views of my luncheon companions, and the dispatch was worded cautiously. Furthermore, a degree of indirection in the use of language was essential if the dispatch was to have any chance of clearing censorship.

The next stage was the critical one. Would the Japanese censor clear the story? Unlike the other correspondents, who filed by cable, I used the telephone to New York (a practice initiated by my predecessor, making the the *Herald Tribune,* I believe, the first newspaper to use the international telephone for the transmission of news). But before I was given my connection to New York, I had to read my story to the censor and wait for him to call me back to let me know whether parts would have to be deleted, whether it could go as written or whether it would have to be suppressed altogether.

My calls were made early in the morning, Tokyo time, which was evening of the preceding day in New York, and close to edition time. It was with no small trepidation on this fateful morning at the end of May that I read my story to the censor. Though I had lived with the story for many weeks, reading it to a Japanese official seemed to make it official; and the meaning of the piece itself again staggered the imagination.

I waited for the censor to call back. There was a long delay. That usually meant trouble. I feared the story was being killed by someone of high authority to whom the censor would have to go with a report of this kind. And I began to speculate on how suppression by the Japanese government might be interpreted. It would not necessarily mean that the report was incorrect. On the contrary, it might be taken as confirmation of its accuracy if the Japanese, acting from a sense of loyalty to their German allies, sought to suppress it so as to preserve the secret.

At last the telephone rang: "Newman-*san,* it is all right. You are being connected with New York."

The Japanese motive in clearing the report lends itself to endless speculation. Were the Japanese annoyed with Hitler because he had not taken them into his confidence and because he was keeping them in the dark as to whether he would change the entire character of the war by invading Russia? Were they repaying disloyalty with disloyalty? Were they also interested in having the report published so they might see what the Nazi reaction might be, and thereby possibly secure some clue to Hitler's intentions? We shall probably never be able to establish the answers.

At the time, however, I was not preoccupied with such intellectual exercises, fascinating as they might be. Having transmitted the report, I started worrying about the consequences. If the reaction from Berlin were violent, the Japanese government might well feel impelled to take measures and to make sacrifices to appease Hitler. And the obvious sacrificial lambs would be the chief censor and the author of the dispatch.

I waited nervously for the next day and the reactions which it might bring. The next day came and went—without a word from any part of the world regarding the report. Then I began worrying about what had happened to my dispatch. Was it published? Did the *Herald Tribune* editors throw it away, considering it to be too far out to be taken seriously?

The days of June began their march, weighing more and more heavily, with cumulative effect, as each passed. The latter part of the month arrived. Still no move by Hitler. By now I was exploding with anxiety. Had I filed a big blooper instead of a big beat?

June 22 was a bright and beautiful day—perfect for our regular game of tennis doubles at the compound where Max Hill, head of the AP bureau, lived. The other partners were Bob Belair, of the UP, and Joe Dynan, second man in the AP bureau.

Max was one who worked hard when he worked, and played hard when he played. On this occasion he was making a most

determined effort to win, and this led to a closely contested
match. In the middle of a heated volley, Max's *ama-san* rushed
out on the court, shouting: "Hill-*san!* Hill-*san!* Telephone!
Domei!"

It was the Japanese Domei news agency, where we all had our
offices, with an urgent message. Max went in to take the call. I
recall marking time by lobbing a few balls over the net. A
moment later, Max, sweet and lumbering man that he was, came
tearing back, shouting: "The Germans have invaded Russia! The
Germans have invaded Russia!"

We stood frozen still a moment, then a wild dash for the car
and a careening trip to the Domei building in the center of the
city. We ran over to the foreign news desk. There was the cable,
with the text of the official communiqué from Berlin announcing
the Nazi invasion.

"Max," I cried, "why don't we all leave for the Russian front?
We're closer to it than anyone in New York or in the West. We
can get there by way of Vladivostok and Moscow. The European
approaches would be closed."

We went off to our respective offices to file cables to our editors
in New York, requesting permission to proceed to the Soviet
front. On my desk was a fresh pile of unopened newspapers
which had just arrived from New York. The papers, coming by
boat mail, were usually about three weeks in getting to me.

I slit open the wrapper of one paper after another, searching
for the *Herald Tribune* of May 31—the issue in which my story
should have appeared. My eyes raced across page one. No sign
of the story. Page two: nothing. Page three, page four, page five,
all the way to the end of the main news section—nothing at all.

I felt a bit ill. Mechanically, in something of a stupor, I kept
turning the pages. I was well into the back of the paper, among
business and routine items, when my eye fell on a headline on
page 21:

"TOKYO EXPECTS HITLER
TO MOVE AGAINST RUSSIA"

It was my story.

I didn't know whether to cry with joy that it had been printed
or with pain that it had been consigned to the paper's posterior.
But there was no time for self-pity or for cursing. The world was

electrified with the news of the new war. Having filed our cables to our New York offices, we piled back into the car and dashed to the Soviet Embassy to submit applications for visas.

The gate was locked. We called out to the Soviet guard inside: "Emergency! Emergency! We must see the ambassador!"

He opened the gate and led us to the main door of the embassy, which was bolted fast. A young Russian woman opened a sliding window in the wall to the right and asked what the commotion was about.

We said we had to see the ambassador.

"He's not here," she replied.

"Then the counselor," we insisted.

"He's not here," she said.

"Then anyone," we pleaded.

"No one is here," she insisted. "It is Sunday."

"But do you know the Nazis have invaded your country? It's war!" we shouted.

"*Pravda?* [Is that so?]," she replied with an air of absolute indifference, as if she couldn't care less. It was a case of supreme sangfroid or of absolute incredulity.

"Come back tomorrow," she advised.

We had no choice but to leave, kicking the pebbles of the graveled driveway in disappointment as we walked away.

Soon after we returned to our offices we received our replies from New York. Worded differently, all said the same: "Stay where you are. Japan cannot be left uncovered."

And indeed it could not. The Pacific theater was warming up. In April, during their meeting in Berlin, Hitler had pressed Foreign Minister Matsuoka to enter the war by attacking the British at Singapore and the Dutch East Indies. The Japanese hedged and played for time. Now, following the Nazi attack on the Russians from the west, Hitler was calling on the Japanese to strike from the east—to trap the Soviet Union in a vast pincers movement which would surely bring down the Stalin regime.

The Japanese hedged again, and again played for time. During the summer months that followed, as the Nazis drove toward Moscow, the direction of future Japanese moves became a matter of supreme importance. There was speculation that the Japanese were preparing to strike north—against Russia. My information was to the contrary, and I filed a report to the *Herald Tribune* that the Japanese were planning to move south—against Singapore and the Dutch Indies. (As we understood it then, their aggressive designs did not extend to Pearl Harbor.)

In October, while I was in Honolulu on a three-week vacation leave, Japanese police raided my office in the Domei building and tried to arrest me on charges of having violated state secrets by having filed such a report as I had. (This seemed a foolish disclosure by Tokyo of its aggressive intentions.) At the insistence of Max Hill and Joe Dynan, Ambassador Grew in Tokyo sent word to the *Herald Tribune* through the State Department advising me not to return to Japan.

The New York office suggested I come home. I countered with a proposal that I remain in Honolulu to await developments. I spent November writing a series of articles on U.S. defense installations in Hawaii. By December, the office was tired of my tarrying in Honolulu. It wired, asking about scheduled sailings. I replied there was one on Friday, December 5, the *Lurline*, and another about a week later. I suggested the latter sailing. The office wired back instructing me to leave on the fifth.

The night before I left, Joe Harsch of the *Christian Science Monitor* phoned to say he had just arrived; that he was having trouble finding accommodations; that he had heard I was leaving; and could he have my delightful cabin at the Halekulani Hotel? He moved in and was there for the Japanese attack on Sunday, December 7.

When the New York office learned of the attack, it tried frantically to reach me by telephone at the Halekulani. It assumed I would know better than to sail for home on the eve of Pearl Harbor. I was, of course, at sea—in more than one sense.

Back in New York on the city staff, I joined an extraordinary group of reporters, including Marguerite Higgins, Bob Shaplen and Homer Bigart, all working under that wonderful city editor, Lessing Engelking. One day I was handed a piece of copy. It was an announcement by Tokyo that Vukie had been convicted as one of the key members of the Sorge spy ring. (He later died in prison.) The Sorge group, spying for Russia, had secured some of the innermost secrets of the Japanese government and of the German Embassy in Tokyo.

Vukie may have been a spy for the Russians. But he shared some of his great secrets with the American public, through the *New York Herald Tribune*.

Henry C. Cassidy writes for the New York *Daily News*. His book, *Moscow Dateline*, gave a comprehensive account of reportage behind the Iron Curtain. He writes here of what it took—a little bit of luck, among other things—to get Josef Stalin to answer a few questions.

Two Letters from Stalin

HENRY CASSIDY

IF I HAD been feeling better and had tried harder, I might have had an interview with Stalin, like everyone else; no one would have paid much attention, and it would have been soon forgotten.

As it was, I was feeling rotten. It was the fall of 1942 in Moscow. The second winter of war in Russia was fast approaching. During the first winter, we had been through the battle of Moscow. For the second winter, we were going into the battle of Stalingrad. And I had an embarrassing boil on my right wrist.

So, instead of what would have been the unmitigated torture of a trip to the Kremlin and a marathon talk with Stalin, I welcomed a letter from him, and then another. They became major documents in the controversy over a second front in World War II. And I became, as an irreverent colleague put it, "a footnote in history."

When Alexander Werth wrote his *Russia at War* twenty years later, there in small print appeared Stalin's words to me, urging the Allies to "fulfill their obligations fully and on time."

Ilya Ehrenburg wrote about it in his war memoirs, describing me as gleeful because the letters so enhanced my reputation among the Russians that I was able to obtain a couple of bottles of wine from the Aragvi restaurant. Ehrenburg had it wrong. The wine came from the official food store for foreigners. But I felt flattered that he had inscribed the episode in the pages of Soviet literature.

In retrospect, it was perfectly natural that Stalin should have chosen that moment to put pressure on the Allies for a second front and that I should have been the unwitting instrument of his will

Foreign Minister Molotov had been to Washington and London in May and June, and the Washington communiqué had said, "Full understanding was reached with regard to the urgent task of creating a second front in Europe in 1942."

That statement should stand as an eternal lesson to writers of communiqués to be careful. The Russians, struggling for survival and desperately in need of relief from the West, took it as an Allied promise of a landing in Western Europe in 1942. Allied military planners said it was merely recognition of the problem, not a commitment.

Winston Churchill came to Moscow in August to tell the Russians there would be no second front in 1942, that the Allies were simply not ready. Churchill was not the popular hero to the Russians that he was among the English-speaking peoples. Stalin gave him a hard time, greeted him with what Churchill later described as "glumness," and even accused him of being afraid of the Germans.

The correspondents never saw Churchill during that visit. Once, we were called to Stary Dom, the "Old House" British consulate where he had his headquarters, for a news conference. But he changed his mind and did not appear. He was known to be in a terrible temper.

The visit ended with a communiqué which did not even mention a second front, the principal subject of conversation, but expressed determination to carry on the war and reaffirmed "close friendship and understanding" among the Allies.

But the Russians did not let it go at that. They unleashed a barrage of propaganda against the British, in press articles, editorials and cartoons, portraying this ally as a nation of Colonel Blimps. But much more serious questions were implied: Were the Allies acting in good faith, or were they yielding to the temptations of anti-Communism and appeasement of the Nazis? Could the Russians carry on, or would they collapse, letting their Allied aid go down the drain?

Inconceivable as it may seem now, the final question arose in many minds: Could the war actually be lost?

Wendell Willkie came to Moscow in September. He did not have bad news to bear; Churchill had already brought it. Willkie was the personal representative of President Roosevelt, the loyal leader of the opposition, on a kind of goodwill mission to assure the Russians that we were still with them and to assure the Americans that the Russians would go on fighting.

The correspondents saw Willkie frequently, individually and collectively. I had dinner with him his first night there at the Soviet Foreign Ministry's guesthouse, near my apartment on Ostrovsky Pereoulok. The dinner was superb—caviar, pigs' feet, fish, roast meat, vegetables and ice cream—quite a sensation after our battle-period suppers of sausage, hard bread and carrot tea. Willkie was in splendid form, talking about politics at home, asking about the war in Russia, obviously collecting information that would be useful in his campaign to support the war effort.

The Russians showed him all their sights—Stalin and Molotov, factories, farms, concerts, ballet, the Lenin Library, the Red Army Museum and the front in the safe, stabilized Rzhev sector, west of Moscow. They also told him—and sold him—their side of the second front story.

When it was time for him to leave, he came to a cocktail party given by the correspondents in the Associated Press office at the Hotel Metropole. He handed out a statement, urging a "real second front in Europe with Great Britain at the earliest possible moment our military leaders will approve." He added, "And perhaps some of them will need some public prodding."

Then it was my turn to be the public prod.

The idea originated neither with me nor with the Russians. It was conceived by the omniscient cable desk of the Associated Press in New York. This is said with no cynicism, because I was then in the field, and with no conceit, because I am now more often a desk-bound creature: the home office always knows best. They can see a story in perspective, view it with comparative knowledge of other events, think it over in tranquillity and come up with better ideas than the fellow in the field who is bogged down in the details of a single assignment and battling such obstacles as censors, transportation, communications and even lack of food and sleep. (May the present crop of foreign correspondents forgive this heresy!)

The cable desk sent me a telegram September 28, saying:

CASSIDY VIEW WILLKIES STATEMENT TRY UTMOST GET STALIN INTERVIEW OR FAILING THAT SUBMIT WRITTEN QUESTIONS SECOND FRONT ALLIED AID SOVIETS ABILITY RESIST ETCETERA ASSOCIATED.

At the time, I was thoroughly unimpressed. For more than a year, I had been trying my utmost, like every other Moscow correspondent, to get an interview with Stalin. Only a few weeks before, I had written him a beautiful letter, telling him I had just been out to see American tanks and planes going into service on the Russian front, and suggesting a statement by him on American aid would be most appropriate. He had not answered. Why should he now?

Not realizing that the time was now more propitious and the subject more interesting to the Russians, I put the telegram in my pocket and forgot about it for a few days. But if a foreign correspondent sometimes resents instructions from an editor thousands of miles removed from the scene of action, he also feels a sense of duty to carry out orders.

On October 2, having a few minutes to wait for the Metropole dining room to open for lunch at two P.M., I typed out a quick note to Stalin. Dutifully, I asked for an interview, but I hastened to add that a written reply would be all right, and I sketched out the questions—second front, Allied aid, Soviet ability to resist. New York's inarticulate "etcetera" I disdainfully dismissed.

I have always been an ardent admirer and user of newspaper reference libraries, but never one to keep a personal morgue. I have subscribed rather to the Walter Duranty theory that a foreign correspondent should keep his files under his hat. But I did make a carbon copy of the note to Stalin, and I stowed it away, together with the telegram from New York, in an old cardboard folder marked "miscellaneous correspondence."

Having no letterhead, I had typed at the top of a page of copy paper:

> The Associated Press
> Hotel Metropole
> Room 273
> Moscow, U.S.S.R.
> October 2, 1942

The letter was addressed:

> J. V. *Stalin*
> *Chairman*
> *Council of People's Commissars*
> *Moscow*

It said:

SIR:
Now that you have talked with Mr. Willkie, and he has given a public statement on the situation and problems of the Soviet Union, the Associated Press of America has directed me, as chief of its Moscow bureau, to ask you for an interview.

We think it would be highly interesting and valuable if you would tell in your own words, for the public which we serve through fourteen hundred newspapers, about this situation.

In case you are too busy for an interview, the Associated Press would appreciate greatly at least written answers to these questions:

What place does the possibility of a second front occupy in Soviet estimates of the current situation?

To what extent is Allied aid to the Soviet Union proving effective, and what could be done to amplify and improve this aid?

What remains the Soviet capacity for resistance?
> Sincerely yours,
> HENRY CASSIDY
> *Chief of Bureau*

That letter, which I would have made much more elegant— probably too elegant—if I had known it would be reproduced a quarter of a century later, had several aspects in its favor that I was not aware of when I whacked it out on a portable typewriter.

By carrying the questions around in my pocket for a couple of days, I had unconsciously made the timing perfect. The furore over Willkie's crack about prodding the military to start a second front had died down, and the Russians were looking at that moment for another means of doing some prodding. The AP offered a splendid public prod.

I had been there long enough to be known to the Soviet leaders. When the Germans invaded Russia, I was in the Caucasus on a vacation, and my story of what I saw getting back to Moscow—a purely factual account of the Soviet mobilization— was one of the first neutral indications that the Russians were not going to fold up in three weeks or three months, as predicted by the military experts. I was not a pro-Russian fanatic, but neither was I hostile, and the Soviet leaders apparently saw no objection to linking my name with Stalin's.

Then, I knew where the mail to the Kremlin was delivered. This was one of those little bits of minor information that a foreign correspondent accumulates if he stays long enough on one assignment. How I knew it, I could not recall. Perhaps one of the sufferers from a prewar purge had told me where a petition to Stalin could be passed through the Kremlin wall. But I knew that the gate in the southwest corner of the Kremlin was the mail receiving room. So I gave my note to George Green, our secretary-courier, and told him to hand it in there.

The very next night, just before midnight, as I was sitting alone in my apartment, reading, the telephone rang. A woman secretary of the press department asked me to come to the foreign commissariat immediately. She would give no reason, except that it was very important. As I walked through the blacked-out city, I wondered what it was all about. I recalled, of course, my note to Stalin of the day before, but if I was ever going to hear from that, it was much too early. I decided it must be some bureaucratic routine.

At the foreign commissariat, it was customary to wait in the press department—wait for credentials, wait for the communiqué, wait for the censor, wait for the copy. That night, I did not wait. I was escorted immediately into the back office of Nikolai Palgunov, chief of the press department. We were not friends. A newspaperman and a censor rarely are. But that night, he seemed to regard me through his thick glasses with a certain amount of respect. And, for the moment, I loved him.

"The document that you are waiting for is here," he said, and he pushed a piece of paper across his desk. At the bottom of it, in what looked like violet ink, was scrawled "J. STALIN."

The letter said:

DEAR MR. CASSIDY,—
    Owing to pressure of work and consequent inability to grant you an interview, I shall confine myself to a brief written answer to your questions.
    1. "What place does the possibility of a second front occupy in Soviet estimates of the current situation?"
    ANSWER. A very important, one might say, a prime place.
    2. "To what extent is Allied aid to the Soviet Union proving

effective, and what could be done to amplify and improve this aid?"

ANSWER. As compared with the aid which the Soviet Union is giving to the Allies by drawing upon itself the main forces of the German Fascist armies, the aid of the Allies to the Soviet Union has so far been little effective. In order to amplify and improve this aid, only one thing is required: the full and prompt fulfillment by the Allies of their obligations.

3. "What remains the Soviet capacity for resistance?"

ANSWER. I think that the Soviet capacity of resisting the German brigands is in strength not less, if not greater, than the capacity of Fascist Germany or of any other aggressive power to secure for it world domination.

With respect
(Signed)
J. STALIN

October 3, 1942.

It was simple. It was crude. But to me, it was beautiful, because it was mine. And it was to create a sensation. Stalin himself had spoken on the second front. He was not satisfied with the apologies and explanations of the Allies. He still wanted a second front in 1942.

There were problems in handling the letter. I received it late on a Saturday night, too late to get a good play in the Sunday papers. Palgunov agreed to let me hold it for release Sunday noon. On Sunday, telegraph communications were down and my own story trailed the Moscow radio announcement. Overnight the bureaucrats had been busy, changing the translation. "Prime place" had become "a place of first rate." "The full and prompt fulfillment by the Allies of their obligations" had been changed to "that the Allies fulfill their obligations fully and on time." But the fussing did not affect the impact of the letter.

On Monday, the Russians demonstrated the importance they attached to the letter by publishing it at the top of page one of *Pravda.* It appeared above the day's official war communiqué under a huge headline, "Replies of Comrade J. V. Stalin to the questions of the correspondent of the American agency Associated Press." Kent Cooper, then general manager of the AP, wired, "Congratulations grand achievement getting Stalin letter which published worldwide."

The contents of the letter were forced to the attention of

government officials. Questions about it were addressed to Prime Minister Churchill in the House of Commons. Wendell Willkie issued a statement, expressing hope that it would receive widespread attention. The U.S. Ambassador to Moscow, Admiral William H. Standley, flew to Washington for consultations.

The commotion could not bring about a second front in 1942. Nor even, as it turned out, in 1943. But the letter parted the Kremlin curtain a little bit, and let the world peek into the minds of the Soviet masters.

There was a significant aspect to the controversy that I did not know about, that Willkie probably did not know and certainly the public could not know because it was a top military secret. While the Allies were not going to open a second front—meaning a landing in Western Europe—in the fall of 1942, they were going to attack in North Africa.

Stalin knew about this. It was called Operation Torch. When Churchill had told him there would be no second front in 1942, he had tried to soften the blow by telling him about Torch. Stalin had continued to protest about the second front, but, singularly for an atheist, he had blessed Torch: "May God prosper this undertaking."

When the Americans landed on the hostile French shores of Algeria and Morocco on November 7, it was not much of a story in Moscow. *Pravda* gave it three paragraphs, reporting that Americans troops under the command of General Eisenhower had landed at several points, the landing was intended to prevent invasion by Germany and Italy, and American and English planes had dropped over France appeals for cooperation. That was all.

New York sent me a routine query, asking for Soviet reaction, and I filed a story, saying the Russian people had heard about the landing, they thought it might be good news, but they didn't know yet—because, I might have added, but the censor would not have passed it, they had not been told. It did not occur either to the cable desk or to me to ask Stalin again—so soon after his first letter—for his own reaction.

That thought grew on me gradually. The Russian people still lacked guidance. But the Soviet press was printing news somewhat more friendly to the Allies, including a speech by Churchill to the House of Commons reporting on the landings in North

Africa and explaining that a second front in 1942 was impossible, no matter how great the pressure of public opinion.

On November 12, I typed out another note to Stalin, asking three questions:

What is the Soviet view of the Allied campaign in Africa?

How effective has this campaign been in relieving pressure on the Soviet Union, and what further aid does the Soviet Union await?

What possibility is there of Soviet offensive power in the east joining the Allies in the west to hasten final victory?

I told George Green to leave the note in the same place as the first one. That was at six P.M., November 12. Somehow, I felt sure this one would succeed. So I was not really surprised to be called to the foreign commissariat from dinner the next evening and to be handed another letter from Stalin. It started:

"I am answering your questions which reached me on November 12th."

Considering the numerous and enormous demands on his time, that was certainly quick service. And no one could ask for a prompter reply.

Stalin's answers to my three questions were:

> "The Soviet view of this campaign is that it represents an outstanding fact of major importance demonstrating the growing might of the armed forces of the Allies and opening the prospective of disintegration of the Italo-German coalition in the nearest future.
>
> "It is yet too soon to say to what an extent this campaign has been effective in relieving immediate pressure on the Soviet Union . . . [but] that campaign creates prerequisites for the establishment of the second front in Europe nearer to Germany's vital centres which will be of decisive importance for organizing victory over Hitlerite tyranny.
>
> "There need be no doubt that the Red Army will fulfil its task with honour, as it has been fulfilling it throughout the war."

This letter did not have the sensational effect of the first one. Already the law of diminishing returns was beginning to apply to letters from Stalin. But the second letter probably had a more profound influence on international public opinion.

Stalin, in effect, called off the clamor for a second front in 1942. He recognized the value of the Allied effort. He predicted a second front, without tying it down to a troublesome date. And he promised his cooperation for the ultimate victory that now appeared assured.

By then, in any case, it was too late in that year for a crossing of the English Channel or a landing on the Atlantic coast.

Moreover, Stalin's men, guns, tanks and planes were moving into position at that moment for a colossal counteroffensive, due to start just one week later on November 19, that would win the battle of Stalingrad. No longer did Stalin need a second front for survival.

From then on, Stalin might even prefer delay in the second front. For the later the Allies came onto the European continent, the less territory they were likely to liberate and the more the Red Army would occupy and place under Soviet political control for decades to come.

More than a year and a half passed before the second front finally was created on D day, June 6, 1944.

That night, a group of us American correspondents decided to go to the Hotel Moskva to see how the Russians were taking the news. The Metropole was our hotel. The National was for important visitors. The Moskva was reserved for Soviet Important Persons. But certainly, that night, we expected to be welcome.

As we sat around a table in the cavernous dining room, having a few drinks and talking loudly to make ourselves heard over the brassy music, a Red Army colonel, quite drunk, came over and demanded belligerently to know what we were celebrating.

The second front, we told him; the Allies have invaded Europe.

"Next, you'll be invading us," he grumbled and stalked away.

He and we had a premonition then of the Cold War.

But none of us knew that little more than a year from then, on July 16, 1945, the first atomic bomb would be exploded at Alamogordo, New Mexico, and after that, in another war, there would be no fronts.

W. Richard Bruner, now the Vice-President, Marketing Communications, for a New York advertising agency, Callo & Carroll, Inc., was on the editorial staff of *Printers' Ink* Magazine for twenty years, the last seven as Executive Editor. He was co-editor of *I Can Tell It Now*, by members of the Overseas Press Club of America published in 1964, and a contributor to that book. Some of his experiences as a war correspondent during World War II are described in this story.

Some of My Best Friends Are MPs

W. RICHARD BRUNER

WOULD YOU believe that a war correspondent hip deep in headlined feuds with the military police would ever consider—just for the sake of a news story—making the supreme sacrifice and masquerading as an MP?

You can bet your little old nightstick he would. And did.

This tale of World War II intrigue, deceit and involvement with the military minions of law and order actually took place in North Africa in early 1943, just a few weeks before the American forces and the British Eighth Army combined to kick Marshal Erwin Rommel's famed Afrika Korps into the Mediterranean. I was assigned to the Algiers and Mediterranean editions of the *Stars and Stripes* and writing, among other things, a daily column called "Yank About Town," which covered the human interest stories and the lighter side of the news about the Allied forces stationed in Africa.

All right. It was a gossip column!

The "Yank About Town" relationship with the MP element had

developed into a campaign of considerable social significance—at least as far as the average GI Joe was concerned. It all began when the weary soldier, after weeks of continual combat on the Tunisian battlefront, traveled to Algiers for a rest period and discovered that the land of the American Red Cross Club and "real" American ice cream didn't quite live up to its press notices.

A substantial portion of this cerebral chafing was provoked by some new boys in town—an MP unit whose nattily attired forces lost little time indicating that they were fresh from Stateside. They began enforcing every regulation in the book plus a few they could only have made up right on rue Michelet. Warnings for minor infractions were a thing of the past. The soldier whose necktie was slightly askew or the soldier whose shoelace was unfastened soon found himself hauled off to the local bastille where he was subjected to a severe reprimand or a comparatively short-term incarceration.

Almost in the nick of time, the "Yank About Town" column, as any reporter worth his salt would, streaked to the aid of the victims of this oppression. Each day the Algiers *Stars and Stripes* carried an editorial attack on military tyranny best described as petulant but pertinent. Typical "Yank About Town" zinger: "What MP unit about town [there was only one—get it?] should read Dale Carnegie's *How to Win Friends and Influence People?*"

Holy heroics!

An eleven P.M. military curfew in Algiers created additional hazards for our war effort in North Africa. The curfew caused a variety of conflicts, but because of our family audience we'll restrict this narrative to the one involving the local movie houses, which American GIs were permitted to attend. Unfortunately, the final show usually ended around 11:30 P.M., or half-past curfew. This of course meant that the MPs, right on cue, would wait until show-break time, then roll along the streets of Algiers in their half-ton trucks picking up all soldiers not tucked in for the night. And so off to the bastille.

One night, after putting the *Stripes* to bed, I attended the late show at one of the local movie palaces, accompanied by Private John Welsh, III, the Army publication's famed "Puptent Poets" editor. Sure enough, on the return walk to our billets, an MP truck pulled over to curbside and two burly military policemen hopped off the tailgate and sauntered over.

The first MP got right to the point. "Okay, you guys, get in the truck."

The second MP was a bit more subtle. "Get the lead out!"

But they didn't reckon with Private Welsh. He decided to try a different tact.

"Pardon, monsieur?" said Private Welsh.

You see, Private Welsh figured this way: (1) our forces had provided the French troops with GI uniforms and it was difficult to differentiate between the Americans and the French (sometimes); (2) Algiers was blacked out, so who could see?

But Private Welsh hadn't reckoned with the ingenuity of MPs fresh from Stateside.

"All right, wise guy, show me your identification card," the first MP demanded.

"*Je ne sais pas.* Chevrolet *coupé. Maison Carrée,*" Private Welsh stammered.

"In the truck!" the two MPs chorused sweetly.

Until then I had remained speechless, marveling at Private Welsh's performance. Visions of a court-martial also danced through my head. Finally I spoke: "But we're *Stars and Stripes* and we have twenty-four-hour passes."

I forget the first MP's exact words, but it's just as well. At that point we got in the truck.

The American forces had taken over a local bastille as military police headquarters and jailhouse, and judging by the filth we GI prisoners encountered, had not deemed it necessary to clean up the Algerian residue. The offices as well as the cells reeked of urine, garbage and stale tobacco. The MPs on duty seemed immune—but the atmosphere did suggest why an MP's disposition usually ran the whole gamut from bad to worse.

The prisoners—some twenty-odd (in number)—were herded into a big room and the decor reminded me of early De Gaulle. It was about fifty feet square, all four walls were beautifully etched with jagged two-inch cracks, a solitary light bulb was positioned at ceiling center and the floors were saturated with diversified and suspicious stains. Along one wall there was a long wooden bench. Six impassive MPs sat slouching and smoking. The only other piece of furniture in the room was a plain wooden table. A youthful second lieutenant and a buck sergeant were seated behind the table receiving their guests.

The sergeant told us to line up single file in front of the lieutenant and to present our dog tags (metal identification discs, to the uninitiated). This request brought me considerable anguish; I wasn't wearing my dog tags. At this point I was about eighth in line, but as the line moved forward I kept moving to the rear. I figured the lieutenant might forget dog tags by the time he reached the last in line.

I was right. He completely forgot my dog tags when he looked at my *Stars and Stripes* pass. Unfortunately, the lieutenant had a good memory—especially for names. He turned to the sergeant and said:

"This soldier's name is Dick Bruner, Sergeant. Now we've heard that name before, haven't we?"

The sergeant nodded. "Yeah. I think he's a columnist."

"Very good, Sergeant," the lieutenant continued. "And you know something else? This jail is awfully dirty. There are cigarette and cigar butts all over the floor. I'm sure Sergeant Bruner isn't accustomed to living in such filth. And whaddaya' now, there's a broom over there in the corner. Think you can handle it, Sergeant Bruner?"

"Yes, sir," I said brightly, this time figuring that any show of antagonism might result in the proverbial book being tossed my way. Well, I cleaned that headquarters to a fare-thee-well. I even got the lieutenant and the sergeant to lift their feet so I could clean under the table. At about 2:30 A.M. the floor was spotless, but not much could be done about the odors. Besides, like the MPs, I was beginning not to notice.

In a report of the incident filed to U.S. newspapers, the Associated Press correspondent then in Algiers continued the story this way: "Eventually the lieutenant called the *Stars and Stripes* office and asked for someone to vouch for Bruner. Down came Sergeant Lewis (Blackie) Blackburn, of Carlsbad, New Mexico, who handles the paper's news service system and who, in the days when he was a New Mexico newspaperman, once gained fame for teaching an officer of the law just west of Pecos the virtues of always leading with his left.

" 'It certainly seemed strange bailing someone else out,' sighed Blackie wistfully. 'I seem to have my roles slightly confused.'

"Back at the office managing editor Hillary Lyons hit the roof. Whether he actually said, 'Those cops don't scare me. You write the story,' is doubtful. But he did tell Bruner to relate what had happened in his column.

"Then Lyons started home from work. Maybe it was pure coincidence, but the MPs picked him up and the whole pass routine was repeated at headquarters. In due time his case came up.

" 'Tsk, tsk, tsk, tsk,' said the lieutenant. 'This man's heart is all right. We must let him go. We certainly don't want to interfere with the publication of the *Stars and Stripes*.'

" 'Of course not,' agreed Lyons, and hurried out before several MPs could convince the lieutenant that, given a few moments time, they could figure out some other charges."

The AP story ran in the New York *Daily News* under this headline: "MPs win first round in bout with Army reporter." But the AP man missed two sequels to the story: (1) First Lieutenant Robert J. Christenson, of the *Stars and Stripes*, visited the bastille the next day and chewed the MP second lieutenant up, down and sideways for not honoring a legitimate pass; (2) The provost marshal general in Algiers, after reading about the incident in the "Yank About Town" column, called me into his office, discussed the plight of the enlisted man "on the town," and then three days later moved the curfew back to midnight. I made a few new friends.

A short time later I was on my way to the battlefront in Tunisia and my second encounter with the military police. From Maison Blanche, the airport in Algiers, I traveled toward Tunisia as far as possible by air. Then I began thumbing rides on various military vehicles. At nightfall I arrived in the town of Tebessa and began looking for a comfortable spot to unfurl my bedroll.

Walking down what apparently passed as the main street, I noticed a group of GIs entering a shabby, shell-pocked building. I walked in, and as my eyes slowly became adjusted to the light, I couldn't believe what I saw. I had stumbled into the headquarters of the military police!

What the hell, I reasoned, I'm tired, hungry and dirty. Where could I possibly acquire more appropriate lodging? I walked over to one of the MPs, Private First Class Ralph Safdieh, of Brooklyn, New York.

"Any chance of getting some chow and a place to spread my bedroll?" I asked.

"Sure," Pfc. Safdieh replied, "you can sack out under that stairway over there and I'll get you something to eat."

I had passed the test. Pfc. Safdieh had glanced at the "*Stars and Stripes* correspondent" insignia on my jacket and neglected to raise even one eyebrow! There was another thing he neglected to mention. I hardly slept a wink that night because of MP boots tramping up and down the staircase.

As I was rolling up my bedroll the next morning, Pfc. Safdieh came over and asked: "How would you like to get an interview with a German prisoner of war?"

I looked at my MP host in amazement. What an ironic turn of events. Only a few days earlier I had been incarcerated by the MPs; last night I had accepted their bed and board. Only a few days earlier the MPs had forced me to sweep out the bastille; today an MP was offering me an interview that might well scoop civilian as well as army correspondents. *C'est la guerre!*

"How do we go about it, Ralph?" I said, in my eagerness using his first name for the first time.

"It won't be easy," Ralph replied. "French doctors are in charge of the evacuation hospital in town and they're tough. There's a story that every time a new group of wounded prisoners are wheeled in the French doctors stand in the doorway sharpening their knives. They'll point to one prisoner and say, '*Italien, bon!*' They'll look at the next prisoner, '*Italien, bon!*' Then they spot the next one and say, '*Allemand! Ah, ha!*' And start sharpening the knives faster."

"That's very encouraging. How do they feel about correspondents?"

"*Pas bon.* They don't like them worth a damn, either. They won't even allow them inside the hospital," Ralph answered.

Assuming that Ralph had a plan that would get me into the hospital or the wounded German prisoner out, I asked: "Do you have a plan for getting me inside or the German outside?"

Ralph chuckled ever so slightly and I began to have some doubts. "Brace yourself, Sergeant. You're going to masquerade as an MP!"

Sure I am, I thought. And Field Marshal Rommel just walked in the door and surrendered. For Ralph's sake I managed a forced grin and requested additional details of his plan.

"It's simple. We'll borrow an MP jacket and helmet from one of the guys. You already have a forty-five. Then you'll go along with me on my regular rounds and I'll introduce you to the French doctors as a new replacement in our unit. That's all there is to it."

An hour later we were on our way to the hospital. Sauntering along the streets of Tebessa in my MP raiment, I could almost feel a surge of power. I curled my lips ever so slightly and thoroughly cased every GI who passed by. Unfortunately, we reached the hospital before I could find one soldier with an untied shoelace.

Once inside the hospital all went according to plan. The hospital was fabulous. It reminded me of a dark, dank, dingy castle. The prisoners were billeted in the basement in a network of curved corridors right out of a Hollywood horror picture. We found Hans, a twenty-year-old pride of the Afrika Korps with an American bullet in his belly, down one of these corridors.

As I expected, as we approached his cot Hans greeted us with the same icy stare that seemed a tradition with all Nazi soldiers. I had expected Pfc. Safdieh to act as interpreter, but this turned out to be unnecessary. Hans had studied English in his hometown, Berlin, and spoke it well.

Hans was extremely bitter about the war in Russia. "The Russians don't fight fair," he muttered. "They fight just like animals. The soldiers of the Reich fighting in Russia are anxious to come to Tunisia and fight the British and Americans. They fight fair."

Hans was enthusiastic about the work of American doctors. "They are very good," he admitted. He stared straight ahead when I asked him about the French doctors. "I'd like to go to a prison camp in America," he exclaimed. "I'm tired of North Africa."

The only sign of warmth crossed his face when I asked whether he had a girl friend back home. "Yes. And she understands what the war means to both of us. She will wait for me until I return victorious." When I suggested that the American troops might reach Berlin before this happened, Hans stared at the ceiling and sighed: "No. It's too far away."

As he talked I became more and more aware that the closest thing Hans had to a God was his former leader, Marshal Rommel. He seemed pretty fond of Hitler, too.

At this point I offered him an American cigarette and he grappled for the pack. I said good-bye and Hans looked me straight in the eye, saying, "Good luck." But, as I later explained to Pfc. Safdieh, Hans said it in a tone of voice that made me reluctant to turn my back on him.

Later that day I filed my story to the *Stars and Stripes* in Algiers. It ran on page one of the April 9, 1943, African edition. The main banner headline that day read: "Yanks, British 8th Army Meet; Allies Swing North After Rommel."

That night at chow I told Pfc. Safdieh about my experiences with the MPs in Algiers. "Maybe I can explain their attitude," Ralph suggested. "I was once stationed in a rest area. You'll probably find this hard to believe, but there are some pretty conscientious guys working those rest areas who are bitter about not being in a combat area. And that's true of many rear-echelon soldiers, not just MPs."

We walked outside to meet the jeep driver who promised me a lift to the American press headquarters at Gafsa. I was still mulling over Ralph's analysis of the MPs in Algiers.

"Ralph, you've convinced me," I said. "From this moment on I have a new slogan—some of my best friends are MPs!"

Richard Tregaskis is the famous author of *Guadalcanal Diary* and *Vietnam Diary*, among other books, and was awarded the International News Service Medal of Honor in 1942 and the George Polk Award in 1964.

Eleven Thousand Feet and No Place To Go

RICHARD TREGASKIS

DISTINCTIONS often come by accident, and that's the way it was with one of my best stories, the story of being involved in aerial combat between American and German fighter planes in World War II.

Other correspondents had flown "piggyback" behind the pilots in fighter planes as a kind of stunt. But never before had it happened that a fighter aircraft carrying a reporter was involved in a dogfight with the enemy.

However, the fates of newspapering are capricious. All the necessary preparations were made, hard work and protracted agony were endured—and the story ended up, for reasons having nothing to do with the content, more like a belch than a battle cry.

The Leibnitzian faith that all's for the best in the best of all possible worlds, and that earnestness pays off in distinction, dies rapidly in the hurly-burly of a shooting war. In a war (maybe in everything), chance turns out to be a fickle lady, or perhaps not even a lady at all.

I had been campaigning for some time, that fall of 1944, to have myself carried along in an American fighter plane on a combat mission. Back in England I'd convinced General Elwood ("Pete") Quesada that I should fly in a "droop-snoot" Lockheed P-38 on one of the tactical bombing missions into Germany.

The "droop-snoot" Lightning P-38 was basically the same kind of silver, two-engined fighter-bomber seen on all our war fronts at that time of the war. But the "droop-snoot" was specially prepared: the guns in the nose had been taken out and a seat substituted, and the nose redone with a transparent Plexiglas cap so that the passenger could see at least as well as the pilot, perhaps better. The objective was to provide a ringside position on operational missions for a "rubberneck" such as a general or intelligence officer. It occurred to me that a correspondent might talk himself into the same privilege.

Until the advent of the droop-snoot, the only way for an extra passenger to be carried on a fighter was the piggyback method: The pilot cranked his seat forward to maximum extent, the passenger crouched behind him. The method was radically uncomfortable, especially if you were more than five feet six inches tall, and I am a foot more than that.

Then I heard from a good source that two of the P-38 droopsnoots had been sent to General Quesada's command, called "Football," which was the code name for the U.S. 9th Tactical Air Force.

General Quesada's Football was doing brilliant and distinguished work supplying close fighter-bomber cover for the forces of the American First Army, sweeping across France and Belgium and into Germany in one of the great blitzkriegs of history.

Back in London, I asked General Quesada for permission to fly in a droop-snoot on an aggressive operation. I had no idea the request would lead to more than a routine tactical bombing—if to that. I furthermore assumed the chances were about five to one that I'd never hear anymore of the request.

Then, on a fall day at the headquarters of the U.S. First Army, in the resort town of Spa, Belgium, I was told that the flight was approved, that I'd have to get myself back to Orly airfield, north of Paris, that same day if I wanted to go on the mission.

It was overcast at Spa, heavy clouds blocking the sun like murky water. I asked my friend, Major "Coop" Cooper, commanding the First Army liaison squadron, for an L-5 to fly me back to Orly, 190 miles to the west.

When we took off in the little L-5 puddle-jumper, a two-place aerial putt-putt, the weather seemed to be clearing. But two hours later, when we should have been sighting Orly, we were in solid soup.

We descended from our customary "contact" flying altitude, about a hundred feet, to fifty to try to find something familiar. In the sloppy gray rainstorm we buzzed endlessly at naught feet, trying to find some recognizable landmark north of Paris. I remember taking a very close look at some oil storage tanks which loomed out of the rain less than thirty feet away and swerving violently away from a succession of undistinguished farmhouses.

I was afraid we would tangle irretrievably with a barn or windmill, and never reach Orly at all.

But at last, there it was, the long paved runway, with P-38 fighters lined up along the hardstand. We taxied to the fighter-bomber group headquarters. I dragged myself from the tiny plane, half dead from three hours of blind flying in the rain. Or more accurately, half-blind flying, contact pilotage in the rain at ceiling zero.

At the P-38 group headquarters I met the pilot who was to fly me in the droop-snoot. He was a bright-faced, eager flyboy, with the rank of captain, a proper drape-shape uniform hat, and I'll call him Bob in this context.

I suppose by fictional standards Bob and I should have got drunk with the pilots that night, but this was fact, not fiction, and we knew we'd be getting up at four A.M. for the mission to Germany. And besides, I was plumb tuckered out. Even the miserable little iron bed in the French billet seemed heavenly.

In the first dawn light we briefed: fifty pilots in sheepskin-leather jackets. The mission was to knock out a rail line well beyond the Moselle River, in the German Rhineland. If we were lucky, we might catch a freight train on the track. Each aircraft had two thousand-pound bombs.

The droop-snoot compartment in our aircraft seemed quite comfortable. There was a brand-new bright yellow cushion for me to sit on, and an instrument panel so I could see airspeed, the plane's altitude, an artificial horizon, RPMs, oil pressure, and so on.

The view was superb. The whole nose ahead of me was

Plexiglas. Whatever was going to happen this day, I should see
very well.

Bob showed me the safety equipment: underneath the yellow
cushion, a trapdoor with a steel handle and cable to engage it.
Bob warned me against pulling the handle unless absolutely
necessary, a joke I didn't much appreciate.

I had a back-pack parachute. It was bulky as I settled into
position for takeoff, but it was also mighty comforting.

I checked the intercom system. To call Bob on my mike I
would say "Hello, Inside" to distinguish the call in the welter of
radio traffic. I tried it successfully.

The only item I didn't think to check was that civilized aerial
concession to biological necessity: a relief tube. On long flights
like this—probably two hours or more to the target, a half hour
messing around with the bombs, and another two hours back—
one should always check into such sanitary facilities. But I was
excited to be in the brave new roaring world of these fifty P-38s
bent on mayhem for the Krauts.

Another item I should have checked, but didn't, was the
oxygen system for me, the passenger. There wasn't any. But I
didn't realize that until a much later and more critical juncture.

On the approach to the target, everything went smoothly. It
was a kick to be sliding so powerfully through the sky—the fleet
of silver, torpedo-shaped fighter-bombers droning through the
clear blue, sailing among tower islands of cumulus clouds.

We progressed over the curving ribbon of the Moselle, over
quaint villages and farms, into Germany. No trouble.

Then everything was happening at once. We were at ten
thousand feet, over railroad tracks like a set of silver threads over
rolling hills. And we were diving, diving on the track, in a great
roaring and whistling, with our nose down, and in the rush and
scream, I saw that there was a toy freight train puffing below us
on the metal band of the track.

The train was growing larger. As it grew, I could see the
separations between the cars, the smoke puffing from the engine.
I felt as if my stomach was dragging on the ground.

We were pulling up. My vision grayed over and grew faint.
The blood was sinking into my legs, leaving my head. I'd known
this kind of grayout in aerobatic maneuvers before, but never this
bad.

We were pulling up sharply, the frantic little engine slipping below us. I was still grayed out as we zoomed toward the clouds. And I was trying to see where our bombs had hit. But no effect was visible. At least, I thought, the bombing was done.

Then Bob told me on the intercom: "Inside—the bombs didn't release. We'll have to try again."

We climbed again, to ten, then twelve thousand feet—and this time, I felt quite shaky up there in the thin air. I had realized now that I had no oxygen equipment in my compartment—and the grayout over the train hadn't helped my state of physical fitness.

But complaint wouldn't have helped anything. I knew that Bob would be flinging the P-38 into another diving attack in a moment. I could see other P-38s strung up and down the sky: one at the top, in the clouds, in a steep bank as he began his dive, two others dotted below, on the way down.

Down we went again. It seemed to be straight down. I glimpsed the airspeed meter. It was reading around three hundred. I gulped for air.

And I saw the train, still frantically puffing, apparently undamaged. I saw a P-38 flash silver below us, pulling up. In the middle of the train, one of those toy freight cars exploded in a dark cloud.

And I grayed out again. The color drained from my vision, but I managed to crane forward so I could see where our bombs would hit. As we leveled, I saw an explosion on one of the cars. The car slowly keeled over and fell off the track.

And as we began to pull up, I saw another bomb explode on the toy locomotive. The engine seemed to explode from the inside. I saw a flash of orange fire, brilliant in the grayout.

Then we were zooming, climbing toward the clouds. I saw that we were up ten, twelve, thirteen thousand feet—fourteen thousand. Too high to be without oxygen.

But there was something more important going on. I heard "Coffin Red" calling "Coffin Yellow," the P-38 element leaders, and the chatter was excited.

Among the auditory garbage of the static, I heard talk about "bandits at three o'clock," "five bandits at angels eighteen, six o'clock."

I looked across the sky luminous with cumulus mountains and

saw the silver torpedo of a P-38 turning fast, with a single-engined, shark-nosed fighter, a Messerschmitt 109, curving after him. I saw them cut a quarter of a circle. A dogfight! We were in a dogfight!

Then we were turning, sharply, way over on our ear, the earth swinging below our wing tip. I glimpsed the altimeter: 15,400 feet.

We flung over to the other side. The wing which had pointed to the earth now reached toward the clouds. We were diving, turning violently. A Kraut must be on our tail. I switched to the intercom channel and asked: "Inside—what's happening?"

But there was no answer. The radio had gone suddenly inert. I fiddled with my switches and the radio was thoroughly dead. Nothing.

And we were jinking all over the sky, the clouds and blue and the brown land flipping from side to side, and up and down like a movie screen gone crazy.

Then I saw a dread pattern. Ahead of me, the sweep of brown landscape was turning slowly. Were we in a spin?

I checked the altimeter: 14,600, 14,000, 13,900. We were going down fast. The airspeed meter was over 300, on the circular dial edging toward the "red line" which indicated the absolute limit of speed to which the aircraft could be flown—after that, it might fall apart. I called into the interphone mike: "Hello, Inside—Hello, Inside. What's going on?"

No answer. I watched the turning brown pattern of the earth straight ahead, and checked altimeter and airspeed. The hundred-foot needle on the altimeter was working fast like the second hand on an electric clock: 12,300, 12,000, 11,500, 11,000, 10,800.

I decided Bob must have been shot, and that we were in a spin. I looked at the German landscape turning ahead of me and set up a schedule: It's only a matter of seconds now, and I'll have to go—or in five or six seconds I'll be dead, on the ground. The dial read 9,500, 9,000, 8,700.

I tried once more with the mike: "Hello, Inside. Hello—" Then I saw that the black plastic jack of the mike cord had slipped out of its socket. I flipped it into place. "Hello, Inside!"

This time, Bob's voice. Very calm. "What you want, Dick?"

I was aghast. I told him: "We're spinning. What happened?"

He laughed. The plane went into a straight dive, then leveled.

"Not spinning. Just a tight spiral. I was losing some altitude in a hurry. No good to be in a dogfight without guns."

I was so wrung out I couldn't talk, let alone wisecrack. Bob sensed I was somewhat discomposed. "Scramble's over. We're heading back to Orly."

But as we headed west, we climbed up among the mackerel clouds, the thin alto-cirrus. I had trouble breathing, I felt light-headed—and cold. And I had sense enough to look at the altimeter. It showed 16,500 feet. For fifteen minutes, I decided to take it without complaint. Then I'd had enough.

I called to Bob: "I don't have any oxygen. Did you forget?"

Silence. We droned still among the alto-cirrus, at 16,600. At last Bob answered: "Okay, I'll ask for lower level." And I heard him talking to "Coffin Red" about going down to join the lowest of our elements.

We went down to 9,000 feet, and I felt considerably better. But by this time I was lamenting the droop-snoot's lack of modern conveniences: particularly, the fact that it had no relief tube.

At that moment, we were passing again over the sunlight-flecked, winding waters of the Moselle—and at that moment, the river chose to look not at all peaceful anymore.

With a loud *Craack! Craack!* two small black clouds spouted in the clear air under our right wing. And the plane rocked with the concussion. I had flown in bombers enough to know that when you can hear them explode over the noise of your engines, they are too damned close.

Another black, cracking burst spewed the air to the right, and Bob flung the plane into a sharp, climbing turn.We went up to 11,000 feet, and stayed there—where the lack of oxygen isn't dangerous, at least if you don't keep it up too long. We sailed back over friendly territory, Belgian villages. But we were still at 11,000 feet, and I knew we had a good 70 minutes to go before we could land at Orly.

I didn't want to be known as a complaining rubberneck—that would be no good for the honor of the press corps. So I hung on to my natural proclivities, watching the slow progress of the minutes.

At last, about halfway through the 70 minutes, I knew the time had come. In irrefutable terms, something vital had to be done.

I looked at the magnificent, lemon-colored cushion which was

my seat in the droop-snoot, and I felt creeping qualms of a
schoolboy conscience. I hung on a few minutes more. Then I
could hold on no more. I thought indignantly: If they could
afford a droop-snoot seat, they could have managed an oxygen
system and a relief tube. Or at least, the more important of the
two. It was their fault. But despite this ego-saving logic, I was
more beat-up than ever, and not a little chagrined—and wet
besides.

When we reached Orly and Bob swept in for a hot landing, I
felt anything but hot. And when we taxied to the hardstand and I
struggled out of the nose compartment, bright-faced Bob sprang
down from his cockpit and bounced over to me, smiling.

"Well, how'd you like it?" he asked.

I had to tell him the truth. "You scared the p—— out of me," I
said, "and if you don't believe me, look at my cushion."

Now that the mission was over, my job was just beginning.
With my notes in my pocket, I found the pilot of the L-5 and
urged him to all possible haste in getting me back to the cable-
head at First Army Headquarters, Spa, to file my story.

It was almost dark when we landed at the First Army landing
strip, two and a half hours later. I dragged myself to the small
auberge where most of the correspondents lived, and, behind
blackout curtains, I glued myself to my typewriter. The resulting
manuscript, in good cablese, ran seventeen and a half pages. This
would represent a healthy press-collect bill for INS, but, I
thought, it would be worth the expense. It was a good news
feature, with my personal difficulties left out.

I found a night-blooming censor, battled the piece to clearance,
and looked at my watch. It was after midnight.

I didn't know till later, but the night cable editor at the INS
shop on East 45th Street, Manhattan, that night was a good and
able friend of mine, Bob Considine.

I wasn't aware I'd have such a distinguished correspondent at
the other end to render my cablese into prose. But I was sure the
story was unique and exciting enough to carry its weight.

Then I suddenly remembered: this was Sunday morning.
Every Sunday morning across the U.S., when the Sunday papers
were all in bed, and only caretaker-type assistant editors (perhaps only janitors) were holding down the deserted city rooms,

tossing out the stained coffee cartons and perhaps sweeping aside the cigarette butts near the slot. Sunday morning!—the death knell to a five-alarm fire or even a great victory at the front. The slim Monday morning papers would pick up the Sunday hard news in their own time. A feature story, even a vivid and exciting one, wouldn't have a chance. And if it was too late for this Sunday, it was too early for the next Sunday's paper where there would be room for good features. By next weekend my story would be lost or strayed, and certainly forgotten, the news-peg gone down the chute.

Years later, I found out that Bob Considine had done the rewrite job himself, and he had liked the story.

"But you know how it is on Sunday morning," he said. "Couldn't be helped."

I did know about Sunday morning. And I was reminded too that fate usually plays capriciously with you, no matter how you may struggle—especially if you don't think of everything. Ever since that droop-snoot mission I have been inordinately conscious what day of the week it is, always. The lessons of newspapering sometimes are pretty damned hard—or pretty uncomfortable and ignominious, anyhow.

Robert Trumbull is chief of the Tokyo bureau of *The New York Times* and an authority on Pacific and Asian subjects.

Hangover on Guam

ROBERT TRUMBULL

A MORNING-AFTER headache resulted in my getting an exclusive story on a major news development of World War II in the Pacific. It was an instance of succeeding by doing everything wrong.

The scene was a crude wooden bunkhouse on the island of Guam; the time, December, 1944. The cast of characters included the late Quentin Reynolds, a Marine general, an unfortunate Army information officer whom we called Doc, and a bantamweight correspondent (me) who found himself in heavyweight company at the Officers' Club bar.

After American forces had recaptured Guam from the Japanese in July and August of 1944, an operation that I had covered for *The New York Times* as a correspondent assigned to amphibious forces, I somehow became privy to a piece of top secret information known to only a few thousand persons in the Pacific theater. This was the plan of Fleet Admiral Chester W. Nimitz, Commander-in-Chief of the Pacific Fleet and Pacific Ocean Areas, to move his headquarters to Guam from Pearl Harbor, Hawaii.

When the transfer to Guam was finally made known to the public, it would be a stirring and significant story that every veteran Pacific war correspondent would want to write. For the move would mean the shifting of the heart of our war effort from the American side of the Pacific Ocean to an island four thousand miles westward on the threshold of Asia, within bomber range of Tokyo. Guam would then become a key staging area for further amphibious assaults on the enemy's inner defenses, and the climactic invasion of the Japanese home islands (of course, at the time we did not know that the war would be ended by two atomic bombs).

All the correspondents based at Pearl Harbor were waiting for the censors to release this story. As with practically all solid news developments involving war operations, this one would be handed out in a formal communiqué and there would be no question of anyone's having the story ahead of anyone else. There was widespread surprise and consternation, therefore, when I broke the story under a Guam dateline.

And no one was more surprised than I when word flashed back to Guam that I had scooped the entire Allied press with a story that I had written under the impression that I was just doing a "local color" piece that might not even be used.

When I arrived at Guam on the way back to Hawaii for Christmas, after a lengthy stint at sea in the forward areas, the first friend I encountered was Doc. A bespectacled young Army captain, Doc had been assigned to Guam from Pearl Harbor with the combined duties of a public information officer and a censor —an admittedly incompatible combination, as Doc was to prove once again. Quent Reynolds, then at the height of his fame, was the only other correspondent on the island.

From Doc I learned that news copy was being sent from the island by a radio-telephone voice transmission direct to San Francisco. This gave me an idea that I hoped would make communications history. If my voice could be pumped into San Francisco, I reasoned, why could it not be relayed to *The Times* office in New York? Then I could be the first person ever to telephone a story to New York from Guam, couldn't I? Doc thought I could, and proceeded to set up the project with the radio boys.

That night, the Marine general commanding the island was having a birthday party at the Officers' Club. Quent and I were present, both with prodigious thirsts, and while we were not competing to see who could consume the most whiskey, neither of us was letting the other get an ounce ahead. Unfortunately,

Quent was approximately double my weight and I had forgotten that a good big man can always beat a good little man at anything. I do not remember that Quent carried me home, but he could have without strain.

The next morning, when Doc shook me awake at dawn, I was feeling about as I deserved. And hangovers are worse in the tropics. But Doc had no mercy.

"Come on, get the hell out of that sack," he ordered brusquely. "I went to a lot of trouble to fix it up for you to make that phone call to New York, and we gotta be at the radio station in forty-five minutes. Where's the story?"

The radio station was nearly a half-hour away by jeep, and I had no story. I gazed limply at Doc, and feebly rolled over.

"No, you don't!" he yelled, hauling me out of the bunk by an arm. "No story, eh? Then, goddammit, you'll write one!"

Defiance was futile. Moaning, I pulled on khaki shirt and pants, somehow got my feet into GI shoes and stumbled across the coral street to the information shack. Doc pushed me into a camp chair in front of a dusty typewriter and slammed down a huge cup of hot coffee at my elbow.

"Goddammit, you write!" he ordered grimly, looking at his wristwatch.

"Oh, Jesus," I whimpered.

"Write, you —— —— ——, write!" Doc screamed.

I sighed and tried to collect some thoughts. "Doc," I said, "has it been released yet that Nimitz is moving to Guam?" I had been out of touch with news for weeks.

"Yes, yes—get busy—it's getting late—*write!*" Doc was brutal that morning. And I did want to make that historic phone call.

So I put my shaking fingers to the keys and painfully tapped out such a story as any correspondent could have written while half asleep, which I nearly was. I datelined it Guam, and went on to say, in effect, that this remote and lush tropical island would become the operations center of the Pacific war when Admiral Nimitz moved his headquarters there, as would happen soon. I continued with a rundown on the nature of Nimitz's headquarters, what Guam was like, what the transfer would mean in the prosecution of the war, and so on for enough wordage to carry the lead but not much more.

When we got to Barrigada, where the radio station was, we

discovered that we had overlooked one little item in our plans for me to make communications history. It seems that you cannot make a telephone call over licensed commercial facilities just because it is physically possible to do so. Such agencies as the Federal Communications Commission have something to say about it, Doc and I were told. In short, nothing doing.

It seemed to me—and it still would, I suppose—that after all that pain I had a story that was worth filing even if it wasn't going to be a new breakthrough in the history of transpacific telecommunications. So we went ahead and sent it off in the ordinary way, addressed to *The New York Times* with the censor's—that is, with Doc's—blessing.

"I imagine there isn't a line in that piece that wasn't written from Pearl when they announced that Nimitz was coming out here, but anyway I got a Guam dateline on it," I remarked to Doc as we headed back.

"Yeah, God knows it's no scoop, but you got a nice little piece there," Doc said, being kind to me.

We soon learned, though, that Doc was wrong in one vital particular. The news that Admiral Nimitz was moving to Guam had not been released, and my story *was* a scoop. Doc had been in the forward area, out of touch with headquarters, just as long as I had.

The appearance of the story on the front page of *The Times* caused a tremendous security flap all the way from Washington to the Western Pacific. I was clear, since Doc had passed the story in his capacity as censor. Possibly because they intended to release the story pretty soon anyway, they let Doc keep his captain's bars.

Stan Swinton is Assistant General Manager and Director of World Services for the Associated Press and was a combat correspondent for *Stars and Stripes* in Africa, Italy and Southern France. After World War II, he became chief of the Southeast Asia Bureau of the Associated Press and then chief of the Middle East Bureau, later becoming a war correspondent in Korea and chief of the AP Bureau in Italy.

The Day Caesar
Hung Upside Down

STANLEY M. SWINTON

THE INCREDIBLE forty-eight hours would end with the corpse of Benito Mussolini hanging by the heels before me in Milan's drab Piazza Loretto. They began when a brunet, pretty even in olive drab, beckoned me to meet her outside the Fifth Army press camp.

In the workaday journalistic world of Seattle, Rita Hume had planned with adroit determination to achieve her dream of becoming a war correspondent. The big hurdle was to get abroad. Rita astutely joined the Red Cross, volunteered for service in Italy and was overseas before she could say "doughnut."

In Naples, Rita sought out International News Service, an organization of fond memory which never flinched or faltered when offered talent already overseas and more interested in bylines than money.

So, beyond the hearing of fellow newsmen in the darkness outside the press tent, it was INS correspondent Rita Hume who offered me a trade that spring evening of 1945.

Thanks to a friendly general, Rita knew when and where American tanks would seek to slash through the German lines next day. But a press camp jeep must be shared with fellow civilian correspondents. Not unnaturally, Rita wanted a scoop.

She offered to share the general's tip with me in return for wheels. Not only did I have a jeep as a *Stars and Stripes* combat correspondent, but my stories appeared only in Italy. It was a fair exchange and I agreed. Rita was elated, confident that she and INS would be exclusive in the United States and the rest of the world on whatever stories we encountered.

In the gray dawn morning a tank column rumbled through Allied outposts and toward the German lines. Its mission: to block the Brenner escape route to Austria so that the collapsing German armies in Italy could be bottled up and captured.

Trailing the grim line of tanks was our jeep, the only un-armored vehicle in the column.

The American breakthrough was perfectly timed. Unknown to the Allied Command, the German rear guard had withdrawn during the night without even pausing to mine the roads. We roared northward unopposed. At Brescia and Bergamo, excited crowds lined the streets. Eager hands proffered glasses of raw brandy. Along country roads peasants looked up from their fields as the armored column roared past and then stared curiously at the lonely jeep tagging behind.

Tagging behind is an understatement. Always capricious, that day my jeep was downright cussed. Each few miles it sputtered, limping along as Rita and I anxiously watched the tanks disappear in the distance. Oil was leaking onto the spark plugs. Again and again I pulled up, wiped off the plugs and chased after the tanks.

Once as I was working under the hood, an Italian major general of the Salo Fascist Republic emerged from his farmhouse hideout and tapped me on the shoulder.

Too furious at internal combustion engines to be startled, I wheeled around.

Briskly the general saluted, handed me his machine pistol and announced: "I surrender."

As I returned his salute, an idea dawned.

"You will remain here until you can be picked up with ceremony befitting your rank," I replied in Italian.

There probably would never be another chance to give orders to a general, so I repeated the command more sharply.

"*Molto bene,*" the general agreed, and again saluted.

Rita was standing beside me. Clustering curiously around us were half a dozen armed Italian enlisted men who had followed the general from the farmhouse.

One, a corporal, motioned to Rita and asked with deep interest:

"Are many American combat soldiers women?"

"In this detachment fifty percent," she answered.

A Neapolitan voice spoke out from behind:

"*Mama mia,* we're in the wrong army."

Back in the jeep, both still giggling, we roared northward toward Como and, we hoped, our missing task force. Soon we were elated to see ahead a convoy of northward-bound trucks apparently loaded with German prisoners, for leading the column was a jeep.

Jubilantly, we cut in and out among the trucks of Germans, a surprising number of them bandaged or wearing slings. We cut sharply around the first truck—to be confronted by two German officers in the lead jeep. These were not prisoners. This was a German convoy.

Everyone in war wonders how he will react to capture. It was simple. There was no time for fright.

From their captured jeep the German officers waved us to halt.

As I braked, Rita removed her steel helmet, letting the dark hair fall back. No giggles now.

"Maybe they won't want a woman prisoner along when they're retreating," she observed calmly.

The German captain suddenly was beside me. He spoke before I could get out the word *Kamerad.* His English was British-accented and excellent.

"This is a hospital convoy. There are three hundred and twenty convalescents. The Italians tell us your tanks are ahead. My orders are to surrender if our retreat is blocked. These men need medical attention tonight."

The captain's face was dust-coated and drawn with fatigue. I pointed to Rita's "War Correspondent" shoulder patch and my own *Stars and Stripes* insignia.

"We are only correspondents, but the tank force is ahead in Como. We are going there and will have them send a patrol to meet you just south of town."

The German saluted.

"Thank you. We will go to Como."

Our stuttering jeep reached Como at dusk. At a roadblock on the outskirts of town, we told an American second lieutenant of the German convoy behind us.

Lake Como was breathtakingly beautiful beneath the star-jeweled sky. Even lovelier were our lost tanks, fanned out in a defense perimeter on the grounds of a Como villa near the lake.

At the command tent they told us there was no way to get the story of our adventures out. We each ate a tin of C-rations. Rita rated a room in the villa. I stretched out on a cot in a staff tent, too weary even to take off my combat boots.

It seemed minutes later when someone shook me awake.

"We've got a real story for you."

Groggily I followed him into the command tent.

There, like Eric von Stroheim in a movie of the First World War, was a German general—Major General Max Joseph Pemsel, Chief of Staff and Deputy Commander of the German Ligurian Army. He was wearing a long, black leather overcoat—and eating a Spam sandwich offered him by an American sergeant. I took one, too.

Pemsel had been entirely out of communication with his five-division force for two days. Through the Italians, the American OSS had made contact and persuaded him to surrender.

The past twenty-four hours had been so theatrically improbable that eating Spam with a German general seemed almost normal.

"Very good," the general said. "May I have another?"

A lieutenant translated.

The war must be nearly over if German generals would eat a second serving of Spam, I thought to myself.

Rita appeared just then. I filled her in and we knocked out stories of Pemsel's capture on the adjutant's typewriter. A major promised to send them back to the Fifth Army on an L-5 liaison plane due in midmorning. Dawn was just breaking.

Outside the command post half a dozen Italian partisans were waiting for the OSS man inside. Rita offered them cigarettes. We talked together for a few minutes until one asked if we would like to see a partisan command post outside Como.

We piled into the jeep. He told us to drive northwest. "Go slowly," he directed. "A mile or so outside town."

A few hundred yards short of a farmhouse, Gino, the partisan, suddenly fired his pistol three times into the air. Half a dozen Italians stood up from behind the low stone walls on both sides of the road ahead, rifles aimed at our jeep. Most had red bandannas tied around their heads—our first hint that these were Communist guerrillas attached to the Garibaldi Brigade.

Gino waved enthusiastically.

"*Amici, amici,*" he shouted. "*Americani amici.*"

Then, to us, with pride, "One of our roadblocks. We are very well organized."

He motioned for me to pull into the farmyard.

Rita and I had been through a lot since leaving the press camp, but the three sudden shots and aimed rifles were too much. My hand shook so that I could barely light a cigarette.

After introductions inside the farmhouse, the partisan commander gave us the shattering news:

"Mussolini has been captured—at Dongo." He pointed to Dongo on his map. "He is a prisoner."

Rita and I looked at each other in stunned surprise. This could be the story of a decade.

"If you would like to go there, I will give you a bodyguard," the partisan officer offered.

Neither of us thought to ask his name, but we would be grateful for the rest of our lives to that stocky little North Italian Communist.

Three partisans climbed in the back seat of the jeep. Two more clambered on the hood, a considerable driving hazard.

For two nightmare hours I was alternately trying to see around the partisans sitting on the hood or flinching when the partisans merrily fired into the air to warn hidden roadblocks a friendly vehicle was approaching. The men manning the roadblocks, uncertain whether the signal meant friend or foe, invariably greeted us with rifles leveled.

The roadblock ritual was repeated every mile or so. Rita and I were introduced proudly as *amici.*

Most of the partisans apparently had not seen a jeep. All were intrigued by their first sight of an American woman in uniform.

At a roadblock ten miles or so from Como, the partisans had real news. Mussolini had passed through en route to Milan—dead. His body was one of many on the back of a truck.

"Colonel Valerio executed him at Bonzanigo," a moustached partisan said. "Petacci is dead, too."

One of our bodyguards explained that Valerio was a senior partisan commander. Bonzanigo was a tiny hamlet near Dongo. Petacci, of course, was Claretta Petacci, the lovely Italian girl who, from her sixteenth year, was Mussolini's utterly devoted mistress.

Memory blurs at how many more roadblocks we passed. Buildings became more frequent. I recall the city-limits sign "Milano" as I drove into Italy's industrial capital.

There were shouted interchanges between our flamboyant bodyguards and passersby as we drove down Milan's streets.

"They say the bodies are in the Piazza Loretto," Gino told us.

Piazza Loretto was packed solid with humanity. I edged the jeep forward while the partisans shouted to make way for the American Allies.

Finally the crowd would give way no further. We left the jeep beneath a shop bearing a big sign, "Gomm." The partisan bodyguard shouldered the crowd aside before us.

As we broke through the first rank, an incredible sight met our eyes. Hanging by their heels from the skeleton of an unfinished gasoline station were seven bodies. Mussolini's face was expressionless, his hands half-clenched. He was wearing blue-green uniform trousers resembling riding breeches. His jacket had fallen back to show a white woolen undershirt. His corpse was poxed with bullet wounds. One slug through the forehead had left a gaping hole in the back of his head where the bullet had emerged.

Petacci hung beside him, lovely even in death. The blouse of her brown suit had fallen away to reveal a blue slip. Her legs were clad in sheerest silk. The woolen skirt had fallen back over her legs. A partisan climbed the steel framework from which she hung by her heels and tied the skirt to her legs—a macabre but very Italian gesture of modesty.

Flanking Mussolini and Petacci were five other bodies, several nude from the waist up, the others wearing long underwear like Mussolini's. Sprawled on the cement below were eleven other bodies.

The quiet menace of hatless partisan soldiers cradling tommy guns in their arms kept the crowd back.

The crowd was huge—from 100,000 to 200,000—no one could estimate or know. Noise is an Italian chracteristic, but there were none of the ordinary sounds of Italian life. Only silence. Absolute silence, as if each individual was trying to comprehend that Mussolini, Fascism's Caesar, was dead and so were his black-shirt lieutenants: Achille Starace, Roberto Farinacci, Nicola Bombacci, Fernando Mezzasoma, Goffredo Coppolo, Alessandro Pavolini and the others, and that these grotesque bodies before them also were the corpse of Fascism and the new Roman Empire.

As I scrawled notes frantically, a bald Milan newspaperman interrupted, quietly asking who we were.

I told him and asked what had led to this incredible scene.

"The bodies were laid out on the pavement at first. They laid Mussolini's head across Petacci's breast so they could be together in death. Then the crowd kept pushing in to see the bodies and so many people were hurt that the partisans tied the corpses to the steel framework," the Milan reporter said.

A photographer snapped us as we talked. I still have the photo. Above us hang the head-down corpses of two of Mussolini's henchmen. Rita is interviewing a partisan to my left. I am in steel helmet and combat jacket, a holstered trench knife and captured German P-38 automatic on my belt.

For half an hour we interviewed the partisans and Italian reporters who had been there since the beginning, getting detailed accounts of how Mussolini was recognized at a partisan roadblock as he sought to reach Austria in a convoy of thirty trucks.

The crowd was becoming increasingly restless. No longer was there silence. Voices cried out. The massed thousands behind pushed forward. Someone ran between two partisan guards and slashed at Mussolini's corpse with a stick.

Gino, leader of our five faithful bodyguards, said: "It's time to get out of here."

The bodyguards steered us back to the jeep, parked beneath the Gomm sign across the square.

Rita and I had a wild hope we could talk Radio Milan into allowing us to broadcast our stories. We would ask Allied headquarters, which for years had monitored the station, to relay our dispatches. A Milan reporter had told us how to reach the station.

No luck. Radio Milan was in the hands of a very cool and friendly British Intelligence major who was broadcasting false information in Italian and German to intensify the confusion of the retreating enemy.

If that was not bad enough, the major had more news. Rita and I believed we had the story alone. Not so. The major politely noted that seven other Allied newsmen were seeking ways to file stories—Stephen Barbour of the now defunct *London News Chronicle*, Christopher Lumby of *The Times* of London, brilliant Milton Bracker of *The New York Times*, James Roper of United Press, John Chabot Smith of the *New York Herald Tribune*, Reg Ingram of *Time*, and Howard Norton of *The Baltimore Sun*.

"We've got to get back to the press camp fast," Rita said. "The only sure communications are there."

Gino understood our problem. He and the other four partisan bodyguards shook hands with us. They waved their red bandannas as we drove off, heading straight south.

After the previous forty hours, what came next was anticlimax. Once just in time we drove across a field and hid the jeep behind a farmhouse as a small retreating German artillery unit with horse-drawn guns passed up the road heading toward Milan. Several times the engine sputtered to a halt and I had to wipe oil from the spark plugs to get us started.

Finally came the silhouette of a Sherman tank ahead. The ultimate irony would be to have an American tank kill us as we reentered our own lines.

I pulled the jeep over against a stone boundary marker. Rita stayed with the jeep. I crawled laboriously down the roadside ditch toward the tank, which remained puzzlingly motionless.

I realized why when I finally reached the tank. It was empty. Literally. This was the spearhead of the Fifth Army—the armored knife which the communiqués ecstatically reported was stabbing into the industrial heart of Italy.

The tank crew, to a man, was across the road in a field with three Italian farm girls.

They did not welcome my interruption but at least they had no objection to our continuing south.

"They certainly can't say there isn't action at the front today," Rita commented with interest as we passed the busy group.

Farther south massed Allied forces were moving forward, men and vehicles by the thousands. A Bailey bridge had been thrown across the Po. Traffic was one way—northward. MPs made us pull over five hundred yards from the river. I walked to the traffic control point and pleaded unsuccessfully for half an hour that we be permitted to cross south.

The MP captain was adamant.

Back at the jeep, I snapped: "It's no damn use. We've got the greatest story in the world and they won't let us across. We'll be here all night."

Rita said she'd give it a try.

Thank heaven for pretty girls, particularly at the front in wartime. Rita returned chatting happily with the same MP captain who had said I was out of my mind if I thought he could stop the blank northbound bridge traffic for one blank jeep.

All smiles, the captain climbed in and escorted us to the bridge. He spoke to the other bank with a walkie-talkie. Voila, the traffic stopped. Rita blew him a kiss as we drove south across the bridge.

Darkness fell before we reached the press camp. Both of us raced for typewriters. I was halfway through my fifth page when Rita interrupted.

"Let's eat," she suggested.

"For God's sake, let's finish our stories first," I said.

"I'm finished," Rita explained. "Jimmy Kilgallen told me never to cable more than three hundred words on a story."

She wasn't kidding. Those were her instructions.

"On this one Jimmy won't mind if you cable three thousand," I told her. "If he complains, I'll pay for it."

She returned to her typewriter. INS was ecstatic. The next day Rita happily was waving cables of congratulations from the INS brass.

My story won unusual distinction, too. The Signal Corps lost it somewhere between the press camp and the *Stars and Stripes* office in Rome. It showed up a day or two later. Journalistic historians will be able to say mine was the only eyewitness account of Mussolini hanging by his heels, first to see print in the following Sunday's *Review of the Week* section in the *Stars and Stripes* magazine section.

Postscript: Soon after the war, Rita Hume married John Secondari, the talented writer and television producer whose novel A Coin in the Fountain, *was the basis for the successful motion picture and hit song,* Three Coins in the Fountain. *She died tragically a few years later in an automobile accident on Majorca.*

Richard J. H. Johnston is a reporter for *The New York Times* and has contributed to several books, among them *The Two Koreas* and *The Pope's Visit to the U.S.* Mr. Johnston is a past president of the Overseas Press Club.

The Last Baton

RICHARD J. H. JOHNSTON

IF THE World War II war correspondent's view of the conflict from Normandy to Rheims was a spectacle viewed through a funnel, the end of the affair had the aspect of a peek into a kaleidoscope being twirled by a madman.

It was May, 1945. Hitler was dead and the German Army was reduced to bits and pieces of rout and confusion, rushing to and fro in what was to have been the great redoubt in Bavaria. Some units fought like cornered prey; others sought someone, anyone—but not Russians, *bitte*—to accept their surrender.

From the press camp of the Seventh Army in Rosenheim, correspondents, British, American, French and even one Mexican, sped off at the crack of dawn in quest of field marshals, Nazi Party functionaries and other big game believed to be scattered through the mountains and small villages. Martin Bormann, they said, was hiding in a gamekeeper's cottage up among the chamois; Göring was roaming the foothills in *Lederhosen*, hopped up with morphine to the eyeballs; and lesser lights of the shattered Third Reich were to be found for the seeking. It was a manhunt with notebooks and cameras and the quarry were the once-powerful, now the hunted.

My constant companion in the closing weeks of the war was Arthur Oakshott of Reuters, a tall, dignified veteran of World War I, with the bearing of Lord Kitchener. We traveled together, roomed together (when there were rooms), slept on heaps of potatoes in dank cellars, laughed together when there was something to laugh at and argued into the night about whether Britain was winning the war with American help or vice versa. In moments of great pique, Oaky was moved to shout:

"Bless me cotton socks!"

This was as close as he ever came, in my presence, to cursing, and when he let fly his imprecation he had a way of looking sheepishly about as though he expected his minister, or maybe his mother, to voice disapproval over his lack of control.

Recollection, aided by faded notes and a few yellowed clippings, would put the date at about May 6. Oaky and our driver, "Shorty" (the notebook recording the name of that GI is forever lost), and I set out from Rosenheim in search of interview material in the persons of German wheels. It was a day for picnics, golf or girls—a stage setting for an act from *The Student Prince;* not a drama reduced to absurdity. The last snowcaps were melting atop the mountains seen from the autobahn leading to Salzburg, skirting the Chiemsee, bisecting lush meadowlands and fields green with carpets of promise for cattle. Now and then a farmer would look up, noting that the passing jeep was not another open military Volkswagen carrying Germans to a place of surrender for their unit. His head lowered, hate in his eyes, he refused to respond to a wave.

"Dicko, old cock," mused Oaky, "I do believe I've got the solution to the 'German problem.' "

"I'm glad somebody has," I said.

"Well, you see, old bean, these chaps get into trouble from time to time because of their forests and mountains. You see, in the forests they brood and think incredibly dark thoughts about how positively awful is their lot. Then they put on those ridiculous pants and climb to a mountaintop. Up there," he said, pointing to a glistening tor, "they develop delusions of grandeur in practically no time at all. Then we're for it—all of us. They come down, get all trussed up in uniforms, organize military bands, march up and down, scowling at everyone and, first thing you know—they begin to rage all about, shooting up everything and arranging the conquest of Europe in quintuplicate. Of course, the whole bloody thing is silly and everyone has to drop what he's doing in order to put them back in the box."

He continued:

"Now, when this nonsense is finished, I am going to propose at the Peace Conference that, among other things, we must remove nine of every ten trees in the German forests and reduce each hill to thirty meters—no brooding, no grandeur, no war."

"I am sure Churchill, Truman and Stalin will be amazed and you will get a Nobel Peace Prize and unshirted hell from the conservationists," I said.

I lost track of Oaky when I transferred to the Pacific a short time later. I have not been back to Bavaria since the war, but friends tell me the forests, the mountains and the Germans are still there.

Salzburg hove into view.

"Look, Oaky," I said, "there's no point going into Salzburg again. It's been farmed completely for field marshals and such. Best we can hope for is a fugitive burgomeister from Tauberbischofsheim or some other town with a name longer than its main street. Even if we find one, he'll claim his brother-in-law is the only Nazi in his family and that he spent the whole war sending Care packages to a rabbi in Chicago. Let's head for the hills, as Zane Grey used to say. Maybe we'll find Goebbel's mother."

"Jolly good suggestion," replied Oaky.

"You guys got any idea where the hell we're goin'?" asked Shorty.

"We are riding into history, my brave one," I said.

"About that General Grey. Wasn't he the chap who ran into all those Indians and lost his golden locks?" Oaky asked, brightly.

"Jesus—these Limeys," muttered Shorty.

"Don't slander your gallant allies, soldier," I said.

"No, Oaky, Zane Grey wrote about the West and cowboys and cattle rustlers and virtuous women. The general with the golden locks was George Armstrong Custer and he lost his hair, his troops and a considerable part of his reputation, but, like your people lousing up in the Charge of the Light Brigade, we still make a big deal about Custer, making like he didn't really screw up at all, because we've got more generals than Indians today."

"*Ausfarht*," proclaimed a sign on the right.

"Turn off here, Shorty, this bucolic byway may lead us to the Pulitzer Prize and a vote of confidence in Parliament," I shouted, pounding Shorty on the right shoulder.

We had developed this primitive means of instruction months before when the crack of mortars seeking to impede our coverage of the war made ordinary conversation impractical. A thump on Shorty's left shoulder meant "turn left," on his right signaled "turn right," sharp thwacks on the top of his helmet meant "use your own judgment and get the hell out of here fast."

"SS, here we come," moaned Shorty.

"This is a tranquil area, secure from enemy hostility, swept of mines, housing only good people with all their bedsheets out the window to tell us they're not mad at anybody. The war, soldier, is said to be over," I soothed.

"I hope these *Kraut* bastards know all that," Shorty replied.

"Don't be bitter. If you hadn't got those three Purple Hearts, you wouldn't be chauffeur to two of the outstanding chroniclers of man's inhumanity to man and confidant of one who can quote Lord Palmerston by the yard and another who can name every state in the union, their capitals, principal rivers, and chief industries and recite their liquor laws," I said.

Suddenly there appeared, coming hell-bent, a German Army motorcycle, churning a cloud of dust ahead of us.

"A goddam *Panzer* division," shouted Shorty.

"Nonsense," observed Oaky, "a man in a motorized bathtub waving a white cloth. He wants to surrender."

Shorty slammed on the brakes. We whipped up a respectable cloud of dust of our own, and since we were victors and had four wheels under us, our cloud was properly bigger than the Germans'.

The dust-covered *Schläger* at the handlebars maneuvered to the side of the jeep.

"Translate, Oaky," I said.

The colonel in the motorcycle bathtub saluted.

Shorty unlimbered the carbine carried in the rack above the jeep dashboard.

"Bless me cotton socks, Shorty, do you want to start this bloody war all over again?"

"When I was in the infantry my CO used to say, 'Don't never

take no chances, specially when dealin' with the enemy.' He's an enemy, ain't he?"

"Was an enemy," corrected Oaky.

"Can't you see the chap's trying to be friendly? He is signifying that, insofar as he is concerned, *der Krieg ist kaput,* and it may be reasonably assumed that his companion holds similar sentiments, although the control of his motored conveyance precludes his waving a handkerchief," Oaky explained.

"Look, Shakespeare," Shorty snarled, "the sonofabitch's got a gun and Eisenhower ain't told me to relax yet."

"Speaking for the Supreme Commander by virtue of the fact that his name is on my accreditation card and I am older than you are, Shorty, and also, since I am a taxpayer who pays your bloated salary, I order you, in the name of the Continental Congress, to relax!" I said, in a manner made persuasive by two years of ROTC training in college more than a decade earlier.

"Jesus God, what a pair of nuts I got hooked up with," said Shorty, letting the carbine slide to the floorboards.

The German colonel dismounted, still waving his dust-flecked, white handkerchief.

"You palaver, we'll eat," I told Oaky.

They talked at great length. Shorty and I broke out two K-ration boxes.

"Pork paste," muttered Shorty.

While Oaky and the colonel talked, we ate. Shorty's *après déjeuner* goody was a fruit bar. He held it for a while, grimacing, then reached over and handed it to the motorcycle driver. He saluted and smiled.

"That's fraternization—*verboten,* Shorty," I said.

"You ain't consortin' with the enemy when you give him one of them goddam things. The CO said it will open your bowels; he forgot to tell us what you get to close 'em. That *Kraut* is going to have one hell of a time between that motorcycle and the bushes, believe me," said Shorty, smirking.

The conversation between Oaky and the colonel, like all conversations in German, went on and on. Parts of it sounded like the lyrics from the second act of *Siegfried.*

"Attention!" shouted Oaky.

Shorty and I stopped crunching our government-issue dog biscuits.

"The chap says that for a pittance of petrol for his vehicle he will give us information concerning the whereabouts of an extremely important person from whose company he has but recently taken leave—without permission, it seems—that person is, he says, Field Marshal Albert Kesselring, lately commander of all German troops in Italy, now in this vicinity waiting to be contacted by General Eisenhower for the purpose of granting General Eisenhower the historic privilege of accepting his surrender, under Mr. Kesselring's terms, of course; and in return for a drop of petrol, he will direct us to the place where Mr. Kesselring hopes to bestow his presence upon General Eisenhower, by appointment," Oaky explained.

"Dump some gas in this guy's tank, Shorty," I ordered, feeling more than a little the CO in complete command of a situation.

" 'Don't never give no aid or comfort to the enemy,' my CO used to say. I'll sure get my ass chewed out for this," said Shorty, unlashing the gerry can on the back of our jeep.

"He advises that Mr. Kesselring is waiting on his train on a little track not far from Keifersfelden, a few kilometers from here. He has given directions that will lead us to him," Oaky announced.

Shorty poured about a gallon of General Patch's gasoline into the motorcycle fuel tank.

The colonel waved; the driver burped and they were off, headed for somewhere else.

"Where the hell is he going, Oaky?" I asked.

"Home. He said he has decided not to wait for the formalities, he doesn't have a clean uniform—thinks his appearance would not be acceptable to his superiors at any historic meeting," Oaky said.

"All right, chaps, away we go. Directions are quite good, if, perhaps, a bit too specific, but you know how these blighters are," Oaky said.

Shorty slammed the jeep into gear, gritted his teeth and muttered cryptic little sentiments about war correspondents, field marshals, generals, the army and dust.

We lurched along the dusty road.

"*Links—rechts—rechts—links—rechts—links,*" called out Oaky.

I translated for Shorty, whose only German word was *Fräulein,* by banging him on the shoulders.

We were fairly deep into a heavily wooded area. The road was deserted. We slowed gradually as Shorty's reluctant foot eased on the accelerator.

"No maps—no people—no mother—no father—no more beer on Saturday nights—we're all gonna get killed—they'll never find our bodies—what a hell of a way to die—what a time to croak— right in the ass-end of the war—I gotta get knocked off because two civilian jerks gotta write for the funny papers," moaned Shorty.

"As La Guardia used to tell us, Shorty, Patience and Fortitude," I comforted.

The jeep rounded a bend.

"He said we couldn't miss it," cried Oaky. "There it is."

"There what is, Arthur?"

Ahead there was a little lane on the right. A German soldier stood at attention, his rifle on his shoulder.

"That's Kesselring?" Shorty asked, disappointedly.

"No, that's his outpost," said Oaky.

"Some outpost—looks like a latrine guard to me. That guy goofed and he got that duty. He's guardin' a goddam tree," snarled Shorty.

"Quiet," I said.

"*Rechts*," shouted Oaky.

I whacked Shorty on the shoulder, he turned into the driveway. The German guard threw a snappy Present Arms. Oaky and I saluted.

Fifty yards into the woods stood a five-car train. A wisp of smoke rose from the engine stack. Guards stood about. Shorty came to a halt near the second coach on the single-track siding. Oaky and I jumped out, looking like a sawed-off Patton and an overstuffed Montgomery.

A German captain appeared.

"You have come from General Eisenhower, *nicht wahr?*" he asked.

"You speak English?" I asked, hoping to steal some fire from my British friend on the historic occasion.

"*Jawohl*," the captain replied, leaving it pretty much on a dead center.

"Well, you might say we come from General Eisenhower. We'll go into that later. Do you have Field Marshal Kesselring here?" I asked.

"Follow me," replied the captain.

Oaky and I mounted the steps of the car, a Pullman-type affair containing offices and living quarters.

"Wait here, *bitte*," instructed the captain as we entered a small reception room. "The Field Marshal is busy at the moment. He is signing awards and decorations for his troops," he added.

We waited for about ten minutes. I looked out the window. Shorty was breaking open K-ration boxes and passing out fruit bars. The Germans seemed to be pleased with Shorty.

"Enter!" said the captain.

I led the way behind the captain. We walked through a second reception compartment and into an office. There were maps of southern Germany on the wall; four or five officers, bemedaled and stiff, stood about. At a desk there sat a chunky man, a great scar lashed across his cheek. It was Kesselring.

The captain said, "I will translate."

Kesselring began to speak. The captain translated.

"You have brought the terms. When will your Eisenhower be here?" Kesselring wanted to know.

"I represent only *The New York Times* and my colleague represents only Reuters news service. We trust there has been no misunderstanding. We are not authorized to negotiate anything but an interview," I said.

Kesselring rose from his chair, picked up his marshal's baton and stepped close to us. Slowly his face broke into a grin. He muttered.

"The Field Marshal would like to have you remain for lunch," the captain said.

Kesselring chuckled and said something else.

"The Field Marshal says he is amused," said the captain.

Oaky turned aside to me and whispered: "Actually, what he said was something like 'Well, bugger me.'"

It was a pleasant lunch of ham, cabbage, potatoes, beer and reminiscence on the part of Kesselring.

He had come up from Italy through the Brenner Pass, on orders from Hitler to take up a position in the Redoubt around Berchtesgaden. His troops were scattered from hell to breakfast; communications with higher authority were long since gone. He had hoped to ride his train into Salzburg, but the bridges were destroyed. He was waiting for someone to tell General Eisenhower where he was. He had sent people out to try to arrange a surrender, but they never came back. It was getting to be quite a bore and his brandy and cigars were running low. He talked long and earnestly about the war.

"Allied air power?" he said. "Ah, yes," he murmured, reaching down to pick up his baton. "Six of these I have left behind in the ruins of command posts, thanks to your air forces," he mused.

I asked, through the captain, if the Field Marshal, considering the state of things, might not give me the baton he was holding.

"Sorry," he replied, "But I think this is the last I shall ever have. I shall keep it."

William L. Laurence is the distinguished Science Editor Emeritus of
The New York Times. He served the *Times* as Science News Editor
and Science Editor from 1930 to 1963. In 1945 he was a staff member of the atomic bomb project. Recipient of two Pulitzer Prizes
(1937 and 1946), Mr. Laurence's published works include *Dawn
Over Zero—The Story of the Atomic Bomb, The Hell Bomb, Men
and Atoms* and *New Frontiers of Science*.

The Greatest Story

WILLIAM L. LAURENCE

Science Editor Emeritus, *The New York Times*

On that moment hung eternity.
Time stood still.
Space contracted into a pinpoint.
It was as though the earth had opened
And the skies had split.
One felt as though he had been privileged
To witness the Birth of the World
To be present at the Moment of Creation
When God said:
Let there be Light!

William L. Laurence as he watched the
Birth of the Atomic Age at Alamogordo,
New Mexico, July 16, 1945.

IT FIRST broke as the story of the dropping of the atomic bomb
over Hiroshima, but the story was much greater than that of the
dropping of a bomb of an explosive force of 20,000 tons of TNT.

It was, in fact, the story of the centuries, the greatest since the legendary Prometheus gave man the fire from Olympus that started him on his march from the cave to the moon and beyond. It was the story of the harnessing by man of the Fire from the Citadel of the Cosmos, the nucleus of the atom; of the discovery of a key for tapping the limitless energy until then hidden in the interior of the sun and in the countless billions of other luminous stars in the vastness of space. It was, indeed, the story of the discovery that assures man the continuance of his progress toward ever-higher goals, eliminating the threat of his return to the cave as the result of the inevitable exhaustion of the limited supply of coal and other fossil fuels.

The story appeared under thousands of bylines and over millions of radios. The lead was an announcement by President Truman, with a more detailed sublead by Secretary of War Henry L. Stimson. But, with minor revisions, everything given out that day by the White House and by the War Department was material prepared by me in advance during four fabulous months in which I had been permitted to visit the secret plants in the secret cities of Oak Ridge, Tennessee; Los Alamos, New Mexico; and Hanford, Washington; the great secret atomic laboratories at the University of California, the University of Chicago and Columbia University; and the fantastic industrial laboratories scattered throughout the land.

The voluminous "press kit" of the "handouts" released that day included my eyewitness account of the successful test of the first atomic bomb at the site named "Trinity" near Alamogordo, New Mexico, as well as a release based on the eyewitness report of the test by Brigadier General Thomas F. Farrell.

But I was not there that day when the stories I had written were released to the world. I was on Tinian Island in the Pacific, the top-secret base from which the atomic bomb was delivered to Hiroshima, and from which I took off two days later to serve as the eyewitness for the bombing of Nagasaki. I listened to my own words as they came over the radio.

How did it come about that I was given the privilege to serve as the exclusive reporter for this unbelievable story? Since it was the greatest of war secrets, it obviously was not given to me by any editor. After the secret was out, some wag remarked that since I knew too much about it, General Leslie R. Groves, the commanding general of the atomic bomb project, had the choice of either shooting me or hiring me. I got my job from General Groves. But as I look back at it, the realization comes over me that the story got *me* long before I got it.

It got me first some twenty-five years earlier by a subtle mathematical net, a simple algebraic equation—$E = mc^2$—the keystone of the Einstein Relativity Theory—which has since become the world's most famous mathematical formula.

When I first learned about it, circa 1919, the formula represented a pure idea that had exploded in the mind of one of the intellectual giants in history. Some twenty-five years later—on July 16, 1945—I watched that intellectual explosion materialize itself into the greatest explosion seen until then on planet earth, that changed forever the lives of its inhabitants.

During two decades from 1919 to 1939 I was engaged in what my friends among the scientists, including the great Einstein himself, regarded as a wild goose chase, in fact, as a futile chase after something that could not possibly exist on this earth. Then, one day early in 1939, the wild goose materialized itself into the equivalent of the legendary Goose that laid Golden Eggs.

That little Einstein formula, so simple that any average schoolboy or girl can master it, represented one of the boldest intellectual concepts in history. Until then it had been a fundamental tenet of physics that neither matter nor energy could be either created or destroyed, so that the total amount of matter and energy in the universe always remained the same, though they might manifest themselves in different forms. For example, if you burn a pound of coal, the smoke and the ashes would weigh exactly one pound. Similarly, one form of energy, such as heat, may be converted into another form, such as electricity, which, if reconverted back into heat, would yield the original amount.

These were known as the basic laws of conservation of matter and conservation of energy. They were the major pillars upon which rested the vast edifice of our knowledge of the material universe, built up through the millennia into the Grand Design of the physical universe as conceived by Kepler, Galileo and Newton.

But this little formula of Einstein, like Joshua at Jericho, blew an "intellectual trumpet" and the walls of the great edifice "came tumbling down." There is no such thing, the formula asserted, as the conservation of matter or of energy as two separate entities, because matter and energy are both two manifestations of only one entity. Matter is energy in the frozen state, while, conversely, energy is matter in the fluid state, just as ice is water in the solid state, while water is ice in the fluid form. When you burn a pound of coal, part of its mass, a very minute part, is converted into heat energy, so that the residue will weigh less than a pound.

This meant that all energy, no matter in what form it appeared, whether as a beam of light, or a current of electricity, or an object in motion, actually had a definite weight. An object in daylight weighed more than the same object in the dark, a cup of hot tea was heavier than a cup of the same tea when cold. The energy of motion of a pitched ball makes the ball heavier than the ball at rest, its extra weight being transformed into heat in the catcher's glove, which makes the glove heavier. The two halves of a broken doughnut weigh less than the whole, the difference being the weight of the energy that held the two parts together, equivalent to the amount of energy spent in breaking it.

All this was startling enough to one trained in orthodox physics, or, for that matter, to one's conventional habits of thinking. But the greatest shock of all came when I ventured to translate the algebraic symbols of the formula, in which E stands for energy, m for mass, and c^2 for the square of the velocity of light, into simple everyday arithmetic. If m stood for the mass of just one gram, I learned, then its equivalent in energy (E) in terms of ergs (the smallest unit of energy) was equal to the square of the velocity of light measured in terms of centimeters, an astronomical figure.

Since the velocity of light is 30 billion centimeters a second, the square of this figure meant 900 billion billion, namely, that one gram (two-fifths the weight of a dime, or $\frac{1}{28}$th of an ounce) of any piece of matter represented frozen energy equivalent to 900 billion billion ergs. As one kilowatt-hour is equal to 36 trillion ergs, the Einstein formula revealed that one gram of matter would yield, if its energy content could be unfrozen, the staggering total of 25,000,000 kilowatt-hours of energy, the energy output of 33.5 million horses or 335 million human adults, working for an entire hour.

"*Wow!*" I exclaimed as I gazed incredulously at the fantastic figures on the paper before me. "Holy Christopher!" I exclaimed a second time after I checked my figures to make sure I hadn't made a mistake.

I soon gained support from Sir James Jeans, eminent British astrophysicist, in his book *The Universe Around Us,* published in 1929. "The amount of energy set free by the annihilation of matter [namely, the conversion of matter into pure energy]," he wrote, "is of an entirely different order of magnitude from that made available by any other treatment. The combustion of a ton of the best coal in pure oxygen liberates about 50,000 trillion ergs of energy (about 1,400 kilowatt-hours); the annihilation of a ton of coal liberates 18,000 million times as much. In the ordinary combustion of coal we are merely skimming off the topmost cream of the energy contained in the coal, with the consequence that 99.999999994 percent of the total weight remains behind in the form of smoke, cinders or ash. Annihilation leaves nothing behind; it is a combustion so complete that neither smoke, ash, nor cinders is left. If we on earth could burn our coal as completely as this, a single pound would keep the whole British nation going for a fortnight, domestic fires, factories, trains, power-stations, ships and all; a piece of coal smaller than a pea would take the *Mauretania* (largest ocean liner afloat at the time) across the Atlantic and back."

Right then and there I began gathering material for a story about what became known as atomic energy. The time was 1930, the year in which I joined *The New York Times* as the first fulltime science reporter. My research supplied me with other figures to supplement Sir James Jeans's "piece of coal smaller than a pea." One-thirtieth of a gram of water ($\frac{1}{850}$th of an ounce) converted into pure energy, I found, would yield enough heat to turn one thousand tons of water into steam; in one whole gram of water there is a sufficient store of energy to lift a load of one million tons to the top of a mountain six miles high; a breath of air could operate a powerful airplane continuously for a year; a handful of snow would heat a large apartment house for a year; the pasteboard in a small railroad ticket could run a heavy passenger train several times around the globe; a cup of water could supply the power of a generating station of 100,000-kilowatt capacity for an entire year.

I wrote several stories about atomic energy for the daily as well as the Sunday feature section of *The Times* until the editors, who regarded the subject dubiously in any case, came to look at it as "old hat." Then came new developments which made the subject newsworthy again. Pioneer experiments, supported by theory, revealed that more than 99.98 percent of the energy in all matter was concentrated in the tiny nucleus of the atom, which occupies but a trillionth of the atom's total volume. At about the same time came the invention by Professor Ernest O. Lawrence of the University of California of the giant accelerator of atomic particles, known as the cyclotron, which hurls atomic bullets, accelerated to nearly the speed of light, at nuclei of atoms as targets.

The purpose of these giant machines, which have since been developed to accelerate atomic, or rather nuclear, particles to energies of 33 billion electron-volts, was not to liberate atomic energy but to learn the secret of the cosmic forces within the nuclei of the atoms of which the material universe is constituted. They are by no means powerful enough to smash up the nucleus of an atom into its constituent parts; the best they can do, and that is a great deal, is, on hitting the target, to knock out a particle or two from the tightly bound nucleus of protons and neutrons, or to have one of the nuclear bullets lodge within the nucleus.

Nevertheless, it sounded good, and it made good copy, to call these accelerators of nuclear particles "atom-smashers." And in my optimism I even harbored the hope that sooner or later an "atom-smasher" powerful enough to liberate atomic energy on a large scale would be built.

That this was a pipedream was made clear to me by none other than the great Einstein himself. "We are," he explained, a touch of sadness in his voice, "poor marksmen, shooting at birds in the dark in a country where there are very few birds." He was referring to the fact that only very few of the many billions of atomic bullets fired by the "atom-smasher" hit the target and that even then only a minute part of the energy in the nucleus was set free.

It looked hopeless that man could ever find a key to what Sir Arthur Eddington, another eminent British astrophysicist, called "the Cosmic Cupboard." Nevertheless the dream persisted. Every good reporter, I know, dreams of the "Big Story," though he may not know exactly what the Big Story would be about. I knew exactly what I wanted my Big Story to be. And when it finally came I was ready.

It was about during that period, sometime in the mid-1930s, when Mike Berger, one of the great reporters of the time, handed me a questionnaire passed on to him by Edwin L. James, *The Times* managing editor. "What is the Big Story you would want to cover?" Mike asked me.

My answer was ready: "The discovery that will make possible the utilization of atomic energy on a large scale."

My good friend Mike didn't know much about atomic energy so I told him the story of the "Cosmic Cupboard" and what it would mean for humanity the world over if only a key could be found to open it.

"It would," I summed up, "provide enough energy for the building of a civilization greater than any ever dreamed of by the wildest utopians. It would turn the earth into a Paradise of Plenty. It will make it possible at last for all mankind to realize to the full its creative potential now largely unrealized by the struggle for a livelihood."

Mike listened politely in evident disbelief.

II

The "big break" I had been dreaming about came late in December, 1938, in the laboratories of the Kaiser Wilhelm Institute in Berlin. It was there that Professor Otto Hahn, world-renowned nuclear chemist, and his collaborator, Fritz Strassmann, came upon, much to their surprise, one of the most revolutionary discoveries in history. Bombarding the heavy element uranium with neutrons, the electrically neutral component of the nuclei of atoms, they found to their amazement that the bombardment had produced radioactive forms of barium, lanthanum and cerium, elements about half the atomic weight of uranium. It was just as impossible as would be the hatching of chickens and pigeons out of ostrich eggs.

The astounding results were communicated by Professor Hahn to his erstwhile collaborator, Professor Lise Meitner, the world's leading woman physicist, then an exile in Sweden because of her Jewish origin. She soon came independently to the same conclusion as did Professor Hahn, though as a chemist, he had found it hard to believe that what had happened was something that the world's leading physicists had regarded as impossible. Faced with the facts, Dr. Meitner, as a physicist, at once came to the conclusion that the "impossible" had, indeed, been proved to be possible. The radioactive elements, half the atomic weight of uranium, were the result of the splitting, or fission, of the heavy uranium atom in two nearly equal halves, she informed her lifelong collaborator and friend.

But the fission of the nucleus of the heavy uranium atom, she further informed him, inevitably results in the release of enormous quantities of the nuclear energy locked up since the beginning of time in the uranium nucleus. Her expert knowledge of nuclear physics made it possible for her to calculate the exact amount of the energy that would be released in the splitting process. The split fragments of the uranium nucleus, she calculated, would each constitute a gigantic atomic "cannonball" of 100,000,000 electron-volts, or a total of 200,000,000 electron-volts, by far the greatest amount of atomic energy ever liberated by man on earth.

Since that constituted one-tenth of one percent of the total energy locked up in the nucleus of the uranium atom, this meant that the fission of one kilogram (1,000 grams) of uranium would liberate the nuclear energy of one gram, which, as the Einstein formula revealed, amounts to 25,000,000 kilowatt-hours.

Lise Meitner communicated the astounding results to her physicist nephew, Otto R. Frisch, also an exile from Nazi Germany, working at the time in the laboratory of Professor Niels Bohr, in Copenhagen. Frisch was visiting her for the Christmas holidays. He was skeptical at first, but she finally persuaded him to carry out a crucial experiment on his return to Denmark to prove whether or not her calculations were correct.

It was on Sunday, January 15, 1939, that Frisch performed in Bohr's laboratory the experiment that proved beyond doubt that Lise Meitner's interpretation of Hahn's experiment—uranium fission—was correct. Professor Bohr, one of the world's greatest physicists, who had been informed by Frisch of the Hahn experiment and its interpretation by Professor Meitner before he left Denmark, arrived in the United States on Monday, January 16. He lost no time in imparting the great news to Professor Enrico Fermi, another Nobel Prize–winning physicist, a self-exile from

Fascist Italy, who was then working at Columbia University, and other American physicists. And on January 25, 1939, the Frisch experiment was repeated at the Pupin Laboratory at Columbia University.

Columbia did not release the story of the pioneer experiment until Monday, January 30, and by that time the news had been leaked out by Bohr and Fermi at a small technical meeting of physicists in Washington. A short report by the Associated Press, a condensation of a page one story the previous Friday in the *Washington Star*, appeared on page two of *The New York Times* of Sunday, January 29, enough to make the Columbia story stale news. It appeared on page one of the second section on January 31.

But the story was by no means dead. On February 24, 1939, I sat in the darkened lecture hall of Columbia University and listened to Bohr and Fermi address an informal meeting of two hundred distinguished physicists on what I described in my report the following day as "the most sensational discovery in modern physics."

The discovery, I wrote, is "a new milestone in man's mastery over the elements, and marks the most important step yet made by science toward the transmutation of the elements and the utilization of the vast stores of energy locked up within the nucleus of the atom. The new method for the release of atomic energy and the transmutation of the elements is regarded as the nearest approach yet made to the finding of the modern version of the Philosophers' Stone of the alchemists."

"The find has been so startling," I added, "that it has left the scientists in a state of breathless wonder and the general feeling prevails that physics is now on the eve of epoch-making discoveries."

I was the only reporter present at that informal meeting, one of the most momentous in the history of American science, and what I heard that afternoon changed the course of my life, as, indeed, it affected the lives of the present and all future generations. And what I learned that day played an important part in my eventual selection to cover the Big Story.

Two of the subjects discussed that afternoon by Fermi and Bohr turned out to be the very keystones in the arch of the atomic bomb project. One of these was the evidence outlined by Bohr

that the uranium undergoing fission was not the abundant form
of uranium, known as uranium 238, which constitutes 99.3 percent of the uranium found in nature, but the much rarer type of
light uranium, known as uranium 235, which constitutes only 0.7
percent of all natural uranium. Since no method was known at
the time for the large-scale separation of the light U-235 from the
heavy, abundant U-238, this meant an enormous obstacle that
had to be overcome before the energy released in fission could be
utilized on a practical scale.

The second subject discussed that afternoon was even more
significant and went to the very heart of the problem of harnessing atomic energy. For just as an ordinary chemical fire needs
oxygen to burn, the release of nuclear energy through the fission
of uranium requires neutrons, one of the two basic building
blocks of the nuclei of all atoms beyond simple hydrogen. The
trouble was that the neutrons are tightly bound within the nuclei
of atoms and there was at that time no known power on earth
that could dislodge them in the quantities required for the large
scale fission of uranium.

But that afternoon I heard Fermi and Bohr utter two simple
words that completely changed the picture.

"Chain reaction!" I heard them say, as they were scribbling
strange symbols on the blackboard. This meant that the uranium
nucleus itself, on being split, would liberate some of its own
neutrons with which to split other uranium atoms, in a chain
reaction that would go on automatically for an indefinite period
as long as the uranium lasted.

As I sat there listening and watching a chain reaction started in
my own brain. Until then I had been considering only the
peaceful industrial and scientific uses of atomic energy. At that
moment it occurred to me for the first time that a chain reaction
liberating large quantities of atomic energy could produce a
tremendous explosive, millions of times more devastating than
TNT. I soon learned from a physicist seated next to me that the
uncontrolled fission of one kilogram of uranium 235 would yield
an explosive force equal to that of 20,000 tons of TNT.

I shall never forget the impact of these figures on my consciousness. This new Promethean fire, I found myself thinking,
could be used by Hitler as the most destructive weapon in
history, which will make it possible for him to enslave the world.

And since the discovery had been made in Germany more than a month before, he might already have ordered the Nazi scientists to work on this very project.

So as soon as the meeting was over I rushed over to ask Fermi and Bohr about this very soul-searing possibility.

"Will the chain reaction make possible an atomic bomb?" I asked.

The two great men looked startled. "Theoretically," Fermi said after a silence, "that may be possible someday, but not for a long time."

"How long?" I persisted.

"Maybe twenty-five, maybe fifty years!" he replied. I noted that Bohr was looking up at the ceiling.

"Maybe Hitler will make one in much less time," I shot back by way of telling him that I took his estimate with a large grain of salt.

I went home that night very much perturbed. War at that time had become a certainty. Knowing the state of our unpreparedness and the tremendous effort it would take to translate uranium fission into an effective military weapon, it seemed to me almost certain that the Nazis would get there first. I was a frightened man.

I did not learn until years later that from the beginning the nuclear physicists had agreed among themselves not to discuss the possibility of an atomic bomb openly. The world soon became for me a vast Poe-esque pit over which a uranium pendulum was slowly swinging down, while the victim remained unaware of his danger. Bit by bit, through my questioning of scientists exiled from the Nazi terror, I learned that the Nazis had set aside a special institute in Berlin to which they had assigned two hundred of their scientists to develop an atomic bomb and an atomic reactor for submarines and industrial uses. The time was the spring of 1940.

I decided that the time had come for the American people, and the rest of the free world, to be made aware of the danger. After persuading my managing editor, the late Edwin L. James, that the story was worth about seven columns, I gave for the first time a complete, detailed account of all that had been discovered about uranium fission since the original announcement in January, 1939, stressing that the Nazis were engaged in perfecting an atomic bomb and outlining the scientific, military and industrial implications of the discovery to the world we live in.

The story appeared on page one, Sunday, May 5, 1940. I had hoped that the facts would galvanize Washington into action. But as far as I could determine at the time, all the article did was to arouse Senator Sheridan Downey of California, who inserted it in full in the *Congressional Record* as part of an impassioned speech urging that measures be taken to stop the scientists from ruining the petroleum industry.

My next attempt to play the role of a journalistic Paul Revere was to write an extensive article for the *Saturday Evening Post.* The editors, after a certain amount of skepticism, finally accepted it. It appeared in the issue of September 7, 1940, and played a major role in my being tapped to cover the Big Story. After the bombing of Hiroshima, the *Post* reprinted the article with the blurb that it "had told the story of the atomic bomb a full five years ahead." The *Post* also revealed that it had been requested by the FBI to take the article out of circulation and to report the names of all those who asked for it.

This was the last story I wrote on the subject. After Pearl Harbor an office of voluntary press censorship was established and any story dealing with atomic energy, atomic weapons, uranium and related subjects was voluntarily suppressed. Story after story I submitted to the censorship office was returned with the request not to publish. Even stories speculating that the secret weapon the Nazis were boasting about was an atomic bomb were also returned with the same request, the reason given being that we did not want the enemy to know what we knew about him.

During that period I lived through a constant nightmare that any day the Nazis might spring a super–Pearl Harbor with atomic bombs. I wanted to eliminate the element of surprise, which I knew would be catastrophic, but the Office of Censorship thought otherwise.

This state of affairs lasted until early in the spring of 1945, when one day "Jimmie" James came out of his office with a letter in his hand.

"A General Leslie R. Groves wants to come here to see you!"

"What do you suppose he wants?"

"Don't know. Better be here. He's coming tomorrow!"

By that time, through a process of piecing together stray bits of information from various sources, I knew in a general way that we had plants in Tennessee, in the State of Washington and in New Mexico working to develop an atomic bomb. "I think I know what he is after," I said.

When General Groves arrived, he first had a long private conversation with James. An interminable time seemed to pass before I was finally called in.

"We want you to come to work for us on a top-secret war project."

"I have been waiting for a long time for an opportunity to serve. When do I start?"

"As soon as possible. We will tell you all about it when you come to Washington." I was to tell no one where I was and what I was doing, not even my wife, with whom I could communicate only through a post office box. I was given to understand that my job would involve some hazard, against which I was to be insured.

Thus began my journey through the Never-Never Land of the Atom. That journey reached its climax at one minute past noon on August 9, 1945, more than six miles in the air above Nagasaki, when I watched the second, and last atomic bomb used in warfare explode in a pillar of fire that reached 60,000 feet into the stratosphere and brought the greatest war in history to a victorious end.

By July 12, 1945, I had visited all the secret plants and laboratories. I had seen things no one had ever thought possible. I had written scores of reports on what I had seen, every one of them marked "Top Secret" and locked in a special top-secret safe.

General Groves had asked me to give him a list of the subjects I intended to write about. Item No. 26 on the list read: "Eyewitness account of the test in New Mexico," to which I added in parentheses: "provided eyewitness survives." Another item read: "Eyewitness account of bombing of Japan," again provided that eyewitness survived.

One of my last acts before leaving for the atomic test was to write a letter to Mr. James, the only one I had sent to the outside world, excepting letters to my wife. It read in part:

"The story is much bigger than I could imagine, fantastic, bizarre, fascinating and terrifying. When it breaks it will be an

Eighth-Day wonder, a sort of Second Coming of Christ yarn. It will be one of the big stories of our generation and it will run for some time. . . .

"The world will not be the same after the day of the big event. A new era in our civilization will have started, with enormous implications for the postwar period, both from a military and from an industrial standpoint."

On leaving for the Pacific I was given an official embossed card bearing my photograph and fingerprints and stating that the bearer was a "simulated colonel," entitled to all the privileges of a full colonel. But stamped on the card in bold red letters was the line: "Valid only if captured by the enemy."

"What a helluva way to become a colonel," I said to myself. I saw myself descending in a parachute, waving my card and proclaiming to the enemy: "Here comes Colonel Laurence!"

As we were circling interminably over Kokura, the target before Nagasaki, I suddenly became aware of large black rings shooting through the white sea of clouds. The black rings, which I soon recognized as flak, kept coming nearer and nearer, closer and closer.

All through the night I had been writing a running story in a small notebook, with the lead to come. I started fingering my parachute, the first I had ever worn, and wondered if I would ever make it, if I had to bail out.

I said to myself: "Well, old boy, this may be the last story you will ever write!"

To which I answered: "If this is to be your last story, could you think of a better one?"

After a brief entry in my notebook about the black rings I wrote in bold letters "L2K. Lead to come!"

Frederick B. Opper is now Athens correspondent for Radio Free Europe, with which he has served overseas since 1953. From 1945 to 1953 he was with ABC as a reporter abroad.

The Open Door Policy—1945

FREDERICK B. OPPER

CORRESPONDENTS flooding into Japan as World War II ended found themselves almost embarrassed by the news riches that were theirs. Closed to Allied eyes and ears for almost four years, the nation almost seemed to go on a talking jag when the Western press and radio appeared.

It wasn't long, though, before General MacArthur clamped down on the freewheeling correspondents.

Arriving at Atsugi Airport in the thirteenth plane of the U.S. occupation, the correspondents commandeered a wheezing Japanese army truck with a Japanese army private to drive it, politely bowing and hissing us aboard. In it we made our way into the shattered capital as housewives and goggle-eyed children lined the roadside to watch in wonder and fear as these august figures from another world went past.

A prewar correspondent in Japan and thus knowing something of Tokyo's geography as well as a smattering of the language, I made my way to the burned shell of the Navy Ministry. There Japanese marines passed me up the ladder of rank until I walked in on Navy Minister Yonai. An admiral without a fleet and a cabinet minister without a ministry, Yonai had the leisure to while away the afternoon reminiscing and recalling, regretting and remembering the details of World War II from the Japanese naval point of view. I left with a notebook full of fascinating stories.

Back at Atsugi, I got a circuit to ABC in San Francisco and passed my stories through. Then, after a few hours' sleep under the wing of our B-17, back through Yokohama, I hoped, to Tokyo and another day of seeing Japan from the inside.

Alas, General MacArthur had by now stepped in. Tokyo was off limits to correspondents, and we were assigned to the Bund Hotel in Yokohama, about as close to important news sources as though we had remained behind on Okinawa or Guam. We were not to go to Tokyo until the September 3 surrender ceremonies, and, to make sure we stayed put, MPs were posted at the Yokohama railroad station and on the main Tokaido highway into Tokyo to seize any would-be stowaways or hitchhikers.

The Bund Hotel was not the world's finest hostelry at the best of times, and this was not the best of times in Japan. Our enforced stay was made no more enjoyable by the C-ration menus and the grousing of scores of correspondents kept in an unaccustomed and, on this occasion at least, unwanted idleness.

The best that could be said for the situation was that when a group of gloomy ABC correspondents gathered in a corner of the dining room to discuss future coverage, Jack Hooley produced a bottle of gin he had hoarded from Manila.

No doubt it was this hospitality bonanza that triggered my idea: an interview with Saburu Kurusu, the Japanese diplomat who had been in Washington negotiating with U.S. Secretary of State Cordell Hull as the bombs fell on Pearl Harbor. He was one of the few Japanese known by name to the American public; he was considered, with ex-Premier Hideki Tojo, the quintessence of Japanese perfidy, the two of them the evil geniuses of the "day of infamy;" he would have a tale to tell worth going a long way to hear; and I had learned earlier that he was now at Karuizawa, the mountain resort up above Tokyo.

Finally, a brain flash born of my prewar knowledge of Japan: it might be possible to catch a Tokyo-bound train at a Yokohama suburban station. Perhaps the MPs were unaware of this hole in their blockade of correspondents.

Buoyed by the Manila gin, I made a devious way to the suburban station, where, I was happy to find, I was the only

Westerner amidst a sea of Orientals. The MPs had not corked this neck of the bottle, clearly. I slunk into the train and hunkered down as inconspicuously as possible. This took some doing. As the only Westerner among several thousand Japanese, and wearing an American Army uniform in a country still technically at war with the United States, I hardly melted into the background. Fortunately, at the main Yokohama railroad station the MPs failed to spot me among the kimono-clad throng, possibly because they were too busy guarding my train against any entry by a number of my expostulating colleagues.

A Japanese lieutenant, whose aid I demanded at the Tokyo central station, jammed me aboard a Karuizawa-bound train, using some American football technique and the remnants of the Imperial Army's authority. A night-long trip over a dilapidated roadbed, in a car crammed to suffocation with village farmers getting on and off at the constant jerky stops, brought me in the dawn to Karuizawa. An unwashed, unshaven, unkempt representative of the conquering might of the United States, I was the first American any of the nervously shying passersby had seen at least since 1941. If I were a representative of the U.S. Army of Occupation that was soon to appear among them, they seemed to be worriedly thinking, then God help them.

I sought out a prewar Japanese newspaper executive friend of mine who, I had learned previously in Tokyo, had left the capital a day or two before for the calmer atmosphere of the mountains. He was known to the first milkman I stopped, who showed me the way with the air of a man delighted to assist what could only be General MacArthur's personal *Gauleiter* for Karuizawa.

My friend talked to me for hours of the political-military maneuvering that had gone on throughout the war, culminating in the final hard-to-come-by decision to capitulate. It was a story of which he knew the full details from a long personal and family friendship with Prince Konoye, a major figure in the drama, and with other court and diplomatic friends deeply involved. It was a background story of our enemies at war utterly unknown to a single American up to that time.

He took me, finally, to the nearby home of the Kurusus and introduced us. Mrs. Kurusu, an American, and her husband, the Japanese diplomat whom Americans equated with an Oriental Iago, took me in with an aplomb that surprises me even now as I look back on it. Certainly Kurusu knew he would be an early target for American investigators and very possibly arrested on war criminal charges. And Mrs. Kurusu must have had some apprehension over the reception she would receive from her former fellow countrymen. But they sat me down, served tea, and made polite conversation. I recall now that in that conversation they passed lightly over what must be one of the most tragic and ironic twists of fate: their son, a blend of East and West, had been a wartime Japanese pilot, choosing the Eastern genes of his makeup by which to be identified. But, shot down over Japan one day in an American raid, local farmers saw him only as a Westerner, and killed him as an enemy.

When Mrs. Kurusu excused herself, her husband began to talk about his mission to the United States that ended in the attack on Pearl Harbor. He told me what instructions he had been given before setting out from Japan, what the cables from Tokyo had said, what he had told Secretary Hull and President Roosevelt, and what they in turn had said to him.

The Kurusu story served to corroborate what my newsman-confidant had told me. I left with what I felt was a comprehensive and authentic picture of Japan on the eve of war, Japan during the war, and Japan ending the war. It was the first "inside Japan" view that Americans had had of the enemy, from Pearl Harbor to surrender.

But the facts in my notebook still had to be voiced into a microphone. By now it was evening in Karuizawa, and I was told that the next and only daily train for Tokyo left the following dawn. I improved the evening hours with additional interviews, and, then, late at night, went to the railroad station, determined to fight my way aboard what I was sure would be a train black with humanity. I slept on the station floor but awoke in time to wrestle my way aboard, though only just.

It was like pushing one's way into a congealing mass of molasses to get a grip by toe and finger on the car's platform. There uncounted Japanese travelers and this lone American were jammed into the coffin-sized vestibule, while at our elbow was a completely empty car. It was preserved in this pristine loneliness, I was informed, in case a member of the Imperial Family should deign to join the train at a later stop. It was at this moment that those Japanese within hearing realized that the war was truly and irrevocably lost.

"Open this door at once," I commanded. Breaths hissed in unison, but authority had spoken. Some may have contemplated hara-kiri at this *lèse-majesté,* but the conductor, representative of the Japanese Emperor, capitulated to the barbarian from across the sea. He unlocked the door. The horde of platform standees stampeded in and dropped comfortably onto the plush Imperial seats.

I like to think that my command to open the door of a railroad car represented the first time in his long history that the Japanese man in the street discovered that the Imperial Family was not really sacrosanct. Perhaps, as they settled into their seats, there may have been some thought that this democratic approach had a lot to recommend it.

In the evening, after an uncomfortable all-day train ride, I got through to San Francisco from the Yokohama transmitter. But I quickly found that American peacetime radio was back in operation. Cut it to two minutes, I was told in no uncertain terms. I voiced two minutes, then cabled the rest.

The next day I had a cable from Bob Kintner, then ABC chief: "Best scoop of the war."

That was cheering, of course. But I felt less happy when I learned that as I had slept on the floor of the Karuizawa railroad station, a special train had inched through toward Tokyo, bearing the first of the American prisoners of war headed home from Japanese prison camps. They had stories innumerable to tell, but I was not to hear them as I slept the sleep of the exhausted.

And the next morning, when I put my hand in my uniform pocket for my wallet, I found that somewhere, on one of those jam-packed trains, a Japanese pickpocket had lifted my money and my papers. Perhaps I had been the victim of the very first sign of a Japanese comeback. Maybe I had the best scoop of the war, but maybe somewhere there was a Japanese thief who didn't feel too badly about my trip, either.

George Weller is a correspondent in Italy for the *Chicago Daily News,* and has written many books on Far Eastern subjects as well as one novel. His awards include the Pulitzer Prize in 1943 and the George Polk Award in 1955, as well as a Nieman Fellowship in 1948. He was also a *New York Times* correspondent in Greece (1932–35).

Back in Nagasaki

GEORGE WELLER

WHENEVER I see the word "Nagasaki," a vision arises of the city when I entered it on September 6, 1945, as the first free Westerner to do so after the war. No other correspondent had yet evaded the authorities to reach either Hiroshima or Nagasaki. The effects of the atomic bombs were unknown except for the massive fact that they had terminated the war with two blows in three days. The world wanted to know what the bombs' work looked like from below.

I had just escaped the surveillance of General MacArthur's censors, his public relations officers and his military police. MacArthur had placed all southern Japan off limits to the press. Slipping into forbidden Nagasaki, I felt like another Perry, entering a land where my presence itself was forbidden, a land that now had two Mikados, both omnipotent.

When I walked out of Nagasaki's roofless railroad station, I saw a city frizzled like a baked apple, crusted black at the open core where the searing sun born at Alamogordo had split open the blue sky of midday. I saw the long, crumpled skeleton of the Mitsubishi electrical motor and shipfitting plant, a framework blasted clean of its flesh by the lazy-falling missile floating under a parachute.

What irony, I thought, in a war of competing velocities, that this slowest-borne of all weapons, falling at a speed little greater than my own descent when I took training as a paratrooper, should in the end out-destroy all the fleetest of the winged killers. The bomb of Nagasaki reversed the rule of war, getting there last and slowest but with the most, a terminal blow riding under a silk handkerchief.

Even now I see the scorched hills ringing the bottleneck of the port. Along the blistered boulevards the shadows of fallen telegraph poles were branded upright on buildings, the signature of the ray stamped in huge ideograms. I can never forget the hospitals where I heard from X-ray specialists the devouring effects of the ray on the human bloodstream and viscera, analyzed as impassively by the little men in white coats as if it had happened to someone else, not themselves.

I felt pity, but no remorse. The Japanese military had cured me of that. After years of unchallenged domination, they were bending a little under the first afterwind of the bombs, a national mistrust, almost contempt, for having led Japan into war. A few sought escape in hari-kiri. The majority blamed the enemy for using weapons that were "unfair."

Had Japan got these weapons first, would they have been unfair, I asked? Was Pearl Harbor an act of Japanese chivalry? The crafty eyes under the peaked brown caps turned unblinking and blank.

In the harbor, I remember, there still burned the last altar kindled by the fireball. A small freighter, crisped like dry bacon down to the waterline, still smoked, glowed and puffed. She was a floating lamp, untended. Bobbing there among the debris-littered dark waters, she spread a light that flickered in eerie unison with the candles and kerosene lamps and little flashlights ashore.

I felt I had a right to be in Nagasaki, closed or not. Four weeks after the two bombs, with no riots or resistance in Japan, it seemed reasonable that MacArthur should lift his snuffer from the two cities. There was a sort of reason for delay, but it had nothing to do with the public's right to know. As something to fall back upon in the event of the failure of the bombs, MacArthur's planners had arranged that the Japanese archipelago was to be invaded in one-two time, first the northern islands and the Tokyo-Yokohama area, then the south, with the two atomic cities. Japan's surrender made little difference. An incredible six weeks was announced as the interval before the southern islands were to be occupied. MacArthur had fought a slow, cautious, methodical war, taking no chances with his postwar target, the presidency. His peacemaking was its twin, with censorship prolonged after victory long after the slightest pretext for it existed.

After submitting to the censors of the MacArthur command ever since I had escaped from Java in March, 1942, I felt I could not take much more. I remembered how his censors, perhaps eager not to offend or alarm the White House, killed a dispatch I wrote criticizing Roosevelt's defeat by Stalin at Yalta. With security no longer in question, I was not going to be stifled again. But I was not unaware that in planning to slip into an atomic city first, I was also risking repudiation by the conformists in my own profession.

My plan formed itself a few hours after we all sat on the gun turrets of the *Missouri,* watching Japan surrender to MacArthur and Nimitz. This measured rite over—almost wrecked by a Russian photographer in Lenin cap who was chased around like Harpo Marx—the correspondents were summoned ashore to a press conference. The war was ended, as we had reported, but the censorship was not. There was no chance, therefore, to ask from Tokyo why the Kurile Islands, regular patrol grounds of the U.S. Pacific Fleet, were to be handed to Russia. What the command wanted covered was the prison camps of northern Japan. The dam was to be opened to one last orgy of hometown stories, more mindless and more alike than the slow molasses drippings of four years of sloppy, apolitical, dear-mom war. Everything had been arranged: destroyers and planes were to take the correspondents north. North, north, north, away from where the war had been decided a month before.

Once, in midwar, I had been able to escape the darkrooms of the four main theaters of war by going home and running off a book called *Bases Overseas,* claiming for the United States a worldwide network of small strong points where her men had died and her treasure had been expended. I did not feel that the right way to end this war was to be herded north, away from

Hiroshima and Nagasaki, to chew more fodder about what-beasts-the-Japs-are and Jimmy-looks-skinnier-today. Only a few days before, but after the Mikado's surrender, a *Saturday Evening Post* writer who wore colonel's leaves refused to pass my story about the 503rd Paratroops on Corregidor, my old outfit, that revealed there were still Japanese bodies unburied in the tunnels. "That's contrary to the Geneva convention, and might make the Japs cancel their surrender," he said. . . . The American psychological grasp of the Japanese was shallow.

I listened as the chief conducting officer, rod in hand, pointed out on a map the prison camps where the newsmen were to be allowed to land and play savior. "Southern Japan remains closed. However, there is a little place down here"—he pointed to the southern end of Kyushu—"where their navy had a Kamikaze base. Anybody interested in the divine wind?"

"Geisha schools next door?" asked a jaded voice.

"Nuh-uh. And the pilots are all in the stockade, I'm afraid." Ah, no interviews, then. Enemy personnel, minimize glorification of.

"What happened to their planes?" asked a hopeful photographer.

"Not much left after the flyboys worked 'em over. But we do have the strip working again. That's a story in itself." Nobody seemed to agree. For *Stripes,* perhaps. Suicide Strip Operative—Engineers in Overnight Miracle. Full of bewildering unit numbers, and ten terse words from the colonel.

No hand was raised for the Kamikaze junkpile. Everybody signed for a prison camp, or nothing, and walked out. At the door I turned back to have another look at the map. The Kamikaze hole was named Kanoya. While the officer was sorting out his camps and correspondents, I cased Kanoya. A railroad came down to it. Kyushu, in fact, was covered with little railroads. But were any operating? Hiroshima and Nagasaki were a long way north, and it was partly mountain country, where bridges had been knocked out.

And then I felt rising in me, like a warm geyser, a jet of confidence.

"I might kill a couple of days with that Kanoya thing," I said. "Who's conducting?" He told me the name of a captain, new to me, not one of MacArthur's little foxes I had been dodging since Buna and Moresby.

"Okay, I'll take a chance."

"Sign here."

The conducting officer, when I met him later, turned out to be a young, friendly captain who had earned a late overseas assignment by impeccable performance somewhere back home. He had already dutifully pulled together everything about Kanoya that could be wrung out of intelligence. Next morning, as we got aboard the plane, I asked him: "What made the general take Kanoya and leave out all the rest of southern Japan?"

He knew, because he had asked. "He had to give back to Eisenhower and Marshall all the C-54s he borrowed to bring our headquarters in from Manila. So we're down mostly to C-47s. They need fuel between Atsugi and Okinawa."

I wanted to get some idea how hard this eager officer was going to press me to produce. "No pain for you, I hope, if I don't find a story in traffic safety," I said.

"It's a gamble," he said cheerfully. "No pain, no strain."

Neither of us mentioned the conspicuous nearness, in flying distance, of Hiroshima and Nagasaki. There had been just enough atomic ferment at the press conference to warn the command that the reporters could not much longer stall off the editors at home. The look-Mom-I'm-free stories couldn't last forever.

As we buzzed south at a safe five thousand feet, keeping offshore as if Japan would strike again, I asked myself how I could shake off this earnest, able officer without souring the end of his war, late and little as it was. What gave me trouble was that I liked him. He really wanted to help me, not throttle me.

When we landed at Kanoya the strip was stiff with Japanese soldiers, drawn up in honorific array. Perhaps they were expecting MacArthur himself. They were ready, if need be, to surrender their ancestral swords. What they got, instead, was a natty, cheerful captain leading a rumpled laundry bag of a correspondent. It was obviously a letdown.

Politely we inspected the smashed hangars, the bomb racks, the dormitories where the pilots slept for the last time before taking off for Iwo and Okinawa. We got almost too much attention. It bonded us together, preventing me from looking around to find a way to escape. Had I had enough of Kanoya? my guide wanted to know. "Because I've made arrangements for us to fly back tomorrow." This was alarming. Unable to think of a reason to stay longer, I began to fear that the trip was all a sterile gamble.

Working around the edge of the base that afternoon, I found that the least conspicuous way to get to the mainland was to hire a motorboat. It was only a few hundred yards. I managed to dig up a railroad schedule. All I could read was the numbers. Kanoya was stiff with ambitious Nisei who could have read it at a glance. But I feared that these loyal patriots would turn me in for an extra stripe.

The help I needed appeared suddenly in a tall thirty-year-old sergeant in Army Airways Communications intelligence named Gilbert Harrison, later the organizer of the American Veterans' Committee, and later still the editor of the *New Republic*. By his easy irony and barbed distaste for military authority, I guessed he might be the outrigger I needed. After some wary soundings to make sure he would not turn me in, I spilled my plan to him. "Can I come?" he said instantly. . . . We arranged for me to get away by motorboat under cover of night and pointed for a rendezvous in Kanoya.

I shook off my captain early, tapped away at my typewriter until he went to bed in a nearby room, and then went to bed myself, fully dressed. In case he ran a bed check, I left my shoes outside the door. Not long before dawn, I slipped past his door, out under the stars. I felt faint pangs. What punishment might MacArthur's dutiful colonels wreak on a trustful, gentlemanly captain, dewy-fresh from the ZI who was given only one, repeat one, correspondent to watch and lost him? To avoid generating alarm and despondency, I put aside my guilt as I stepped into the boat to cross the stream.

When I landed on the opposite shore, the village lights were winking out. Nobody was awake but a few fishermen, coiling their nets after the night's catch. I don't remember Harrison being with me, and I think he spent the night in camp, to avoid causing any alarm. As I remember we formed up at the railroad station in Koyama, the end of the line. The gentle captain seems to have assumed that I went out for an early morning walk and got lost, delayed or shacked up.

Harrison protected his disappearance by sending a dutiful service story about Kanoya's redemption to his commanding officer in Manila. Actually the sergeant was in better legal shape than I was. He had orders allowing him five days to reach Tokyo, means unstated. The orders didn't say that he couldn't visit southern Japan any more than a powder room says "Ladies, No Men." So he chose to imagine that his superiors didn't care how he went. Nothing happened to him, indeed, until ten days later when his colonel found him in the officers' mess in Tokyo and asked: "Are you enjoying yourself here, Sergeant?"

The first train north did not leave until four in the afternoon. We kept worrying that the Americans at Kanoya might be willing to smudge their image as liberators by asking the Japanese police to pick us up. They were ubiquitous, the only government Japan had. By train time I felt confident enough to order the soldiers around the station to carry our bags.

For the conquerors to choose to travel in third class, which was crowded as a cage of monkeys, seemed puzzling to the soldiers, passengers and train crew. But we had no Japanese money, and it seemed to me that there, where a fuss would cause maximum trouble, we had the best chance of brazening our way through. We also were protected, by this eccentric self-abasement, from the prying questions of passengers of rank who might have the brains and inclination to turn us in.

Harrison had brought a box of rations, including plenty of coffee, a barter article better than gold. Spectacled students kept plying us with questions. Where were we going? I refused to say. I wanted to leave a cooling trail. Fumbling for direction, we changed four times. At one junction, all lanterns, rumors and whispers, we found that we had to make the decision: Hiroshima or Nagasaki. The nearer to Hiroshima was the nearer to Tokyo. I was afraid that there we might run into some party of bombing assessors. Nagasaki, being remoter from MacArthur, seemed safer.

Already I had a formula that held off the most officious questioners. I looked them in the eye and said very softly, "Please consider your position." When they did, they blanched and departed.

We were aristocrats in a series of slow rattlers whose locomotives and coal cars were draped with clinging deadheads, mostly homebound soldiers. Each time we changed trains, at Shibushi, Yatsushiro and Tosu, the good-humored trainmen saw that we were protected by soldiers with fixed bayonets. The trains were filthy and we were hoarse with soot, our arms weary from

opening and shutting windows at tunnels. The trainmen filled our
canteens with clean water and showed us the *benjo,* or latrine. At
Shibushi we met our first escaped prisoner, a private from Utah.
He was not eager to accompany us to a bombed city, feeling that
we were inviting a necktie party.

A few hours after daylight we reached Yamaguchi. Here, after
eighteen hours of travel, we picked up the train for Nagasaki. We
also took in tow three Dutch prisoners captured in Java—as I
almost had been, too—four years before. A week earlier, three
weeks after Japan surrendered, on August 28, their camp of six
hundred starving men had been "bombed" by B-29s with food
and pamphlets warning them not to eat too much. MacArthur's
cautious pace in liberating Kyushu excited their derision more
than their anger. They were simply ignoring orders to stay in the
camps, and wanted to see Nagasaki.

We needed numbers. I accepted them. The trainmen moved
us to a baggage car, roomy and airy. As we click-clicked along, it
occurred to me that the authorities of Nagasaki might be more
difficult than train crews. Here we were, an atomic mission,
highly classified, but also oddly bereft of orders. Nor did we have
side arms. We were headed by an untidy reporter and a gangling
sergeant, with three alien privates whose rice-gray faces and
merriment revealed their ex-prisoner status. I saw that the first
Japanese official who guessed our real identity would get the
police to put us in custody "for your own protection," exactly as
MacArthur was doing with my colleagues, and telephone to
Tokyo for the MPs to come and pick us up. Lacking even a
revolver, we could not defend our mission with force. There was
only one protection we could assume: rank.

Rank! In war it will get you everything but mail.

I therefore awarded all members of my command spot promo-
tions, starting naturally with myself. I became Colonel Weller. In
hardly an hour, between Yamaguchi and Nagasaki, Harrison rose
from sergeant to major. He could not have done better in Cuba.
The three Dutch privates became lieutenants in an interallied
working party so dense with secrecy that they communicated
with me part of the time in German, the enemy language.

I took off my brass shoulder tabs, lettered "War Correspondent," and put them in my back pocket, ready for use if Colonel
Weller were compelled, by some emergency, to turn his force

around and lead it back into humbler status. The needles kept pricking me in the behind during the following week in Nagasaki. They hurt especially whenever a Japanese called me "Colonel." I felt like one of those Caesars in triumph, who had an elderly slave standing behind him in his chariot, murmuring, "Remember thou art only a man."

On September 6, exactly four weeks almost to the hour since the bomb dropped on Nagasaki, our little train of toy cars flustered its way into the remains of the station. For the last ten miles the buildings were in ruins on both sides of the track, and I assumed the whole city was flat. I was wrong. The blast had traveled out along the railroad gulch, instead of being deflected upward as it was by the hills in the city's heart.

There were no taxis, no rickshaws, no wagons. Defeat had leveled the Nagasakians into a city of walkers, except for the lucky officials who had bicycles. By firm language with the police sentries and introductions from the trainmen, we managed to intercept a truck. I asked to be taken to the military commander. The volunteer pointed up to a hill flecked with villas: "The general lives up there." "Get him down here. I must talk to him," I said. The police were impressed, but offered to take us up to him. I showed annoyance, but consented.

As we climbed the graceful curves into the little-damaged suburb of the executive class, Nagasaki came alive. The long inlet of the main harbor looked eerily deserted, with the floating lamp of a single freighter smoking off the blistered, sagging piers and twisted derricks. We could see the main Mitsubishi plant, a long fallen Zeppelin of naked, twisted steel, bent like a child's structural toy crushed by a passing foot. Its form was still almost intact, though it was almost directly under the bomb. The sturdiness of the ceilings had taken the blast and blocked the ray. The workers were more fortunate than their families in the one-story bungalows around the plant. They did most of the dying.

When we arrived at the arch-roofed villa of the general, I left my staff outside and marched up the broad front stairs. Leading me was the general's aide, a sharp lieutenant around twenty-five with an eye full of cool appraisal. He guided me into the general's office. He was a square-built, impassive man in his forties, guardedly cordial, warily courteous. I explained my mission: to obtain the facts about Nagasaki. I did not say for whom.

The lieutenant translated, and appended a suggestion of his own. The general nodded. "General say he like to see your orders," said the lieutenant.

I did not look at the general, but I spitted the lieutenant with a glance. "If the general doubts our authority," I said icily, "I suggest that he telephone directly to General MacArthur for confirmation." The general, who understood more English than he let on, glanced at the lieutenant, inviting comment. The lieutenant scrutinized me a shade more respectfully. "But in making such a call," I said, "the general should *consider his position.*" Now I looked at the general. There was a nervous pause. The general said something low and rapid.

"General says you are very welcome in Nagasaki, Colonel. He will give orders to show you everything." I nodded casually, as if no other result was ever thought of.

"You have only three cars left, I understand," I said directly to the general, to let him know I realized he had notions of English.

"General says that is true," said the lieutenant at my shoulder.

"Then my party will take only two of them, the two Fords," I said. "I realize that the general must have one car for himself. He has the very important task of keeping discipline and order, and preventing looting." This remark seemed to reach the general. He nodded with vigor. "And I shall require two Kempetai every evening to take my daily reports to Tokyo."

"This is a difficulty," said the lieutenant. "Many of our men have gone—have been released. Why two? One is enough."

"One is not enough," I said. "One Kempetai must be awake while the other sleeps. My reports go straight through Tokyo to Washington."

A consultation. "General says it is difficult, but you will have two Kempetai."

"Good. Now would the general give us the two cars and send us to our quarters?"

The general sent us down to a hotel. This was our baptism in the new Japan, where the army was spurned. The manager simply refused to book us. He did not like the vagueness about who was going to pay, and who we were. The lieutenant, abashed, called the general. Colonel Weller and his staff were transferred to a villa of their own where we bathed and lived on lobster, rice and sweet little slices of canned tangerine.

Before this muddle about quarters cooled him, the lieutenant took me out on the terrace of the general's villa. We stood at the top of the long, templelike flight of steps, overlooking the prostrate, battered city from which rose only the tinkle of bicycle bells. The arrogance habitual to the military caste, sitting uneasily on him as an educated civilian, was now plated with a new veneer, freshly applied, of compassion for the bomb's victims. He was not cringing. The Japanese had studied Americans for enough years to know that Oriental cringing was not the way to subdue them. You had to play at being American. He was aiming at that underlying strain of compassion that makes the American review all his acts of force, even against assassins.

He pointed at the sky at a point not much higher than we stood. "One enemy plane fly right over city," he said. "We sound no alarm. Think maybe he is lost. Another plane off there. Seem like he watch first plane. But maybe he lost, too. No formation."

Did the people take shelter? "No. Only some prisoners lie down in slit trenches. No alarm, so good people keep working." Did they know about the Hiroshima strike three days before? "We know. General and I know. Police know. But few people know."

This was a lie, I learned later. At first the Nagasaki newspapers were ordered to censor out Hiroshima, but this was pointless. The trains were still running—nothing can stop the Japanese railroad system, which has a life of its own—and too many people were moving around. Hiroshima was terribly and mysteriously stricken, that much was known. But it did not seem worse than the great fire raids on Tokyo.

Nagasaki, people felt, would be spared. Why? Because in the face of all logic, it had been spared so far. It was a complex of industrial plants. It was a feeder port for the campaign in Southeast Asia. It was the nearest major Japanese city to the American bombing bases. And yet it had been left almost intact. Streams of B-29s flowed north and south around it, but this prime target remained mysteriously untouched. Perhaps, people guessed, it might be because it had a large Roman Catholic population. But Rome's railroad yards had been bombed, with Catholic bombardiers at the pips. More likely, they thought, it was being saved as the logical port for a coming invasion, a Cherbourg. They did not know MacArthur had decided to hit the north first, then work down. That decision put Nagasaki on the bombing list.

"Police ring our telephone," said the lieutenant. "They say me: 'Tell general enemy plane drop parachutist. Please to watch the falling.' I see big parachute, with man hanging underneath, not moving legs, falling like dead. He seem about eight hundred meters tall. Plane flying away fast, not watching. Very strange, to drop spy over city in daylight. Not fool anybody. Police say, 'You watch, tell us where parachutist fall.' I find binoculars quick and watch. Lucky, because binoculars save me from blindness for my life." He gulped.

He closed his eyes, then went on. Suddenly he was talking like a civilian. "Big light. Too much. I drop glasses. Fall down. Blind. Fall right there." He pointed. "General in back. He all right, I think. When get up, still cannot see. Parachute should still be falling. But gone. Man gone, too. Police phone not working anymore. I go tell general. He say it is big bomb, like Hiroshima. We come back on terrace. My eyes better. We can see damage to buildings, bodies in streets. Ships sinking, sailors swimming. Mitsubishi plant, roof gone. General says, very bad."

Did a wave of fire sweep the city?

"No wave. Only little fires. No big ones. Just few little ones where workers live next to plant. There, see?" he pointed to the still, lifeless acres of charred beams and blackened walls, a hopeless tangle of burned-out debris.

The vision of the outside world of the bomb as whipping the city with a single, all-killing sheet of flame was wrong. Even the awful heat of the bomb, being only instantaneous, did no more harm than an opened furnace door to anyone who had any solid protection: a roof, a wall, a door. Yet most of the dead had been incinerated right there in the ruins. If not the bomb, what killed them?

He explained. The bomb fell almost at the noontime break in the factory when wives were preparing rice over charcoal fires in kitchens and tiny gardens. The flame burst on high. The ray swept their roofs. Neither did much harm in themselves. But the blast pressed the roofs down, broke the timbers, sent the ceilings crashing onto the open hearths, scattering red-hot embers amid bodies and firewood.

People not wounded tried to fight the first small fires. But the water lines were broken. Firemen got as far as the edge of the district, then were stopped. They could not get inside, either with hoses or shoulder-pack chemicals. Walls had fallen across streets. Alleys were flaming tunnels. The wounded nearest the edges were dragged or crawled out. Inexorably the smoke spirals turned to flames. The flames spread. In half an hour it was out of control, a broad, orange-red, crackling pyre. By then the last cries had long ceased, as suffocation mercifully preceded incineration.

Now came the lieutenant's epilogue. "What do you think, Colonel," he said, "of the culture of a people who could drop such a terrible weapon on the people of Japan?"

I wanted to cut this experiment off early. I waited a moment. Then I said, as gravely as I could, "To give you an honest reply," I said, "I would have to ask my own people. And of course I would have to begin with those who were walking to church on Sunday on Red Hill in Hawaii when your planes struck them."

We got along much better after that.

Nagasaki was never, strictly speaking, "destroyed." Nagasaki had about 300,000 people, about the size of Worcester, Peoria or Tacoma. About 20,000 died, the majority by concussion from falling buildings or by burning in ruins, not by concussion of air or direct singeing. I was told 35,000 had been hurt, mostly by burns. Harrison's figures were 25,000 and 40,000. About 18,000 homes, mostly two-room bungalows, were destroyed, for perhaps $20 million worth of total replacement.

Soon after the Soviets consolidated their booty in the Kuriles and the Rosenberg spy case developed, the atomic bomb became a "horror weapon." The ideology of the Japanese army became that of the Communist International. Since then, Nagasaki's casualties have been rising in multiples of five and ten thousand. At the most recent ban-the-bomb meetings the dead tripled to 65,000.

Before the bombs fell, Nagasaki was getting ready to lose the war but win the psychological recovery. American prisoners working in the Mitsubishi plant were naturally told that, if defeated, the entire nation would commit hari-kiri. But the executives of the plant had taught their foremen some highly unsuicidal terms, such as, "How are you today?" and "We workers want to save our plant." They had also shown disbelief in Nagasaki's immunity by moving their most expensive machinery to a hole in a hill two miles away.

I found these instructors, many of whom had brutal records in prison camps, now fawningly eager to serve the new colonel in town. They mistook me for their bridge into the MacArthur command. The general himself saddled me with the most repulsive of these double-tracked vehicles, an unctuous character who, Harrison discovered, had been one of the roughest straw bosses over the Allied prisoners. These swarming aspirant-interpreters did not, like those in Germany and Italy, try to prove that they had been oppressed democrats all the war. They imitated the army's pitch: that the United States had won unfairly and owed Japan generous help to come back. Their hands were out to collect the first slice for themselves.

When we entered the ruins, I had my first showdown with my interpreter. The ruins were "poisoned" and "dangerous," he said. Luckily, in the hospitals I had asked the X-ray specialists. "We don't think so, not if you wear thick-soled shoes like yours," they said. When I led the way in, he tried to take my camera. "Photos are forbidden," he said. "Not to me," I said.

I got rid of the interpreters in the hospitals because their officious manner got between me and the doctors, earnest, dedicated scientists, with nothing to sell. As fast as the pathetic patients squatting in the corridors died, the interns took them into the back rooms and dissected them for the doctors. Already they knew precisely what the effect of the ray was.

A doctor who had survived Hiroshima explained to me: "The main effect seems to be on the bloodstream. People say that the red and white corpuscles are killed. But we do not find it so. What are killed are the platelets. Do you know what they are?" I didn't. "They are the third important element of the blood, which gives it the capacity to coagulate. See that man?" He pointed to a thin figure with a paper-white face propped against a wall, surrounded by kneeling, intense relatives. "He was already a tuberculosis case, with minor hemorrhages. He was exposed about a quarter mile from the explosion. He was knocked down, but not apparently hurt. Then, after a few days, his coughing began to increase. He began raising more and more blood. We looked at it, and found the platelets were all dead." "Is there nothing you can do?" His eyes fell, as if in apology for his inadequacy. "Nothing," he said.

The most valuable thing I got in Nagasaki was a careful

analysis of the effects of the ray on each organ: heart, lungs, kidney, liver, stomach. In all cases there was some deterioration. But often they were almost intact, and the patient died of some insignificant scratch whose bleeding could not be stemmed.

When darkness fell I spent three hours each night tapping out my stories by lamplight. Then, about a half hour before the train left on its 24-hour journey—at least—to Tokyo, two Kempetai arrived at my door. I addressed the stories to "Chief Censor, American Headquarters, Tokyo."

I considered trying to smuggle my stories out of Japan, but rejected it. I had made the point I wanted by getting into Nagasaki and proving it could be done safely. Now I wanted to give the MacArthur command the least possible excuse to hold up my research. I eschewed all horror angles. I intended within five days to be in Tokyo myself. I wanted to be prepared to defend every line. If the stories were blocked as reprisal against me, I intended to take the case to MacArthur himself. Only if he blocked them would I consider smuggling them out myself.

One thing that made me feel extra secure in my laboratory, able to work methodically and broadly, was that Nagasaki's airfield was supposed to be damaged beyond repair. And then, on the fourth or fifth day, when I had pumped off about ten thousand words to Tokyo—research, interviews, damage reports —my laboratory was burgled, my monopoly ended. The lieutenant phoned me the awful news. "Many American reporters have landed," he said. "They have two planes." I hurried downtown with my staff. Indeed there they were, about two dozen old friends from all the war theaters of the world, wandering up and down the pitted boulevards in their go-to-hell Air Force caps, talking Pentagonese. They looked like yacht passengers who have stopped to buy basketry on an island. I had an impulse to hide, but they already knew about Colonel Weller. "You dirty dog, how did you get here?"

I told them. "Well, you better not go back to Tokyo. They're sore as hell at you. Get aboard with us. We've got two Forts— yes, two, one to ride, one to transmit our stories. We take off and sling them straight into Washington. The straight stuff, no censorship."

How could I close up my atomic laboratory, with the work only half finished? Where were they going? "Right down the line,

Hong Kong, Hanoi, Saigon, Singapore, Indonesia, maybe even Bali."

Up sauntered the small, slim commander and deviser of the expedition, Tex McCrary, former New York editorial writer turned colonel, a friendly, dynamic ex-Texan who later married Jinx Falkenberg and turned himself into a breakfast-hour TV star. "Did MacArthur clear you for Nagasaki?" I asked hopefully. There might be a loophole there for me. He shook his head. "Never asked him. Didn't have to. We're flying right out of Washington, under worldwide orders from Joint Chiefs. We can go anywhere, write anything. We have our own censors, and we transmit while airborne. No local clearances."

"We just throw it over their heads into Washington," growled a voice. "In three hours from now, all our Nagasaki stuff will be on the desk."

"Stuff!" I felt like a Robinson Crusoe, reluctant to be rescued, but half-sensing, from these new-dateline-every-day boys, that my obsession with history was getting out of hand. My Dutch forces had quit Nagasaki and gone back to their camp, where movie projectors and films were now being dropped in. Harrison had run out of time and was leaving. One of my cars had disappeared, and the night before the lieutenant had sent only one Kempetai, not two. Was it time to cut my losses and go?

But the deep fullness of the Nagasaki story was still emerging. I was beginning to look ahead to something free, big and formal. I considered deferring fighting the censorship in Tokyo, and going north to Hiroshima. My mind was fumbling for something ample, leisurely and magnificent, such as John Hersey was to do several months later for *The New Yorker*.

McCrary, kindness itself, offered to take carbons of my stories and file them when airborne. In my stubbornness I refused. First, my work wasn't over. Second, I had spent four years bucking the MacArthur blackout (minus intervals in European and African fronts). This was my fight and I was going back to see it through. The circus shook their heads as if I were mad, and they were right.

When I looked up, alone again in Nagasaki and saw the two B-17s swing over the city, and imagined the typewriters talking as they swept southward, I had that bite of shame that comes when you have missed your communications. A few hours later, on the old radio in the villa, the playback of "the first correspondents in Nagasaki" began to come through.

What remained fascinating for me was the constant revision of my own ideas of total devastation and no-escape-from-the-bomb. The sharpest correction came from 120 prisoners I interviewed on an island in the harbor, and another camp of workers—Americans, British, Dutch, Australians and Javanese—next to the Mitsubishi plant. Of these several hundred men, only eight had been killed by the bomb. Why so few, when so near the supposedly all-pervasive doom? "Those eight wouldn't have got it, either," explained an American dentist, "but they poked their heads out of the slit trench to watch the parachute falling. Just too curious."

They showed me the slit trench, hardly two hundred yards from where the bomb went off high above their heads, and barely four feet deep. "Whenever there was an air raid warning, we would bugger off and hunker down in the slit trenches till the all clear sounded, or the foremen drove us back. That's what saved us. For the last weeks there were so many planes passing north and south around Nagasaki that the warnings and all clears got all mixed up. The workers stayed at their machines, but we claimed our rights. And they needed our skilled work so much they didn't force us."

Blast and ray flew harmlessly over their heads. They had lain prostrate almost directly under it, and only forty claimed to be wounded, few severely.

A few, who happened to be looking that way, saw the mushroom cloud climb over Hiroshima. But they had then been in the mad camp at Omuta, where an insane Japanese captain with a mania for baseball kept the diarrhea patients running bases in a lavatory league of his own. It was a week after Nagasaki's bomb, when the prison authorities began burning the medical records, that they knew the war was over.

Not a word came back from Tokyo about my dispatches. The Kempetai returned to Nagasaki, but they had no message for me. A feeling of hopelessness about my stories began to drag me down. Perhaps they were already locked in some censor's safe. If so, what sense was there in leaving southern Japan for Tokyo,

to start this tedious battle? Why not, instead, mine what there
was around me? The camps of southern Japan, six weeks after
the Mikado's surrender, were still not opened.

So, about four days after McCrary's flying circus departed,
Colonel Weller packed his bag and started up country, sans staff.
Two American officers who had wandered into Nagasaki furnished me with a list of unopened camps, each with its weird
story. For a week I roamed from camp to camp. Then the
grapevine of errant prisoners brought me another blow. The
Marines had landed in Nagasaki. I raced back south. What a
change!

In three days Nagasaki had undergone the full transformation
from crushed worm to brave yellow butterfly. A ruin was changing into a hostess city. Destroyers, transports, LSTs crowded the
harbor. My floating lantern was gone. Salvage operations had
begun. Jeeps and trucks hustled through the stream of bicycles.
Marines leaned on the sagging sills of the harbor buildings,
lovingly cleaning their carbines.

But still there were no correspondents from Tokyo. The Navy
had landed, but even they were under MacArthur. And still,
going on seven weeks after the bombs, the world was waiting.
What was the reason? To keep the victory of two nuclear
weapons from eclipsing a general? To prevent its being said that
the Pacific war was finally won in the Manhattan Project, not in
Manila? I could imagine the two hundred correspondents, still
bottled up in Tokyo, being told that there were "no facilities" for
them in Nagasaki, and that the ruins might be infected. Meantime I was leading Navy doctors and nurses through the now
cleared, sorted and arranged ashes.

By this time it was not really necessary to become a casualty of
Nagasaki myself, but I managed to do so. On a hospital ship's
deck I caught a medicine ball thrown by a burly Navy doctor,
and felt something crack. In an hour Dr. Malcolm Stevens, the
former Yale coach, had me mummified in a plaster cast from the
neck to hips. The ship carried me off to Guam.

But I still had my smudged carbons. A month later I started
trying to get them through the Navy censorship. "We can't clear
this stuff, but we'll be glad to send it to Tokyo for you. I'm sure
they'll release it there." "Thanks, but never mind."

As soon as I was able to walk, I received orders to go back to

China. I was somewhere in Manchuria, I believe, when I received news that parties of correspondents were now being taken to Hiroshima, and yes, Nagasaki, too.

They won. At least I was not busted by my organization for bucking the system, like dour, funny Ed Kennedy, who was too early for Eisenhower with the signing of the armistice. Ed, who had covered the fall of Greece with me, had set up communications that were too good. I threw away my one good chance to communicate, trying for a fuller, more perfect story.

Oh, Nagasaki! What a way to lose a war!

Margaret Bourke-White's name is synonymous with photo journalism. The first *Life* magazine cover and its first photo essay were by Margaret Bourke-White. Here, in words as splendid as her pictures, Miss Bourke-White describes how she got a photograph of Mahatma Gandhi.

How I "Shot"
Mahatma Gandhi

MARGARET BOURKE-WHITE

PHOTOGRAPHY demands a high degree of participation, but never have I participated to such an extent as I did when photographing various episodes in the life of Gandhi.

I arrived in India in 1946 on a *Life* assignment. At that time, India stood shining and full of hope on the threshold of independence. Gandhi was the heart and soul of this.

I shall always remember the day we met. I went to see him at his camp, or *ashram*, in Poona, where he was living in the midst of a colony of untouchables. Having thought of Mahatma Gandhi as a symbol of simplicity, I was a bit surprised to find that I had to go through several secretaries to get permission to photograph him. When I reached the last and chief secretary, an earnest man wearing horn-rimmed spectacles and dressed entirely in snow-white homespun, I explained my mission. I had come to take photographs of the Mahatma spinning.

"Do you know how to spin?" asked Gandhi's secretary.

"Oh, I didn't come to spin with the Mahatma. I came to photograph the Mahatma spinning."

"How can you possibly understand the symbolism of Gandhi at his spinning wheel? How can you comprehend the inner meaning of the wheel, the *charka*, unless you first master the principles of spinning?" he inquired sharply. "Then you are not at all familiar with the workings of the spinning wheel?"

"No. Only with the workings of a camera."

The secretary fell into rhapsody. "The spinning wheel is a marvel of human ingenuity. The charka is machinery reduced to the level of the toiling masses. Consider the great machines of the factories, with all their complex mechanisms, and consider the charka. There are no ball bearings; there is not even a nail. The spinning wheel symbolizes what Gandhi calls 'the proletarianism of science.'"

It was useless for me to protest that I had a deadline to meet, that this very evening a package of film must be at the airport to be placed on a certain transoceanic plane that would be met at the airfield in New York, rushed to the *Life* photo lab, processed through the night, and in the morning, forty-eight hours after the taking of the photograph, finished prints of the Mahatma at his spinning wheel must be lying on the *Life* editor's desk.

As the secretary became more involved in his oratory, I grew desperate. "The charka illustrates a major tenet of Gandhi's. When individually considered, man is insignificant, even like a drop of water, but in the mass, he becomes mighty and powerful like the ocean."

"You will make me drop photography and take up spinning," I said politely, wondering when we could get back to the appointment.

"That is just what I wish to do," said Gandhi's secretary.

I know when I'm licked. "How long does it take to learn to spin?" I asked wearily.

"Ah," said the secretary, "that depends upon one's quotient of intelligence."

I found myself begging for a spinning lesson.

"I must compose editorials for Gandhiji's weekly magazine, *Harijan*," said the secretary. "I have a deadline to meet. Come back again next Tuesday."

Somehow I persuaded Gandhi's secretary that my spinning lesson must start this very afternoon. It embarrassed me to see how clumsy I was at the spinning wheel, constantly entangling myself. It did not help my opinion of my own IQ to see how often and how awkwardly I broke the thread. I began to appreciate as never before the machine age, with its ball bearings and steel parts, and maybe an occasional nail.

Finally, my instructor decided I could spin well enough to be brought into the presence of the Mahatma. There were two injunctions I must faithfully follow. I must not speak to the Mahatma, as this was Monday, his day of silence. And I must not use any form of artificial light, as Gandhi disliked it. I could see from the outside that Gandhi's hut was going to be very dark indeed (a perfect job for Tri-X and souped-up developers, which then we did not have). I pleaded with Gandhi's secretary to allow me some lighting equipment, and finally he allotted me three peanut flashbulbs.

I found the inside of the hut even darker than I had anticipated. A single beam of daylight shone from a little high window directly into my lens and into my eyes as well. I could scarcely see to compose the picture, but when my eyes became accustomed to the murky shadows, there sat the Mahatma, cross-legged, a spidery figure with long, wiry legs, a bald head and spectacles. Could this be the man who was leading his people to freedom— the little old man in a loincloth who had kindled the imagination of the world? I was filled with an emotion as close to awe as a photographer can come.

He sat in complete silence on the floor; the only sound was a little rustling from the pile of newspaper clippings he was reading. And beside him was that spinning wheel I had heard so much about. I was grateful that he would not speak to me, for I could see it would take all the attention I had to overcome the halation from that wretched window just over his head.

Gandhi pushed his clippings aside, and pulled his spinning wheel closer. He started to spin, beautifully, rhythmically, and with a fine nimble hand. I set off the first of the three flashbulbs. It was quite plain from the span of time from the click of the shutter to the flash of the bulb that my equipment was not synchronizing properly. The heat and moisture of India had affected all my equipment; nothing seemed to work. I decided to hoard my two remaining flashbulbs and take a few time exposures. But this I had to abandon when my tripod "froze" with one leg at its minimum and two at their maximum length.

Before risking the second flashbulb, I checked the apparatus with the utmost care. When Gandhi made a most beautiful movement as he drew the thread, I pushed the trigger and was reassured by the sound that everything had worked properly. Then I noticed that I had forgotten to pull the slide.

I hazarded the third peanut, and it worked. I threw my arms around the rebellious equipment and stumbled out into the daylight, quite unsold on the machine age. Spinning wheels could take priority over cameras any time.

The secretary was waiting outside, all smiles. I had been in the "presence"; I belonged. He asked graciously if I would like to see a demonstration of spinning on Gandhi's own personal spinning wheel—the portable one he carried when he traveled.

"I would enjoy that very much," I replied. I enjoyed it even more than I had anticipated, for, in the middle of the secretary's demonstration, the spinning wheel fell to pieces. That made me feel better about the machine age.

This was the first of many occasions on which I photographed the Mahatma. Gandhi, who loved a little joke, had his own nickname for me. Whenever I appeared on the scene with camera and flashbulbs, he would say, "There's the Torturer again." But it was said with affection.

As time went on, I saw this incident of the spinning wheel in a different light. Translated into the many situations a photographer must meet, the rule set up by Gandhi's secretary was a good one: if you want to photograph a man spinning, give some thought to why he spins.

In the case of Gandhi, the spinning wheel was laden with meaning. Nonviolence was Gandhi's creed, and the spinning wheel was the perfect weapon.

Ansel E. Talbert is managing editor of *Air Transport World* magazine, and former military and aviation editor and syndicated columnist of the *New York Herald Tribune*. A war correspondent during the Korean conflict, he has been decorated with the Legion of Honor of France and is a trustee of the Overseas Press Club Foundation. He was the first newspaper man to fly over both poles.

News "On the Rocks"

ANSEL E. TALBERT

IF I HAD BEEN smart, perhaps I would have remembered the old U.S. Army maxim:

"Never ask for anything you're not sure you want—you might get it."

But, on the other hand, I would have missed the "pleasures" of living through blizzards, ice fogs, and "white-outs" (thicker and more deadly than London pea-soup fogs) on Ice Island T-3. This kidney-shaped mass of freshwater glacial ice 9 miles long, 4 miles wide and 160 feet thick was about 250 miles from the geographical North Pole when I first landed there.

This oversized ice cube, composed of a congealed hunk broken off a glacier in the Canadian archipelago, was floating slowly across the North Polar regions at the rate of two to three miles a day, propelled by winds and currents, and grinding through less substantial Arctic Ocean sea ice frozen mostly to a depth of eight feet. T-3 had no competition for its claim of being the world's most northerly inhabited outpost.

Come to think of it, if I had not been sent there, I would also have missed being buzzed by the first Soviet aircraft in history to

be sighted visually by Americans on the Canadian-American side
of the North Pole since World War II's end. And Poncho, the
only Alaskan husky dog I ever got to know personally, wouldn't
have lived to meet the beautiful husky bitch who became his
mate.

But to start at the beginning: The first time I ever heard of Ice
Island T-3 was in the Officers' Club at Anchorage during a
stopover in Alaska. As part of a newspaper assignment, I was
traveling the shorter Great Circle Route by air to the Far East a
year or so after the fighting simmered down in Korea. I had been
a war correspondent during the first seven months of the Korean
War. My newspaper now wanted me to pay a return visit with a
view to writing some powerful pieces already tentatively entitled
"Korea—Twelve Months After Cease-fire." My own working title
was, "Howgozit in the Land of the Morning Calm?"

My Officers' Club informant, a chance acquaintance, mentioned
a remarkable plan already in the early stages of development: to
try to land a small group of Air Force volunteers and civilian
scientists on a floating ice island called T-3, somewhere in the
vicinity of the North Pole. The idea was to see whether this
relatively stable ice mass could be kept under continuous American habitation for a period of months and possibly years. Actual
aircraft landings on the island and air drops of supplies were to
be a major part of the project.

An Arctic Ocean ice island, it should be explained, differs
considerably from an ice floe, the latter being simply a large hunk
of frozen sea ice.

Ice floes have a disturbing tendency to split apart suddenly
after developing "leads" or cracks, with little or no warning. In
1937 polar flyers of the Soviet Air Force had landed directly at
the North Pole on the frozen sea ice and planted the Red Flag
there, but didn't remain to colonize the area. Small Soviet scientific parties were known to have camped on ice floes.

But landing and building a permanent or semipermanent
settlement on one of the several huge ice islands of the Arctic
Ocean was something else again. These islands—at least those
on the Canadian-American side—follow relatively fixed paths in
floating year after year across the top of the Canadian archipelago toward Alaska, then back in the opposite direction across
the North Polar area toward Greenland, and back once again

toward Alaska. As a veteran of nearly a dozen trips to various parts of the Arctic and one of the first two commercial air passengers to travel from New York City to Nome, Alaska, I was tremendously excited by the plan.

I suddenly lost interest in returning to Korea, and immediately began pulling all possible wires to join the Ice Island T-3 landing party. The commanding general of the Alaskan Air Command, General Kepner, was an old friend. After a conference, he readily agreed that the inclusion of a working daily newspaperman would be a good idea. Permission of Air Force Headquarters in the Pentagon would be necessary, however, and I fired off a telegram to Washington, giving all possible reasons why I should be allowed to go. General Kepner's endorsement went with it.

In a happy mood, I informed my newspaper of my proposed change of plans and started looking for more Arctic gear and any background information available on ice islands and their history.

There was a small fly in the ointment: nobody knew for sure when the first landing on T-3 would take place. It already had been scheduled, cancelled and rescheduled. Emphasis now was on making sure that the expedition was a success, regardless of how much preparation it required. It might come off in a couple of weeks, or it might be several months. Opinions differed, and even the general couldn't promise anything.

Time passed, and after receiving several plaintive communications from my foreign editor asking: "Any news, pal, on ice island landing date?", and "How do you feel about Korea now, ice island later?", I decided reluctantly to proceed to Tokyo, Seoul, Pusan and Taegu, leaving behind future addresses where the Air Force could reach me if anything developed.

Nothing did, as far as I was concerned. I completed my Far Eastern tour, returned home by way of Hawaii with a stopover to study the defense situation at Waikiki Beach, and forgot I ever had planned a trip to Ice Island T-3.

Two years later and two days before Easter Sunday, for which I had extensive plans, the telephone in my New York apartment rang early. A deep voice said: "This is United States Air Force Headquarters in Washington. Some time back you applied to pay a visit to Ice Island T-3. Do you still want to go?"

"Certainly," I said, without considering.

"Would it be pushing too hard," the voice queried, "to ask you to be at Westover Air Force Base in Massachusetts not later than tomorrow night, to catch a plane going through to Thule, Greenland?"

I told them to count me in. I still hadn't figured out why they happened to think of me, after so long.

Thule in northwest Greenland was a military city of several thousand inhabitants—an engineering miracle which included an air base capable of handling four-engined bombers, only seven hundred nautical miles from the North Pole. Arriving there after a tedious flight of nearly three thousand nautical miles by way of Labrador—not exactly as a crow would fly—I reported immediately to the executive officer of the base command.

He regarded me with a suspicious eye when I identified myself and named my proposed destination. The exec said:

"Ridiculous—no newspaper correspondents are or have been authorized to visit T-3. As a matter of fact, we have specific orders to the contrary. Who sent you here, anyway?"

Knowing the ways and habits of the military from long exposure during World War II, I showed him my travel orders and suggested politely that he go through his incoming mail basket. About an inch or so down he found the TWX from the Pentagon saying that "by order of the Commanding General, Ansel E. Talbert, newspaper correspondent, is authorized to visit Ice Island T-3." This changed matters. It resulted immediately in (1) assignment of an officer to show me around, (2) provision of Arctic gear suitable for life on an island of ice, and (3) quarters in one of the prefabricated aluminum buildings of Thule.

The following day, when I received a summons from the operations officer to be out for a 6:30 A.M. takeoff for the ice island the next morning, I began to feel that matters now were straightened out.

In a light snowfall, I climbed aboard a ski-equipped Douglas DC-3 twin-engined transport plane (called a C-47 by the Air Force) and was off at the scheduled hour. The flight of more than five hundred nautical miles was to require approximately four and one-half hours, over some of the wildest and most beautiful Arctic areas of snow- and ice-covered mountains I had ever seen.

After striking up a conversation with some of the crew members, I was mildly shaken to learn that all services, including the Royal Canadian Air Force, were observing a period of radio

silence each hour in the hope of picking up distress signals from a
United States Navy Privateer aircraft carrying eight. This had
taken off ten days before from Thule bound for Ice Island T-
3—and disappeared.

The wreckage of this Navy plane, which had struck an icy peak
in the Canadian archipelago on lonely Ellesmere Island—the spot
from which Rear Admiral Robert E. Peary began his successful
dash to the North Pole in 1909—was discovered some days later.
All its occupants died in the crash, apparently caused by a sudden
"white-out" of a type capable of confusing even a veteran instrument pilot.

Two months before, I was informed, an Air Force plane,
carrying supplies, two civilian scientists and crew to T-3, had
failed to pick up the island due to a navigational error and had
run out of gas on the attempted return flight. The pilot was able
to make a forced landing on the relatively smooth surface of a
snow-covered glacier in Northern Greenland. All the plane's
occupants were picked up by the efficient Air-Sea Rescue unit at
Thule, after a night and a day on the glacier. My own luck now
seemed to be in high gear, for exactly at the estimated time of
arrival, we were over T-3. The ice island's outline could be distinguished from the surface of the sea ice pack because the island
surface appeared white, smooth and unbroken. The ice pack, by
contrast, appeared darker and full of cracks. It resembled the
surface of a giant mirror that had been shattered.

The runway on which we landed, made of packed snow that
had been rolled laboriously and stomped down by the snowshoes
of the ice island's inhabitants, was about a mile from the tiny
camp at the northwest end. From the air the camp had the
appearance of an Eskimo village, with all buildings now snow-
covered mounds. The pilot never cut his engines after landing,
but kept gunning them while the mail and supplies were unloaded by the permanent party of eleven.

In less than forty minutes, he taxied to the end of the runway,
turned about, gave the engines full power and took off on the
flight back to Thule, with only a few feet of runway left. The
wreckage of another DC-3 that hadn't lifted off in time some
months before, and crashed, killing the pilot and several occupants, served as a grim runway marker for all air operations to
and from T-3.

Two Air Force enlisted volunteers for T-3 duty came in with me. Another went back with the plane, bringing the total human population to thirteen, including two civilian scientists and this correspondent. It might have been an unlucky situation for the superstitious, but for the presence of Poncho, an Alaskan husky of the breed used by Esquimaux to haul sleds. He had been brought as a small puppy to the ice island from Alaska by the first group to occupy T-3, and obviously considered himself human rather than canine.

Immediately after the landing I had taken off a fur-lined mitten in order to scribble a note to the Foreign Desk back home, saying "Arrived T-3 safely—wish you were here", and other observations. But my fingers swiftly stiffened from the sub-zero cold, so that I could no longer hold the pen after a sentence or two.

I was taken aback by the lack of enthusiastic greeting for the new arrivals until I noted that each member of the permanent party had received a packet of from thirty to fifty letters. After completing the unloading, each was busy tearing open envelopes and scanning the contents with an eager enthusiasm which banished other interests for the moment.

Poncho was the only one without letters from home to read, and eager to make friends immediately. Thereby a lasting friend-ship began.

On reaching the camp on foot I found that it consisted of two prefabricated structures, each about the size of three medium-sized rooms placed end to end—and almost entirely covered by snow. One was for working, studying, recreation and eating. The other, kept darkened inside and quiet at all times, was for sleep-ing. It was used around the clock, since weather observations and the collection of other scientific data were matters carried out on a 24-hour basis.

A tunnel with a boarded roof connected the buildings. There also were several small one-man tents available to the camp's fresh-air fiends, who might prefer a sleeping bag in a tent in sub-zero cold, and privacy, to a more comfortable cot in the bunk-house.

Poncho was among the fresh-air fiends. Nobody had been able to coax him inside either of the huts within memory of any then living on the ice island. He liked raw steak, but even the promise of one held a foot or two from his nose failed to make him cross the huts' thresholds. No matter how many degrees below zero the temperature went, Poncho would locate the windward side of an oil drum or some other wind-breaking structure. Then he would curl up in a ball and go to sleep.

After all the mail had been read, the atmosphere became friendly and convivial. Everyone wanted to know the circumstances that had brought me to the ice island, and someone finally asked me how long I planned to stay. When I replied that three weeks might be about right, the laughter was uproarious. For a time I didn't get the joke.

In ignorance I had assumed that by now a "milk run" with regular flights two or three times a week was in operation. I hadn't tarried long enough in Thule to get a briefing on what the situation really was. From the T-3 party I learned that there had been only two flights involving landings on the ice island in the past three months. During one period not far back, there had been none for approximately five months. Landings depended on the weather and on whether there was any real pressure to make a flight.

Each morning the Air Force radio operators on T-3 would receive an early call from Thule, asking for weather conditions at the runway area. Thule was in the habit daily of scheduling a flight to the ice island and requesting a flow of reports on how the weather was holding up.

If the initial report told of sunny weather with ceiling and visibility unlimited, fog invariably would make its appearance before long and further rapid weather deterioration would cause the mission's cancellation. It was a good working example of the old British jest: "If you don't like the weather, wait awhile." There was nothing imaginary about the swift flying-weather changes, but it also was a fact that Air Force operations officers at Thule tended to be conservative rather than risk needless losses of aircraft.

In a day or two I became resigned to an indefinite and possibly lengthy stay on the ice island, and decided to let fate arrange my departure date.

There was no way to get personal messages back from T-3 except through the courtesy of ham radio operators in various parts of the United States. They talked with the two T-3 operators at night when the military traffic was at a minimum, and forwarded brief personal communications. When conditions were particularly good, they sometimes arranged for a "telephone splice," allowing the T-3 party members to talk with their wives and children back in the States. This, however, was a rare occurrence.

On the theory that I ought to get to know the place where I was staying, I decided to explore the ice island thoroughly. Usually I went alone on skis or snowshoes, for the other twelve had piled more than fifty feet high off the island's edges, I experi-campsite. On one long trek to the opposite side, where the sea ice had piled more than fifty feet high off the island's edges, I experienced the most frightening event of the trip.

One of the civilian scientists, Norman Goldstein of Cambridge, Massachusetts, had sighted freshly made Arctic fox tracks near the ice island's edge. Since Arctic foxes habitually follow polar bears to make meals of whatever food the bears leave after a kill, the possibility of a surprise visit by strangers wearing white fur coats entered the minds of all.

On my solo ski and snowshoe trips, I began to experience fantasies involving sudden and unexpected meetings with large and aggressive polar bears. What do you do on such an occasion? I asked myself. Run like hell? Stand your ground and calmly stare the bear into cringing submission? Or what? The only positive suggestion came from the wag of T-3 who suggested helpfully: "Just show him your press card."

Not long after the fox-track sighting, I was pondering these matters while blazing a new ski trail with long, sliding steps. Behind me I heard distinctly the patter of padded footsteps apparently following me at a running gait. But when I turned, expecting to face the teeth and claws of a hungry polar bear, I was knocked flat into a snow drift by Poncho, who had been following my trail from the camp and wanted to frolic.

Never underestimate the capabilities of an Alaskan husky! Poncho, as it turned out, had a built-in aircraft warning system difficult to explain in scientific terms. Some days later, when the radio was bringing in the usual weather report requests, preliminary to the cancellation of a flight from Thule, Poncho suddenly began to bark furiously outside in a manner he never before had done. A slice of beefsteak failed to quiet him.

Fifteen minutes later we were made aware of what caused the canine outburst. Even inside the huts, the roar of approaching aircraft engines became audible. All hands rushed out into the 24-hour daylight which then was prevailing. Coming in low at below five hundred feet was an unusual-appearing transport-type aircraft. Somebody who hadn't looked carefully yelled: "It's the pony express from Thule—they finally made it."

Another saw the first letter of the plane's markings in large letters—CCCP—and shouted: "It's not an American plane—it's Canadian."

At that moment I remembered that the markings corresponded exactly to those on Soviet aircraft I previously had seen in various parts of world, and I shouted: "No! It's Russian!"

For a moment nobody did or said anything. Was the mission from the other side of the North Pole friendly? Did the Soviet Union, which had stated officially at the time its bombers landed at the North Pole before World War II that "the North Pole now belongs to the Red Air Force," really mean this boast? Was it now in the process of taking care of any interlopers?

There were no armaments on T-3 except rifles for hunting, but there was no thought of using these until friendly overtures had failed. Spontaneously, everyone in the T-3 camp removed their canvas-covered caps with built-in earmuffs, and waved them.

The Soviet pilot responded by dipping his wings in a salute of peace as he roared directly overhead and then began a wide turn after passing the ice island. This brought him back across the camp a second time exactly at right angles to the path of his first crossing.

Apparently the Soviet plane was carrying out a photo run. Following his second pass at the camp, the pilot headed in the direction of the North Pole and disappeared over the horizon.

A radio report of the incident soon was on its way to Thule, and back came a barrage of queries beginning with: "Did you get any photographs?" On receiving an affirmative answer, other messages inquiring about the weather conditions began arriving in great profusion. This time the mission from Thule wasn't scrubbed, and in about four hours a ski-equipped plane arrived, followed by a second.

I decided to arrange to fly back with the pilot carrying the photographs, and to try to clear my stories as soon as possible.

Before my departure I had agreed to submit all stories to the Air Force and the Defense Department for security clearance. Although I regretted the arrangement, I felt it had to be kept. Because of the delicate diplomatic situation involving Danish sovereignty in Greenland, where the air base at Thule was located, and the sensitivity of Danish Cabinet and Parliament members to reading reports in American newspapers about events on their territory of which they had no knowledge, it was considered tactful to show the stories to the Danish ambassador.

From one of the pilots from Thule, I learned that because Ice Island T-3 had been under continuous American occupation and inhabitation for twenty-six months, Air Force headquarters had decided to close up shop temporarily, leaving the huts and all facilities on the island for future use. For the record, they did come back.

This decision, I learned later, had no connection with the Soviet visit from across the North Pole, and actually had been made weeks before. I inquired immediately: "What's going to become of my pal Poncho?"

The base commander said: "It's too bad, but he'll have to be destroyed. They don't allow dogs of any kind, particularly huskies, in Thule. No Eskimo would have him for a sled dog even if you paid him, because he's been spoiled as a pet. We'll just shoot him quietly."

I was outraged, and at once brought the Power of the Press to bear. I made it plain to anyone who would listen that if a home wasn't found for Poncho, I would rouse every dog lover in the United States in protest. In short order, radio messages went out to all Arctic stations. It soon developed that a three-man weather party at Alert, a tiny weather station on the northern tip of Greenland, would be glad to have Poncho join them.

Considerably relieved, I flew back to St. Johns, Newfoundland, to persuade the commanding general of the Northeast Air Command to help me secure "urgent clearance" for the story of the Soviet reconnaissance. This had been classified Top Secret, for what reason I could not fathom, since the Russians obviously knew about it. The general concurred.

When released, the story made page one in New York and in cities all over the world to which it was syndicated. My later

"Life on an Ice Island" series did equally well, even in Alaska and Scandinavia.

Some months later, I was in New York and had forgotten Poncho when an Air Force message arrived through official channels from Alert. Signed by the officer in command, it said:

"Your friend Poncho involved with beautiful husky bitch, but has stiff competition."

Several weeks later a second came in from the same source, and this read:

"Poncho badly chewed by competition but will recover."

The final message proved that my faith in Poncho was not misplaced. It informed me: "Poncho nosed out competition; now father of five. Will you be godfather?"

Benjamin Fine's scholarly achievements and long list of authoritative books in the field of education have earned him a formidable reputation. As education editor of *The New York Times,* he won a Pulitzer Prize. He is presently a practicing educator—headmaster of the Sands Point Country Day School at Sands Point, New York.

When Does a T-Bone Become a Scoop?

BENJAMIN FINE

(Special to The New York Times)

Clay, Ky., Sept. 12 (1956) . . . "This little community of some 1,400 population became an armed camp today.

"Two Negroes were the only students in the previously all-white school here.

"Acting in secrecy, Gov. A. B. (Happy) Chandler ordered the National Guard and state police here. Some 500 Guardsmen and sixty state police officers arrived in the center of town at 3:55 o'clock this morning.

"They immediately deployed their forces along the roads leading to the Clay consolidated school, on top of a steep hill. The men were under the direction of Maj. Gen. J. J. B. Williams, Adjutant General of Kentucky."

So began my front-page exclusive ten years ago. A new era in the Southern integration battle had opened. It was the first time that a governor had called out the militia to protect Negro children who sought entrance into an all-white school. Here were the ingredients of a news thriller—state troopers, militiamen, army trucks, guns, bayonets, a circling army plane overhead! What more could any newspaperman want?

A frozen T-bone steak and a friendly state trooper combined to place me in the center of this front-page thriller!

The 1956–57 school year opened on an uneasy note. Two years previously the United States Supreme Court had ruled that separate but equal schools must be scrapped with all deliberate speed.

"One thousand years is deliberate enough to integrate," said Southern diehards.

The North shrugged its shoulders. "The Supreme Court doesn't mean us," Northern leaders held.

It would be several years before integration hit the North with a blizzard of boycotts, demonstrations, strikes and civil disobedience. But in the fall of 1956 the big issue remained: would the South comply with the Supreme Court ruling? Angry segregationists pledged a bitter last-ditch fight. Their slogan was "Never." They wore buttons that said "Never." Never would the South permit its white children to go to school with Negroes.

One of the first big tests of this policy took place in Louisville, Kentucky. I was education editor of *The New York Times* then. Harold Faber, our national editor, called me into his office.

"We want you to go down to Louisville," he said. "The schools are set for an integration test."

So off I went to Kentucky for a two- or three-day assignment. Would the white parents challenge the plans to integrate the Louisville schools?

They would not. Segregation died quietly. Its passing created no more than a token ripple of protest. Integrated classes, from elementary through high school, took place throughout the city. Fortunately, the superintendent of schools, Dr. Omer Carmichael, had done his job well. He had prepared the city for integration. White and colored citizens took integration in their stride. White and Negro children sat together in the classroom. They played together in the schoolyards, ate together in the cafeterias, studied together in the libraries.

But there were rumblings in another part of Kentucky. In Clay, some 160 miles away, a skirmish had taken place when segregationists turned away two Negro children, a brother and sister, who tried to enter the all-white school. At nearby Sturgis, several state troopers escorted seven Negro students to the local high school. These were minor squabbles. Louisville, apparently, had been the big test. There was not a single arrest, though hundreds of Negroes entered the previously all-white schools.

I was ready to return to *The Times* when I received a call from Hal Faber. "We'd like you to go to Clay," he said. "Take a look at the situation. Come back in a couple of days."

Hal informed me that our Washington correspondent, John D. Morris, was at Clay. Morris would fill me in on details. He was staying at the Forty Winks Motel, some five miles from the town of Clay itself.

I arrived at Forty Winks about 5:30 on the afternoon of September 11. Unfortunately there had been a mix-up in signals. Morris had departed before I arrived.

A stranger in these parts, knowing no one in Clay or any of the tiny surrounding towns, I had no way of getting background information. I did not know what to expect. Other reporters were already on the job. Where were they staying? I couldn't even get in touch with them. Indeed, I didn't know how to find the school, nor did I know the issues involved.

Since it was now past six o'clock and I was hungry, I left my room and sauntered over to the Forty Winks dining room. It was virtually deserted; one or two other guests were waiting for their dessert.

I ordered a T-bone steak special, and pondered my immediate future. How would I get to Clay? Was there a story brewing there? I felt good about Louisville, with two front-page stories. But there I knew the superintendent and had full cooperation of the school's public relations office.

In a brief discussion with the Forty Winks manager, I soon discovered that if anything was happening at Clay, neither the manager nor any one else with whom I spoke had any inkling of it. They were as uninformed as I. They showed little interest.

In fact, I gathered that I was looked upon as a freak. Plainly, they questioned the judgment of a *New York Times* reporter coming all the way to a little out-of-the-way place called Clay for a nonexistent story.

"I heard that two colored children want to go to a white school," the manager said. "Of course, they won't get in. They have their own school. What do they want to go to a white school for?"

Then he added: "But that's all over now. Nothing much is happening far as I can tell."

I became impatient, waiting for my T-bone. I had been waiting almost an hour.

"Miss," I protested to the waitress, "what's happening to my steak? I've got work to do. I'm wasting too much time."

"Oh, I'm sorry," she apologized. "We have only frozen steaks left. You have to wait an hour for a good T-bone to unfreeze and broil just right."

Upset, hungry and worried about getting my story, I acted gruffer than I normally might have done: "I wish you had told me it would take this long. I would have ordered a hamburger and been out of here by now."

Only later did I realize that the frozen T-bone steak, with an hour or more for broiling, had helped me stumble upon one of the top education stories of the 1956 school year.

At half-past seven, about an hour and fifteen minutes after I had entered the motel dining room, two blue-coated state troopers, erect and businesslike in their uniforms, walked in, sat down and they, too, ordered steak.

"You'll have to wait an hour," I said, smiling. "They're frozen."

One of the troopers looked up, grinned and answered: "We're in no hurry. We got all night."

My T-bone arrived. It was delicious, well worth the waiting. The platter of homemade hot buttermilk biscuits, dripping with melted butter, provided the extra touch of goodness. Southern cooking and Southern hospitality, I thought, certainly deserved praise.

While digging into my steak, I looked up to find at least 15 or 20 blue-coated state troopers in the dining room. They came in groups of twos and fours.

What, I wondered, were so many officers doing in this out-of-the-way motel dining room? Was a convention taking place? Any arrests to be made? What's up?

I became curious.

After I ate my fresh blueberry tart and drank a delicious cup of hot Kentucky coffee, I walked over to one of the tables where the two troopers whom I had warned about the long wait for frozen T-bones were still waiting. They were in serious conversation and didn't seem the least bit impatient.

"I'm a reporter from *The New York Times*," I began. "Is anything going on here? Quite a few of you men eating here tonight."

Silence.

The waitress came up with two sizzling platters of steak and a mess of hot biscuits.

"So long," I said, as I left. "Enjoy your dinner."

Silence.

I walked through the L-shaped motel yard. On one side, opposite my room, I came across another group of blue-coated state troopers. Slowly I sauntered among them, hoping to find out what was taking place. By this time I was more than curious; I was determined. But all I heard was small talk about the lovely fall weather, the growing recklessness of teen-age drivers and the favorite brand of pipe tobacco.

I was more puzzled than ever. By now I had counted some forty troopers.

Slowly, I walked back to the dining room. My "friends" had just about finished their dinner. They were talking quietly and obviously they wanted to be alone.

"A glass of beer," I told the waitress. I wanted an excuse to remain in the dining room.

I took the plunge, not knowing whether I'd be rebuffed. "There's quite a few troopers here this evening," I said. "Anything special happening tonight?"

One of the troopers half-smiled as he answered: "Nothing that we know of. Have you heard anything?"

"No," I answered ruefully. "But I can't help but wonder. Are you here because of the Clay situation? Do you expect trouble there in the morning?"

All I got in response was a half-smile from one of the officers. The other looked off into space.

By this time I was convinced that there was something brewing. Either a state police officer's convention or the making of a story. By midnight most of the state troopers had left the dining room and gone back to their rooms.

My two friends arose and walked over to the cashier's corner to pay their bills. I followed. As the three of us walked out of the room one of the troopers said so softly I could barely hear: "You might want to get up at two o'clock."

He said it so quietly that I took a double take. "What?" I shot back. "Where? What time?"

The two men walked off without answering.

Here I was, at the Forty Winks Motel, away from any center of activity, in a strange town that was bathed in shadowy moonlight. Only the chirping of crickets and the croaking of frogs in a nearby brook broke the silence. To me it seemed as though I was the only one left in the world.

I went to my small motel room. What should I do next? It was midnight. I was tired and sleepy. What did the state trooper mean when he suggested I should wait up until two o'clock? I didn't undress but threw myself on the bed, dozing off and on, restless, not daring to fall asleep.

I didn't need the alarm clock to awaken me. I heard the ticking and watched the illuminated dial glow 12:15, 12:30, 1:00, 1:30. I arose, washed, put on my jacket and stuck my notebook in my coat pocket. I hoped I would be able to use it before the night ended. Since there were no other reporters at the motel, I was unable to compare notes or discuss the situation with anyone else.

At about 1:45 I walked out of my cabin door and stared at the courtyard. I saw nothing but the dreary, cold darkness. Even the moon was lost behind murky clouds. Bravely, I paced the motel grounds, heading toward the section where I had seen the state troopers congregate earlier.

Suddenly I became alive! Before me, barely visible in the darkness, stood a dozen or more army trucks. And near them were the state troopers that I had met at the dinner table several hours earlier.

Hastily, I walked over to the trucks. The troopers were evidently preparing for a morning raid—or better still, active duty! Peering into the trucks, I could see rifles and other army equipment. A military atmosphere pervaded the quiet night.

Again, I pleaded with a trooper nearest me: "What's happening? Where are you men going?" And once again I got the snub treatment. No answer. I found the officer who had given me the tip earlier and asked him in a half-whisper: "What's taking place? Thanks for the tip, but what's next?"

He just looked up at me, said nothing for a moment, and then

answered quietly: "Why don't you follow us? You may find
something interesting to report."

That was all I needed. I got into my Hertz car, checked my gas
gauge, made sure that all was in order and sat back to wait. It
was cold and damp. Everything seemed eerie, unreal, night-
marish.

Nothing happened.

Then, the roar of motors. The signal was given for the caravan
to begin its unknown journey.

The trucks rumbled along, going onto the main highway. A
dozen or more trucks were now filled with state police. Some of
the trucks, I noticed, held militiamen! Where had they come
from, and where were they going? By this time I knew. Why, to
Clay, of course! But to do what? The question remained un-
answered.

I started my car and pulled into the driveway. The captain,
evidently in charge of the convoy, walked over to me. "Where do
you think you're going?" he snapped. And before I could answer:
"How in hell did you get here?"

Swallowing hard, I replied: "I'm a reporter for *The New York
Times,* out on assignment." I showed him my police pass, observing that it allowed me to pass police and fire lines.

The captain shook his head in disbelief. "Well, I'll be damned,"
he said; "you here all the way from New York? How did you
manage to track us down? No one knows that we're headed for
Clay."

"I'm just lucky, I guess," I retorted.

"Guess you're not," he replied. "We can't let you come along.
Better get back to your room and get a night's sleep. We'll be
back in the morning. If you want to talk with me then, I'll be
ready for you."

"Why are you going to Clay?" I persisted. I still did not know
what to expect, but by now I realized that something big was
about to break. What would troopers do at Clay? And what
about the several trucks filled with National Guardsmen? Where
were they going? How had they come here?

Why so many troops? Up to this point, troops had not been
used to enforce integration. This was such a little issue! Only two
little children at Clay. Who would need an army of troopers and

militiamen to protect them? I did not realize that I was witness-
ing a precedent-shattering phase of growing segregation conflict.

The captain said icily (I had forgotten he was still with me):
"I advise you to go back to your room. Otherwise you might get
hurt. We can't let you come with us."

"Thanks, officer," I said. "I'll be careful."

He stared a moment, shrugged his shoulders, then walked
away. Soon the first of the trucks, loaded with state police and
National Guardsmen took to the road. Since I was a stranger here
and hadn't the faintest notion where to go, nor did I know where
the trucks were going, I returned to my car, bided my time and
then headed toward the main highway. I managed to squeeze my
car between two heavy trucks, and made certain not to get my
fenders clipped.

We moved along slowly on our secret, mysterious mission.
Then, about four in the morning, we reached the center of the
sleeping town of Clay. The men jumped out of their cars and
immediately began to deploy their forces along the road leading
to the Clay Consolidated School, on top of a steep hill. I parked
my car along a small roadway and caught up with a group of
state troopers.

I pieced together the bizarre story. Acting in secrecy, Governor
A. B. (Happy) Chandler had ordered the National Guard and
the state police to move into Clay. Some five hundred Guardsmen
and sixty state police officers arrived between 3:30 and 5:30
under cover of darkness. The strategy was under the direction of
Major General J. J. B. Williams, Adjutant General of Kentucky.

It was dark, without even a moon overhead, when the troops
began pouring into town. To avoid awakening the unsuspecting
residents, they came in quietly, by two different roads, the
Guardsmen from one direction, the state police from another.
They met in front of the school and then took preassigned
stations.

By this time I was wide awake! As the only newspaperman in
Clay at four in the morning, with an exciting, dramatic story
breaking before my eyes, I had a reporter's dream come true—to
be on the spot to get an exclusive, historic front-page story.

For three hours the men, many of them boys of seventeen or
eighteen on their first call to active duty, sprawled on the grass or
sat on the hard curb. They seemed weary and looked sleepy.

Most had been up all night. Some of the militiamen and state troopers traveled five hundred miles to arrive on time. Not a sound could be heard in the night.

But at 6:30, with the streets now bathed in a shadowy light from a half-awakened sun, the men sprang to alert. They straightened their shirts, adjusted helmets, placed their bayonets in rifles and hugged their submachine guns.

A parade of army vehicles roared into town. This was a hundred-man escort for Mrs. Louise Gordon and her two children, Theresa Gordon, eight years old, and her ten-year-old brother James. Only the day before Mrs. Gordon had been turned away from the white school when she attempted to enroll her two children.

"No niggers wanted," was the stinging cry of the townspeople.

But now it was different. In the vanguard of the parade was General Williams. The Gordon escort consisted of eight jeeps, four National Guard trucks filled wtih soldiers and three state police cars. A military plane circled over the town. With amazement I watched the rapidly developing saga. Suddenly the sun broke through the clouds.

Windows popped open, and closed with a bang. Window blinds were raised and then just as suddenly pulled down tightly. A door opened, a head peered out, and then just as quickly the door closed. An incredible look appeared on the half-asleep men and women as they gazed out in astonishment. They could not have been more amazed if they had seen a ghost.

And just as quickly the streets were lined with clusters of questioning persons, little clusters of five or ten, deeper, more vocal groups of fifty or sixty. They stared in astonishment and disbelief at this amazing display of militiamen with drawn bayonets lining their streets, army trucks stacked with machine guns and military weapons. Angry groups quickly formed in front of the troops, in this quiet little rural town of western Kentucky, just 160 miles west of Louisville.

I spoke to General Williams, whose headquarters were in front of the school. He was astonished, dismayed and annoyed that I had come here.

"General, you didn't expect to keep this mission secret, did you?" I asked.

"Oh, no," he answered, "but we don't want any reporters here at this time. Newspapermen, asking questions, might upset the apple cart and incite some of the townsmen to riot."

I promised that I would not incite anyone to illegal or dangerous acts of violence!

But the townsmen didn't need me to get excited. They were furious at the "invasion" of their community.

"What are they bringing these troops in here for?" the townsmen kept asking each other, and all who would listen.

One brawny, angry millhand snapped: "It seems like we had settled the whole mess, didn't we? We told Mrs. Gordon to keep her nigger kids away from this school and she did. Now why is she bringing them back for? We don't want them."

I asked General Williams why he had engaged in this secretive, warlike maneuver.

He answered honestly: "Many of the people in the crowd are armed. They are pretty rough and they are tough. If we are not careful, we will have a dangerous situation on our hands."

I walked up and down the line of troops, talking first to the young National Guardsmen who appeared scared and ill at ease, and then to the townsmen. It wasn't easy to talk to either.

"What's happening?" I asked. "Anything going to take place here this morning? What are you doing here?"

One of the boys answered: "We're just doing what we've been told."

"Obeying orders," another said.

Then I walked over to a group of townsmen who were bitterly denouncing the soldiers, the police, the Governor, the state and reporters in general. I found myself in the midst of fifty or more men arguing violently. They were angry, belligerent, ugly.

"Get the hell out of this town before we throw you out," was the way they greeted me. "What do you want of us?"

"Just want to know how you feel about these soldiers and the Negro children in your school."

I got the answer—in colorful four-letter words.

"Why you causing us all this trouble?"

I answered simply: "I'm only a reporter here covering a story."

"Listen, Mac," one of them said, sneering, "are you a nigger lover?"

"Mister," another one said menacingly, with his fists clenched, his eyes snapping fire, "You had better get out of town fast before you get hurt."

By this time three or four men surrounded me and began poking me in the ribs. I guess I was scared. I had not seen such raw, naked prejudice in many years of reporting. Only the day before in Louisville I had been treated courteously and with respect while covering the integration story.

The mob kept growing. It was at least a hundred strong now. I was deep in the center and all around me I could see vicious, ugly faces.

"Let's beat the bastard up right now," one of the overalled men cried out, clenching his fists menacingly. "What are we fooling around for?"

"Sure, the son of a bitch deserves his lumps," another agreed. "He's just a troublemaker, asking a lot of questions, trying to show us up."

"He won't be able to come back once we're through with him," a brawny, red-faced man—he could not have been more than nineteen—snarled.

"I just came here as a reporter," I tried to explain. "I want to report the news, nothing more."

"Yeh, a reporter, huh?" another piped up angrily. "Let's show this son of a bitch that we don't want nigger-loving reporters here."

Just as the mob began to inch me toward a side street, where they were prepared to give me the "lumps," two state troopers, with revolvers drawn, pushed their way toward me. What a welcome sight! The only other time that I experienced a comparable sense of relief came a year later, when I watched the United States troops roar into Little Rock at the request of President Eisenhower.

"What's going on here?" one of the troopers snapped as he came to my side. "Let this guy alone. He's not doing you any harm."

A grumbling and murmur of protest arose from the mob. A big, brawny, red-faced, red-shirted man shouted: "Let's get the troopers, too. They're with this New York troublemaker."

But the crowd made way as I was escorted between the two men, out of the crowd. "You can't fight a man with a revolver," one said, sullenly. "But wait until these nigger-lover cops leave us. We'll show this son of a bitch what we'll do to him."

Slowly, the two officers backed me out into the main street. What relief when I reached the row of National Guardsmen, their bayonets fixed on army rifles, standing at alert!

One of the troopers gave me Dutch uncle advice. "These men are fighting mad," he said. "They're rough. They'd just as soon string you up as not. Don't go off by yourself again. Better stay close to us. That way no harm will come to you."

"Thanks a lot," I answered. "You men saved my life."

Around eight o'clock several busloads of children chugged up to the school. By this time the crowd had grown larger, uglier and angrier. Some four hundred to five hundred men and women milled along the streets leading to the school. They jeered each time a bus brought its load of children. They shouted at the youngsters, some only six or seven years old, urging them to go home. They set up a chant, "Go home, go home, go home."

"Don't go into the school," mothers yelled as the buses unloaded their cargo. "There's niggers in that school. Stay out."

Several groups of children entered, but they soon walked out. By the time the school bell rang for the opening morning session, the only ones in school were the state troopers, several teachers, the principal and Mrs. Gordon, hovering over James and Theresa. Every one of the white children, at the insistent urging of their elders, had boycotted the school.

Mayor Herman Z. Clark of Clay rode up to the school in his auto. He seemed in a daze, bewildered, flustered. "What's happening here?" he demanded. "What's taking place? What are all these men doing here, carrying guns? Who asked the army to come here?"

He was full of questions but had no answers. I walked over to the mayor. "Any comment?" I began. "How do you feel about the Governor calling out the National Guard to protect the two Negro children?"

"I'm against all of this," he spat in disgust. "And I'll do everything possible to get these soldiers away from here. We're going to keep our school all-white. We won't let any Negro children sit with our white young ones."

Mayor Clark entered the school, talked with the few remaining teachers and urged them to leave. All but three teachers walked out. This left the school with only three teachers and the two little children. An attempt was made to hold "classes," but at 1:30 school was dismissed.

Booing, hooting and catcalling continued throughout the day, but no violence took place. One or two men were arrested for breach of the peace, nothing more.

The townspeople were surprised and hurt at this show of force. A clean-cut farmer of forty said, more in sorrow than anger: "Looks as though the army is in charge here, but why did they come? We haven't had any fighting here. We never hurt anyone. The army waded in on us, came in the dark of the night, and is staying here. I'm a respectable citizen. I own a farm. My father lived on it before me, my grandfather and yes, his grandfather. We never had any trouble before. We go to church, we tend to our business, why can't they leave us alone?"

That was the general attitude. "Why can't they leave us alone?" Even the children took up the refrain, parroting over and over again: "I ain't going to school with niggers." One youngster, not more than twelve years old, said viciously: "I'd rather grow up to be an idiot than go to school with a nigger in it."

Throughout the morning and late into the evening, there was an ominous threat in the air.

"Sure," said a young, husky farmhand, "we'll keep quiet while the troops are here. We won't argue with loaded guns. But after they leave, watch out!"

By midmorning news of this display of arms, state troopers and national militiamen had reached beyond Clay. Reporters began streaming in about ten o'clock. By this time, the early excitement had lessened. But the state troopers, the National Guardsmen with fixed bayonets, the army trucks and army plane circling overhead, and the mobs of angry townsmen were still very much in evidence.

General Williams had the situation well in control. He was satisfied at the way things were going.

"We'll stay here as long as we have to," he said. "We're here to maintain order."

I filled in the other reporters as best I could. The thrill of being on the scene and getting this exciting story was worth whatever dangers and threats I had received. I found my car, where I had parked it six hours earlier, and rode back to the Forty Winks

Motel. In the quiet of my room I began to pound out copy on the morning's fantastic developments.

"Kentucky Troops Guard Two in School," *The Times* front-page headline read next day. "Whites Quit Classes at Clay. Militia Deployed There at Night in Secret."

I stayed with the story for three weeks. The town raised many objections, demanding that the militia and state troopers be removed. The white children continued to boycott the school. Not a single white child entered or remained in class while the two little Negro children were there.

I had a series of front-page stories dealing with the Clay incident. What had appeared at first as an incidental one-day story developed into the foremost integration story of the year. This was the first time that the governor of any state had called out the National Guardsmen and state troopers to enforce a court order for integration.

"Why, there are only two niggers involved," some of the townsmen protested. "Why can't they go to their own colored school?"

But a principle was established, a principle that I saw reversed a year later at Little Rock, when Governor Orville Faubus called out five hundred National Guardsmen to keep nine Negro children out of school. This, in turn, forced President Eisenhower to call out the Federal troops to enforce integration.

The Clay story did not have a happy ending. The school board at Clay went to court and received a court order requiring James and Theresa Gordon to go to the all-Negro Rosenwald school in nearby Providence, Kentucky. The Clay residents won the first round in their battle to keep their schools lily-white. They called it a great victory. They vowed that regardless of future court action their school would remain white now and for all time. They were, of course, wrong. Negro children are now attending white schools throughout Kentucky and, on a token basis at least, throughout the Deep South.

Those who took part in the early battle felt the brunt of the conflict. The fight for integration was lost when James and Theresa were ordered out of Clay Consolidated School, but the fight had really just begun. It was one setback in the long battle, still continuing after a decade, to gain equal opportunities for all American citizens regardless of race, creed or color.

Those who participated in it suffered, of course. James Everett Gordon, a $55-a-week automobile washer in a local garage, soon found himself unemployed. For three days, from September 12 to 15, his two children had attended the white school, the first Negroes to do so. This upset the town of Clay more than anything that had ever happened in its century of existence.

James Gordon knew that by sending his children to the white school his livelihood might be endangered. He knew that revenge might be taken by the powerful White Citizens Council. And revenge it did take. He lost his job at the end of the week. He was told there was no place in the garage for him, even though he had worked there for years. No one in or about Clay dared hire him or was brave enough to do so.

The Gordons had to leave town to seek employment elsewhere. Mr. Gordon told me: "I'm a Christian man. I obey the laws of the land in the best way I know how. I think I did the right thing for my children. Maybe it will help other children, too."

I learned that the Gordons lived in a small frame house in Wheatcroft, some four miles from Clay, in the Negro section of town. Despite warnings from General Williams and others that it was dangerous to venture into this section alone, what with tempers running high, I wanted to meet the Gordons in their own home. I drove my car into Wheatcroft and tried not to let the stares of curiosity and suspicion I found on every side upset me too much. Finally, with the aid of directions from a number of Negro residents, I reached the weather-beaten, sad-looking wooden shack. I found a dozen or more neighbors seated in the parlor, concluding a prayer session. (The Gordons belong to the Mount Pisgah Baptist Church.) After the "Amens" were said, Mrs. Gordon turned to me and said quietly: "I've turned to our Lord a lot since all this started. This is a big fight. We will need God's help to win."

Then she added: "You know, we are not the kind of people who use force of weapons. We do not want to harm anyone. Sometimes I don't understand it at all. I only tried to do what was right for my children. They deserve a good school. I don't see what we did wrong. Now my husband is the one to suffer. I feel sorry for him. It's not good for a man to lose his job and see his family go hungry."

That was ten years ago. I haven't seen or heard from the

Gordons since. I hope that they are well settled now and that the emotional scars have faded.

The five hundred National Guardsmen and sixty state police troopers who took over the little town of Clay, under the direction of General Williams and at the command of Governor Chandler, made American history. But the manner in which they "captured" the town made the story fantastic drama.

I can still see the look on the faces of the farmers, miners, sleepy housewives and storekeepers as they peered out of their windows and saw row upon row of soldiers in army uniform, bared bayonets at their side, trucks rumbling through their main street, an army airplane overhead!

"This is war," exploded one of the men as he opened and just as quickly banged shut his front door.

Yes, war it was: a war against ignorance, prejudice, intolerance and violence.

It was a war to provide every American citizen, regardless of race, creed or color or religion, equal educational opportunities. I found out later, in Little Rock, New York City, Chicago, Boston, Birmingham, Selma, New Orleans and other towns, villages and cities, that the war has not yet been won. But Clay showed the way. Democracy triumphed over hatred and prejudice.

A frozen T-bone steak and a friendly state trooper combined to give me an exclusive, history-making, front-page story!

Enrique Meneses is director of Fotopress in Madrid, and has been bureau chief for *Paris-Match* in the Middle East. He is the author of numerous books and articles dealing with Cuban affairs.

First Days of the Cuban Revolution

ENRIQUE MENESES

WHEN I arrived in Havana from Paris toward the end of 1957, few Europeans were even aware that an armed insurrection had broken out in Cuba. The distance, as well as a traditional attitude of condescension toward all Latin-American revolutions, were the main reasons for the scant coverage given by the European press.

Seven months had elapsed since Fidel Castro's landing in the Niquero area of Sierra Maestra, and Batista's army was becoming more and more violent in its efforts to combat the insurgents. As the rhythm of revolutionary activity increased, so did the police repression, and this in turn produced waves of indignation which resulted more often than not in additional recruits for the revolution.

In the midst of all this, Fidel Castro and his men were, for many Cubans, like a ray of hope burning bright on the peak of the country's highest mountain, the Pico Turquino in Sierra Maestra. There were nevertheless those who doubted whether Castro was still alive. Others thought he and a handful of men were probably fleeing for their lives through the jungle and would not be able to hold out for long. Cubans were, in general, pretty skeptical about Fidel Castro's chances and were therefore reluctant to participate in the fight for fear of being caught on the losing side. This attitude was much more prevalent in the capital than in Oriente Province, which was the cradle of all the independence movements of the last century and most of the uprisings against political regimes.

In March, 1958, the first extensive account of life in Sierra Maestra, complete with pictures of the rebel army and its leader, appeared in the press. Although I began work on the story just before Christmas, 1957, I was not able to get it through to Paris till February. Even so, in spite of all the material I had gathered, Fidel Castro's revolution was still regarded in Europe as just one more Latin-American political upheaval.

For American newsmen it was relatively easy to establish contact with the anti-Batista movement. Miami and New York have long had large Cuban communities that have always taken an active interest in the political upheavals of their homeland. Fidel Castro's couriers frequently passed through Miami, and Mario Llerena was in New York raising funds and buying arms, as well as acting as general public relations man for the "26th of July" movement. In Europe, however, what few Cubans were living there were too far away and out of touch with things to be of any help to a journalist. So I departed for Cuba hoping to make the best of it once there.

I booked in at the Hotel Pasajes in front of the Capitolio, Avenida del Prado 515. Here in these modest lodgings I was just one more Gallego come to Cuba in search of a job. My profession: lawyer, but prepared to accept any kind of work. The proprietor of the hotel had immigrated from Galicia some years before and had two student sons aged sixteen and eighteen. After some prodding, the elder boy, Orlando, confessed to me his one ambition—to join Fidel Castro in Sierra Maestra. I suggested that the first step was to establish contact with the underground and he eventually admitted that a certain blond-haired woman living in the hotel was the wife of the secretary general of the Revolutionary Directorate, who had recently found it advisable to take refuge in the Costa Rican Embassy. I asked Orlando to introduce me to her.

Señora Chamón was about forty and rather scruffy in appearance. I told her I wished to visit her husband at the embassy and she agreed to accompany me. We went by separate buses and met inside, after passing the scrutiny of the Cuban guards posted to check all those entering and leaving. Señor Chamón, wearing pajamas, soon joined us. I explained that I was a journalist and wished to enlist the aid of the underground in getting to Sierra Maestra. The man rather halfheartedly tried to dissuade me, explaining the many difficulties I would encounter, and then gave me the address of an office on L Street where I was to enquire after a certain person using his *nom de guerre*. He also gave me a necktie that I was to wear for the occasion.

Next day I went to the address I had been given. I entered a room containing seven or eight men. A meeting was in progress, but my arrival silenced the proceedings. Over the fireplace were a bust of the poet Martí and a Cuban flag. Sitting behind a large desk was the man I assumed to be the head of the group. I introduced myself to him and explained that I was on assignment for *Paris-Match* and that my mission was to get a story on Fidel Castro in Sierra Maestra. After letting me talk for about half an hour, one of the men who up to then had been sitting quietly in a corner got up and said he was the person I had been sent to see.

I was told to go back to the hotel and forget where I had been and whom I had seen. My request would be studied and an answer given in a week's time.

When I left, one of the conspirators said he would accompany me to the bus stop. He seemed quite friendly and told me he was none too happy about the way his *compañeros* were handling things. He was from Santiago in Oriente Province but had fled to Havana once his face became too well known to General Chaviano and his men. But he had discovered that the way the revolution was being directed in Havana was disastrous; no one would make a decision and no one was prepared to take risks. In Santiago things were different—the rebels got help from men, women and children. When we parted the man told me to take care since my every move would be watched to make sure I was not one of Batista's agents.

For a week I went about my usual business, which was doing nothing. I did not even go to have my visa extended as I did not want to arouse suspicion by a trip to the police station.

When my morale was beginning to droop and I thought I was

on the wrong track, I received a visit from the man who had accompanied me to the bus stop a week before. He said he was called Luciano, though I doubted it was his real name.

Luciano was even more nervous than I was. He began with another speech about how much better revolutionaries the Santiagueros were and I told him that for my part I was pretty annoyed by the fact that several Havana papers had published a report that "an envoyé special from *Paris-Match* had arrived in Cuba to cover the revolution." The news could only have been leaked by someone from the group I had seen the week before. Luciano agreed and offered to help me. We arranged to meet at his house next day.

I arrived at the appointed hour in a modern apartment building. Luciano introduced me to his wife and the three of us set about planning my ascent into Sierra Maestra.

Luciano's wife would make a quick trip to Santiago next day, taking with her a photo of me so I could be identified when I arrived. The Windsor Bar, which was run by Luciano's mother, was to be my rendezvous.

A problem yet to be solved was how to get my photographic equipment to Santiago. A number of foreign journalists had already tried to get to Sierra Maestra, but as soon as they landed in Santiago they were picked up by General Chaviano's men. They were then usually hosted around town by the army for several days, visiting all the night spots and being shown how peaceful everything was. It was totally impossible for the resistance to contact the newsmen under these circumstances, and Santiago was as far as they got. It was therefore essential to land there as discreetly as possible and the first thing *not* to do was to arrive with a string of cameras around the neck (it is surprising how many did just this).

My equipment would therefore have to be sent ahead of me and when Luciano's wife got back from Santiago and gave us the all clear, we devised the following plan. Cameras and film would be sent by bus, since, in their efforts to put a halt to the heavy traffic in arms across the country, rail and air freight were subject to much more thorough inspections by the police and the army. I suggested using the bottom of a crate of rum, but Luciano explained that rum never traveled eastbound, since Santiago was the capital of Oriente Province which was the chief rum-producing region in Cuba. So we settled for a whiskey crate, in the bottom of which I was able to put only a minimum amount of equipment and film. We covered the lot with straw and then a top layer of Johnnie Walker. In a corner of the address label we scrawled a prearranged sign that was to indicate to Luciano's mother that this was not just an ordinary consignment of whiskey so she could make sure it was not pried open by any of her employees, several of whom could not be relied upon.

A few days after dispatching the crate via the Havana-Santiago *guagua* (Cuban slang for "bus"), I boarded the seven A.M. plane from Rancho Boyeros airport. We figured that Batista's soldiers would not calculate on international newsmen traveling so early in the morning when they could get planes on the hour all through the day. I wore a guayabera and clenched an unlit *tobaco* (cigar) between my teeth throughout the flight. When I had to speak I Cubanized my accent so as, I hoped, to be undistinguishable from the other half-million *Gallegos* living in the country.

When I arrived at the Windsor, I sat at the bar in front of the cash register. An elderly woman, rather heavy and untidy, came toward me wiping down the counter. I ordered a coffee, staring her square in the eye. I kept on staring until she moved away and began filtering the coffee, not sure whether she had recognized me. When she brought me the coffee I looked around quickly to make sure there was no one within earshot and said I was a friend of Luciano's. The woman made no reply and went on wiping down the counter.

After about half an hour I got up and asked how much I owed, putting down a five-peso bill. She brought back the change on a saucer—on it were a note and a key. I emptied the lot into my pocket and walked out. There was not much traffic and no one nearby; I read the message. It said I was to go to a house two doors away, Room E second floor. I found myself in a gloomy room with a washstand against the wall and the bed unmade. I waited about two hours before Luciano's mother appeared with food and news. "El Rubio" had been informed of my arrival and had in turn contacted "Deborah." My cameras were in a safe place. Some time later "El Rubio" showed up, hair dyed platinum and dressed all in white. He was quite young, looked nervous but spoke little.

Outside was a black sedan which was to take me to see
"Deborah," who I gathered was the leader of the Santiago
underground. I was taken to a house and led into the living room
where a woman and several teen-age girls looked me over
suspiciously. I sat down in a cane rocking chair, and before long
a young woman came in and said she was "Deborah's" sister.
Then in came "Deborah"—Vilma Espín, now Mrs. Raul Castro—
wearing simple clothes, no makeup, hair pulled back straight. We
discussed the possibility of my getting to Sierra Maestra and the
difficulties involved. The number one problem, she told me, was
the shortage of guides. I would have to be kept hidden in
Santiago for a while, changing hideouts frequently so as to avoid
arousing suspicion. I explained that *Paris-Match* was an important international magazine, with particular weight in Europe.
Deborah smiled and said she knew it quite well—her grand-
parents had immigrated to Cuba from France many years earlier.

For the next two weeks, regardless of however much I protested at being kept waiting so long, I was shifted to a new
hideout every day or so. I never knew when I would have to
move or where. However, in this way I was able to get to know a
lot of people from all walks of life who were generally happy to
tell me what they were doing to help Castro's revolution and
why.

One day when I was alone in a new hideout, I heard over the
radio that a group of Canadian journalists en route for Sierra
Maestra had been turned back at Santiago airport by General
Chaviano. I decided I had wasted enough time, and when my
host arrived I arranged to send an urgent message to Deborah.
Either she provided me with a guide immediately or I would set
out on my own in spite of the twelve thousand troops surrounding all the approaches to Sierra Maestra. That night I got a phone
call from Deborah. "What size shoes do you wear?" she wanted to
know. "Forty-three," I replied, not knowing what she was getting
at. She arrived shortly after with boots, sweaters and fatigue
pants. "You set out at five in the morning."

I spent my last night in Santiago in the home of Dr. Antonio
Busch, an important figure in the Santiago underground. The
house had been empty for months, as Dr. Busch was hunted by
the police, so I could not put on any lights, radio or television.
From what I could see in the moonlight, the house was expen-

sively furnished. I fell asleep around two A.M. and awoke, amazingly refreshed, two hours later. In a few minutes I was dressed and ready to go. A Land Rover pulled up across the street. The driver, a Negro, got out and came toward the house. I went out. Dr. Busch was waiting in the Land Rover with our guide "Napoleon." I was on my way at last.

The road we took to Sierra Maestra was the old Via Real which had been built right across the island by the Spaniards in the seventeenth century. It was not too frequented these days, probably because the pavestone blocks made very bumpy traveling. We generally had to stop before passing any farms or villages along the way, while Napoleon went ahead to make sure the going was clear. We spent one emotion-filled night at a farm owned by Castro sympathizers. We had just sat down to dinner when we heard the whistle of an approaching train. The owner of the house briskly ordered all lights out and told us to get down on the floor. The train passed within forty feet of us, and as it went by a burst of machine-gun fire splintered what remained of the windows on that side of the house. "Batista's soldiers on their way to the front line," explained our host, helping one of his small sons up from the floor. "They always try out their weapons on us as they go by."

Shortly after we had settled down for the night, we were awakened by voices outside the house. It was a band of Senator Masferrer's henchmen looking for the owner of the house, who was suspected of anti-Batista activities. They were drunk and wanted nothing more than to gun down their prey there and then. Napoleon, who had preferred to sleep outside alongside the Land Rover, managed to convince the men that the farm they were looking for was another five kilometers farther on. As soon as they left, we decided we too had better be on our way. Our host had earned a short reprieve—but not for long. While I was in Sierra Maestra I learned that the entire family, children and all, had been liquidated.

The following day we made a halt while Napoleon went on to see if the road ahead was clear. He came back looking worried. We could not go on by road as the bridge over the Yara River was held by the army. And the river itself, swelled by recent rains, was too deep to cross. We decided to go down to have a look for ourselves. There was a strong current and the water was over our heads. We decided to camp there for the night and pray that the level of the water would go down by morning.

We awoke early; the river was a little lower but not too much. We took a vote as to what we should do. Those of us in favor of continuing won, and we went to work securing the Land Rover with ropes. Napoleon waded across the river with two ends of the ropes and set out for help. He came back in about half an hour with a peasant and two zebus. Dr. Busch remained behind, looping the two remaining ropes around a tree while the Negro driver and I waded into the river to prevent the vehicle from overturning or being carried away by the current.

Napoleon, aided by the peasant and his zebus, heaved on the ropes from the other side with Dr. Busch slackening on his end just enough to let the vehicle advance. It was not an easy matter, with the rapidly flowing water up to our chests, keeping the Land Rover upright, and it took us easily two hours before we got it safely across to the other side. The peasant refused to accept any payment for the invaluable help he had given us. It was only then that I learned Dr. Busch was carrying a quarter of a million dollars for Fidel Castro inside his shirt.

We were already in the foothills of Sierra Maestra when we came to a halt at a wooden hut built in a clearing. Its owner was a coffee merchant, and there were about a dozen men, mostly planters or traders, negotiating their wares. We were invited in for coffee. The area was on the outer fringe of what was practically regarded as rebel-controlled territory. By the time we finished our coffee, horses had been prepared for us and the Land Rover hidden in the undergrowth nearby. We said good-bye to our friendly coffee merchant and set out on the last lap of our journey.

At nightfall we reached a mountain refuge where I saw my first rebel in uniform. He was convalescing from a leg wound and was being cared for by two women, one of whom was a prisoner obliged to act as schoolteacher to the children of the region (for most, this was the first schooling they had ever received). The place was called *Minas del frío* (Mines of Cold), and it was certainly an appropriate name. We hardly slept at all because of the gusts of icy wind that penetrated us to the bone and threatened to carry away the roof at any moment.

All next day we continued our ascent on mules and arrived at dusk at a clearing with a cluster of wooden huts. A band of rebels welcomed us. I dropped, exhausted, on the floor of the nearest hut, half propped up on a sack of potatoes. All my bones were aching from the hours of unaccustomed riding. My eyes were half closed already when the shadow of a huge bulk of a man filled the doorway.

"Enrique Meneses?" he asked. I nodded. "My name is Fidel Castro."

It was Christmas Day, 1957.

Life in Sierra Maestra had, when I arrived, settled down to a more regular, though by no means comfortable, existence. Fidel Castro had divided his small force into various columns; one group, under the command of Ernesto ("Che") Guevara, had set up camp in a valley near the Yara River. Here they established a hospital, a bakery, an arms repair shop, a newspaper, a garment factory to make uniforms, and in February, 1958, a Collins radio transmitter mounted on top of a nearby hill. Under Guevara's command were about fifty men, including the well-known lawyer Humberto Sorí Marín who had formerly represented Cuba in the Inter-American Bar Association, and Luis Orlando Rodriguez, owner of the Havana newspaper *La Calle,* which had been shut down by Batista—Fidel Castro was among its former contributors.

The group led by Fidel Castro was known as *La Comandancia* and numbered about twenty-five. Among these were Dr. Martinez Paez, one of the most prominent Havana bone specialists, Celia Sanchez, Fidel Castro's faithful secretary and assistant, Captain Almejeiras, later to become Castro's chief of police, and Castro's mulatto bodyguard, Juan Almeida. *La Comandancia* was flanked by two other smaller groups led by Raul Castro and Ramiro Valdés (now chief of the G-2 secret service). Finally, there was a group of *Escopeteros* armed with ordinary shotguns who were led by an individual called Larita and operated on their own in the foothills of Sierra Maestra around Bayamo, Manzanillo or Estrada Palma.

Batista's army had withdrawn to peripheral positions, leaving the whole Sierra Maestra area, some 2,400 square kilometers, with a population of 50,000 *guajiros* (Cuban peasants), entirely under the control of the rebels. Only one garrison remained in the Sierra—Pino del Agua. In the middle of February, 1958, I witnessed a battle that lasted 24 hours between the rebels and the 250 men of the garrison.

Right on the summit of the Maestra is a long narrow platform of land about 300 yards by 7 or 8 in width. The rebel force assembled there consisted of not more than 25 men. Our hammocks were stretched between the trees on the slopes leading up to the platform; Castro had ordered mine to be put up directly under his as I had no nylon cover to protect me from the heavy dew of the Sierra. I was at least dry, but got little sleep with Castro bombarding me with questions well into the night. He knew I had been stationed for some time in the Middle East, and most of his questions were about Nasser and his land reform.

At five in the morning we were awakened by a light tap on the shoulder; it was a Sunday, and if I recall correctly, February 14, 1958. It was raining and a heavy fog hung over the Maestra. We headed for the extreme edge of the platform facing the peak of Pino del Agua. We took more than half an hour to cover these three hundred yards, stumbling our way over fallen trees and rocks in the fog. The battle line was formed with Che Guevara on the left manning the rebels' one and only mortar (81-mm.) with a supply of exactly eight shells. Fidel Castro, with his telescopic rifle, took the center. On the right was a Thompson machine gun. I took my place beside the rebel leader, who was to give the signal for battle by opening fire. Banks of mist were moving slowly between us and Pino del Agua. Finally there was a break, and we could see the thirteen buildings that made up the garrison. Castro fired, and bullets hailed down on the sentinels, many of whom died without ever awakening. The weather made it extremely difficult to shoot pictures, particularly of the enemy position, which although only about two hundred yards across on the adjacent peak, kept disappearing in the fog.

After about two hours of fire we heard the drone of approaching aircraft. All day we sustained the bombing and 50-mm. machine-gun fire from the planes, but rebel losses were nil thanks to the cover of dense foliage.

Castro had no intention of taking the position, but had prepared two ambushes for the reinforcements he figured would be sent to back up the garrison. Although these showed up however, they withdrew without presenting battle. So at six A.M. Monday, after being drenched in rain all night, we started to move out. Late that afternoon, when we were already some distance away, we saw clouds of smoke shoot skyward from Pino del Agua. Since reinforcements could not get through, the army was abandoning the position and had set it ablaze. Batista's last stronghold was thus dislodged from Sierra Maestra.

We marched without a halt until we reached Che Guevara's camp. After resting for a couple of days, Castro set off again at the head of a column of men. Toward evening, when I thought we were due to stop and make camp for the night, I saw Castro just ahead of me wade right into the Yara River. The column followed, and for more than half an hour we waded waist-deep up the river. A truck awaited us in a clearing and drove us to a village just a few miles outside Estrada Palma.

Castro established his GHQ in the house of the village doctor and immediately started making plans for the coming battle, which was scheduled for two A.M. For the first time Castro's officers refused to let him take part. He lost his temper, but with Celia Sanchez helping, they finally managed to convince him that he was too important for the revolution to take unnecessary risks at that stage. Castro gave me permission to go along with the advance party of rebels, although I knew I would not be able to get any pictures in the dark.

Captain Delio Ochoa led his men to their objective—a sugar refinery that was occupied by about one thousand troops. Escalading the barbed-wire fence, we entered the compound and the rebels dispersed to surround the position. We crawled to within about twenty yards of the sentry dugouts and could see the guards making coffee and hear their radio. At two A.M. Delio Ochoa, who was just to my left, opened fire. Tremendous confusion developed.

This time, the reinforcements sent from Estrada Palma fell into the rebel ambushes. One Captain "Guajiro" destroyed six armored cars, killing more than two dozen soldiers, using Molotov cocktails and then firing on the men as they tried to escape from the flaming vehicles.

At four A.M. we began to withdraw, making all possible haste to be as far off as we could before the aviation was set on our heels.

Whereas Che Guevara preferred to remain in a fixed camp, Fidel Castro and his two flanking groups liked to keep constantly on the move and usually did not sleep twice in the same place. The marches began at six A.M. and did not come to a halt until seven or eight in the evening. Marching through Sierra Maestra, with its heavy undergrowth, was not an easy matter, and conditions were not improved by the frequent rainstorms, but Castro did not want to be caught by surprise in a bombing raid because he remained too long in one place. He was also a sportsman and took pride in maintaining a fast pace; I was not in such good form and had great difficulty keeping up with him.

The food was abundant though monotonous, consisting mainly of boiled yuca and malanga (both root vegetables) with an occasional piece of meat thrown in. News from the outside world arrived by messenger or via the numerous transistor radios the rebels had somehow managed to get hold of.

A week after the battle of Estrada Palma, I decided it was time for me to go back to Havana to dispatch to Paris the material I had gathered in the hills. Also, the underground was preparing to launch a general strike throughout the country and it would be a good opportunity for me to get material on how the revolution was making out in the cities.

Arriving back in Havana without incident, I learned at the hotel that the police had been there to arrest me. The underground offered me a hideout in the home of an engineer by the name of Capó. He was an amateur photographer and had a darkroom which was a godsend for me. I developed all my black and white film and typed out some fifty pages of notes.

Later I was hidden in the home of Piedad Ferrer, a seventeen-year-old resistance worker. Her father, a retired army colonel, was bedridden and totally unaware of his daughter's activities or of my presence in the house.

Preparations for the general strike were well advanced. A radio transmitter was installed in Piedad's house, which was also stacked with arms, ammunition and medical supplies. A steady stream of "visitors" filed through the house, and the servants, who were ardently pro-Castro, had their hands full keeping them plied with food and coffee. Accompanied by Piedad, I visited several churches that had agreed to act as first-aid centers, each equipped with a doctor and a nurse. Hospitals were under close police surveillance and therefore out of bounds for wounded rebels.

The strike was set for April 9. Faustino Perez, head of the Dirección Nacional del 26 de Julio, had given me a sealed envelope that was not to be opened before eleven in the morning of April 9. I opened it as soon as I was alone and learned that the strike would begin at eleven and that a bomb had been placed in a tunnel under the sidewalk just in front of the Escuela de Televisión. At the same time a rebel commando squad was to capture the CMQ TV station and broadcast an appeal to the nation. I was to photograph the take-over on the TV screen and then head for downtown Havana, where the 26th of July student commandos were to make an attack on the naval barracks.

The strike was a total failure. At eleven o'clock the opera program faded from the TV screen, a jumble of voices could be heard in the background and then the station went off the air. Just as I was about to head downtown, the commandos who had attempted to capture the TV station arrived at Piedad's house. They were unanimous in accusing the Communists of sabotaging the strike, and had had to escape through the police lines that had encircled the building rather too soon. They all made ready to seek refuge at whatever embassies they could reach.

Meanwhile I drove through the city; in Avenida del Prado a crowd had gathered to watch a column of smoke and fire shooting up from the sidewalk—the bomb had exploded and set fire to the gas pipes. In the old part of the city everything was over in fifteen minutes. Several youths had been killed by the police and others fled for their lives, disposing of their arms in garbage bins so as not to be caught red-handed.

I returned to my hideout and tuned in to the clandestine radio to learn how the strike was making out in the rest of the country. By the evening of the ninth however, it was clear that all was lost: the strike had been successful everywhere except in the most vital spot—the capital.

During my stay at the Ferrer house, a continual stream of underground members came to see me to inquire after friends and relatives who had taken to the hills. For my part, I was keeping my eyes and ears open for an opportunity to get my stories out of the country without running any risk of their being seized. Parcels airfreighted out of Cuba were carefully inspected by the authorities in order to intercept any instructions or messages from the underground to exiles abroad. It was by now common knowledge that a *Paris-Match* correspondent had spent months with Castro in the Sierra and the police were on the lookout for me and my material.

As no better occasion presented itself, I decided to accept an offer made by Piedad Ferrer. She had good friends living in Miami and by pretending to visit them, she could take my material with her and dispatch it to Paris as soon as she arrived. Piedad was to carry the films and text on her person; we decided to sew the lot between two petticoats, leaving a free area in the back so she could sit down. A friend of Piedad's by the name of Conchita helped with the sewing. When everything was ready, Conchita and I accompanied Piedad to the airport so as to be able to report to the underground if anything went wrong.

Fortunately wide skirts, usually worn over starched petticoats, were the fashion in Cuba at the time, so there was nothing amiss in Piedad's appearance. We went to the bar and waited till we saw her head toward the tarmac. We got up to leave but froze on the spot when we heard her name being paged over the loudspeaker. Thinking all was lost, Conchita went over near the counter to try to find out what had happened. She came back all smiles—Piedad had boarded the wrong plane and the hostess had just noticed her mistake in time. The change-over was made minutes before the Miami-bound plane took off. That night I received a call from Piedad in Miami telling me that her boy friend was fine and had left for Paris as scheduled.

The stories I got through to *Paris-Match* depicted all the aspects of life with the rebels in the Sierra and the resistance workers in the cities that I had seen, explaining who these men and women were and why they had been moved to take up arms against Batista and his regime.

The day after Piedad's flight to Miami, we were back at the airport to meet her returning plane, and had a scare I shall not easily forget. On seeing us, Piedad rushed toward us and in her haste dropped a cardboard box that resounded on the floor with a tremendous crash. The carton broke and the floor was dotted with dozens of small-caliber bullets. I looked around in horror; the airport was reputed to have more government informers per square yard than all the rest of the island. The girls' aplomb saved the day. Squatting down on the floor, their wide skirts fanning out and all but covering the box and its treacherous contents, they proceeded to pick up the bullets and put them in their handbags as calmly as though they were nothing more than lipstick tubes.

Shortly afterward, I began to plan my departure from Cuba. The failure of the strike was bound to set the revolution back for months, and I had other assignments awaiting me. The problem was how to leave the country without being arrested. I tried to get diplomatic help, but the Spanish Embassy said I should try the French Embassy as I worked for a French magazine, and the French said they could do nothing as I was a Spanish citizen. The U.S. consul said he would like to offer me his help but would have to consult Washington first.

Meanwhile the police raided Piedad Ferrer's house. I was arrested and taken to the investigation bureau to be interrogated by Comandante Medina. For twenty-four hours I was manhandled and interrogated. My cameras were smashed against the wall "for having photographed Fidel Castro." I spent almost a week in jail, believing every moment would be my last. The underground, however, had notified the Spanish Embassy of my arrest and finally Señor Capdeviella, Press Attaché, came to visit me in jail; I was taken to see him in the office of Colonel Orlando Piedra, head of the investigation bureau. He told me that the Spanish ambassador, Lojendio, had negotiated my release on condition that I leave Cuba via the next Iberia flight four days hence.

The day of my departure finally arrived. Before leaving the investigation bureau I insisted that my cameras be returned to me, battered though they were. With great reluctance, my jailers agreed; they then offered to collect whatever baggage I might have scattered throughout the city. I declined, preferring to leave behind a number of things I was sorry to lose rather than compromise any of those who had risked a great deal to help me.

At the airport, I learned that a journalist from Ecuador by the name of Bastide had been tortured to death in the cell next to mine just after I had been arrested.

As we flew over Oriente Province, the hostess explained on the microphone: "On your right are the mountains of Sierra Maestra with the highest peak in Cuba, the Pico Turquino."

I looked down on the jungle where I had spent more than three months and where the men I had come to know so well were still waging a war that was to grow in scope beyond anything I could have imagined at the time. It had been a tough assignment, but my stories had filled three issues of *Match*, as well as a cover, and had been syndicated to most of the leading newspapers and magazines throughout the world.

Nearly nine years have gone by since my rendezvous in Sierra Maestra with Fidel Castro, and I am still amused today by the fact that nearly every Cuban I meet went to school with Castro and later joined him in the hills, and nearly every journalist who ever went to Cuba claims he got the first international scoop on the rebel leader in his mountain hideout.

But as we winged out over the Atlantic, all I wanted to do was to set foot in the quietest corner of Europe I could find, and sleep for a month. Little did I suspect that within a fortnight I would be plunged into the midst of the Algerian uprising. And I never did get that month's sleep!

Martin A. Bursten's activities encompass news-gathering in the European Theater of Operations during World War II and numerous overseas assignments for the *Bridgeport* (Conn.) *Herald, Parade* and other publications, in Europe, Africa, the Mid-East and Latin America.

Assignment: Find the Invisible Man!

MARTIN A. BURSTEN

"BERLIN—What I actually had to do to get to meet the man I will call Hans Braun, a leader in Germany's anti-Communist underground, must remain untold at this time. His real name, if mentioned here, could be dangerous in the hands of the Reds. But there was Braun at our rendezvous and, as he talked, the details of an intricate and delicate segment of the underground operations began to fall into place and form a coherent pattern."

THIS WAS the opening paragraph of my September 16, 1956, feature story, which the *Sunday Herald,* of Bridgeport, Connecticut, titled "Outwitting the Soviet Masters" and touted as: "An Exciting Herald Exclusive."

To understand better the significance of the *Herald's* "exclusive," let's look at events in the summer of 1961.

Three million disenchanted Germans had fled their "workers' paradise" in the East Zone of the Fatherland for new homes in the "decadent democracies" where wurst, and beer, and freedom were unrationed.

In an attempt to stem this tide pouring over the "German Democratic Republic's" borders, the Kremlin hastily replaced its Commander of Soviet Forces in East Germany on August 10, 1961. Three days later, the new Muscovite general, Ivan I. Yakubovski, ordered the erection of the now infamous twenty-foot-high Berlin Wall.

If you asked, at that time, what motivated the East Germans to uproot their families from their ancestral communities to seek new lives in West Germany, you would have been told that it was the result of an underground counterpropaganda movement.

Although the German Reds were able to jam broadcasts of Radio Free Europe, The Voice of America, Radio Télédiffusion Français, and RIAS (Radio in American Sector of Berlin), they never could stop inflammatory printed messages from being delivered into the hands of the East Germans.

For ten years the underground movement, which for convenience had labeled itself "The Society of Free German Workers and Peasants in the Soviet Occupation Zone," disseminated millions of printed messages in countless varied forms. The East Germans were told the truth about their unsuccessful farm collectives, crop failures, shortages, repression, rationing, labor conditions, conscription, police terror, and the like.

Their stirring and sharply electrifying messages called, in simple and unclouded phrases, for precipitous dissent, open revolt or abrupt defection.

They urged the Soviet victims to rebel. They beseeched them to cast off their mantle of herd spirit and to break with the traditional German worship of authority and discipline.

The man in charge of this intricate propaganda and psychological warfare operation, which reached into every hamlet, village and city of East Germany through varied means, was high on the "MOST WANTED" list of the Soviet executioners. But he knifed through the Iron Curtain at will, directing the maneuvers of his network of operatives, defying the most perceptive Red intelligence agents. He was known as "Hans Braun," and only very few of his lieutenants ever came in contact with him.

In August of 1956, I was enjoying the lavish facilities of the Bristol-Kempinski Hotel, on Berlin's fashionable Kurfürstendamm, which had been rebuilt with Marshall Plan dollars. I was writing the last of a series of articles on the East German refugees for the Bridgeport *Sunday Herald*. In the initial installment, I had briefly mentioned "Hans Braun" and his phantom underground operations. It apparently had intrigued Lee Danenberg, my publisher, for he fired off a cable to me suggesting, if not ordering, "TRY OBTAIN EXCLUSIVE INTERVIEW CUMHANS BRAUN."

It seemed like an impossible task. But, as Damon Runyon's characters would say, "I got lucky." I got the interview.

Here, then, is—how I got *that* story.

When I received Lee Danenberg's cable, I started my search for Braun by handing out "contracts" all over Berlin—I enlisted refugee camp leaders, military intelligence agents, local journalists, and even a couple of double agents who were serving both sides of the border and who would sell their own mothers for Deutschmarks or rubles.

None of these "contracts" bore fruit. But what finally led me to Braun was a recollection that I had seen large quantities of the propaganda leaflets at the various refugee camps in West Berlin. I therefore had speculated that some of the newly arrived refugees who best knew their way around East Germany were in all probability part of the underground operation and might lead me to Braun.

The UN International Refugee Organization's man, at one of the larger camps, put me in touch with a number of the "pamphleteers," but all of them denied knowing Braun. Each time I pursued a lead I wound up in a cul-de-sac.

But then, as Sigmund Freud maintained, "Nothing happens by accident."

On Sunday morning, September 2, I set out to visit the fabulous Museum Island in the East Sector.

As I drove through the Brandenburg Gate, into the Red domain, nostalgia gripped me. I parked my car and got out to look at the partial repairs of the damage caused by the shelling, back in 1945, by Soviet troops advancing toward the last redoubt in the Zoological Gardens. I stood there for the longest time, it seemed, studying the historic gate which had been built in the eighteenth century on the model of the entrance to the Acropolis in Athens. And I recalled a day, in July, 1945, when war photographer George Grebb, who had shared a SHAEF jeep with me, photographed me with my arms around a group of joyous, smiling, and extremely friendly Russian officers in front of the battered monument.

My pensiveness was abruptly interrupted by a slight man

wearing a frayed jacket, a faded blue shirt and no necktie, who asked me for a match. As I lifted my lighter to his cigarette, I spied his wide eyes peering up at me.

"I may be able to help you find Braun," he said slowly. "Where shall I meet you?"

"At the Pergamon Museum," I finally answered. "In an hour."

The little man nodded his head, and sauntered off. From his accent I deduced he was not a German. Perhaps a Pole, Czech or a Russian.

I crossed the canal to the "Museuminsel" and walked toward the lofty Pergamon Altar, which was being restored. Most of the other museum buildings in the complex, including the Bode Museum and National Gallery, from which priceless art treasures had been removed to Russia "for safekeeping and painstaking restoration," were almost completely destroyed. The Bode had contained the Early Christian Byzantine collection of sculptures, and the National Gallery had boasted fine arts from the Gothic period to modern times, including paintings by Cézanne and Goya.

In a short while, my man arrived. As we strolled leisurely about the grounds, I learned how he had sought me out. He had seen me at the refugee camps, and also at the Berlin offices of United Hias Service, an American migration agency which resettles people in all parts of the world, and with whom I was closely associated. From other refugees he had learned of my search for Braun, and had therefore followed me that morning from my hotel.

Could he put me in contact with Braun? Yes! He had checked me out, and I was a "genuine American correspondent and definitely not a Communist agent." He would help me, but there was a slight *quid pro quo* involved. He wanted my help to expedite the immigration of his sister to Australia, through United Hias Service. He and his sister had miraculously survived the Nazi occupation of Poland and had come to West Berlin in the hope of migrating to a land of sanctuary somewhere overseas. He was willing to remain behind, to continue helping Braun, but he wanted instant security for his sister. She was a Polish textile worker, and since Eastern European refugees were establishing a vast textile industry in Australia, she chose to go to that country.

I consented to help him, and he said he would put me in touch with Hans Braun. Actually, I would have helped him at any rate, for Murray I. Gurfein, former OSS colonel, who was president of United Hias Service, had told me that his organization had sufficient visas and funds with which to move a sizable group of refugees to Australia. I mused about the strange mentality that drives people to seek influential pressure even when it is unnecessary.

For the next two days I stayed close to the Kempinski. On the morning of the third day, at about six o'clock, there was a muffled knock on my door. When I opened it, two men politely pushed their way into the room and bolted the door behind them. The younger and slimmer of the pair offered his hand, smiled lightly, and said: "I hear you have been looking for me. I'm Hans Braun." The heavyset man, apparently Braun's bodyguard, also offered his hand.

Braun had brought with him a bulging and tattered portfolio of heterogeneous samples of the types of printed material disseminated by his clandestine organization. He stressed that this was not the work of amateurs, that the people responsible for producing the material were professional writers, editors, research specialists, political analysts, artists, engravers and highly skilled printers.

I watched Braun as he recounted with obvious excitement and genuine delight his many exploits. He was lean, dark and mildlooking except for his eyes. He spoke with philosophic calm of things that had to do with life, death, revolt and freedom from totalitarianism.

We talked into the afternoon, and although he never identified individuals, he outlined his operations in sufficient detail for me to understand how it is possible for agents to carry out their inordinately perilous assignments and somehow manage to elude the ubiquitous Communist police.

To understand fully the modus operandi of Braun's pamphletbarragers, let's take one incident that Braun related:

Kurt is a factory worker in the East Zone of Germany. They work pretty hard there. They are constantly exhorted to work faster to increase the output, for the greater glory of the East Reich. The Communists call it "Stakhanovism," and it is considered patriotic to be a "Stakhanovite." In the "war-mongering democracies" however, the unions have a word for it, too. It is called the "speedup."

It was payday. Kurt's wife tore open the pay envelope and counted his meager earnings. Her face brightened. There was one bill more than usual.

"Kurt, you've been promoted?"

He shook his head. "Not that I know of. Here, give me that money." He took the bills from her and counted them slowly, carefully. One bill looked funny. He examined it closely. At the bottom, in small letters, was a superscription he had never before seen on German money: "Please turn over."

He turned the bill over. On the back was the following message:

"This is as valueless as the rest of your pay. Bolshevism exploits you and brings you hunger and despair. Chase the Red henchmen out of the land—the ones who make your money valueless."

At this point in Braun's absorbing recital we were disturbed by a knock on my door.

Braun motioned to me to bang on my typewriter while he headed with drawn gun for the bathroom. His associate flattened himself against an inside wall and motioned for me to open the door. Nervously I pulled the door open. A bellhop stood there with a jar of glue that I had ordered the previous day. The bellhop departed, my visitors returned to their chairs in business-like fashion and the interview continued.

Braun was one of the first, back in 1946, to volunteer to organize an underground network of propaganda distributors throughout the East Zone.

In 1947, he was on a train to the Baltic. He was arrested by two Russians who surprised him as he was hiding two rockets stuffed with propaganda pamphlets in a washroom.

It was not the prison sentence that bothered Braun so much as the fact that the rockets had failed to accomplish their task. They were intended to catapult thousands of leaflets into the island city of Rugen, which faces out toward the Scandinavian countries, where thirty thousand slave laborers were reportedly being forced by the Russians to build fortifications and canals.

Braun was first sent to Sachsenhausen, an erstwhile dread Nazi concentration camp. However, even here Braun kept in constant touch with his boys and girls, and he reported that even some Red guards had passed him copies of the latest anti-Red leaflets that had infiltrated into the prison.

He recruited short-term prisoners for underground service in their various home communities after their release.

In October, 1953, he was being transferred to the Brandenburg penitentiary, just outside of Berlin, for a spirited third-degree "seance" with the Russian Secret Police. The prospect of torture and brainwashing was more than Braun cared to face. "I'm very sensitive, you know," he told me. "So I thought I'd escape."

Braun escaped to the West, rejoined his group, met the newcomers in the ranks and started reorganizing the "fieldmen."

There were many ingenious devices developed by Braun's resourceful minions. He recounted them with the delight of an old college alumnus recalling his campus pranks. For instance:

A housewife returning home from the grocery store, irritated by high prices and shortages, would unpack her shopping bag and find a counterfeit ration card. A message on the back placed the blame for food shortages on the East Zone's Communist masters.

A typical scare poster, designed to be pasted surreptitiously over street posters announcing Communist meetings, bore the inscription: "Bolshevism Tears Germany Apart and Brings Us Death." Even that did not appreciably reduce the attendance by a people familiar with death and terror, so Braun played a trump card.

A great Red Party meeting was to be addressed by Wilhelm Pieck, president of the "German Democratic Republic." On the night of the meeting, the hall was practically empty. The infuriated Communist collaborators couldn't understand it. Finally, they discovered the answer. Pasted across the face of each of the posters announcing the meeting was a streamer, which read in bold type:

"CANCELLED—Consult Your Local Papers."

Some thirty such meetings were broken up, and eventually police stationed a 24-hour guard at each poster.

But there were other ways of breaking up meetings. Some gatherings were enlivened by explosions from roof rafters which released showers of leaflets proclaiming:

"MOSCOW LIES."

When the leaflets were collected by the Red stooges and the meeting had regained its composure to some degree, a second explosion would occur in another part of the hall. This time the leaflets would read:

"MOSCOW CONTINUES TO LIE."

Party functionaries were urged to defect with the following message:

"Functionaries and appointees of the Kremlin—think about Beria's murder. The same fate awaits you. Save your life by joining the fighters against Bolshevism."

The leaflets were tailor-made for special circumstances. After a Communist meeting that all peasants had been ordered to attend, a shower of leaflets proclaimed:

"Collective farms annihilate the peasants' freedom. Collective farms bring misery and widespread hardship and slavery. Collective farms are only valuable to the Red slave regime to create slaves."

Braun's organization was largely credited with having incited the June 17, 1953, riots in East Berlin, riots which were finally put down by Russian tanks of the type later used to quell the Hungarian revolt of 1956.

A different line was taken with Russian occupation troops. They were urged to go AWOL and defect to the West. Such propaganda recalled numerous celebrated and well-publicized cases of defection. It spoke of Victor Kravchenko, a captain in the Russian Army who, while working in Washington, D.C., with a Soviet purchasing mission, had abandoned his post and asked for political asylum. He had later—with Victor Lasky—written a book, *I Chose Freedom*, in which he exposed the machinations and double-dealings of high-level Red bureaucrats.

On New Year's Day, 1954, Wilhelm Pieck, East Germany's president, found a printed proclamation on his desk. It was a genuine-appearing proclamation from Pieck over his own signature. It was the first time Pieck had ever seen it.

The proclamation wished Pieck's constituents well for the coming year, and disclosed that he hears from them "constantly by various means and through devious ways and channels." After stating that he is "depressed to learn about the hardships" they have to endure, it goes on:

"As a stooge of the Kremlin I have had to study our Republic

. . . I have found that the people have suffered from hunger for years . . . that clothing is lacking, and there have been no medicines."

The proclamation "sympathetically and compassionately" concluded:

"You have all suffered hunger for years and years, and I don't think it is too much to ask you to wait just a little longer. So cut down your resistance against our system of terror and we will reach our goal. Meantime, be calm, because the symbols of blood, the hammer and the sickle, will be scrapped soon. I greet you with hopes that we will be reunited with our brothers and sisters in freedom in Western Germany."

Pieck offered a generous reward for the capture of the author of this New Year's message and an equally large reward for the apprehension of the intruder who placed it on his desk. The rewards were never claimed.

The young underground leader finished our interview, shook my hand and paused a moment at the door.

"There's a job which must be attended to tonight—part of the unfinished business, you know," he said, and departed.

When I returned Stateside several months later, Jess Gorkin, editor of *Parade* magazine, asked me to do an updated feature on Hans Braun, so I queried my source in Berlin for a summary of Braun's most recent activities.

The reply I received would have, at one time, shocked me into disbelief. But I had learned to expect the bizarre and the fantastic from Braun.

My source reported that Hans Braun, whose real name was Ernst Greiss, was in a West Berlin prison. He had turned double agent and was apprehended while in the process of kidnapping a West German official.

As I said, double agents will sell their own mothers for Deutschmarks or rubles.

Albert E. Kaff is general news manager of the Asia division of United Press International and is based in Tokyo. He has a long history of distinguished reporting in the Far East.

Fire Arrows
Over Quemoy

ALBERT E. KAFF

A MESSENGER delivered my dispatch paragraph by paragraph to the Chinese Government Radio Administration for transmission to United Press International in New York. I slugged each take "urgent."

"TAIPEI—Thirty-two Nationalist Sabrejets fought their way out of a Communist trap over the China coast today and shot down 10 Soviet-built Mig 17s.

"Six other communist jet fighters probably were damaged in a battle against 100 Red planes.

"The Nationalist air force reported no losses among its Sabrejets in the biggest aerial battle of the Quemoy war.

"There were unconfirmed reports that the Nationalists used new American air-to-air missiles."

But were the reports true? Did Generalissimo Chiang Kai-shek's air force launch their "fire arrows" for the world's first missile battle? That was the question which plagued my Chinese colleague, Shullen Shaw, and me while we confirmed and then denied and then reconfirmed our reports of history's first guided missile warfare. Our story was so dramatic and our account was so exclusive that we came close to doubting it ourselves.

The time was September, 1958. For one month, Communist

Chinese shore batteries had been bombarding tiny Quemoy, the Nationalist outpost island located within eyesight of Red China's coast. Heavy artillery shelled the island from three sides in an attempt to prevent air or sea resupply from Formosa, one hundred miles to the east. The Communists expected to starve Quemoy into surrender.

On September 24, thirty-two Nationalist Sabrejets were flying patrols along four hundred miles of the China coast, searching the skies north and south of Quemoy.

Without warning, an estimated one hundred supersonic Mig-17s attacked the slower, older and heavily outnumbered Sabres from several altitudes. The Mig pilots fought with new tactics. Instead of battling above the Formosa Strait as in the past, the Red jets attempted to force the Sabres to fly over the China mainland, where they could be shot down over land. The Communists then could claim that Chiang's aerial forces attacked the mainland and were repulsed in a glorious victory for the People's Republic.

Formations of red Migs lured the Nationalist jets toward the coast. Migs then boxed in the Sabres on three sides, leaving an escape exit open only in the direction of the China mainland.

But something went wrong, badly wrong, with the Communist scheme. Suddenly a Mig exploded in midair, then another. Wings, tails and fuselages burst apart and fell into the blue waters of the Formosa Strait. In just a few seconds, ten Russian-built jets were blasted to smithereens. Every single Sabrejet escaped without a scratch, and the Nationalist pilots turned toward home to report one of their biggest victories since World War II.

Back in Taipei, newsmen were summoned to a heavily guarded brick building with a center tower that dominates the city, the headquarters of the Ministry of National defense.

Smiling, Major General I Fu-en, air force chief of intelligence, announced the Nationalist victory, so lopsided that several foreign correspondents greeted his claim with considerable skepticism.

"But the Mig-17 is a faster and far more maneuverable plane than is the Sabre," one newsman told General I.

"Our pilots are better trained," he replied.

"General, you were outnumbered three-to-one."

"In Korea, the Americans scored against similar odds because of superior training."

"General I, did your planes fire guided missiles?"

He snapped his reply. "Discussions of such matters benefit only the enemy."

The chief of intelligence made it clear he would disclose no details of how the Nationalist pilots achieved what he called their "glorious victory."

Shullen Shaw is an alert, energetic Chinese newsman who taught himself English from the pages of the *Reader's Digest* and popular American detective novels. He grew up in China's vast western province of Szechwan, the nation's rice basket. With two million other Chinese, he fled to Formosa in 1949, when Mao Tse-tung's armies completed their conquest of all China. Shaw joined Nationalist psychological warfare teams which were sent to Panmunjom, Korea, in 1953, in an attempt to persuade Communist Chinese war prisoners to defect to Formosa. He worked for the English department of the Central News Agency of (Nationalist) China before UPI hired him to assist its resident American correspondent in Taipei.

During the 1958 Quemoy crisis, Shaw spent about eighteen hours a day in military headquarters. He made friends with all key officers in the army, navy and air sections. He gulped down his rice, tea and noodles inside the headquarters, rarely leaving the building until after midnight when fighting around Quemoy usually waned. He became almost a part of the headquarters staff, answering telephone calls and even reading official communiqués to his stay-at-home competitors when they called in. Tenacity led Shullen Shaw to the *ho jien* or "fire arrows."

The ancient characters of the Chinese language are ideal for poetry and philosophy. In my own study hangs a scroll presented to me by a Chinese scholar on my wedding day. Its six characters are brushed in black on gold paper: "Albert, labor one thousand years, peace." Pleasant, vague. The Chinese invented gunpowder about 1,500 years ago, but they run into trouble today when they try to put mid-twentieth-century science into their ancient calligraphy.

Several days before the big Sabrejet battle, a Nationalist air force officer told Shaw, "We've had some pretty good luck dealing with the Migs, but just you wait for the next air battle. Then you will really see something."

He refused details. Shaw checked other sources and learned that some Nationalist jet fighters had been equipped with *ho jien*—fire arrows. The trouble with the phrase *ho jien* is that Chinese use it to describe both conventional rockets and sophisticated guided missiles.

Meanwhile, American sources told me that the United States had given the Nationalist air force several Sidewinder missiles. The Sidewinder is an air-to-air guided missile. It is equipped with an infrared device that seeks out the heat from a jet's exhaust. Fired in the direction of an enemy plane, the Sidewinder locates the jet's heat trail and roars down that trail until it hits the plane with a mighty explosion.

For the record, neither the Chinese nor the Americans would confirm officially that Nationalist fighter planes had been armed with *ho jien* Sidewinders.

After General I Fu-en described the 10-to-0 supersonic victory, Shaw sought out his best private Chinese source. "That was it," the source said. "*Ho jien.*"

I cabled New York that apparently the first guided missile battle had just been fought with a resounding victory for an American ally. "It appears," I wired, "that the Nationalists were able to win this lopsided battle by firing Sidewinder missiles for the first time in anger."

My competitors received urgent cables from their head offices: "UPI claims missile battle over Quemoy." No one had the story except us. Were we too exclusive? Were we exclusive because we were wrong?

Queried by my competitors, the official spokesman for the Ministry of National Defense firmly denied my report. "No Sidewinders were fired," he stated.

Shaw and I huddled. That confounded term: *Ho jien.* Old-fashioned rocket? Or the slickest missile in the armory? Our original Chinese source was highly competent, but he would say no more than "*ho jien.*" He would not spell it out in English. Faced with an official denial, we had no choice but to row back and hope that somehow our New York editors would be understanding. "There were unconfirmed reports, officially denied—" I cabled, knocking out the headline meat from my original Sidewinder dispatch. Most other newsmen pooh-poohed our Side-winder claim, and the official defense spokesman continued for days to deny it.

Somehow, Shullen Shaw and I always believed that we were correct. That astounding aerial battle, better than Hollywood, left little doubt in our minds that *ho jien* was in fact the heat-seeking Sidewinder.

Our vindication came from unlikely quarters: the People's Republic of China and the then U.S. Secretary of State, John Foster Dulles. Peking's New China News Agency accused the American puppets of fighting with inhumane missiles. Weeks later, in a speech, Dulles identified the missiles fired by the Nationalists over the Formosa Strait: Sidewinders.

Valiant is the word for Dickey Chapelle, who was killed in Vietnam while covering the war. In 1962 Miss Chapelle received the Overseas Press Club's George Polk Memorial Award and in 1963 she was honored with the highest award given by the U.S. Marines Combat Correspondents Association. Following is a portion of the material for a new book she was preparing at the time of her death.

The Trouble I've Asked For

DICKEY CHAPELLE

I WAS the first reporter accredited straight from America to a rebel fighting force in Algeria.

My clandestine journey from New York to Algeria was a proper cloak-and-dagger operation. Before I left, I received two presents from Abdel Kadar Chanderli, the UN delegate for the rebels. One was a code name. "You are a guinea pig for us, but 'guinea pig' has no poetry as a name. So we'll call you 'Squirrel' . . . after those I saw in Central Park this morning," was Abdel Kadar's verdict.

The other gift was a handwritten piece of white cardboard. The language on it was French. I could translate the words *squirrel* and *a friend* and *unafraid of risk*. This was to be the credential by which the Algerian underground could identify me as their correct kidnapee in Madrid.

Of course my final acquisition before I left New York was a contract for the publication of my stories, if any. It had to be with a press association willing to gamble at least $630—the round-trip air fare to Madrid. Abdel Kadar had said the big services were out. I knew of one news service run by a father and son. There

only one family would need to know where I was going. I
appealed to them and they approved the project and an advance
of more than I needed.

My last instructions were from Abdel Kadar.

"Offer the white card to a man you'll meet outside the
Moroccan Embassy the morning of the third day after you arrive
in Madrid," he said. He told me how to identify him and added,
"Don't let anybody know you're on your way to the Embassy
building."

When the TWA plane landed me there, I mentally reviewed
the plot of every cloak-and-dagger thriller I'd ever read, and
checked into a hotel other than the one to which the airline
delivered me via a cab other than the one from in front of the
hotel, if that's clear.

I gave myself the identity of a tourist interested in Valencian
dancing and Andalusian oranges—no, the other way 'round. For
twenty-four hours I reveled in having nothing at all to do. Then I
thought I'd look in the telephone book in a niche beside my hotel
bed to find the street address of the Moroccan Embassy.

In ten minutes, I was sure of the bad news.

There wasn't any Moroccan Embassy in Madrid.

I glared at the telephone book. And my eyes focused on the
four numbers on the bottom of the cover. They were big and
black. They read 1953.

I came back to life.

There hadn't been any nation of Morocco in 1953. That was the
year France first freed the two colonial countries on each side of
Algeria—Morocco and Tunisia. The Algerians had begun to fight
in 1954 because they had not been freed also. So of course there
was no diplomatic establishment from Morocco in Madrid the
year the phone book had been printed.

The next day I strolled out to a bookshop, bought a tourist map
of the city and, sure enough, found the address of the Embassy of
Morocco.

So I did present at the right place at the right time to the right
person the little white card which said the squirrel was a friend
unafraid of risk. I at once discovered that being "kidnapped" only
meant I'd be escorted to the airport at Madrid, then onto and off
a commercial airliner landing in Rabat, by two men in business
suits with briefcases who looked a little too capable for peddlers

—which was what they said they were. They delivered me to another young Arab man and my kidnapping began in earnest.

My first few days being smuggled from harem to harem in the Arab world taught me that here women did not sleep alone.

"You will not leave this room until and unless we come for you. Maybe today. Maybe tomorrow. You will not speak to any person. Any person at all. Please repeat these orders back to me."

I did, and the young man with the torn shirt and tousled black hair turned on his heel and walked away across the courtyard. The midday August sun of North Africa made me squint as I watched him leave the compound.

I had always wanted to live in an Arab quarter, a *medina*—someday. Before I was done photographing the Algerian rebels, I did it several times. But this was the first day. And with the uncompromising words of my orders still echoing between the white walls of the room where I had been left, I could not seem to remember why I had ever considered being hidden in a harem such a desirable adventure.

I looked around me slowly and realized that I was not actually in one, at least not yet. Undoubtedly, there was a *harem* (a women's part of the household where no male but the husband went) in the compound. But this room obviously belonged to the master of the house. Apparently he had vacated it for my use out of hospitality. I knew that was what he would have done if my news syndicate back in New York had sent a man out here.

But instead they had sent me, for whose sex—outside the harem—there is no traditional Arab code of etiquette. Unshaken by its lack, the doughty Algerian refugees who made up the underground in this little town on the Sahara frontier simply had decided to treat me as if I were a man.

Hence these spacious quarters. The room was long and bare and high; the tile floor red and polished. One of the end walls showed the flag of "free Algeria," the unborn state that was my social host. Under the flag hung a calendar in both Arabic and French characters, a large poster showing an Arab leader on horseback, and a set of small clear color photographs of nine children in rising lines facing the camera. The prints were marked EASTMAN KODACOLOR.

There was one piece of furniture in all the vast expanse of tile—a mahogany cabinet wide as the room and higher than my head. It was pushed against the farther short wall. Its center panel supported a full-length mirror. Spread before it on the tile lay a thick pad, like a comforter, wide as a bed and covered with pink flowered percale.

I sat down cross-legged on the pink comforter and started to turn toward the mirror to see if my nose needed powdering. Then I remembered that I was not wearing any makeup. My blouse was rumpled, my skirt was out of press, my sandals were unpolished and dusty. I had not been told just who I was supposed to be. I did know that my nerves were not unshaken, and when I looked into the mirror after all, I was pleased that it didn't seem to show.

It had all come about because I was being moved like a package through the Algerian underground between neutral soil and the war front. The night before, I had been driven a long way in a fast car en route to a destination beyond this little town. About an hour before dawn, the wiry man at the wheel of the car pulled it off the narrow road and slumped forward.

"Please wake me in a quarter of an hour," he said, not emphasizing any word in his weariness. "My eyes see two roads. That is dangerous."

At the time I chuckled inwardly at the last word. I had never thought to hear Ali call anything he did dangerous. He was a revolutionary who had fled a highly professional job as a scientist in Oran. His prewar background was no less "Western" than my own. But his present assignment was ammunition smuggling, preferably large scale. The hours of work ran to twenty in a day and I never found out what the pay was. I did know the price the French were rumored to have put on his head—$20,000.

I watched the luminous dial of the huge military watch on his wrist and called his name in a low voice after fifteen minutes. He did not stir and it occurred to me that of course the name by which I knew him was not entirely familiar to him, being a pseudonym. I repeated it anyway at a near bellow and he sat upright instantly.

"It's no use. I still see two roads. We will stop in the next town where we have friends and I must sleep."

When our tires slithered through the mud of the village before a building marked simply HOTEL, I was preoccupied with a new worry. A hotel meant a clerk, a clerk meant a passport examination and a police registration card to fill out. And I was now several hundred miles beyond any border where I wanted the police to know that an American reporter assigned to the Algerian rebels existed.

I mentioned the problem as Ali opened the car door. "You don't need to worry," he said offhandedly. In a few minutes he and a sleepy clerk led me to a small room, furnished with a bed, desk and curtained-off washbasin. With the clerk holding an oil lantern which showed Ali's face gray with fatigue, the smuggler said to me almost under his breath, "At eight o'clock in the morning, I'll knock on your door. Be ready to leave at once."

When I woke up, it was not eight o'clock. It was after ten, the sun was pouring hotly through the window and no one was knocking at the door. I tried to imagine what slipup had occurred. Where had Ali gone? Had he been arrested? Shot?

I was hungry, very hungry. But I realized that there would be no breakfast here for me. Not knowing who I was supposed to be, I didn't know what language to admit I spoke, so I would not dare to ask for food or leave the hotel.

I started to play solitaire with a deck of cards that had been in my luggage, murmuring to myself that I could forgive the life of high adventure everything but its ineffable boredom.

And then a new matter of language made me anxious to be bored again. From outside my window I had been conscious of many voices, men's voices. Now I listened and recognized the tongue—French. I wondered idly why, here in North Africa, I heard not one Arabic word. So I risked a long glance past the shutters of my window and, instantly, I understood. The men who thronged the sidewalk wore the uniform of the French Army. They carried rifles and submachine guns. From the building adjoining the hotel there was a constant coming and going of trucks and jeeps, all in war paint and all bearing on their broad front bumpers the tricolor of France.

On assignment to the rebel Algerians, I had been sleeping in the shadow of a French military headquarters.

I reminded myself that guerrilla warfare is traditionally fought in the vest pocket of the enemy. But I added mentally that I didn't know that meant *this* close.

For two more hours, I played solitaire. I kept winning, which further unnerved me. Finally, there came a soft knock. I hoped it was no clerk or maid and opened the door. Ali came in quickly without making any noise at all.

"I am sorry I am so late. But we have to change the route for you. We think the French expected you in the place we were going." He continued to explain but I hardly listened. I was busy watching his hands. He took out a U.S.-made .45, checked the clip (it was full), put it back and worked a shell into the chamber, then reholstered the gun.

Between the General Motors army trucks grinding by outside the window and the Colt in my guide's possession, I remember thinking U.S. arms obviously were indispensable to the conduct of the war—on either side.

"How was your breakfast?" Ali asked.

I told him why I hadn't had any. "Maybe you better tell me how I'm registered."

"Oh, I just said you were a German tourist. I gave the clerk the idea you were of such—such—questionable virtue that I wouldn't want anybody to know I'd driven you here." He paused. "But come—you deserve a good lunch."

Quite formally, Ali escorted me to a large cool restaurant a few blocks away. There were white cloths and flowers on each table. Most of them were occupied—by French officers.

Remembering the .45 and the $20,000 rumor, I did not eat slowly. As soon as we were safely away from the restaurant, I asked with horror why he had chosen to lunch there.

"It is the best place to eat in town. All those officers always eat in that restaurant; it's become their mess now." Then, abruptly: "Do you want to see some French troops leave for the front?" He inflected "French troops" as a curse.

He parked the car, and a military convoy headed toward the border in full battle array passed in front of us. In the lead jeep sat the officer whose table had adjoined ours in the restaurant.

While I was still counting troops—I reached two hundred—a little green sedan had parked behind us. As soon as the last army truck had disappeared, the sedan's driver gestured a greeting to Ali and wordlessly moved my baggage from Ali's car to the back seat of the green one.

"You go with him now. Good luck and *bon courage*," was Ali's farewell. And the sedan's driver, the young man with the torn shirt, unhesitatingly nosed his little car into the *medina*, the Arab quarter. He circled and backtracked among its winding narrow streets until he was sure I had become thoroughly disoriented. Then he parked before a red door in a high compound wall, and led me through it into the room of the mirror and the pink comforter.

There, I had thought I was alone and I started to lean back on the pad. But I caught sight of a boy's face peering gravely through the door of the room.

I knew who it was; my escort had introduced us in the court-yard as we came in, saying, "This lad will be here all the time. If you want anything, please clap your hands"—he demonstrated, twice—"and M'hammed will see to it." The "anything" I might want, my escort amplified with shy gestures, was the use of the washroom on the far side of the court. M'hammed's task was to make certain each time that there was no one in the courtyard to see me as I crossed it.

Now I looked at my young warder. He was probably fourteen and his bones were too big for his flesh. His shirt and trousers had belonged to someone a foot taller, but that had been a long time ago. On his button nose rested a pair of thick-lensed glasses with great black plastic frames. From behind them, bright blue eyes regarded me with the frankest curiosity.

Maybe I had been staring, too.

M'hammed regarded my appraisal as a sign of loneliness and stepped into the room. He took one of the color prints off the wall and brought it to me, holding it close to his face because he was nearsighted even with the glasses. The picture showed two tiny children, a boy holding the Algerian flag and an erect soldier carrying a submachine gun. M'hammed pointed to the flagbearer.

"Me. In Algeria, before we come away," he said. Then he indicated the soldier. "My brother. Killed now." And he walked back to replace the print on the wall, not seeming to hear my murmur of sympathy.

He was still determined to provide me with company. He sat down cross-legged on the tile floor in front of me. I had already taken my deck of cards out of the gray camera case. I dovetailed the edges of two half-decks with a riffle, then made a bow of my hands and let the cards flip from my palms to my thumbs; it was a shuffle I had learned from a Missouri gambler whom I was sent to interview when I was a tyro newspaperwoman.

M'hammed was fascinated. He hitched himself closer to me and reached for the cards. I divided the deck in half and pushed the two piles toward him. He found the riffle difficult and it took him perhaps half an hour to master it. He was a hard taskmaster to himself, beginning the whole trick over each time he failed to get the cards to whirr as I could.

By this time, we had an audience. There were two barefoot little girls hanging in the doorway, one in a pink smock and the other, very tiny, in a blue dress short by inches of modesty. "M'hammed," breathed the older respectfully.

This earned her a spate of Arabic which was clearly, "Go away, woman; this is no business for girls."

But after M'hammed was sure he had the shuffle down pat, he relented and invited the girls in, first pointing out to me their faces on the color prints. They sidled across the tile, stepping shyly to a point just short of my outstretched hand. After M'hammed had demonstrated the Missouri shuffle to them, he recollected gruffly that they had names—"Soroya. Amina," he said—and they were torn between giving me their hands to hold for a minute and giving him their wide-eyed, giggling applause.

So then there were four of us sitting cross-legged shuffling cards.

When M'hammed wearied of this, he decided it was time for me to visit the washroom and he directed me to it a little like the traffic policeman at Times Square.

In the courtyard, I had noticed a whole wall of woven reed containers, huge and perfectly cubical. I thought they were provisions, and on my second walk through the court I looked again. In a way, my hunch was right; each was stenciled heavily in black ink GUNPOWDER SECOND GRADE 50 KILO. I tried to count the containers with a glance—seven across and five high. Almost two tons.

My mental arithmetic reminded me of something. I did not yet know how to count in Arabic. So I sat down on the pink comforter again and separated the ace to the ten of spades from my cards. I laid them on the tile before me and counted out loud in English and French. M'hammed got the idea at once and transferred to me the iron discipline he had shown in learning the shuffle. First he made me say the numbers, then copy them into my notebook in figures and phonetics. Finally he took the note-book out of my hands and wrote into it the numbers from one to twenty, and the entire graceful 29-character Arabic alphabet. He was critical of my accent as I read the pages back to him.

When I protested that *wahid* to *hashrah* (one to ten) was enough to memorize in one afternoon, my youthful teacher kibitzed my solitaire game. But he did not let my scholarship suffer. Each time I put down a card, I had to say its number aloud in Arabic; if I forgot, he simply picked up the card and handed it back to me. He also figured out the rules for building on aces in my game—I was playing patience—and correctly pointed out every move I missed. Within an hour or so under his steady gaze, I grew afraid to cheat myself.

I began to wonder about the wisdom of having received the little-girl visitors. What if they described the stranger in their father's room to a neighbor's family? My orders had been to talk to "no person."

I was still concerned with this when the doorway of the room suddenly darkened. The presence was a woman—barefoot, huge, magnificent. I guessed from her features that she must be M'hammed's mother. Her face was wreathed in flesh as well as headdress and she was great with fat and pregnancy. She weighed perhaps three hundred pounds and wore a rumpled full-skirted dress of blue flowered print. Almost buried in her round pink chins were half a dozen necklaces of beads and gold.

On the threshold, she hesitated a moment, erect and smiling. I could see that she was cradling a baby in one vast elbow. She did not waste a word of greeting, knowing we had no language in common, but simply undulated across the room to where I was rising and performed the one gesture that most expressed trust.

She thrust the baby into my arms.

I used some words but I knew they were not needed; Earth Mother on the spot had established a better kind of communica-tion. I found I was deeply touched. I was overtaken by a rush of feeling that I had known her since I was a little girl myself.

The baby was a black-haired boy in blue blanketing wrapped to a point below his feet. He had been sleeping, and he paid me the compliment of waking up on my lap without crying while his mother stood before me, beaming and nodding.

Now that I had Earth Mother's blessing, the other daughters

paid me a visit. There were two, and they shook hands gravely
before settling on the floor to admire M'hammed's Missouri
shuffle. Fatima was thirteen and Fawzia, a willow tree of a girl
whose heavy braid of brown hair fell far below her waist, was
sixteen, they said.

I had just come to realize that the "you will talk to no one" in
my orders evidently did not include the women of this household
when the man of the house came into his usurped chamber.

Earth Mother and the two daughters arose and disappeared
instantly and silently. M'hammed went as far as the door, hesitated, then stepped outside.

His father was a tall, bony man, hawk-nosed and graying, bent
a little about the shoulders. He was tieless, wearing a neatly
pressed striped shirt and trousers which bore a crease. We
discovered we could manage something like conversation in
pidgin French.

He asked me if I had eaten, if I was comfortable, if M'hammed
was taking good care of me. Then he gestured out the doorway,
indicating the virtual wall of gunpowder. He spoke at some
length but too fast for me to understand. Finally he gestured for
me to follow him.

He led me into another room off the courtyard and here, for
the first time, I met a group—there were six men in the room—
of Algerian rebels. They were all in their twenties and though
they wore disheveled, Western-style civilian clothing, there was
no question of their vocation—or avocation. A field-stripped BAR
gun lay across a little table just inside the door, and every man
there wore a gun or had just laid his holster aside as he sat down
on the floor.

I was presented to them with some ceremony. The six young
men and the one old one formed a circle and indicated I was to
join them. A chunky blond man in a rumpled blue shirt such as a
sailor wore spoke English, and he welcomed me on behalf of the
rebel forces.

"It is very dangerous for you to be here," he finished with an
approving smile in which his colleagues joined him. Perhaps he
and I were not thinking of the same danger, but I was tempted to
agree with him, considering the number of loaded weapons in the
small room and the casualness with which they were being
handled, almost fondled.

"What do your people believe about our revolution?" and
"When will America stop arming France?" were the opening
gambits of our conversation. Feeling as much interviewed as
interviewer, I asked for the men's stories and they frankly volunteered them. All had fled Algeria and two said they were the only
survivors of their respective families. Three told me they had
been studying in French universities before becoming "freedom
fighters." One of their questions was, "Why did the Hungarian
revolutionaries stop fighting the Russians? Why didn't they flee to
the mountains as we have?" They seemed surprised when I told
them Hungary was almost all one great plain.

I asked each of the six in turn, "Are you a terrorist?" As I
framed the question, I thought how almost any Westerner would
answer it in this situation with only a stare or perhaps a flip
"What do you think?"

The Algerians did neither. A simple yes—in French—was one
answer. "Against terror one uses terror," said one man placidly in
German, speaking for himself and the men next to him. "I am a
counterterrorist," said the man who was acting as interpreter.

M'hammed's father had poured us tea, and we had exchanged
cigarettes by this time. M'hammed himself came hesitantly into
the room. He studied the circle; finally it was clear that he did not
approve of a woman sitting with men through the traditional tea
ceremony, and he had never seen it happen before. He whispered
something to his father, and the father gestured for me to follow
M'hammed out into the courtyard.

As I was making my farewells, the translator said, "I must not
forget to tell you something. Did you understand what the old
man said about the gunpowder?"

"No."

"As long as you are staying here tonight, he thinks you ought to
know that if the French Army raids the compound, he will
explode it. He does not want to be taken alive. He has been in a
French prison before, for a long, long time."

I said, "I understand," and stepped into the court. The sky was
very dark and near and the stars in it very bright and close.

It was the evening meal for which M'hammed had fetched me;
I might sit with the men but apparently I was to eat with the
women.

Not exactly with them, I quickly saw, but in the same room as they. And this room was indeed the heart of the household, the *harem*. That I knew from its one piece of furniture—half chest and half sideboard, upon whose shelves were gleaming glasses and china. Otherwise, the room was a match to the one I had been occupying.

But here, it was crowded. There was Earth Mother and Grandmother, whom I now met for the first time, the four girls and the baby, and M'hammed and I.

My hostesses had set my place on a small high table at one end of the room, and a straight chair stood beside it. The table was covered with a flowered plastic cloth. A knife, fork, two spoons, napkin and glass of water were on it. So were bread, butter, grapes and marmalade.

The rest of the women began to eat as they usually did, from a single huge enameled basin set on a raised wooden tray at the other end of the room. They sat on the floor and used only spoons. M'hammed first ladled my dinner into two small china plates and carried them carefully over to me. There was a drumstick of roast chicken and a bowl of stewed peppers in oil.

I cut off a piece of meat and it was delicious, but I decided the splendid isolation of a table and chair was too lonely a way to eat. I picked up the plates, carried them back to the circle of women, emptied them into the common basin and sat down with my spoon in my hand. It was a very friendly meal.

We women took our evening tea afterward, sitting cross-legged on the tile of the courtyard. The rooms of the men were dark and silent and again I felt the intimacy of feminine communication-without-words which Earth Mother had first brought to me in the afternoon.

Then the great red gate of the compound banged open, announcing the return of the man of the house. By this time I was so thoroughly immersed in *harem* custom that I hastily fell silent and scrambled to my feet exactly as the rest of the women did.

The father was not alone. Beside him walked an erect figure in a gleaming white hooded robe, the traditional Arab *djalabba* of the area.

The two men motioned me into the room I had occupied all afternoon. They lighted an oil lantern, then closed the door and the shutters. The old man's companion threw back the hood of his robe. It was lined with azure satin. As it fell, the neckline of the

robe opened back; under it I could see that the man wore a khaki
army shirt with insignia on the epaulets. The face above them
was brown-bearded, improbably even-featured. The eyes were
blue and heavy-lashed.

The officer did not identify himself, pointedly. By bearing and
speech, I could imagine him in no other role but that of a tactical
commander. When he began each sentence with the traditional
military formula, the words, "You will . . . ," I was sure that I
was right. One sentence he used twice was, "You will not have a
jeep when you photograph us in Algeria."

He also praised me, warned me, checked every item of my
personal gear from boots to cameras for its ruggedness, and
handed me a document and a ballpoint pen so I could sign it.
He laughed long and low when I wryly commented that it was
the same kind of document every army in the world seemed to
have in generous supply—a release form saying that if I were
killed or wounded neither I nor my heirs could sue the Algerian
government.

Then the lantern was extinguished, the concealing *djalabba*
again hid the uniform and the shutters were opened. The old man
said, sweeping his hands wide to indicate the whole room, "My
home is your home," and "I will return tomorrow," and the two
men melted into the night.

When the gate had closed behind them, M'hammed came into
the room. "You sleep now," he instructed me.

I nodded and removed one of my sandals, sitting cross-legged
on the edge of the pink comforter.

"No, no," said M'hammed. I was puzzled. I removed the other
sandal.

Where my behavior had only bewildered M'hammed before,
he was now clearly scandalized. He continued to shake his head.
Finally he burst into a torrent of Arabic, checked himself and
picked up my sandals one in each hand.

He motioned me to follow him, leading me to the room of the
women. Now there was hardly room to step in it, for each of
them was already lying on a comforter on the floor. In their midst
was a single empty place marked not by a thin pad but by a thick,
worn mattress.

Now I understood, and sat down on the edge of it. As I swung my bare feet onto it, M'hammed set my sandals neatly at its foot and declaimed, satisfied that all was right with the world again:

"Women do not sleep alone."

He left the *harem* with a firm tread. And I had officially arrived at my new assignment.

Gertrude Samuels is a staff writer and photographer for *The New York Times*. She is the author of *B-G: Fighter of Goliaths: The Story of David Ben-Gurion*, and her award-winning articles have appeared in many magazines.

Hitler Slept Here

GERTRUDE SAMUELS

THE FOLLOWING excerpt is the lead from my 4,000-word story in *The New York Times* magazine of January 5, 1964, headlined:

GERMAN DEMOCRACY—A REPORTER'S NOTEBOOK

WEST BERLIN

Every night at the Porcupine, the popular satirical cabaret here, one skit that gets roars of approving laughter goes this way:

"Of whom are the Russians afraid?" one actor asks another.

"Of the Americans." (Laughter.)

"Of whom are the Americans afraid?"

"Of the Russians." (Laughter.)

"Of whom are the French afraid?"

"Of de Gaulle." (Laughter.)

"And of whom should the Germans be afraid?"

"The Germans don't have to be afraid of anyone but themselves."

The punch line convulses the house.

Partly, the reaction seems a reflex to the actors' exquisite timing. But mostly the roars of approving laughter reflect the new mood of self-confidence and self-satisfaction of a people who no longer fear that they have anything to fear. Conversely, the skit and its reception seem to point to another truth: the awareness that a good deal of distrust of Germany remains in the world outside.

Industrial West Germany, 1964, is again the most populous, the wealthiest, the most industrious and disciplined nation of Europe. But, many individuals among her neighbors and allies wonder, is the abstract ideal of the Federal Republic—democracy—truly established? Could the German people again turn to dictatorship?

I had not been back to Germany for many years, and, in fact, had come to feel that Germany was one country I could live without forever. But late in 1963, I was asked to cover a unique mission of "understanding" to that land—comprising a dozen representatives of the American Jewish human relations agency, the Anti-Defamation League of B'nai B'rith. Their main thrust was to attend conferences with German experts in government, education, justice and labor groups to exchange knowledge and techniques of democracy—so that, they hoped, Nazism could never happen again. Some members of the American mission were refugees from Hitler's Germany; some had fought the Nazis in the battlefields of World War II. By living with German Gentile families and studying youth groups, schools and the government-in-action, the mission wanted to see for itself the effectiveness of German democracy and its attitudes toward the Jews.

We spent a month in Germany, moving around official circles, touring towns and villages, talking wherever we could to the people. I wrote several stories for *The Times* daily and magazine and for *Harper's* magazine on those experiences. The Americans' findings illustrated basic contradictions in German life today, above all, that while Germans regarded a parliamentary form of government as democracy, there was yet little awareness that democracy must become a way of life that permeates all personal relationships.

The mission eventually recommended that more responsibility for social action be shifted to private groups to encourage more initiative, at the citizens' level, for their own affairs; that greater emphasis should be put on early teaching in school of respect for other people; that all Nazi war criminals should be prosecuted and appropriate punishment given (the Federal Supreme Court itself having rebuked the courts for imposing sentences that were "too mild").

Altogether, as the harsh spotlight of the German mass media of press, television and films still keeps warning Germans, much remains to be done to clean up the Nazi record.

Wherever I went in Germany on this trip, I found that I could do nothing about the ache that was always near the surface of my feelings. There are only about 30,000 Jews left in Germany (compared with 560,000 Jews in 1933). Nearly all live in the major cities of West Germany, and almost none are in East Germany. The Nazi death machine had managed to kill nearly 6,000,000 of prewar Europe's 7,500,000 Jews.

Certainly the ache was there, in part appeased, in part deepened, by human contact with the Germans, young and old. The story-behind-this-story is not so much one of ingenuity and initiative in "getting the story"—for Germans are only too eager at this point in history to accommodate visiting Jews—as it is of human interest and human frailty. It concerns (1) Wolfgang, who met his first Jew; (2) some schoolgirls' reaction to a Jewish poet; and (3) Herr Dreesen, who knew Hitler.

One Sunday morning, our team was traveling by chartered bus from the hotel near Bonn to Frankfurt. In Frankfurt we were to go to the cemetery with its rows of 1942 markers—commemorating the mass suicides of Frankfurt Jews who had preferred death to deportation. Our young German driver, who spoke no English, rolled the bus along the autobahn, passing cyclists peddling furiously down to the river; past the neat, geometric patterns of green and yellow fields; past storybook houses with their local flags waving; past the remarkable number of Mercedes-make cars. A sunny Sunday morning in Germany—with everyone going somewhere.

Perhaps because of the memories we were all carrying, the "Senator," so called because he was a civil rights attorney in Washington, tried to break the mood in the bus. In Yiddish, which is sometimes understood by Germans, the "Senator" asked the bus driver: "How do you like driving these American Jews around?"

The young driver took his eyes off the road momentarily. He turned to the "Senator" with a pleasant shrug. He hadn't understood. A German-speaking member of the team translated. The driver looked at the translator steadily for a moment.

"I can't find a difference between people—between Jews and non-Jews," he replied quietly.

The traffic was getting heavier. Farms came down to the roadside. Cows lazed near the highway. The generous sunshine warmed the hills and pines and clearly marked traffic signs.

Suddenly, effortlessly, the driver identified himself with the mood of the group.

He was, he told us, 33-year-old Wolfgang Arndt of Mecklenberg, which was now in the Russian zone. His father had been killed in the war by the Russians. He had a wife and a small son. His great hope, he said with a smile, was one day to be able to emigrate to America like some of his friends.

"Did you ever meet a Jew before this group?" the "Senator" asked him, through the translator.

"*Nein.*"

"Did you know we were Jews?"

"*Nein.*"

The blue-eyed, blond young man, lean and muscular in his brown sweater and slacks, threw the "Senator" an engaging grin.

"You don't carry signs on your bodies."

The travelers smiled with him.

What had he thought a Jew looked like?

Wolfgang's peasant face reflected honest puzzlement.

"I remember vaguely having seen pictures of Jews," he replied, "and everyone in the other times tried to indoctrinate the children. But nothing has remained with me."

He took a hand off the wheel to gesture.

"*Ja!* In 1933 the people were taken in. The people didn't realize what policies Hitler would actually follow. Making war was the big mistake. I can't find a difference between people. I can't understand why a people tried to exterminate another group of people."

The translator told Wolfgang—who was three years old when Hitler came to power and fifteen years old when Hitler lost the war—how his family had been killed in concentration camps. Wolfgang bent his head, listening, nodding, frowning, believing.

"I had a deep compassion—*mitgefühl*—for the Jews," he said, "who were gassed in the camps and perished. But I would like not to forget that there were quite a number of non-Jews trying to help Jews. My father was killed by the Russians, but I don't hold that against the Russian people. Maybe," he said earnestly, "one cannot forget. But one should try to forgive."

"One can try," said the "Senator."

Some teachers are trying to go beyond the inadequate textbooks on the recent history of Germany, and so deliberately work against what is a conspiracy of silence in many areas.

I saw this at the Elly-Heuss-Knapp Schule in Bonn, a modern lyceum for girls. A class of sixteen- and seventeen-year-olds were studying the works of Else Lasker-Schuler, the lyrical German Jewish poet of Weimar Republic days. (She fled to Palestine in the thirties and died there.)

Once a month, their teacher, Frau Meyer, the wife of a Protestant minister, used great literature in this way to focus attention, though obliquely, on Germany's Nazi period. I asked the girls how their parents would feel if they were told that the class was studying the poetry of Lasker-Schuler, a Jewish poet. One dark-haired girl answered with surprise: "She is not just a Jewish poet. She is a very great poet who has written a beautiful poem."

Another told me, in a proud tone: "We do not distinguish today between Germans and Jews."

Was that because of the teaching in this class?

"Partly," she told me. "But mostly because of our own convictions. We weren't yet born in the Second World War, and we didn't know Hitler. But we try to go further than our parents, and we try to understand more than our parents did."

That these girls wanted—needed—to identify with positive causes that foster understanding was clear to me in the way they described certain missions of "penitence" that some scores of German youths have made to countries once overrun by Hitler, and to Israel. When they learned that I had been to Israel several times, they asked eagerly:

"What is a kibbutz like?"

"Can one really build in the desert?"

"Where will the water come from?"

The poetry lesson stopped.

I spent the rest of the period telling the class about Israel, about the land and the people, and about the Anne Franks who never got to Israel.

The 55-year-old headmaster who listened, too, told me with a

candor rare among the older Germans: "Looking back, I know
that my generation were cowards. We feel that these children
must be interested."

The story of Herr Dreesen, who knew Hitler—was, in fact, Hitler's host—is linked in a way to the German statute of limitations
on war crimes. West Berlin's attorney general finally charged Hitler with mass murder between 1933 and 1945. It has always been
presumed that Hitler, with his mistress Eva Braun, committed
suicide in the bunker behind his Chancellory on April 30, 1945.
But just in case he should show up, this legal step, which
interrupts the statutory period of twenty years, now insures that
Hitler can be prosecuted for quite some time.

Not only can Hitler be brought to court, but while awaiting
trial he can even be offered his old bed. I learned, while in
Germany, that Hitler's favorite retreat on the Rhine—Herr
Dreesen's inn, also called the Rhein-hotel Dreesen at Godesburg
—has been saving it.

This historical hors d'oeuvre was dished up to me while being
taken on an inspection tour of the hotel, in particular, Rooms 106,
107 and 108—Hitler's one-time suite. The hotel has remained in
the Dreesen family, and my guide was one of the brothers
Dreesen.

The hotel is in a spot that is sentimental to Germans. This is the
neighborhood of the Wagnerian operas and part of the German
mythos—the legendary story of gods and men. From the hotel's
balconies on the west bank of the Rhine, one looks out on the
castled crag of Drachenfels (the Rock of the Dragon) and,
behind the great rock, usually lost in mist, the chain of the Seven
Hills, the Siebengebirge.

Here Hitler was wont to brood, as he stared out from the
flower-decked balcony of his bedroom, Room 106, listening to the
Lorelei, and planning his plans. Here it was that he decided on
the "blood bath" of June 30, 1934. Here he came, savoring his
triumph, when his troops went into the Rhineland in 1936. Here,
on September 22, 1938, he gloated over his pre-Munich conferences with Britain's Prime Minister Neville Chamberlain.

For obvious reasons, the Dreesen was interesting to the mission
which I was covering. Our first request, after settling into the

hotel, was to see the old Hitler suite. And there at last were the rooms that had held the man and had known his thoughts.

I don't know what I expected to find, but they were quite ordinary rooms. Occasionally, I was told, they are rented to hotel guests.

Room 108 is a conference room, with a long, oval table for the conferees, a few plants and some nondescript prints on the walls. No portraits. Adjoining it, Room 107, is a small reception room, furnished with a small sofa and chairs. And adjoining that, Room 106—the bedroom.

In Room 106 were dark mahogany twin beds, a small table and two chairs, and French windows that opened to the balcony and splendid views of the Drachenfels. The storied river was humming with traffic—French and Swiss and German barges of coal, oil and wheat, looking like freight trains on the water. Almost unbelievably as we stood there, a storm broke over the Seven Hills, lending a nice Wagnerian obliggato.

"All the furniture in the room has been changed," Herr Dreesen was saying.

He was a tall and intensely civil man. Everyone in the hotel was intensely civil. The reception desk people had been apprised of our arrival, but it was clear from their muted, earnest reaction to us that if they were not seeing Jews here for the first time, at any rate they had never seen them en masse as now, and their best foot was forward.

Now Herr Dreesen described to us how the rooms had been changed, and where Hitler liked to stand on the balcony, and there seemed to be—could I be wrong?—just a tinge of historical pride, such as one can hear in Morristown, New Jersey, when a guide intones that "George Washington slept here."

I found his information fascinating.

"All the furniture replaced?" I asked.

"Yes, all thrown out."

Someone cracked, apparently to relieve the emotions that we were feeling, "That's so no one can say that the Germans don't throw things away."

Herr Dreesen joined in the laughter.

"Well, I should add," he added, "that everything has been thrown out except his bed."

There was a silence.

"You didn't throw his bed out?" I asked.

"No, we kept that."

"Why?"

He stared back at me, seemingly perplexed. He shrugged his shoulders.

"We decided to keep it."

"What is it like?"

"It's a usual bed, a big bed. We have it in the cellar."

"Why have you kept it? Out of sentiment?"

"Oh, no, no, no," he said. He turned away.

"May I see it?"

"Yes, certainly. Later on."

I stayed at the hotel for several days, meeting the government people in nearby Bonn as part of the mission's studies, visiting university students. But though I asked several times over the next days to be taken to the cellar to see the bed, that part of my tour was never arranged. I left Godesburg without seeing Hitler's bed.

In case the Führer should turn up, I hope the sheets have been changed.

Tad Szulc is Madrid bureau chief for *The New York Times* and the author of many published works. He was awarded the Maria Moors Cabot Gold Medal in 1959.

The New York Times and the Bay of Pigs

TAD SZULC

SOME OF the best stories, I believe, are the result of fortuitous accidents that, blindly, lead the unsuspecting reporter to his first clues. In the case of the Bay of Pigs—a story that involved *The New York Times* and me in a controversy that still seems to be alive more than five years later—it all started at the Mac Bar in the MacAllister Hotel in Miami during the cocktail hour of Friday, March 31, 1961.

The reason I was having a martini at the Mac Bar was utterly unrelated to Cuba or any planned invasions of Cuba. Instead, it was my first drink after arriving in Miami from Panama to spend the Easter weekend with an old friend and his wife. At the end of six years as a *New York Times* correspondent in Latin America, I had been transferred to our Washington bureau, but the paper agreed it would be a good idea if on my way home I paid farewell calls in all the capitals where I had worked and visited all these years.

Actually, Miami was not on my original itinerary: the plan was to make the last two stops in Panama and Caracas, Venezuela, and then head for New York. As it happened, however, I caught my final tropical bug in Panama and spent a few days there recovering. With the Easter weekend approaching, there seemed to be no point in going to Caracas to see officials, so I decided to hop over to Miami to see the couple I had known intimately during my earlier reporting tours in Cuba.

As I landed in Miami, nothing could have been further from my mind than Cuba or the exiles' plans to launch an invasion to topple Premier Fidel Castro's regime. Having covered many phases of the Cuban story after Castro's capture of power, I was naturally aware of the exiles' activities in general. I had even read a story in a November, 1960, issue of *The Nation* on the training of anti-Castro guerrillas in Guatemala and, subsequently, a confirming dispatch by my colleague Paul Kennedy in *The New York Times* of January, 1961. But, for all practical purposes, Cuba no longer was my story and I had no reason to concern myself with any of it.

Yet, even before I finished that first martini, I was suddenly and deeply enmeshed in the invasion story. My Miami friend had professional reasons to be closely in touch with the Cuban situation, and, as we sat at the bar, he was telling me that events in which I might be interested were beginning to shape up in Florida and elsewhere. My ears perked up—it is a professional reflex, undoubtedly—but before I could ask any questions, another man joined us at the bar. He was a young Cuban whom I had known well in Havana as an active underground worker and one of my best contacts with the emerging anti-Castro groups.

We chatted pleasantly for a moment, then I asked what had brought him to Miami. His answer, in effect, ended my restful Easter weekend. He told me that he and his friends were engaged in a new effort to oust Castro and that the United States stood behind them. He was in a hurry just then, he said, but he would be glad to meet me the next morning to fill in the details. He left, but a few moments later an American whom I had known in Cuba as a navy officer walked past me with a quick greeting.

All this was becoming very intriguing—sufficiently intriguing for me to decide to do some nosing around Miami before resuming my trip north. My first notion was to gather enough general information to pass it on to my editors in New York so that, if warranted, a correspondent could be assigned to the story while I reported for work in Washington in a few days, as scheduled.

But after twenty-four hours of intensive reporting—including conversations with a half-dozen Cuban friends whom I trusted—I knew that I was on top of a major story. The existence of training camps in Guatemala was confirmed to me. I discovered that intensive recruitment was underway in the Miami area and that, every night, young men turned up at the Coral Gables head-quarters of the Cuban Revolutionary Front—the exiles' principal organization—for departure for an unknown destination. My second evening in Miami, I, too, appeared at the Front's building to find a group of young men saying farewell to relatives and friends before boarding trucks for a trip somewhere in the area. Having by then already rented a car, I discreetly followed one of the trucks to what turned out to be the old airfield of Opa Locka. There were armed civilian guards at the gate, so just as discreetly I went back. The suspicion was confirmed: the young Cubans were being flown somewhere, and somewhere could only be Guatemala.

Other conversations produced the fact that the preparations for an invasion were widely known in the large Cuban community in Miami, which meant, among other things, that agents of Castro's G-2 military secret police knew at least as much as I did. I discovered that several Cuban physicians of my acquaintance were on standby to report for duty aboard a hospital ship, and that a number of young girls I knew were being trained as nurses. There was an air of urgency about all this activity: secret meetings, people vanishing in the night, blood plasma being collected.

I also became aware that the moving power behind this whole operation was the Central Intelligence Agency. My Cuban friends spoke freely—and proudly—of the CIA's backing, and, one evening, I even received the telephone number of a mysterious personage known as "Frank Bender." This "Mr. Bender" was described to me—quite accurately—as CIA's chief representative in the exile movement and the man running the whole show. Just for the hell of it, I phoned him. As I had been told, he spoke English with a foreign accent, probably German. And as I had been warned, he refused to see me. "Mr. Bender," it seemed, saw people only if they were brought to him by his American or Cuban associates. I might add that I never met him and that, to this day, I am not sure I know his real name.

In any event, it was now obvious to me that I had reached a point in my reporting when something had to be done about all that material in terms of a story. But, just as obviously, this was not something I could just sit and write and spring on New York out of the clear blue sky. Likewise, I felt that it would not be advisable to discuss the story over an open telephone line with my superiors. The details were too startling and too unbelievable. On the morning of April 2, therefore, I called *The New York Times* to request permission to come up to New York to discuss something of a highly urgent and confidential nature. That same afternoon I was in New York, telling my story to foreign editor Emanuel Freedman and managing editor Turner Catledge. Orvil Dryfoos, our late publisher, was asked by the managing editor to join the discussion because of the tremendous implications of what I had to say.

The first decision that afternoon—one that pleased me greatly —was that I was being assigned full time to the invasion story, no matter how long it took and what it called for. I was to go back to Miami, but stopping in Washington on the way to confer with James B. Reston, our Washington correspondent, and with such Administration officials as it seemed prudent to discuss the story, even by indirection.

Arriving in Washington the following day, I realized that the Administration—and the CIA—knew that some of us in the press corps had more than an inkling of what was being prepared in Guatemala and Florida. Howard Handleman of *U.S. News & World Report* had done some investigating in Miami even before my arrival and, as I was to find out later, raised the matter with Arthur M. Schlesinger, Jr., then one of President Kennedy's Special Assistants.

Schlesinger played possum—as he was to do for days to come with all informed callers, including correspondents from *The New York Times*—but chatting with some friends in the new Administration, I received enough careful hints to convince me that I was on the right track. Although the operation was Top Secret, quite a few people in Washington seemed to know something about it. After I briefed him, Scotty Reston went to see Allen B. Dulles, then CIA director. My recollection is that Dulles did not deny to Scotty that something like an invasion was in the works. But he did deny that followers of former Cuban President Fulgencio Batista—many of them men with criminal records—were a part of the invasion force. I have no reason to doubt Dulles' sincerity; it was one of many instances before and during the Bay of Pigs when one hand did not know what the other hand was doing.

On Tuesday, April 4, I was back in Miami, at the MacAllister Hotel. Stuart Novins of Columbia Broadcasting System, Hal Lavine, then of *Newsweek,* and Howard Handleman were there, busily tracking down the invasion story. Some of the better Miami reporters—two or three of them—were also on to the story. As their editors told it later, it was *their* concept of their sense of responsibility *not* to report the story that was unfolding before their very eyes, in their own territory. For us, on *The New York Times,* journalistic responsibility meant reporting facts, even though—as I was to find out soon—our editors, too, were troubled by the implications of the situation and of the information we were now receiving at an accelerated rate.

The next four days were taken up by more feverish reporting. Novins and I worked closely together. We were not competing in a direct sense—he was a network man and I was on a newspaper —and for my part, at least, I found it useful to exchange thoughts with another correspondent in a situation as bewildering and controversial as the Miami story was becoming. There was a moment, however, when I was to regret this cooperation, though through no fault of Stuart's.

By noon of April 6—a Thursday—I felt I had the story in good shape. I had more interviews with Cubans, more information from other personal sources and a reasonably clear idea of what was about to happen. I also developed a fairly good notion that there was a deep and dangerous split within the Cuban command, and that the CIA was openly favoring right-wing elements against the progressive exile groups identified with the concept of a social revolution in Cuba but opposed to Castro and Communism.

On practical and realistic grounds, this CIA policy struck me as dangerous and self-defeating. If the invasion I knew to be in the final stages of preparation was to be successful, support for the invasion by Cubans in Cuba evidently would be a vital factor.

But, for reasons of its own, the CIA chose to support fairly unpopular groups whose arrival in Cuba would be rather unlikely to evoke the backing of the population. This was only a little more than two years after Castro's victory, and I knew enough about the mood of Cubans to realize that—at this point, at least —they were not likely to throw away *their* revolution in favor of what smacked as the return to *status quo ante 1959*, courtesy of the United States.

My contacts with the progressive anti-Castro groups—notably the MRP (Peoples' Revolutionary Movement) of former Public Works' Minister Manuel Ray—opened my eyes to the fact that the CIA was cutting them out of the operation, even though they ran a highly effective underground operation on the island. Ray, a member of the Miami-based Cuban Revolutionary Front, was kept out of most of the planning, and, in Guatemala, his people were being arrested by the CIA to make sure they stayed out of the invasion.

Thus, with considerable misgivings about what the United States was about to undertake, I sat on April 6 to write my first major story of the approaching invasion. The story emphasized the imminence of the invasion, told of the CIA's role in it and went into considerable detail of what was about to happen. At this stage, my own belief was that the invasion would occur within the next week or so.

A parenthesis is required at this juncture to take account of my own feelings about the story I was handling. Let it be said at once that, just like my editors in New York, I was deeply troubled by what I was putting down in story form. This, to be sure, was not a routine story, not even an unusual story. It was a situation in which an American reporter is faced with the dilemma between telling what he knows—and what he thinks the American people should know—and the highly disturbing considerations of what is commonly known as national security and the national interest of the United States.

To sit on the facts in the name of national interest—as Miami editors subsequently were to justify their posture of silence—would be, of course, the easiest way out. This is what the Kennedy Administration would want us to do, at *that time*. But, on the other hand, I had the ominous feeling that—because of misinformation or other reasons—this new American Administration was about to commit United States prestige to an operation that, as seen from Miami, seemed awfully dubious, politically and morally. Worst of all, I feared that it would not succeed because of the way in which it was being staged.

The moral, philosophical, ethical and patriotic quandaries of this situation were amply discussed by Stuart Novins and myself. That Thursday afternoon, we both concluded that—weighing all the pros and cons—we had no alternative but to go ahead with a full report of what we knew. For my part, the preparations for the story included some fairly agonizing telephone discussions with Manny Freedman who, as our foreign editor, had the perfectly understandable concern that I might be going overboard on my story.

Finally, the story was written and telephoned to *The New York Times'* recording room in New York. Simultaneously, Novins had CBS in New York tape his broadcast saying essentially (if in fewer words) the same thing. We agreed that CBS would hold Novins' broadcast for the eleven P.M. newscast, to give *The Times* time to put out its city edition which hits the streets shortly after ten P.M. If nothing else, I was not going to be scooped on my own story.

But, in a sense, I was scooped. What happened to my story that evening was best told by Clifton Daniel, the present managing editor of *The Times*, in a speech before the World Press Institute at St. Paul, Minnesota, on June 1, 1966. Daniel had chosen this opportunity to illustrate, with the example of the Bay of Pigs story, the dilemmas that face a great newspaper at crucial moments in history. Let me quote from his speech:

"His [my] article, which was more than two columns long and very detailed, was scheduled to appear in the paper of Friday, April 7, 1961. It was dummied for page one under a four-column head, leading the paper.

"While the front-page dummy was being drawn up by the assistant managing editor, the news editor and the assistant news editor, Orvil Dryfoos, then the publisher of *The New York Times*, came down from the fourteenth floor to the office of Turner Catledge, the managing editor.

"He was gravely troubled by the security implications of Szulc's story. He could envision failure for the invasion, and he could see *The New York Times* being blamed for a bloody fiasco.

"He and the managing editor solicited the advice of Scotty Reston, who was then the Washington correspondent of *The New York Times* and is now an associate editor.

"At this point, the record becomes unclear. Mr. Reston distinctly recalls that Mr. Catledge's telephone call came on a Sunday, and that he was spending the weekend at his retreat in the Virginia mountains. . . . As there was no telephone in his cabin, Mr. Reston had to return the call from a gas station in Marshall, Virginia. Mr. Catledge and others recall, with equal certainty, that the incident took place on Thursday and that Mr. Reston was reached in his office in Washington."

(My own recollection is that Manny Freedman in New York told me Thursday afternoon that Scotty Reston was being consulted. I also recall that he had doubts about publishing any references to the CIA.)

But Daniel's account goes on:

"Whichever was the case, the managing editor told Mr. Reston about the Szulc dispatch, which said that a landing on Cuba was imminent. 'I told them not to run it,' Mr. Reston says. He did not advise against printing information about the forces gathering in Florida; that was already well known. He merely cautioned against printing any dispatch that would pinpoint the time of the landing.

"Others agree that Szulc's dispatch did contain some phraseology to the effect that an invasion was imminent, and those words were eliminated."

(My dispatch very definitely did say that the invasion was imminent—the word "imminent" was in my copy as phoned from Miami that afternoon. Daniel accurately quoted my recollection five years later that this and other stories were toned down, "including the elimination of statements about the 'imminence' of an invasion.")

The Daniel narrative continues:

"After the dummy for the front page of *The Times* for Friday, April 7, 1961, was changed, Ted Bernstein, who was the assistant managing editor on night duty at *The Times* and Lew Jordan, the news editor, sat in Mr. Bernstein's office fretting about it. They believed a colossal mistake was being made, and together they went into Mr. Catledge's office to appeal for reconsideration.

"Mr. Catledge recalls that Mr. Jordan's face was dead white and he was quivering with emotion. He and Mr. Bernstein told the managing editor that never before had the front-page play been changed for reasons of policy. They said they would like to hear from the publisher himself the reasons for the change.

"Lew Jordan later recalled that Mr. Catledge was 'flaming mad' at this intervention. However, he turned around in his big swivel chair, picked up the telephone, and asked Mr. Dryfoos to come downstairs. By the time he arrived, Mr. Bernstein had gone to dinner, but Mr. Dryfoos spent ten minutes patiently explaining to Mr. Jordan his reasons for wanting the story played down.

"His reasons were those of national security, national interest and, above all, concern for the safety of the men who were preparing to offer their lives on the beaches of Cuba. He repeated the explanation in somewhat greater length to Mr. Bernstein the next day."

Daniel went on to say that, "ironically," although the mention of the invasion's imminence was eliminated from *The Times'* story, "virtually the same information was printed in a shirttail on Tad Szulc's report. . . . That was a report from the Columbia Broadcasting System. It said that plans for the invasion of Cuba were in their final stages. Ships and planes were carrying invasion units from Florida to their staging bases in preparation for the assault."

That, of course, was Stu Novins' broadcast. I heard it on the eleven o'clock news that night in Miami, not knowing what decisions had been taken on *The New York Times*. Needless to say, I was overcome with indescribable frustration when I looked the next morning at my copy of *The Times*—with the shirttail on Stu's broadcast.

But events were moving fast and I had no time to dwell on frustrations. For one thing, I was not aware of the drama that had taken place the night before in the newsroom of *The New York Times*.

In Miami, in Guatemala and in Nicaragua preparations for the actual landing were quickening. I received word that Cuban paratroopers and commando units were being trained near New Orleans and that new camps in Florida were being activated. On the strength of all this, I suggested to Manny Freedman that reinforcements for *The New York Times,* too, might be in order. The next day, "Long John" McCandlish Phillips from the city staff joined me in Miami.

Yet, the week that followed turned out to be the most depressing of the invasion assignment. The trouble was that *The New York Times* suddenly began doubting that an invasion was really going to occur. McCandlish Phillips' failure to locate the New Orleans camp coincided with a press conference announcement by the Cuban Revolutionary Council in New York that no invasion was being planned. In Washington, the Administration likewise pooh-poohed our preinvasion stories. Manny Freedman ordered Phillips back from New Orleans without any further consultations. The tone in my editor's voice was one of cold doubt about my tireless forecasts of things to come. It suddenly struck me that my credibility was at stake and that my whole Miami operation was about to be canceled.

I imagine that you can sustain the suspense of an invasion scare for only so long before your editors start getting fidgety about the paper's prestige being committed to a story that may never come off. And we did commit ourselves and we were under attack, not leastly from our Miami colleagues.

I think it was on April 12 that one of my intelligence sources confided that the invasion was set for the eighteenth. His forecast was based on the fact that broadcasting stations in the whole Caribbean region were being asked to stay off the air on the dawn of April 18, in order not to interfere with certain "priority" communications. To me, it was the final confirmation that the invasion was approaching. I phoned the bullpen in New York to warn that the invasion *really* was imminent this time and that the paper should stand by for possible late-night developments. As I recall, I was met with highly courteous skepticism.

For the next three days, my problem was as much to keep up my reporting as to convince New York that I was not simply refusing to come off a long, long limb. I knew time was running out on me, and unless the exiles moved immediately, I would have to move—away from Miami. On Saturday, April 15, the exiles and the CIA took me off the hook.

This was the raid on Havana by a brace of B-26s that purported to be defecting Castro aircraft but in reality were CIA planes from Guatemala flown by exile pilots. I heard in the morning that one of the planes had limped to Miami International Airport, its engine and wings shot up by Cuban bullets. At the airport, the Immigration and Naturalization Service dropped a curtain around the pilots, forbidding interviews. But photographs could be taken, and this gave away the whole show.

For one thing, the pilot could be identified. As soon as the Miami News was out that afternoon, I took copies to a group of Cuban fliers who had been sent away from Guatemala for the CIA's ideological reasons. They were able to identify the pilot as an ex-colleague from the training camps. Later, the pilot's wife provided additional identification. She had not known her husband was back in Miami, and she was delighted to see the Miami News photograph.

This incident again posed the moral issue. Was it honorable to publish the story and, again, to puncture the official U.S. denials that we had nothing to do with all this strange activity in the Caribbean? Or should we silence the facts and thus contribute to the misleading of the American public (and, as we found out later, of President Kennedy as well)? Even before my filing deadline that Saturday afternoon, the story was all over Miami and knowledgeable Cubans laughed at the official cover story that the pilots had defected from Cuba and requested asylum in the United States. The final touch to the collapse of the official fiction surrounding that famous "First Strike" was the minute fact, revealed in the news photographs, that the CIA's B-26 had a different nose from the B-26s in Castro's air force. This detail, evidently overlooked by the CIA in planning the operation or in handling its public relations in Miami, was at once spotted by the Cuban fliers, familiar with the Castro aircraft.

With all this in hand, I had no choice—it seemed to me—but to write the story straight, taking account of the official cover version of the day's events while spotlighting all the other pertinent and disturbing facts.

The New York Times, I was sorry to see the next morning, toned down this story, too. Looking back on this whole situation, however, I can sympathize with editors in New York who might have felt some qualms over the fantastic story pouring in day after day from Miami. And, after all, it takes courage for a newspaper to call its government a liar. Though I would have been happier at that time to see my story intact, I believe that we did get the facts across and this is what really mattered.

One of the immediate byproducts of the abortive air strike on Cuba was the restoration of faith on the part of *The New York Times* in the belief that we really had a story in Miami. Instantly, another correspondent, Sam Pope Brewer, was rushed down from New York to work with me.

What happened subsequently is now history. The Cuban brigade began landing at dawn of Monday, April 17 (my early tip had been off by only twenty-four hours), and seventy-two hours later it lay defeated at the Bay of Pigs along with a good part of United States international prestige.

The New York Times covered the story from what by then had become a full-fledged field bureau at the MacAllister, complete with three correspondents and a radio-monitor girl. We installed direct telephone lines to bypass the jammed hotel switchboard. It was probably the only modern war episode to be covered entirely by radio and telephone from nearly 150 miles away, but, really, there was no choice. Manny Freedman and I briefly discussed the possibility of hiring a private plane to fly over the area, but we dropped this notion when it developed that the FAA would not approve flight plans from Florida toward Cuba. Besides, we both felt trepidation about sending a correspondent in a Cessna or Piper Cub into the middle of aerial dogfights over the beachhead.

Many of our competitors and colleagues, who initially derided our preinvasion coverage, now seemed determined to grab the story and run away with it. Dispatches were filed—complete with wirephoto maps—describing nonexistent pincer movements across Cuba by nonexistent rebel "Second Front" forces.

After first being suspected of recklessness, I was now accused of being overcautious and conservative. Night after night, the foreign desk in New York read to me wire service and other stories, rich in fanciful detail, asking whether we could match them. To remain self-disciplined in the face of all this provocation was, in a way, as difficult as winning credibility for our earlier coverage. And there was, of course, the nagging thought that perhaps we were misreading the situation and, indeed, there were pincer movements all over Cuba. . . .

But we stuck by our guns. Much of our information came from Radio Havana, which we monitored around the clock, but, of course, we were aware of its bias dangers. The big piece of luck came when we were able to break into the internal microwave network of the Cuban government. This network, operating in open voice transmissions, was used by the Cubans to order and report their own troop movements, request supplies and, often, to describe quite vividly certain battle situations. Working with a detailed map, we could plot most of the military movements as soon as our transcripts of the microwave output were rushed to us from our secret monitoring source.

The microwave monitoring also produced some superb side-bars that gave the only real flavor of the war to our reporting.

The data obtained from this combination of Cuban radio sources suggested to me by noon of Tuesday—the second day—that the invasion was failing. I spent a good part of the afternoon checking with certain Miami sources with good access to intelligence and operational reports—I still cannot identify these sources—and late in the day I was in a position to file a lengthy and detailed story indicating that the invasion had failed.

Because at this stage my reporting was running completely against everybody else's reporting (the pincer movements were still a big thing on the wires), I had to do a goodly amount of selling to our foreign desk in New York. I remember the frantic one-minute-before-deadline calls from the desk to ask once more, "Are you sure? Are you really sure? And what about the new air strikes against Castro that the Blank-Blank is leading with to-night?" But *The New York Times* went along with my judgment each night and we were never stampeded.

All the postscripts to our coverage of the Bay of Pigs are now history. They include President Kennedy's personal remark to managing editor Turner Catledge two weeks after the invasion fiasco that "if you had printed more about the operation you would have saved us from a colossal mistake."

On September 13, 1962, Mr. Kennedy said to Orvil Dryfoos, our late publisher, in a conversation at the White House: "I wish you had run everything on Cuba. . . . I am just sorry you didn't tell it at the time."

In his book *A Thousand Days* and in a television appearance in 1965, Arthur M. Schlesinger, Jr., charged *The New York Times* with acting irresponsibly because it had cut or, as he said later, "emasculated" some of my preinvasion stories. The unusually frank account of the agony in *The Times* newsroom that April night was given by Clifton Daniel in his St. Paul speech, from which I have quoted above, as a reply to the Schlesinger charges.

I would like now, as an accidental actor in this whole drama, to offer my own conclusions on my work and *The New York Times'* handling of it.

As for the first part of it—my reporting—there can be no question that I would do exactly as I did in 1961, if a similar situation were to arise again. I feel strongly that a reporter in the field must tell the facts as he sees them, though he must, inevitably, participate in the moral judgments that his stories make necessary.

As for *The New York Times,* in perspective I have no real quarrel with the handling of my stories. I wish, of course, as the President later did, that they had been published in full. But, on the whole, I think we did our job correctly and, if the Administration had wanted to be warned by our reporting of the impending disaster, they could have easily done so. Instead, the official effort was to deny everything we were saying.

For this reason I believe that Schlesinger's accusations are unfair, to say the least. In charging us with irresponsibility, he overlooks the crucial fact that the full power of the Administration—including his own efforts on behalf of the White House—were centered on exploding my reporting. In a sense, it was the word of the Government of the United States against my word. To say, under these circumstances, that *The New York Times* had failed in its mission to inform fully and accurately is highly irresponsible in itself. To say, further, as Schlesinger did, that "I, at least, had the excuse that I was working for the government," seems to me to border on the ludicrous.

If a newspaper like *The New York Times* approaches great issues of national interest with caution, as it should, it seems just a bit too facile for a repentant former government official to come up years later, in effect, with the startling commentary that we should have assumed from the outset that we were dealing with a bunch of liars. If we do feel, as we do, that there is something increasingly wrong with the relationship between the American press and the American Government, I still do not believe that the solution lies in an across-the-board assumption—which, in effect, Arthur Schlesinger recommends—that the government always lies.

I continue to think so even after my experience in 1965 with the United States intervention in the Dominican Republic, when the Johnson Administration had certainly divorced itself from the truth for long periods. In that situation, incidentally, *The Times* did nothing to tone down my stories, mainly because my reports could be fully documented and verified. We were not working in a murky area as we did in 1961, in covering the Bay of Pigs.

My final postscript to the Bay of Pigs story relates to a conversation I had with President Kennedy in November, 1961. Speaking in the presence of Richard N. Goodwin, his special assistant, the late President also told me at his White House office that while he had been "mad" at me at the time for printing the preinvasion stories, he now wished that we had published all we knew or, at least, told him about it personally.

But in the end, he added, "the responsibility was of course mine."

Hugh Mulligan's career as a feature writer for the Associated Press has taken him from the Gallo brothers' hangout in Brooklyn to St. Peter's Square in the Vatican; from T-3, a floating ice island in the Arctic Ocean, to a leper colony in South Vietnam. After covering President Kennedy's assassination and funeral, Mulligan, with three other AP reporters, wrote *The Torch Is Passed*, which sold more than four million copies.

Hi There, Space Fans!

HUGH A. MULLIGAN

AMERICA'S SPACE program has come a long way since Alan Shepard and Gus Grissom went tourist class to the Bahamas on the head of an old Redstone rocket and a chimpanzee named Enos, with a nasty disposition and a fondness for banana pellets, went skipping around the world strapped to a reclining couch. Astronauts now take ghostly walks in the nothingness of outer space, do calisthenics in the open hatchways of their capsules and make dramatic rendezvous with bits of hardware that have been clattering about in the wild blue yonder for a year or more.

Even more amazing, if less dramatic, all sorts of long-legged things land on the moon and send back fuzzy photographs and eerie radio signals that induce learned men to make all sorts of conclusions having nothing to do with green cheese or rhyming with June or the celebrated cow who reputedly made the first orbital pass at the moon. Missile shots are the greatest science story of our age, and will continue to be so until man finally plants a trembling toe and a few earth germs in the terra incognita of a neighboring planet or in the dusty glitter of a wandering star.

Even with Gemini twins dashing off to blast-off every few weeks, public interest in the space program seldom seems to flag. There is a hypnotic excitement about every countdown, but to the old hands on the Cape Canaveral beat, the 400-odd reporters and science writers who regularly cover the space shots, there probably never will be another launch like the Glenn launch. History can never again duplicate the combination of a bashful, balding hero trying to catch up with the Russians on a dangerous, death-defying mission carried out amid the bizarre carnival trappings of early Cape Canaveral, a wild and woolly frontier town that served as the final border to outer space. The Glenn story was exciting to witness, fun to cover, hard to get. All that, and bikinis, too.

First of all, it took John Glenn exactly two months to be up and going. Originally, America's first manned orbital space shot was scheduled for December 20, 1961, but a combination of bad weather, mechanical breakdowns and heavy seas in the primary recovery area kept postponing the launch date. It wasn't until February 20 that the soft-spoken Marine finally got off the pad. Any man who can keep four hundred reporters in Florida on expenses through the better part of the winter is bound to be a national hero.

During the long wait, reporters from all over the world sat despondently around the kidney-shaped swimming pools and in the dimly lit cocktail lounges trying to think of sidebars, peripheral stories, that would keep their editors happy until the big day finally arrived. Cocoa Beach, the little community that served as press headquarters for the Cape, was then a garishly impromptu collection of cardboard motels, neon-blazing bars, surprisingly excellent restaurants and pastel-painted resort cottages arrayed in a three-mile strip along Florida Highway A1A.

To the strip at missile shot time flocked an improbable admixture of scientists, technicians, military men, reporters, campers, tourists, college kids on vacation, surfers, beach bums, belly dancers, hucksters peddling "Go-Go Glenn" buttons, prostitutes and assorted camp followers.

The beach at Cape Canaveral was then hard-packed and relatively primitive, but that was in 1961–62, several hurricanes and at least a dozen new motels ago. Cars could drive up and down the sand at night, so that lovers frequently got washed out to sea; and early in the morning, along that empty stretch of white sand, all sorts of exotic birds left their nests in the mangrove swamp to cavort at the edge of the ocean: pelicans, herons, sandpipers, even rare roseate spoonbills. The motels, in those pioneer space days, were all named for the various missiles, "Vanguard," "Polaris," "Starlight," Saturn," and the bars along the strip featured space age concoctions like the "Atlas Highball" and the "Titan Toddy," some of which were compounded of 190 proof alcohol and could send a man into private orbit at first contact.

On the night before a missile shot, tens of thousands of people camped out on the beach, singing songs around open campfires, and keeping watchful eyes on the ghostly glare of the floodlit gantries, where technicians labored around the clock to ready the launch vehicle. A blinking red light on the end of the rock jetty warned the Cape's large shrimp fleet that a launch was about to take place and that they must head back to port once a large white ball began its slow descent down a tall tower at the very tip of the Cape.

Even in such bizarre surroundings, sidebars were hard to find by the end of the second week of waiting. John Glenn was a laconic man, not easily accessible. He was friendly, invariably cheerful, but Spartan in his public utterances. Lieutenant Colonel John ("Shorty") Powers, the voice of Mercury Control, attempted to skim the top off Glenn's occasional remarks for the benefit of the assembled press at the daily weather briefings, but even when the delays became exasperatingly monotonous, Glenn apparently never said anything more incendiary than "Aw, shucks," or as one of the more imaginative writers paraphrased him, "words to that effect."

Still, we covered John Glenn from every possible sidebar angle. This story had more sidebars than a corner suite at San Quentin. John Glenn's low residue diet. John Glenn's form-fitting couch. John Glenn's backup pilot. John Glenn's environmental control system. John Glenn's elimination system (sometimes known as "John's other John"). John Glenn's reaction to waiting. John Glenn's lack of reaction to waiting. John Glenn's lack of reaction to other people's reaction to waiting.

Sometimes, we even saw the great man in person. John Glenn

runs at dawn along the beach. John Glenn gets a haircut (reporters and photographers had the little clapboard barbershop down in town staked out like a scene in *The Untouchables*). John Glenn goes to the bakery (two autographs, seven loaves of onion pumpernickel, his favorite). John Glenn goes to church (some of us put in enough time at Riverside Presbyterian to qualify in the next vestrymen's election).

The competition for such trivia became so great that if anyone broke out a typewriter at the swimming pool, he could ruin the whole day for hundreds of his colleagues. He might only be writing a letter to his wife, but then again he might be banging out a bulletin, like "Yellow Bird" being John Glenn's favorite song or John getting a touch of athlete's foot in his morning shower. There was a camaraderie about the space-shot press that bred mutual respect and mutual suspicion. You saw pretty much the same crowd every shot and got to know them pretty well: Walter Cronkite of CBS, Roy Neal and Frank McGee of NBC, Dick Witkin of *The New York Times*, Stu Lurie of the *Herald Tribune*, Howie Benedict, John Barbour and Al Blakeslee of AP, Bill Hines of the *Washington Star*, Bob Considine of Hearst Headline Service, Jules Bergman of ABC, Doug Dederer of the Cocoa *Tribune* and dozens of others who became experts at ferreting out unlikely sidebar material. If an AP man went out with the shrimp boats, *The Times* staff would be distraught for days; if a photographer caught Alan Shepard doing the twist or Annie Glenn building a sand castle for the kids, he would be lionized as if he had just scooped the Iwo Jima flag raising.

The days of waiting followed a meaningless routine that seldom resulted in much of a story. Each morning, promptly at nine, but more often at ten, we attended weather briefings, eagerly separating the calms from the squalls, the freshets from the swells. By the time John Glenn finally rode into orbit, most of us knew more about weather conditions in the mid-Atlantic than a school of Beluga whales planning their annual picnic. Each evening, promptly at five, we attended the flight briefing, where the baroque prose of "Shorty" Powers hung in the air like a summer smog: "The Atlas is go, the capsule is go, the pilot is go, only the weather is marginal. We have cloud cover at three thousand feet and a space window of less than thirty minutes."

And each midnight, save one, we scrubbed. And the whole thing started over again.

Then, right in the middle of our numbing monotony, a real story broke the even tenor of our ways. A murder, of all things. Perhaps you remember "The Missile Murder." It won't go down as one of the great crimes of the century, but it grabbed more headlines than low residue diets and the aerodynamics of retro-rockets. One murky night, close to closing time, a fellow walked into the bar of the Starlight Motel, where the NASA press headquarters was located, and pumped seven slugs into a waitress who happened to be his estranged wife.

The British press, which had been somewhat critical of our space efforts in those faltering days, called it the "most successful shot at Cape Canaveral in six months." The killer left his own car in the motel parking lot, cut across the mangrove swamps to the state highway and hitched a ride to Orlando, fifty miles to the west. The first deputy sheriff on the scene made a thorough fingerprint check of the murderer's car, then began a door-to-door search through the motels for a man answering his description. Two hours later, the bloodhounds arrived from the Florida state prison farm, sniffed greedily at the steering wheel, picked up the scent and proceeded to chase that poor deputy sheriff all over Cape Canaveral the rest of the day.

Surely one of the most incongruous sights in all the Cape's boisterous history was the bloodhound pack tearing through the lobby of the Vanguard Motel, dragging their keepers along behind them with AP photographer John Rooney in hot pursuit, as startled tourists checked in at the front desk and an army helicopter beat overhead, searching the surrounding mangrove thickets.

Despite sinister allegations of "all that free time" from the home office, sleep was hard to come by on the Glenn assignment. The foreign press, because of pressure of time zone deadlines, kept all sorts of weird hours. Saul Pett and Bem Price of AP shared a room that backed up on one occupied by two British journalists. Each morning, somewhere around four, which was really nine London time, Her Majesty's scribes placed a transatlantic call to their Fleet Street editors. The conversation, shouted through the paper-thin walls, went precisely like this:

"'ello Rodney, Wilson here. I say, have you seen Ruth lately? Oh, is she? Rotten luck, that. And do say 'ello to Daphne, will you, old boy?"

After ten or more minutes of social chitchat, Wilson informed Rodney that he had "a bit of a story 'ere, nothing much, really, but you might have a go at it"—and then proceeded with two thousand or so laboriously shouted words.

But despite the hours they kept and their preoccupation with the missile murder, we all had an affection for the British press. Only a Londoner, fluent in the mother tongue, could cut intrepidly through the jungle of Shorty Powers' prose to report that "the weather is still a bit mucked up, but all systems in the American mis-aisle are tickety-boo!"

The foreign press gives the space assignment a unique flavor. Each manned shot brings at least two hundred reporters and photographers from the great newspapers and news agencies around the world, including an occasional representative from behind the Iron Curtain, like the Czechoslovakian radio man who ignored the Glenn blast-off to continue a tape recorded interview with a college intellectual advocating joint Soviet–U.S. space efforts. For some reason the Japanese are avid space fans and sent a large delegation of newsmen to the Glenn shot. My motel room was right next door to one that served as a combined office and dormitory for a large Japanese news agency. About six o'clock every evening five diminutive Japanese reporters would gather around a single diminutive Japanese typewriter to pool their creative talents on a single story. One of them, a studious-looking type with thick beer-bottle eyeglasses, would preside at the keys while the others, standing behind him, all dictated at the same time in a piercing high-pitched singsong. It was like the Kingston Trio, except there were five of them. The Japanese were superbly informed on space matters, asked highly intelligent questions at the press conferences and knew the names of all the top American science writers, especially AP science editor Alton Blakeslee, who has visited Japan several times and is known in the inscrutable and unpronounceable East as "Or-ton Brakes-ree."

Then one day the John Glenn mission was planned, duly scheduled, and this time there was no scrub. The electric thrill of a Cape Canaveral countdown is something that no reporter ever forgets. It makes no difference how many missile shots he has covered, the drama and the excitement are always there. It's something that even the most blasé and cynical can't get blasé and cynical about. Even the most hard-boiled reporter melts a little at the knee joints on shot day.

From the time the public address system leaps to life at seven A.M. with the somber announcement that "this is Mercury Control; the clock now stands at T-minus sixty minutes and counting," the spectacle builds in an increasing crescendo of tension and suspense to its inevitable fiery conclusion. At T-minus five, the lines disappear completely from the coffee stand out at the forward press site. The reporters grip their telephones, lines open all around the world. The photographers lean into their cameras. The missile is loxed, topped off with its final infusion of liquid oxygen. It turns shivering cold, frosting over like a popsicle and trailing plumes of white vapor.

Here indeed is the world of fire and ice that the poet Robert Frost spoke of.

As the countdown slips portentously down to zero, the huge silver missile, more than ninety feet tall—the height of a ten-story building—sends out a lick of orange flame, trembles slightly on its pad before righting itself, then rises slowly, majestically into the vast blue sky. An eerie silence falls on the press site, after the first hectic shouts of blast-off bulletins into the phones. Suddenly, conversation seems to die everywhere: up range and down range, in the little concrete blockhouse where Mercury Control is monitoring the flight, in the forward abort area where ambulances and rescue planes have been warming up, ready to rescue the astronaut if something goes wrong, on the beaches where the all-night vigil has ended for the campers, on the roads clogged with sightseers, and in the far-flung tracking stations and on the recovery ships all around the world, where 19,000 technicians are deployed in a fabulous communications network.

Then the loudspeaker barks out the good news: "We have a successful orbit."

Sometimes a cheer goes up in the forward press area, more often it's a prayer, a silent prayer sent heavenward by blasé reporters too moved to realize that someone might consider such emotions corny. The contrail breaks up like a languorous pretzel

in the sky; Phantom jets scream off to photograph the rocket as it
breaks off its booster, and the long wait begins at the press site,
the wait for the splashdown and recovery.

The press site, for the benefit of those who have never seen it,
is a little grassy hill overlooking the launching pad from a
distance of less than a mile. Here the several hundred reporters
and photographers train their telescopes and cameras on the
foaming missile, or sit in little wooden bleachers, like a Little
League stadium, with notebooks poised, or clack out overnight
stories or early night leads on typewriters and teletype machines
set up on rickety wooden tables in a big circus tent.

Inside a smaller tent, more on the order of a sideshow tent, a
large electrified map marks the astronaut's voyage around the
world and serves as a backdrop prop for television commentators.

All in all, a pretty incredible place. You come out of the men's
room at the base of the little green hill and find a couple of
hundred television and movie cameras trained right on you. Pete
Andrews, of Hearst Headline Service, met me on the way out one
morning and cautioned, "Smile, you're on Telstar."

Each shot draws a huge outpouring of reporters of varying
degrees of brilliance. Phone space at little wooden stalls arranged
in an amphitheater style is provided for more than a hundred
newsmen. But the Glenn shot seemed to have the corner on
characters. Bob Considine drew a slot next to a radio man from a
small Florida station, who came on the air just about the same
time as Mercury Control with the folksy greeting, "Hi there,
space fans in eastern Florida!"

Man will get to the moon one of these days soon, and I hope
I'm there to get in on the story, at least on the blast-off end.
There'll probably be a press corps of more than a thousand
covering that one, but only the old Cape Canaveral hands will
remember the gay, golden days of John Herschel Glenn, Junior.
We'll gather in a talkative little knot, like old prospectors around
the post office stove, reminiscing about the frontier days of outer
space, when everything was A-okay if not downright tickety-boo.

William R. McAndrew reigns from the summit of broadcasting journalism—as president of the NBC News division of the National Broadcasting Company.

Suspense and the Tunnel

WILLIAM R. McANDREW

THROUGHOUT THE summer of 1962, three of us at NBC News, New York, shared a burdensome secret.

We were privileged to know about a project so bold, so risky and so difficult that it was hard to accept as a reality. We knew that if it succeeded, NBC's filmed record of it would make one of the most engrossing television news stories of our times. We also were well aware that if it failed two of our cameramen, along with many other brave young men, might lose their lives.

The project was an attempt by a group of West Berlin students to tunnel under the Berlin Wall and provide an escape route for some friends on the Communist side.

Like many secrets, it was a frustrating one. Here we were—Julian Goodman (then vice president, News, and now president of the National Broadcasting Company), Reuven Frank (then an executive producer and now vice president, News) and I—sitting on a fantastic story, and we couldn't talk about it except among ourselves. For security reasons, no information came through from our news bureau in West Germany.

Before I get into the story, I would like to make it clear that none of us connected with NBC took part in the planning or building of the tunnel, nor recruited anyone for this undertaking,

nor induced anyone to help with it. NBC bought the right to film
the tunnel, and this only after we were assured that the tunnel
would be continued whether or not we filmed it.

That summer, after other escape routes were cut off, more than
a score of tunnels were dug under the Wall. Usually they were
like rabbit burrows—ten or twelve feet long—mostly in open
places. This meant that the refugees had to come close to the
border, and close to the People's Police—the Vopos—who patrolled every foot of the forbidden zone along the Wall. Some of
these tunnels were discovered and their builders were killed or
captured.

The tunnel we were filming turned out to be the most professional and provided escape for the most people—fifty-nine men,
women and children. It became more sophisticated as it progressed, and came to be equipped with electric lights, a telephone
line, ventilation, air and water pumping systems and a cart that
traveled on steel rails to remove the earth.

The program we telecast, "The Tunnel," was not what we originally intended. We planned to do a study of what was going on
in East Germany, and the escapes and escape attempts were
meant to be part of this overall theme. So, as the tunnel-building
activity increased that summer, Gary Stindt, who was then chief
of NBC's news film operation in Central Europe (now director,
NBC News Operations, Central Europe), spread the word among
students he knew that if anyone was building a tunnel, and
wouldn't mind having it filmed, NBC would like to hear
about it.

As a result, in May, 1962, a young American approached
Stindt and said, "Are you still interested in a tunnel?" Stindt
assured him that he was. "Well," said the American, "I know
where there is one, and it's being dug now by engineering
students. They're very serious about it and doing it right—
planning it with charts, surveys and everything else."

Piers Anderton, then our bureau chief in West Germany, came
to New York the first week of June to get married. While the
wedding reception was in full swing, he backed Frank into a
corner and, in a conspiratorial tone, said he had to talk to him
privately. As Frank tells the story, "I thought that was a little
strange—hardly the occasion for business—but he insisted." They

went back to Frank's office and, again at Anderton's insistence —closed the door. Anderton said, "I've got a tunnel."

He had actually been inside it. By this time the tunnel had been under construction for about a month and had progressed some sixty feet toward the Wall.

The most daring refugee rescue operation in Berlin's history was being planned by three young men, led by Luigi Spina, an Italian art student at West Berlin's Technical University. His co-conspirator was his roommate, Domenico Sesta, also an Italian, who was an engineering student. They had met in high school in Gorizia, near Venice, seven years before, and had pooled their money to go to college in Germany. In the room next to them was Wolf Schroedter, who was reputed to know something about tunnels. The Italians approached him because they felt they needed a German partner.

The reason for digging the tunnel was to provide escape for Peter Schmidt, an art student who lived in East Berlin with his mother, his wife and an eighteen-month-old daughter. Spina and Sesta had known Peter at school before the Wall stopped his studies in West Berlin.

The site selected for the tunnel opening was a cellar under the Bernauerstrasse, one of the busiest streets in West Berlin. The building was a bombed ruin which was still usable and therefore had not been repaired. Upstairs there was a plastics factory that manufactured swizzle sticks for cocktails.

In New York as elsewhere our primary concern was maintaining security. No sooner had we set the ground rules than Anderton floored us by announcing that the students wanted $50,000 for the right to film their tunnel. We agreed on a much smaller figure which he was to offer on a take-it-or-leave-it basis. The offer was accepted.

The negotiations were conducted in a cloak and dagger atmosphere. Some of the things we did were ridiculous, but we felt this was better than taking chances. Meanwhile, the students were meeting in hotel rooms and setting up more meetings through intermediaries. But after Anderton and then our two cameramen, Peter and Klaus Dehmel, won their confidence, the students became a little lax and had to be warned about their own security.

We maintained rigid security. The tunnel was never mentioned in any telephone call. West Berlin is 110 miles inside Communist territory, and telephone communication with the rest of the world is by microwave. We naturally assumed the Communists were monitoring these transmissions.

Frank, who was supervising our coverage of the project, did not visit West Berlin until the day before the expected breakthrough. There were perhaps a dozen English-speaking newsmen there, and we felt that if Frank were to spend a lengthy time in Berlin, his presence would cause comment. He didn't ask the location of the tunnel. That information wasn't necessary for his job or ours, and it made sense not to tell someone something he didn't need to know.

When it became important to have production meetings, Frank would meet Anderton and the Dehmel brothers in London or Paris. They would talk in hotel rooms or in the noisiest nightclubs they could find, where they couldn't be overheard.

NBC News filmed the digging only when the students who had planned the tunnel were doing the work. It wasn't possible to call a meeting of all the diggers—who included students from other schools—and explain the situation. Not many of them were in the mood for meetings anyway, considering they were digging eight hours a day, seven days a week.

The negotiations were carried out without the knowledge of the NBC legal department. Signed papers were exchanged between us and the tunnelers, but I question whether they would have been held legal in a court of law here or in Berlin. Frank got an NBC accountant to work outside company channels from a kind of blanket account to which we could charge all the raw stock, the money for lights, an extra camera we had to send, transportation fees and other items. This man simply refused to tell our NBC business executives—his own bosses—how the money was being used, and—surprisingly—got away with it.

The Dehmel brothers had volunteered to film the underground work. It was no easy task. At its entrance the tunnel went down vertically about fifteen feet, then leveled off in a passageway one yard wide or one yard high—or, as Frank pointed out, "not much roomier than a coffin." Peter Dehmel had to lie on his back behind the man digging and point his camera forward. Klaus

Dehmel would lie on his stomach with his head against his brother's and hold the lights.

So tight was the working space that Peter could not use the usual 400-foot film magazine, but had to use a 100-foot magazine instead. This meant that he had to change magazines after every two and a half minutes of shooting. A further complication was that, with each change of film, he had to unwrap and rewrap the entire apparatus with a plastic cover to keep the dirt out.

There was rarely room for a sound recorder and never for a third man to operate it, so very few sounds were recorded. The film crew did record some of the street sounds overheard, and it was frightening to think that if these noises could be heard, the Vopos also might hear the digging noises below. Especially since the Vopos were equipped with listening devices.

The digging went on seven days a week for four months, with each day divided into three eight-hour shifts. The members of each shift relieved one another at the toughest job—excavating at the face of the tunnel. To carry the earth to the opening, they laid a single steel rail on which they ran a small rope-drawn cart. They timbered every few feet with a crossbeam and two uprights. Where the tunnel cut through sand instead of clay, they covered the floor and roof completely with planking. They bought and carried and secretly unloaded twenty tons of wood, and each piece had to be sawed and fitted. The digger was in front of the timber, of course, and risked the danger of being caught in a collapse of the earth.

Although the equipment was fairly primitive to start with, it was mechanized by the time we were halfway through the filming. The students strung electric lights along the tunnel and rigged a telephone line so that the spadesmen could call to have the dirt removed. After they had passed under the Wall, they called this line "the only direct telephone connection between East and West Berlin."

When the tunnel was thirty yards or more long, the air became a little foul. The builders bought an air compressor and devised a ventilation system that blew fresh air from one end to the other.

The work was impeded twice by breaks in Berlin's water system. As we said it in our telecast: "It was a cold, rainy summer all over Europe—the worst in years (very bad for the beach resorts) . . . and June was the cruelest month. The cold rain beat on Berlin two days out of three . . . sparing neither the just nor the Vopos . . . seeping into the soaked earth. The ground relaxed, settled . . . and a crushing weight fell on the water lines below the surface . . . and on the tunnel supports below the water lines."

The tunnel supports disintegrated. The builders bought a hand pump and a hundred yards of hose. With Sesta doing most of the pumping, they pumped—at half a pint a stroke—eight thousand gallons in one week. But the tunnel did not become dry.

With a fine show of impudence, they bored a hole in the city pipe running through the cellar and pumped the excess water into East Berlin. They had already taken a sample to friends at the Technical University, who mistakenly analyzed it as rain water. But after a week of pumping, the tunnelers realized their friends were wrong. The water had to be coming from a broken main. The problem was to notify the West Berlin Water Department that a main had broken without revealing the existence of the tunnel. It took about three weeks to manage this and get action. Meanwhile, the activity in the tunnel was confined to pumping. Finally, a city work crew repaired the main and the flood stopped.

The second flood, much worse, came from a broken main on the Communist side. Since there was no chance of repairs, the tunnelers bought an electric pump, primed it, and, working night and day, pumped out forty thousand gallons. The water stopped suddenly—they never knew why—and the pump caught up. The tunnel dried.

Between these floods, Spina was rushed to a hospital to have his appendix removed. Sesta, who visited him daily, learned from Spina on one visit that a co-worker had been captured while helping out on another tunnel. It must be assumed that this man would reveal the existence of the tunnel under Bernauerstrasse. A new breakthrough point and a new rendezvous location had to be planned. The original point was two blocks from the Wall. The tunnelers decided to make their breakthrough only one block from the Wall. They scheduled the escape attempt for September 14.

The original date had been June 30. There had been many postponements. Frank met Anderton in Paris the last week in

August. Anderton said they would be ready for him in about two weeks. When Frank expressed disbelief because none of the other scheduled dates had been met, Anderton said, "No, but this time you'd better do it." So, on September 13, Frank and a film editor arrived in West Berlin.

They were met at Tegel Airport by Stindt and Anderton. Frank asked how long he would have to wait. He was told, "They go through tomorrow night. The tunnel's finished."

There were twenty hours of film to view. Frank and the film editor, Gerald Polikoff, worked from early afternoon until well past midnight, then started again the next morning and worked throughout most of the afternoon. Frank called me about noon. All he said was, "I think we need ninety minutes, but I'll tell you better tomorrow."

The cameramen went out to film Sesta's fiancée, a 22-year-old secretary, who was going into East Berlin to meet with several refugees. Because she was a West German, not a West Berliner, she was allowed to go into East Berlin. The cameramen stayed on the elevated train with her until the last stop before the border. Of the ten couriers in the project, she was the only girl—but the other nine missed their assignments or got frightened off, and she ended up bringing all of the refugees to the tunnel herself.

About three o'clock that afternoon the Dehmels left to get what film they could of the refugees' escape. They were supposed to be back by seven o'clock. When they still had not returned by 11:30, Frank couldn't stand waiting around any longer. He got one of Stindt's assistants to drive past the location of the tunnel. They drove by, not even slowing down, so as not to arouse suspicion. There was no police activity on the West Berlin side and, as far as they could tell, none in the East. The tunnel had not been discovered.

The Dehmels came in about two A.M. with the film of the escape. They got it into the lab and screened it Saturday morning. The lab was owned by a man who was a friend of Stindt's late father. He didn't ask questions.

One of the reasons for editing the film in West Berlin was to get the identities straight. Stindt and the Dehmel brothers were there to sort out the many people who appeared in the film. When it had been edited down to a workable length, Frank personally carried it on the trip home. He put it behind his seat, which was the last seat in the first-class compartment. Then he was asked if he would mind changing his seat. Berlin Mayor Willy Brandt and three assistants wanted the four seats across. There was no gracious way to refuse, so Mayor Brandt sat on this film all the way from Frankfurt to New York.

The Gulf Oil Corporation was tentatively approached about sponsoring the telecast. I left word at the airport for Frank to call me as soon as he arrived. I told him I would like him to go to Pittsburgh on Sunday to meet with the Gulf management. He was somewhat reluctant, having been away from home for some time, but I persuaded him. He met several Gulf representatives in a hotel room and told them what he had. In about fifteen minutes the program was sold. And throughout all our later problems, Gulf did not waver once in its desire to sponsor the telecast.

During the final editing, we edited out or, where this was not possible, blacked out the faces of all except those who had clearly consented to be shown on the film.

As I said, there were many tunnels in Berlin that summer. CBS made a deal similar to ours to film another tunnel. But that one was compromised in August and blocked off by West Berlin police. After this happened, we received a visit in New York from a deputy assistant Secretary of State who warned us that the tunnel we were filming (or so he thought) had been discovered by the East Germans and that further work on it would be dangerous.

We announced the program on October 11. Frank and his editors were doing the final "mix" in a recording studio, putting music and voice portions together, when a UPI story broke that the State Department had said the program was "not in the national interest."

The State Department's stated objection was that if the tunnel had been discovered, the presence of an American company there would have proved an embarrassment. There was no specific objection to the program itself. They said many times, in writing and to us personally, that once the film was finished, any objection would be academic. They did not want to interfere with the program and had no objection to it being aired.

We were certain the film would not endanger those who built the tunnel or escaped through it, nor their relatives in East Berlin.

We were equally sure it would not compromise American–West German relations. We told the State Department this.

On October 19, press officer Lincoln White told reporters:

"When apprised of the Department's view that involvement of American television personnel in clandestine tunnel operations was both dangerous and irresponsible, the Columbia Broadcasting System promptly and laudably withdrew from a tunnel project. This was greatly appreciated.

"NBC was made equally aware of the Department's view that such involvement was risky, irresponsible, undesirable and not in the best interests of the United States. NBC chose to continue with its tunnel project. . . ."

White rested his case largely upon opposition from German officials, who apparently had been led to believe that the telecast would endanger people still in East Germany One of our vice presidents met with these officials in Berlin. After he assured them that all identities had been carefully concealed, they withdrew their objections.

The day after White's remarks, the West Berlin Senate issued a statement acknowledging NBC's assurances and adding:

"In its attitude, the Senate respects that NBC is guided by the wish to bring by an authentic report to the public of the United States a direct impression, which is in the interest of Berlin. The decision to show this documentary naturally lies with NBC alone."

Support from NBC's plans came three days later from Ernst Lemmer, West Germany's Minister for All-German Affairs, whose cabinet post dealt with relations between East and West Germany. After relating NBC's assurances on the security aspects, a statement released by his office said:

"Minister Lemmer stressed that he had not given any comment on the disputed showing. However, he could only welcome it if the events in Berlin were reported to the world public as extensively and precisely as possible."

"The Tunnel" was scheduled for October 31. But the Cuban crisis came along, so, the day before, we postponed it. Our announcement said: "In view of the critical international situation that has developed in the last twenty-four hours, the National Broadcasting Company has concluded in its own judgment that this is not

an appropriate time to broadcast its documentary program showing the construction of a tunnel under the Berlin Wall and the
escape of East German refugees."

"The Tunnel" was presented on the NBC Television Network
December 10. It had been a long project and, like Spina, Sesta
and their friends, we were happy to "break through." The program received one of the highest ratings ever recorded by a
public-affairs program and praise from television critics throughout the country and abroad. It was the first purely journalistic
undertaking to receive the Emmy Award for "Program of the
Year." The U.S. Information Agency edited the program down to
a half hour and distributed prints overseas.

Waverley Root, as chief of the Paris Bureau for the *Washington Post* and president of the Anglo-American Press Association of Paris, occupies a distinguished position in overseas journalism. He has had a long and notable record as a foreign correspondent and has written many books which have been published internationally—on topics ranging from *The Food of France* to *The Secret History of the War.*

Why Go
to the Kabylia?

WAVERLEY ROOT

"YOU WON'T go into the Kabylia, will you?" my wife asked.

"I have no such intention," I answered.

This is known as maintaining mobility. She was under the impression that I had promised to leave Kabylia strictly alone. But I had reported only on present intentions. Intentions change.

You get into the habit of talking this way if you spend much time around diplomats.

I was just leaving for Algeria and, eventually, Morocco, to look into the border conflict of 1963. But there was also another conflict going on, an internal mutiny against the government of Ahmed Ben Bella. It was led by Hocine Ait-Ahmed, a former fellow prisoner with Ben Bella in France, and a fellow member of the pre-independence Algerian Provisional Government. Now he was accusing Ben Bella of having betrayed the revolution, and was in armed rebellion against him, making his headquarters in the Kabylia Mountains, Berber country, always ready to fight the Arabs.

My dusty answer left me quite free to respond when another American correspondent sprinted through the dining room of the

Aletti Hotel in Algiers, tossing me on the way the information that Ait-Ahmed had called a press conference for six P.M. in Michelet, about a hundred miles east and five thousand feet up from Algiers, as the crow flies. The crow possesses the only means of transport adapted to this region.

I reflected. I was in the middle of an excellent lunch in a comfortable hotel. I can recommend the Aletti, even since nationalization, as an excellent place from which to cover a war. I had an appointment that afternoon with a member of the government. But I had already seen one cabinet minister that morning, plus the British ambassador, and I thought Ait-Ahmed would provide a change of pace. I launched a hurry call for my driver, whose station was theoretically just outside the hotel, ready to move at a moment's notice, but who in fact used to slip in a little extra revenue by occasional taxi jobs when he judged I would not be needing him for an hour or two. He had so judged. I had plenty of time to shift from clothes suitable for meeting ministers to clothes suitable for meeting rebels before he was captured. It was then about three P.M.

I asked him if he could make Michelet by six. He assured me he could. I had not yet realized that he considered it impolite to return any answer likely to be unwelcome to me. I wanted to be in Michelet by six. Therefore he told me we could be in Michelet by six. That was what I wanted to hear, and it would give me pleasure. Details like distance, state of the roads, and state of his car were irrelevant. We were off.

A week earlier, the Information Ministry had told me that I would require a pass to enter the Kabylia region, but the day before a partial truce had been announced between the government forces and the rebels, whose terms included a lifting of the road blocks which had shut off Kabylia. Sure enough, as we approached Tizi-Ouzou, we found the bar that the day before had blocked the road lifted, and the barrier unmanned. We went by unchallenged, and at Tizi-Ouzou turned south and started into the hills.

Up to now the road had been wide and well kept. Now things changed. The route was up—up, up, and again up, with never a downgrade, a succession of hairpin curves executed by a road which was a sort of narrow ledge following the flanks of the mountains, the ground rising swiftly above our heads, and on the other side, a deep section of nothing. I could see why it was difficult to scotch a rebellion in the Kabylia. Every few yards provided a dandy place for an ambush. There was no reason why anyone should ambush me—except maybe for practice—but I began to doubt that I would reach Michelet alive in any case. I was not afraid of the rebels. I was afraid of the driver.

He drove with brio. We roared around those narrow curves without so much as sounding our horn. If there had been a car coming the other way around any of them, we would have come to an abrupt end. No doubt my driver knew that nobody was using this road anymore, but there could have been an exception. We were using it, for instance. And as six o'clock came and went, it occurred to me that some of my colleagues might be on the way back from the conference I had missed, undoubtedly with Arab drivers too. They would be, like mine, fatalists. I was not a fatalist, or anyway not his kind of a fatalist, but I had become an assimilated fatalist willy-nilly, by the grace of Allah and my driver. It was all right for him to trust to the mercy of Allah, but I was afraid I didn't qualify. I didn't belong to the club.

We finally reached Michelet about seven. There had been no sign of anyone returning from the conference, though to get back to Algiers it would have been necessary to take the road by which we had come. Perhaps the others came down out of the hills and sped away behind our backs while we were becalmed in Michelet, perhaps their wives had told them not to enter the Kabylia and they had decided to obey. I never did find out whether there had really been a press conference, for I left for Morocco the following morning and saw none of them again.

The problem now arose: how do you find a rebel leader when you don't know where to look for him? There was a policeman standing in the center of the main street to direct traffic, but there was no traffic, except us. So I asked him how I could find Ait-Ahmed, though it seemed a little odd to ask the representative of the law how I could get in touch with an outlaw.

"Ait-Ahmed? Never heard of him," he answered unconvincingly. "Why don't you ask at the town hall, over there?"

I asked at the town hall, where nobody had ever heard of Ait-Ahmed either. But they told me to sit down and wait. The driver and I sat down on an uncomfortable narrow wooden bench and waited.

"There's no way of finding him," my driver said. "We might as well go back."

I thought he was probably right, but having come this far I didn't want to give up without a little effort. I poked my head into an office where some of the persons who had told me to wait were in a huddle. I asked again about Ait-Ahmed.

"Wait," they repeated. "We're telephoning."

"To Ait-Ahmed?" I asked.

"We're telephoning," they said. "Wait."

We waited.

The hour of the evening news broadcast arrived. We got into the car and turned on the radio. As we were listening, a closed delivery truck, the first car we had seen since we started into the hills, swung to the curb in front of us. A man got out and came to our car.

"Follow us," he said.

He made a U-turn and we fell in behind.

It was dark now. Toward the edge of the town, he swung right and so did we. From the side of the road a flashlight winked. Another one in the delivery truck winked back. A truck emerged from nowhere and swung in behind us. It was filled with men in uniform, with rifles slung across their backs. Pinched between the two cars, we moved upward, into the bush. I was making progress. Either I was going to see Ait-Ahmed or I was going to get my throat cut. At the moment, I assessed the chances at about fifty-fifty.

I didn't know where we were going, and to this day I don't know where we went. All I know is that we rose higher and higher, on a narrow dirt road which kept us feeling our way through the great cloud of dust thrown up by the car ahead. Twice jackals darted across it in front of us. It led us into a sort of opening occupied by a village, where we were taken to what seemed to be another town hall. It consisted chiefly of one large room, decorated by Arabs sitting on the floor along all four walls.

"Ait-Ahmed?" I asked.

"Wait," they said.

We waited.

Eventually a door opened and a group of men in uniform oozed in. None of them wore any insignia, but I recognized the tall man in the center as Ait-Ahmed immediately from his pictures. His mouth curls up characteristically at one side so that he seems to be wearing a perpetual sneer. He struck me, however, as being anything but a sneerer. We began talking in French, when suddenly he shifted into excellent English. He talks with a soft voice and in a cultivated manner. He told me that when he had been in Washington he read the *Washington Post* regularly.

"A first-rate paper," he said.

The cabinet minister I had seen in the morning had said the same thing. This seemed to make it 100 percent for Algeria. We were all right with both the ins and the outs.

I cannot say that I learned anything of great interest from our brief talk. He repeated his position concerning the government, which was familiar. He reiterated his intention to continue his fight against it in the hills, where he said he could hold out indefinitely, which was easy to believe. He gave me a copy of the communiqué he had prepared for the press, and then excused himself.

"I have to go out on patrol," he said.

What there was to be patrolled was hard to imagine. I had seen no sign that government forces had dared to penetrate these forbidding mountains, and I couldn't blame them.

We then returned to Algiers by the same road, at the same speed, with the same lack of concern for anyone else who might be using the road, with the difference that now it was pitch dark. We got back at midnight.

I was now listed officially by home and family as missing. My secretary's instructions were to phone me every night at seven so that I could dictate my story. My wife usually came to the office to talk to me at the same time. On this occasion, I had told the hotel to explain at seven that I was out working on a story, and to ask the office to put in a call every hour on the hour until I got back. I had also instructed the hotel not to give any further information, but when the night man came on, he said to my wife, who had become pressing, "We don't know where Mr. Root is, but he asked us to call the Ministry of Economy and excuse him for not being able to keep an appointment with the minister because he had been unexpectedly called out of Algiers."

"Out of Algiers!" my wife thought instantly. "The Kabylia!"

She is equipped with 150 percent feminine intuition.

When the midnight call came through, I was eating dinner and

writing my story at the same time. When I told my wife I was
dining, I meant it for a simple statement of fact, but she recounts
with indignation to this day that when she finally reached me
after an evening of anguish I scolded her for interrupting my
meal. That's domestic life.

When I returned to Paris and caught up on back numbers of
the paper, I found my story. It had been pared down to nothing
—a résumé of the far from sensational communiqué which I
could have obtained in Algiers without ever leaving the comforts
of the Aletti. True, it wasn't a very hot story, or at least, not the
part they ran. But I had thought it made not bad reading for
color, and that was the part they cut out. Besides, it established
the fact that they had a man on the spot.

Well, all right. The *Washington Post* is not a great admirer of
the Richard Harding Davis school of reporting, and neither am I.
But in that case why did they print, some three weeks later, a
long press service story from the same region which had nothing
but color in it, not even an anemic communiqué to excuse the
purple prose?

That's journalistic life.

Madeline Dane Ross is a world traveler and freelance journalist who has been a magazine editor and reporter and an UNNRA and U. S. State Department information specialist. She won the Overseas Press Club Distinguished Service Award in 1955.

The Jaguar Scoop

MADELINE DANE ROSS

IN THE SPRING of 1965, little Tunisia (population under 4,500,000) was front-page news. Her outspoken President—Habib Bourguiba—had told a group of newsmen in no uncertain words that Israel was a nation here to stay; and that the sooner Mr. Nasser and the Arab League admitted the fact and got down to the business of living and working with the reality, the better it would be for everyone. To this he added that he would not attend any further Arab League conferences until he saw progress. For many Americans who believed that the minds of all Arabs thought as one, Bourguiba's statements made exciting news.

I already had plans to be in Sicily when this flurry came out. Since Tunisia is not far from Sicily—as the plane flies—I decided to go there too and try my luck at a bit of headline hunting. Through a friend, I got two letters of introduction: one to Habib Bourguiba, Jr., foreign minister and son of the president; and a second letter to the minister of information. Then I got a letter of assignment from the North American Newspaper Alliance expressing "interest in an exclusive interview with President Bourguiba or his son, preferably on some controversial subject."

Receiving my letters of assignment and introduction only one day before leaving for Europe, I had no time to dig for background material and was really on the spot. However, in the two weeks before reaching Tunis, I "picked all the brains" available and pored over European editions of *The New York Times* and *Herald Tribune*. Tunisia for the most part had dropped out of the news.

I arrived in Tunis on a Saturday and was fortunate to meet the district sales manager of TWA—John Van Enige, Jr. His office was in the Majestic Hotel where I was staying. I told him why I had come to Tunis and asked his advice on getting my interview. He told me there was no use trying for an appointment until Monday and suggested that I spend the time until then seeing the sights of Tunis and Carthage and visiting the markets. All this could give me a feel of the country which was new to me.

Then he invited me to a cocktail party to be given that evening by U.S. Ambassador Francis Russell for the retiring area head of the Peace Corps. Since I had been a member of the United Nations Relief and Rehabilitation Administration in Germany and Austria, I was curious about the young people doing a comparable job today. The party, Van Enige suggested, might also help me get more background material, and it did. I met informed people whose observations on Tunisia were of special interest, and they willingly answered my questions. Through them I learned some positive and some sensitive spots in the country's current program.

Sunday, a mild sunny day (luckily, for it is usually hot and humid in June), I spent going through the great Bardo Museum —looking at the fabulous mosaics, tiles, art and culture of centuries; watching natives on their day off enjoying the displays— many women still wearing the veil (*chefcherie*), and most men wearing litle red felt caps (*chiaches*) and loose gowns resembling nightshirts (*jebbas*). There were family groups obviously happy with the free day and the opportunity to see the displays. I sponged up the atmosphere, attitudes, dress, manners and condition of these Tunisians. I noted particularly that I saw no one —man or child—without some form of footwear. Then I went to the markets—the *souks*—fascinating for the goods and wares offered in them, the conglomerate odors, and the vendors who called to passersby. I burrowed through the maze of twisted alleys.

Monday at nine A.M., I went to the TWA office and met Mr. Van Enige's secretary—Elyane Bismuth—a lovely girl who spoke English, Arabic and French fluently. Just the help I needed! Arabic and French seemed imperative for getting an appointment by telephone and Mr. Van Enige offered me her services for the calls. I told her what I wanted and sat beside her. But even with her linguistic ability and patience, after talking on the phone for one hour to seemingly countless people she had got nowhere.

"I think," she suggested politely, "we had better go to the government offices. They are near."

"And to save time from here on," I added, "since I have a letter to Bourguiba, Jr., let's go directly to his office and skip the minister of information." Fortunately we did just this and I presented my letters.

Then began the choreography of the aides—dressed in Western sack suits—appearing and disappearing, returning, stalling, everyone nicely polite, but no appointment. Finally, another man emerged with my letters. He regretted that Mr. Bourguiba was "very busy with commitments all day," and he seemed to sigh as he told me that "on top of a full day's work, the Foreign Minister would have to be in Kairouan at six P.M. for a Youth Festival." Kairouan, 150 miles from Tunis, is an ancient and revered city famous for its great mosques. Seven trips to Kairouan are equal to one trip to Mecca.

Thinking fast, I persisted, "I was going to Kairouan tomorrow! If I went today, would there be any chance of interviewing Mr. Bourguiba there?" I tried to look enthusiastic, pleading, earnest. The aide studied me. I thought I detected a faint smile into which I read, "These amazing American women—middle-aged too." He said, "A moment please," and left. When he returned, he reported, "*The* car will pick you up at four this afternoon."

It was great to get a hitch to Kairouan. Gasoline is very expensive in Tunisia. Consequently, driving to Kairouan is considered quite a haul. Elyane reserved a room for me in Kairouan and I spent the time until four P.M. going over clips I had, framing questions, asking questions and packing an overnight bag.

What should I wear? Would I be invited to the Youth Festival? What was a Youth Festival? How much warmer would the weather be? In a land where many females wear veils, are uncovered arms appropriate? I finally decided on my best blue and white cotton suit—which in my copy-writing days I'd have described as "restrained elegance." If it became too warm, I'd slip off the jacket and take a chance on the bared arms of a shell blouse. (In this I had chosen well, for later I was *included* in all the ceremonies for Mr. Bourguiba. Only my skirt proved a hazard —it was straight and short and definitely not designed for sitting cross-legged on rugs at a formal Arab banquet.)

Leaving my room at 3:45, I told the desk clerk that I was keeping it and would be back the next day. Then I sat in the large white marble lobby that contained no guest but myself and waited for *the* car. I thought of the scurrying of the morning and mused, "What am I letting myself in for?"

At 4:07, a nice-looking, olive-skinned man mounted the elegant stairs to the lobby. I could see him as he rose up the flight, coming to fuller view with each tread. His hair was black. He had dark, alert eyes, a small, neat moustache and a serious expression. He was well turned out in a light tropical suit and I thought, "This must be the man calling for me." He was followed by a smartly liveried chauffeur. Coming directly to me, he asked quietly, "Miss Ross?" When I nodded, he told the chauffeur to take my bag. As I rose, I said softly, "I'm sorry, I didn't hear your name." Of course I hadn't heard his name, because no one had said it. The man looked startled for a moment, stared at me for another, and then in a faltering half-whisper said, "I'm Bourguiba."

I'd have been happy to sink through the cool white marble! Following him down the steps, I lamely explained, "When I met your father at the Overseas Press Club seven years ago, you were with him. I remembered you as having blue eyes. It's your father who has the blue eyes. . . ." Imagine not knowing what the second most important man in a country looks like, especially when you are going to interview him! Had I bought a Tunisian newspaper, it never would have happened. The very next day, the papers seemed full of photographs of him and his father. I was impressed with the absence of irritation or arrogance on his part.

We got to the car—it was a Jaguar limousine. I was asked to sit in the back. Mr. Bourguiba sat in front beside his chauffeur. He then apologized for being late. He had just taken Mendès-France, "a great friend of Tunisia," to the airport and was a bit delayed;

some of the speeches ran overtime. Then he remarked, "We will have to drive rapidly to Kairouan to get there by six o'clock." In Arabic, he directed his chauffeur briefly and then asked me, "What do you want to talk about, Miss Ross?"

This was all going much faster than I had anticipated. Before *the* car arrived, I thought, "On the drive, I'll have time to plan my interview." Suddenly, I was faced with immediate action and at great length. I reached in my purse for my small looseleaf notebook. The Jaguar had little folding tables such as they have on the backs of airplane seats. I pulled one down and started the interview, taking notes leaning on a table in a car going at least eighty miles an hour.

"My letter of assignment," which I was sure he had seen, "called for some timely or controversial subject." He replied, "Oh, we've had too much controversy already," which I took as a cue to stay away from the subject of Israel for a while. Since our trip would take at least two hours, I felt I could bide my time.

It was really exciting flying over good roads that seemed to have no traffic—in a posh car, through open country, with a personage all to myself for two hours! I used very little time for discussion and spoke only enough to explain a question and to keep Mr. Bourguiba interested and talking. I got information about his country, numerous direct, revealing and pithy quotes, and a fairly good profile of the man. He speaks English well, and coming from him, many of our American clichés sounded charming. For instance, in a brief discussion of Israel, he said, "Israel is a reality and we must face today's problems with today's thinking. We cannot wish our problems away." When asked about the admission of Red China to the UN he answered, "We can get nowhere behaving like the ostrich. Red China should be accepted for UN."

One car going toward Tunis—the first I had noticed—passed us and stopped. We stopped. Mr. Bourguiba got out and walked to the other car. After two minutes he returned and explained, "That was my wife and family. I had to tell her I would not be home for dinner."

Mr. Bourguiba had been in Washington, D.C., for two years, serving as Tunisian Ambassador to the U.S. He made many American friends. Although one might find it difficult to place the accent of his English, I venture to say that it is more American-

oriented than English. After my "controversial" questions such as:
"What kind of aid does Tunisia get from Russia?" "Were there
any repercussions following Tunisia's absence from Arab League
meetings?" And "Will you succeed your father as president?" I
launched into questions about today's Tunisia which he seemed
to enjoy answering. I asked about child welfare and child labor
and the rights of women. I asked about birth control, and he reported a highly realistic and successful program. "There are
twelve birth control clinics in Tunis—a city of half a million." On
compulsory education he said, "We do not have it now, because
facilities are not available for everyone, but by 1970 or 1971, we
will have a place in school for every child. At present, 85 percent
of the boys and 40 percent of the girls are in school."

We talked of the public health program, which sounded as if
it were well under control. Drinking water is potable everywhere
in Tunisia. Trachoma and malaria have been practically eradi-
cated. Noting many new buildings, schools, youth centers, farm
communities where cement housing had replaced mud huts, fine
hotels, private housing developments and the attractive external
state of the buildings in Tunis and its environs, I asked if taxes
were high. He replied, "Yes, but the people can easily see what
they are paying for and each year we have taken in more taxes
than we anticipated. We do not promise them the moon. We
offer them a candle and they can see that they are getting it."

About halfway to Kairouan, Mr. Bourguiba asked me if I
would like a Coca-Cola. I did not see any sign of such in the
pristine countryside, but soon we arrived at a roadside stand
surrounded by tables. We stopped just long enough to purchase a
few bottles which were brought to the car. By this time I had
taken off my jacket. It was warm. When I did, Mr. Bourguiba
asked if I'd mind if he removed his. While the men—only the
men at the roadside rest—did look at us, none seemed to stare.
There seemed to be a remarkable and natural democratic in-
formality about the foreign minister, who is serving his country in
many ways. It was obvious that they all knew who he was, yet
there were no outward signs of it. No one except the Cola vendor
came to the car. The people just let us come and go, as though
they saw limousines all the time and as though the president's son
was just another citizen doing his job. Speaking of the limousine,
Mr. Bourguiba confessed, "Some people criticize me for having

such an expensive car." When I commented, "It holds the road better and will last longer," he seemed pleased.

I told Mr. Bourguiba that I had noticed only one person in Tunis without some form of footwear and thought it was remarkable. He replied, "I am happy to hear you say this. To me you have made an eloquent remark, because it dramatizes with simplicity the great change in the standard of living for most of our people since the revolution."

A few minutes after six P.M., when Mr. Bourguiba was due in Kairouan as the guest of honor for the annual Youth Festival—an event held in every large city of Tunisia in an effort to encourage young people to better themselves through hobbies, education, trade training, athletics, scouting and similar programs—he turned to me, slipped on his jacket and said, "There is a delegation ahead waiting on the road for me. I have to leave you now," and he gave me a most rewarding smile. I held up my ballpoint and pleaded, "One more question. Do you make it a practice of having interviews while you travel about your country?"

As Mr Bourguiba got out of his car to be greeted by the mayor of Kairouan, he replied, "No, you are the first."

Barrett McGurn tells here the story of a memorable scoop. Mr. McGurn was the New York *Herald Tribune's* bureau chief in Rome for thirteen years and in Paris and Moscow for three years. A past president of the Overseas Press Club, he is now American Embassy press attaché in Rome.

A Scoop—Twenty-five
Years in the Making

BARRETT McGURN

THE STORY was boxed on the top of page one: Pope Paul VI would come to the United States within six weeks. Under the banner headline was the start of a column-and-a-half story containing almost every major detail of the first papal trip to the Western Hemisphere:

The Pope would address the United Nations General Assembly on peace and world poverty.

He would conduct a dramatic outdoor religious service for peace, probably in Yankee or Shea Stadium.

It would be a very short visit, not more than three or four days, and the Pope would not set foot outside the city of New York.

The pontiff might see the President of the United States, in New York, of course.

And he might go to the New York World's Fair, where Michelangelo's *Pietà* in the Vatican Pavilion was one of the exposition's great hits.

It was all exclusive, each word of it. I went to sleep on that September, 1965, evening elated with the great scoop, and then passed a fitful night. I began having doubts. It is a maxim of journalism that "it's good to have stories first, but they mustn't stay exclusive too long." The beats that are not confirmed quickly are sometimes denied successfully.

How comforting it was to wake up to a television news announcement: "The Vatican said this morning that Pope Paul will go to the United Nations on October 4 and . . ."

The broadcaster had one thing more than I had—the exact date—but he was short of many of the significant details. The Vatican, as I learned later that day at the office, had confirmed the bare minimum of my story, and had left many important angles untouched. It was ten days before all the main features of the beat were released officially.

How was it possible to get a scoop on such an unusual and colorful story? There are some who say that exclusives are impossible nowadays, that the news agencies count their beats in split seconds and that little better is possible. The story of the Pope's coming trip stayed exclusive for seven delightfully long hours, long enough so that *The New York Times*, our omnipotent opposition, went to bed without so much as a paragraph about the big event.

Even now I can't tell in precise detail just how I got the story. Sources must be protected even at this late date. But some of the background is no secret.

Essentially the scoop grew out of a long time on one beat— Catholic news. When I started as a cub reporter on the *Herald Tribune* in New York, no one else knew much about Catholic ritual and doctrine, whereas I had just finished a year as editor-in-chief of the student newspaper at New York's largest Catholic university, Fordham. On the *Tribune*, Sunday was one of the six days I worked each week. The *Tribune* had the theory that if the Catholic Church wished to announce anything it would probably do so in the sermons at the eleven o'clock high mass in St. Patrick's Cathedral or at least at the half dozen communion breakfasts in the midtown Manhattan hotels. Soon I found myself responsible for covering the St. Patrick's mass and a fistful of simultaneous communion breakfasts each Sunday morning. If it had not been for the kindness of *Times* men staffing each one of the events I would have been hard put to touch all my bases. Somehow I did, and usually the pickings were slim.

Still, it was a specialty, and I enjoyed exploring the ramifications of what I found to be a limitless area of inquiry: the whole range of Catholic organization, attitudes, teaching and history. In 1939, when Pope Pius XI died, I filled pages in the *Herald Tribune* summarizing the late Pope's encyclical letters, and describing the ancient pomp associated with the end of one pontificate and the beginning of another.

"Why don't you go to Rome?" a colleague teased.

The thought of being in on such a climactic moment in Catholic, European and world history so excited me that I could not write another word on the five "spreads," the five long articles that I had promised to contribute to the next day's paper. To recapture my peace of mind I asked the city editor to let me go to Rome. After all, I reflected, as soon as he said no, I could get back to calm work again, and there was not much time until the deadline.

"That's out of my area. I'll have to ask the managing editor," plump Charlie McLendon told me gravely.

Twenty minutes later elderly Grafton Wilcox went by on the way to the office of Ogden Reid, the owner.

"That's out of my area," was the gist of the message from the managing editor.

At noon next day, passport and ticket magically in hand, I was on my way to what turned out to be thirteen fascinating years in Rome.

Covering the Vatican, I soon found out, was one of the most frustrating of news assignments. The Vatican thought in terms of thousands of years. Newsmen, especially the large corps of agency workers, did not even measure time on so broad a scale as thousands of seconds. The news people in general were close to despair. The Vatican had the idea that Italian journalists would jump the gun on release dates, so there were no advance texts on papal speeches, not even at the moment at which the reading began.

One news agency had two male stenographers who would tune in to Radio Vatican, copying down as much of the Pope's talk as either of them could understand. They would pass it along page by page to an American "staffer" who would start writing without letting the pontiff get to the point of what he had to say. Sometimes the reception was flawed by static. Occasionally the stenographers had to leave holes in their versions of the text. The American was expected to "write around" the missing parts.

"It's awful," one agency "Vaticanist" told me one day. "You can't write a really hardhitting story. You've got to fudge it. How can you be sure of what he said? How can you know what the point really was? Then when the end of a 45-minute talk comes along you find out what he was really driving at. You do a new lead but by that time editors and radio stations around the world have gone in with your first story. The papers especially don't like to reset type. They stay with what we sent first."

An agency head managed to wangle an interview with an officer of the Secretariat of State. He explained the mangling to which the pontiff's speeches were being subjected. The officer of the Holy See was astonished, but he had a suggestion.

"Why don't you wait?" he asked. "What's your hurry?"

When Pius XI, between the two world wars, wanted to publish a denunciation of Fascism, he and the Curia fretted over the problem. How could Mussolini's vigilant censorship be evaded?

"Simple," said a young monsignor from Massachusetts. "There isn't any Mussolini censorship in France. Give it to me and I'll hand it to the AP in Paris."

To curial minds adjusted to ways rooted in an ancient Roman past, the proposal was startling, but the American was given his way. The Pope's denunciation made the world headlines, via the Associated Press bureau, and a new star, that of Francis J. Spellman, began a rapid rise in the Vatican sky.

The future Cardinal Spellman had another recommendation about the same time: "Organize a Vatican press office."

That was a bit too much for the Curia to take, but an unofficial press office of the Vatican newspaper, L'Osservatore Romano, finally was opened on an eight A.M. to two P.M. basis. It wasn't what the newsmen wanted. It was not an "official Vatican press office," even though it was well inside the Vatican walls. It *was* official, though not in name. It was, at least, a start, even though it closed for the day two hours before the daily issue of L'Osservatore Romano hit the newsstands with the half-told stories about which each newsman had a score of questions he would have liked to ask.

By the next morning, when the unofficial press office reopened, all of *Osservatore*'s stories would be old hat, too old to merit much further checking. Reporters began to adjust to the idea that even the unofficial press office was only of marginal value to them and that they would have to take their chances, often as not, with their own guesses of what the hints in *Osservatore*'s pages really meant.

That was the Vatican I covered for 13 years. I found a few supplements for the unofficial press office. There was, for instance, an Irish-American monsignor in the Secretariat of State, a successor of Cardinal Spellman in that office. I called him one day about a phrase Pius XII had used in a speech:

"We grieve about the frightful conditions in an area so filled with sacred memories. . . ."

"Monsignor," I said, "I am correct, am I not, that he is speaking about Palestine, and that he is worried about the breakdown in his effort to obtain the internationalization of Jerusalem and the other Christian Holy Places?"

"Use it the way he said it," was the answer. "That's the way he meant to put it."

"But it is of course about Palestine?"

"The way it is is the way it should be."

I gave up. There was no point trying to explain any further that the papal words would not fit in a headline or even in a lead paragraph or a story. They were transparently clear to the uncommunicative monsignor, but they would have been meaningless to nearly every reader and certainly to all editors. I wrote my lead accordingly:

"Pope Pius XII, who has been trying to internationalize the Palestine Holy Places, said today that he is bitterly disappointed. . . ."

The lesson was to use every opportunity to interview Vatican officials on every step of the curial ladder, from the humble ushers to the popes themselves, and to talk endlessly about every phase of Catholic and Vatican diplomatic, theological, organizational and other problems. Beyond that it was clear that every paragraph of every issue of *L'Osservatore Romano* had to be scanned and, sometimes, read and reread. A wide range of other Catholic periodicals, especially the Jesuits' *Civiltá Cattolica*— Catholic Civilization—had to be studied. And in between times it was clear that as broad a library of Catholic history as a reporter could explore should be pondered for a comprehension of the small hints that could mean big stories.

This meant learning Italian, of course. There were even times, I found, when a brisk command of Latin would have helped too. I tried for both. My Italian became fluent if not always grammatical. The Latin limps but offers some help in a crisis.

All of this is background to the telling of "how I got the story" of Pope Paul VI's coming trip to the United States.

I suspected at least twenty-one months before my scoop that Pope Paul might come to America. The tip was in his January, 1964, trip to the Holy Land, the area whose Israeli war of national birth so worried Pius XII. If the Pope would fly there, breaking a tradition of 150 years during which no pope had left Italy, then, I thought, an American journey was a possibility too. It was possible but not sure. There was a chance that the return to the land of the Bible, the first trip any pope ever had made to Palestine since the time of St. Peter, the first of the popes, might have been a onetime thing. It might be a pilgrimage to the place of Christianity's origins, to be followed by no other journeys. That was possible, but I kept watching the wording of Vatican comments and kept talking with many friends on many levels of church life and associations, both persons inside the Church and diplomats and others in contact with it.

The tip-off on the sensational visit to the Western Hemisphere came, I felt, in the fall of 1964, one year before my scoop. That was when Pope Paul announced a second trip out of Italy, this time to Bombay in India, the first trip of a pope to Asia. Paul called himself "an apostle on the move." The very name he had chosen as Pontiff was that of the great traveler who had spread Christianity throughout the critical Mediterranean area in the Church's first decades. Paul, I was convinced, was a journeyer who would cross the Atlantic, the first pontiff ever to do so. I did a piece for the Sunday supplement, *Family Weekly*, piecing the clues together and concluding with the comment:

"If he receives any indication that he would be welcome, it is my bet that Pope Paul will come to America."

It was still a good twelve months before the fact.

I began corresponding with friends in the Vatican. My assignment by then was New York but Rome is only days away via the mailbox. The answers were provocative: "Nothing is definitely arranged as of this moment."

In translation that was sensational:

"For the first time in history it is not unthinkable that a pope will call on the Americas."

I kept watching and checking.

Then a second vital ingredient of the scoop went to work for me. It was the character of Pope Paul. This pontiff likes to dot all the *i*'s and cross all the *t*'s before any important announcement is made. Like Pius XII, whom he served at first hand, he prefers to conduct most of the Church's major transactions personally. That meant that the Pope worked almost alone as he made his preparations for the great New York trip. He supervised even small details. The effect was that the few weak channels leading to the newsmen who cover the Vatican were, in good part, plugged up. It preserved the secret. But the Pope could not work wholly alone. Contacts had to be made with the Italian government, with the United Nations, with the United States, with the police of New York.

The "package" for the trip was almost completely assembled, with no leak as yet to the press. The great story was ripe for a scoop. Then I managed to break it.

The story made page one across the country that night, but only in the papers subscribing to the *Herald Tribune* news service. To be sure that *The Times* would have the hardest possible time confirming the scoop, the *Herald Tribune* kept the news out of its first edition. Those were the days of Hurricane Betsy. Two big storm pictures were boxed on the top of page one. To *The Times*' editors they must have seemed like a plausible feature display on a day with no other great news. The hurricane photos vanished for our late city edition when the scoop plopped in.

Though the precise details of how the "package" was picked up and opened cannot be given, there is no problem about telling how the scoop was protected. It was a time-honored custom for *The Times* and *Herald Tribune* to buy copies of one another's editions the instant presses began to roll. The late city edition surely went on the usual fleet feet from the *Herald Tribune* plant to *The Times*, two blocks distant, but it was one A.M. in New York by then and seven A.M. in Rome. It was hard to get anyone at the

New York Chancery office, Cardinal Spellman's headquarters, and it was an unseemly early morning hour in the Eternal City. The *Times,* the news agencies and the networks did all they could, but most news sources were in the dark about the Pope's "package" and no one who knew even small bits would talk.

No one would say anything, but the Vatican's machinery began to turn. As Rome began to come alive to another morning, diplomats of the fifty nations accredited to the Holy See were summoned to the ornate, high-ceilinged apartments of the papal secretary of state, Cardinal Amleto Cicognani.

"You should be the first to know," the eighty-year-old prelate said in effect, "that the Pope will go to America. . . ."

The hundreds of thousands of readers of the *Herald Tribune,* of the *Boston Globe,* of the *Chicago Sun-Times* and of the other papers of our news service were ignored in the cardinal's words.

Two hours later a one-paragraph announcement from the Vatican's still unofficial press office said in effect:

"Diplomatic protocol was respected here today when the countries accredited to the Holy See were informed by the Cardinal Secretary of State that . . ."

The great news was spelled out in the dependent clause: news gatherers of the world would be offered one of the most remarkable of spectacles, a Pope on United States soil. A quarter of a century of talks and of reading had paid off in the sort of scoop a reporter does not manage every day.

One of the world's authorities on Latin America, the late Jules Dubois died before his article could see print. The events he describes will, we believe, make fresh news.

Exclusive—Washington
Tries a Bribe

JULES DUBOIS

ON SUNDAY September 5, 1965, in an exclusive story from Santo Domingo, I reported that an attempt had been made by representatives of the American Embassy to offer Brigadier General Elias Wessin y Wessin, the then anti-Communist military leader of the army, a bribe to leave the country at once.

Two days earlier Dr. Hector Garcia-Godoy, the carefully selected candidate of the Political Committee of the Organization of American States which was headed by American Ambassador Ellsworth Bunker, assumed the office of Provisional President to govern, ostensibly, for an interim period of nine months pending elections.

The day after my story was published, every correspondent in Santo Domingo tried to interview Wessin to confirm or deny. Some of them had received rockets from their home offices when the wire services picked up my story from *The Chicago Tribune*. Wessin refused to see them.

American Embassy officials maintained their silence and there was no comment from Washington.

Space limitations prevent my telling the entire Wessin story. That will have to await the book I plan to write about the Dominican Revolution. Nevertheless, I will try to relate the highlights of how I got the story.

Although Ambassador Bunker had two other members on the Political Committee—Ambassadors Ilmar Penna Marinho of Brazil and Ramon de Clairmont-Dueñas of El Salvador—they had instructions from their governments to go along with whatever the United States wanted.

Before dinner on Saturday night September 4, 1965, I encountered Ambassador Bunker in the lobby of the Hotel El Embajador and we exchanged greetings. A brief conversation followed.

"You may not know this, Mr. Ambassador," I ventured, "but notwithstanding the fact that Wessin never has been to the United States and speaks no English he is very pro-American."

"Is that so? Hasn't he even been to Panama?" Bunker asked.

"No, except possibly to fly through there on his way to or from Peru, where he was assigned to the Los Chorrillos Military Academy in Lima to take an advanced course."

"That is very interesting," Bunker mused. It was 7:15 P.M. and I left him. I noted that he headed for the exit and entered his automobile and rode away.

The next morning I decided to drive to the San Isidro Base to interview Wessin. His base was located twelve miles east of the capital on the outskirts of the San Isidro Air Base and was separated by it by a secondary macadam road.

One of Garcia-Godoy's first decrees, issued on September 4, 1965, abolished the independent command of the Armed Forces Training Center (called by the Dominicans the CEFA for the short title of the Spanish name: Centro de Enseñanza de las Fuerzas Armadas) and ordered all personnel and installations integrated into the army as the Fourth Brigade. Immediately, unfounded speculative stories were written that Wessin would rebel.

Knowing Wessin as a professional soldier who had the interests of the welfare of his country at heart, I was certain in my own mind that he would accept the change in good grace, but I wanted to interview him so I could write a follow-up story on the presidential order.

At nine A.M. I was cleared through the outer gate of the CEFA by the sentries, after having driven through the San Isidro Air Base, a shortcut, to reach Wessin's headquarters. At the main sentry gate outside the headquarters I was informed that Wessin had left the center for the headquarters of Brigadier General Juan de los Santos-Cespedes, the Chief of Staff of the Air Force. I reversed my car and drove back to the air base.

I climbed the flight of stairs and knocked on the door of General de los Santos's office. He was not in and neither was Wessin. The office was filled at the time with senior staff officers and several squadron commanders. Yes, they told me, General Wessin had been there, but after a brief conversation with General de los Santos, they had both left immediately for the Palace of Congress, where Commodore Francisco Javier Rivera-Caminero, the Minister of Defense, still had his office. They would meet with the latter and the other chiefs of staff, Brigadier General Jacinto Martinez-Arana of the Army, and Commodore Ramon Emilio Jimenez, Jr., of the Navy. They should return soon, I was assured, and it was suggested that I wait.

"Do you know what happened last night?" several of the air force officers asked me almost in unison.

"No, I don't," I admitted.

"Well, the American Embassy tried to bribe General Wessin," the officers replied. "They offered him and his whole family a trip around the world and a hundred thousand dollars for expenses for himself and his family, plus a visit to all military installations in the United States and Panama, if he would leave the country immediately. That is why he and General de los Santos have gone to the ministry to confer with all the others."

They embellished their versions with a few more details. It was evident they were angry and their ire contributed toward the exaggerated versions which they offered. But one fact became immediately clear. It was that Ambassador Bunker had lost no time in submitting a recommendation for what might at that moment have been a tempting offer to any Latin-American army general other than Wessin: an invitation to tour United States military installations and those in the Panama Canal Zone. He had apparently obtained the idea after I ventured the information that Wessin had never been given such a tour.

The only person mentioned by the air force officers as having called at Wessin's home was Lieutenant Colonel Joe C. Weyrick, Army Attaché of the American Embassy. They added that he was accompanied by a civilian. Then three of the senior officers simultaneously blurted out:

"Yes, and the Americans had offered General de los Santos, Rivera-Caminero and Martinez-Arana half a million dollars each to leave the country."

That sounded incredible.

"When was that done?" I asked.

"When the men who were sent here in May by the White House were here," one staff officer replied, and the others nodded in confirmation.

(That was the team that was headed by McGeorge Bundy, Deputy Secretary of Defense Cyrus R. Vance, Undersecretary of State Thomas C. Mann, and then Assistant Secretary of State for Inter-American Affairs, Jack Hood Vaughn. At that time my oldest son, a first lieutenant of the Tactical Air Command who was on duty at the San Isidro Air Base, was assigned by Major General Marvin L. McNickle to act as interpreter at a high level meeting of the White House team with the Dominican military chiefs. I am proud to reveal that he never uttered a word to me about it at the time.

The return of De los Santos and Wessin was delayed and my questions to the air force officers produced a general discussion of the latest military developments that revolved around future potentialities and obligations that had apparently been contracted by Garcia-Godoy with the military chiefs as well as with the rebels of Colonel Francisco Alberto Caamaño-Deño.

In the interim Colonel Pedro Bartolomé Benoit, who as president of the first military junta had on April 28 requested in writing that the United States send "temporary assistance" in the nature of troops to the Dominican Republic, arrived and participated in the conversation. He, too, was angry over the latest Wessin development, attributing it as a maneuver to surrender to Communist demands and expressing bewilderment that—with Garcia-Godoy already installed as Provisional President—the American Embassy would take it upon itself to produce the exit of Wessin. His comments, though, were measured and serene.

De los Santos did not return until after 12:30 P.M. Wessin was not with him. We shook hands as he took his seat behind his desk, which had been vacated by his executive officer.

"Where is General Wessin?" I asked.

"He has gone home."

"What is the story?"

"You will have to ask Wessin."

"I intend to do that. But please let me ask you something else. Is it true that you were offered a bribe by a representative or representatives of the United States some months ago to leave the country?"

"Yes."

"Was it five hundred thousand dollars?"

"No."

"Was it more or less?"

"It was less." I decided to slash the figure in half.

"Was it two hundred fifty?"

"No, a little more."

"How much?"

"Three hundred thousand."

"What did you do?"

"I rejected it."

"Are you disposed to mention the name or names of those who made the offer?"

"No."

"What about Rivera-Caminero and Martinez-Arana? Was the same offer made to them?"

"You will have to ask them."

I said good-bye to General de los Santos, Colonel Benoit and to all the officers who had remained in their chief's office during the three hours of my visit there. I descended to the parking area in front of the headquarters building and drove off toward the secondary macadam road and turned westward to speed a distance of seven miles to Wessin's residence.

Wessin had built a three-bedroom house that had a small living room, a dining room and a modest patio. The home was still mortgaged and he was paying off the mortgage from his salary. He owned a lot across the road. Wessin was in one of the bedrooms with a group of friends. Several friends were also at the fringe of the patio and entered the living room, greatly agitated, when they saw me.

"We have drafted something for him to read over Radio San Isidro," they said in agitated voices, "but he refuses to do so. We beg you to convince him to read it. He will be able to arouse the entire country to support him."

"The general is a man who makes his own decisions," I replied with a snap in my voice. "I am a newspaperman and it is not up to me to try to convince him to do anything."

Just then Wessin emerged from the bedroom and the emotional friends withdrew to the patio. The general invited me to accompany him to the privacy of the dining room, which had not yet been prepared for luncheon.

"Those men," Wessin said, "have drafted a harangue for me to broadcast over Radio San Isidro and they are pressuring me to do so. I won't do it, because the only purpose it will serve will be to inflame the people of this country against the United States. I have the draft here—read it."

He handed it to me. I read the five pages. It was an inflammatory denunciation of alleged devious operations of the CIA, and invoked operations in Southeast Asia, Malaysia and now Santo Domingo. I returned it to Wessin and asked:

"Are you going to make the broadcast?"

"Of course not. I am not crazy."

Wessin then remarked that his friends were endeavoring to persuade him that, in desperation, he could be assassinated by order of the Americans.

"I have taken care of that possibility," revealed the general, who wore his uniform slacks and a khaki shirt open at the collar. "I have prepared a series of documents that are sealed and which I have placed in safe hands to be made public only in the event I should meet foul play at the hands of an assassin."

"What is the story about last night?" I asked. "I have been told that you had visitors from the American Embassy and that you were offered a hundred thousand dollars in cash to take your family on a world tour as well as other things."

"That is not true," Wessin replied.

"Can you tell me the story?" Wessin began to furnish the details:

"Last night, at a most unusual hour—ten-twenty P.M.—I received a telephone call from Lieutenant Colonel Joseph Weyrick, the Army Attaché of the American Embassy, who asked if he could come over to see me as soon as possible on an urgent matter with a friend. It was a very strange hour to call for an appointment but I agreed to receive him. He arrived after midnight with a civilian, whom I shall not name, who I later learned is from the CIA.

"They sat down here at this table. The civilian did all the talking, Weyrick just listened and did not say a word. I immediately realized that they were acting on orders from their superiors. I had never met this CIA representative before. A few days earlier, though, another American civilian, whose name I do not remember, came with an interpreter and offered to buy my house and lot across the street for forty thousand dollars provided I would immediately leave the country. That was before Garcia-Godoy assumed office. He said he would give me eight thousand dollars in cash when I boarded the plane and the balance when I landed at my destination. I turned him down and told him I had no intention of selling my house and much less of leaving my country.

"Last night my civilian caller offered me fifty thousand dollars for my house and lot across the road if I would agree to leave the country. I told him that my house was not worth fifty thousand dollars and that I was not going to accept a bribe. He also offered me a trip as guest of honor of the United States at all military installations in the U.S. as well as in the Panama Canal Zone.

"Pounding animatedly on the table, he insisted that I had to leave because the Communists refused to surrender their arms and ammunition until I left the country. I told him that the Communists were not going to surrender their weapons anyway and that if he or anybody else thought otherwise they were very mistaken and were dreaming.

" 'What if you are canceled by the President?' he asked. ["Canceled" means cashiered and/or separated from active duty.]

" 'That is something entirely of my incumbence,' I answered, 'and I will cross that bridge at the proper time.' He continued to insist that I accept and I told him that my house was not worth twenty-five thousand dollars and I would not accept what I considered to be a bribe to satisfy the Communists. Then after two o'clock in the morning my two visitors left."

Early in the month of May the American Embassy had vainly tried, based on the "war of propaganda" that was directed by ex-President Juan Bosch from his comfortable sanctuary in San Juan, Puerto Rico, to persuade Wessin to leave. Wessin had been summoned to the 82nd Airborne Division headquarters at the Batalla de las Carreras Military Academy near his own base to meet with American Ambassador W. Tapley Bennett, Jr., and

Lieutenant General Bruce Palmer, Jr., Commanding General of the 18th Airborne Corps. (This was prior to the creation of the Inter-American Peace Force). The State Department was running the war at the time.

Richard I. Phillips, who had been sent from Washington to act as the embassy spokesman, made the startling announcement that afternoon at a press briefing that Wessin had resigned and would be leaving the country forthwith. The State Department was the only source for this announcement. There was no official word from the Government of National Reconstruction, presided over by Brigadier General Antonio Imbert-Barrera, the formation of which had been urged by Special Ambassador John Bartlow Martin and which was sworn in by the President of the Supreme Court on May 7, 1965. Asked about the State Department announcement the next morning by the press, Imbert said: "I will be glad to accept his resignation if he should submit it."

Wessin had other plans. He told me that what he said to Bennett and Palmer and what he wrote to Bennett in a longhand letter under pressure that critical afternoon, he did with mental reservations.

"I wrote a letter in longhand, at his request, to Ambassador Bennett," Wessin said, "in which I agreed to leave 'after a prudent time' provided some of the corrupt military commanders were shipped out of the country because they were a disgrace to the armed forces and to the Dominican Republic. I listed their names and the day after Imbert took office they were shipped out.

"A few days later the embassy continued to pressure me to leave and sent Colonel Weyrick to tell me that the Americans had kept their part of the bargain and every one of the officers I had listed had been shipped out of the country. I reminded Colonel Weyrick that I had recorded 'a prudent time' in my letter to Bennett, and by that I had meant after we had rid ourselves of the Communist danger.

"The pressure did not cease and in order to get the Americans off my back, I wrote another letter by hand to Bennett, this time asking the outlandish price of forty thousand dollars for my house, without any intention of accepting the sum," Wessin concluded. "An emissary came a few days ago from the embassy and offered me that sum at the conditions I previously stated. I told him that if I took the money—which I would not—it would be to build another house across the road. That is the whole story."

With that I thanked Wessin and entered my car and drove back to the Hotel El Embajador. I was about to call the embassy to attempt to check out the after-midnight visit by Weyrick and the civilian to Wessin's home, when I met in the lobby a USIS officer assigned to the embassy.

"Is it true," I asked, "that two men from the embassy called on Wessin late last night at his home?"

"We have already been asked that question and we checked it. Nobody at the embassy has any knowledge of it." That was the denial.

There was no need, then, to pursue my questioning. It was quite obvious that the embassy had no intention at the time of confirming the visit.

I wrote my story in the press room and filed it by Telex to Chicago. As I could not locate Rivera-Caminero and Martinez-Arana that afternoon to check out the other bribe story which had been confirmed only by De los Santos, I did not mention that in the Wessin story. I did manage to interview Rivera-Caminero and Martinez-Arana on September 6, 1965. Both flatly denied that they had been offered any bribe. I wrote the De los Santos story and quoted the denials by the other two officers.

A few days later, two correspondents, Edward Scott of NBC and Robert Berrellez of AP, interviewed Wessin in his headquarters after the latter insisted that they obtain permission from Rivera-Caminero. Rivera granted the permission and Wessin confirmed to them what he had told me.

The anger of the embassy and Bunker became evident. They asserted that Wessin had held a press conference that morning, and they voiced their obvious displeasure. It was no press conference. It was a joint interview, duly obtained through Dominican military channels, via the simple expedient of journalistic enterprise by two correspondents.

There were two other postscripts to my bribe stories. The first came less than a week after the Wessin story. I was making the rounds of my Dominican military and political contacts prior to my return home. Wessin had already been booted out of the country.

"We have been warned not to talk to you anymore," I was

informed by the highest sources I visited. "We don't dare to talk
to you because we don't want the same thing to happen to us
that happened to Wessin. We have been admonished to boycott
you on the grounds that you already have caused a lot of damage
to Dominican democracy."

I later learned that those warnings emanated from American
Embassy sources. But the resistance that those sources attempted
to build up against me vanished by the first week of November,
when I returned to Santo Domingo, as my Dominican contacts
became convinced that it was not I who had caused "a lot of
damage to Dominican democracy," for Wessin had been proved
right and the Communists had failed to surrender their arms and
ammunition.

Such reprisals are one of the calculated risks of documented
reporting by the foreign correspondent. In journalism there is no
substitute for courage and accuracy. And in diplomacy there is
nothing more stupid than trying to dry up a correspondent's
source in Latin America.

The second postscript came in January, 1966, when I was
interviewing Rivera-Caminero in his home in Santo Domingo. I
happened to mention the name of one of the members of the
White House Advisory Group who had been there in May.

"He is the man who made the three-hundred-thousand-dollar
offer to De los Santos," Rivera broke in and chuckled at the same
time.

When I pressed Rivera to repeat that and confirm it to me, he
promptly retreated, and, still chuckling, refused to do so. Hence,
because of lack of confirmation by the man who was then still
minister of defense and is now naval attaché in Washington, I
withhold the name he mentioned.

The Editors

DAVID BROWN, who has had a distinguished career as an editor and author, today is Vice President, Director of Story Operations, for Twentieth-Century Fox Film Corporation. Previously he served as Editorial Vice President of New American Library of World Literature, Inc., Managing Editor of *Cosmopolitan* and Editor in Chief of *Liberty* magazine. Mr. Brown has been a contributor to major national magazines over the years. He was the co-editor of the book *I Can Tell It Now*, by members of the Overseas Press Club of America, published in 1964.

A biographical note on W. RICHARD BRUNER appears on page 147 at the head of his story, "Some of My Best Friends Are MPs."

PN
4781
.09

Overseas Press Club of
America
How I got that story

Date Due

89021977